HORI-san and MIYAMURA-KUN

HORIMIYA

HERO × DAISUKE HAGIWARA

05

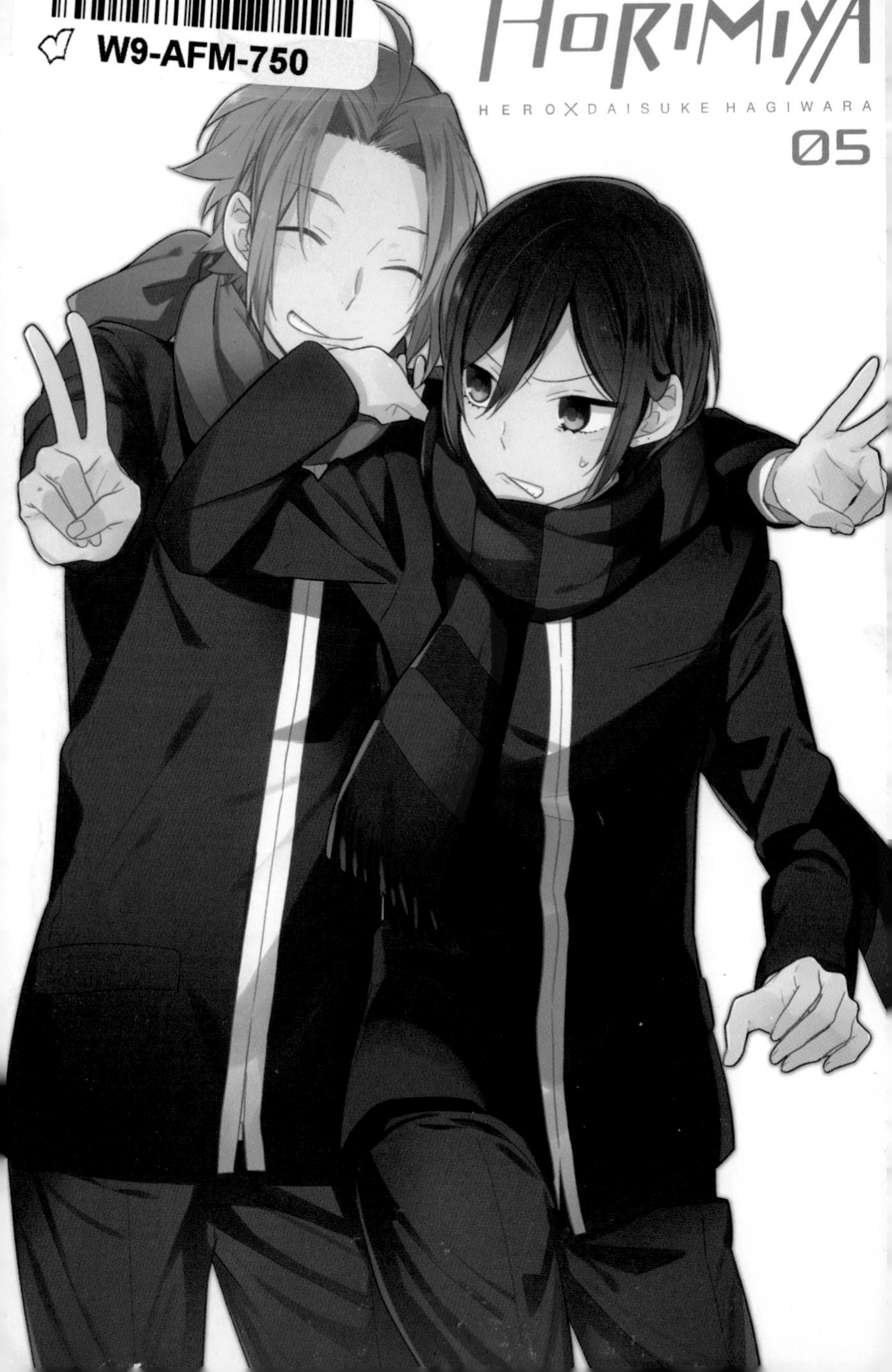

HORI-san and
MIYAMURA-kun

HORIMIYA
05

CONTENTS ★

Page·27

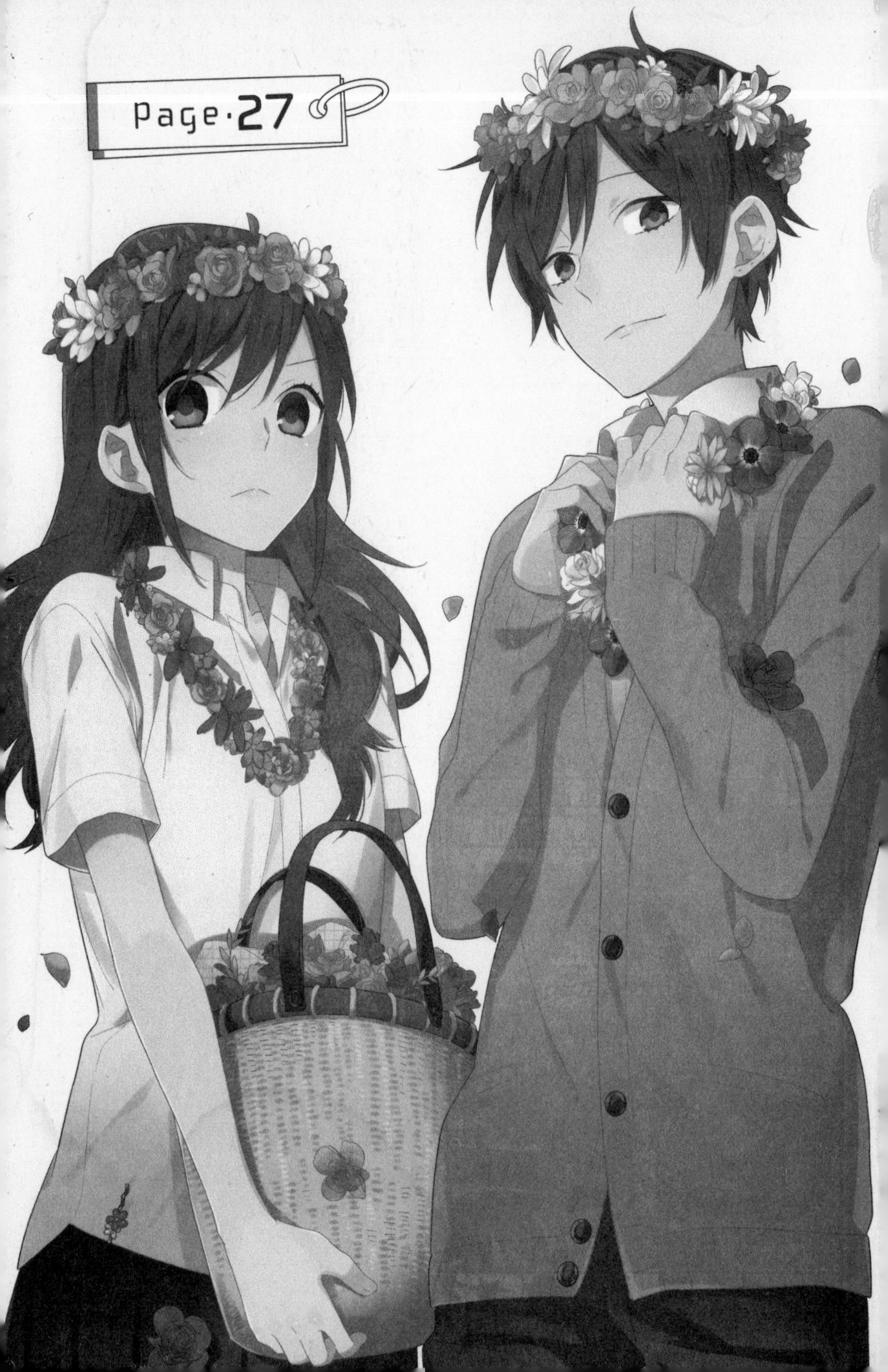

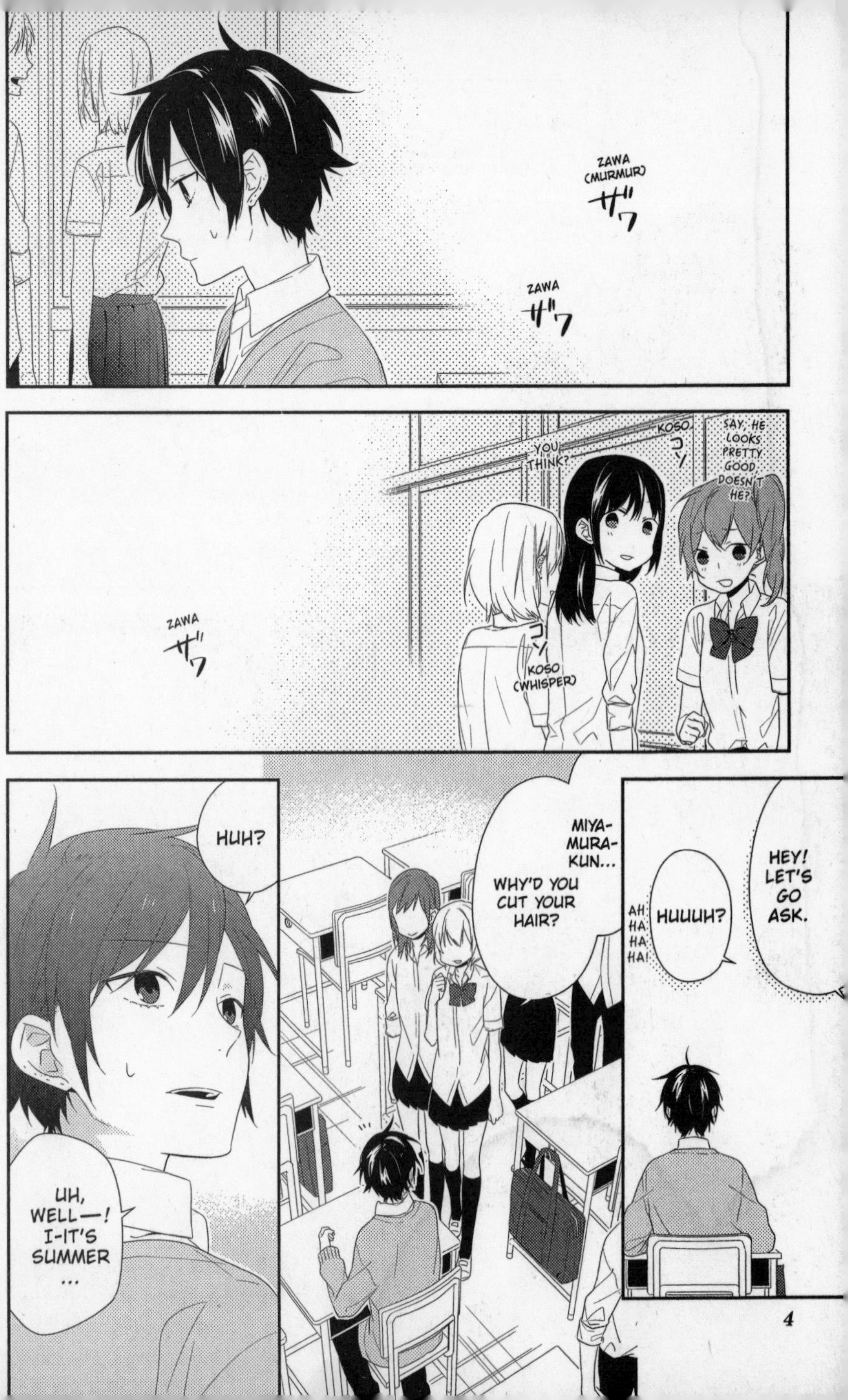
ZAWA (MURMUR)
ザワ
ZAWA
ザワ
SAY, HE LOOKS PRETTY GOOD, DOESN'T HE?
KOSO
コソ
YOU THINK?
コソ
KOSO (WHISPER)
ZAWA
ザワ
HEY! LET'S GO ASK.
HUUUH?
AH HA HA HA!
MIYA-MURA-KUN... WHY'D YOU CUT YOUR HAIR?
HUH?
UH, WELL—! I-IT'S SUMMER...

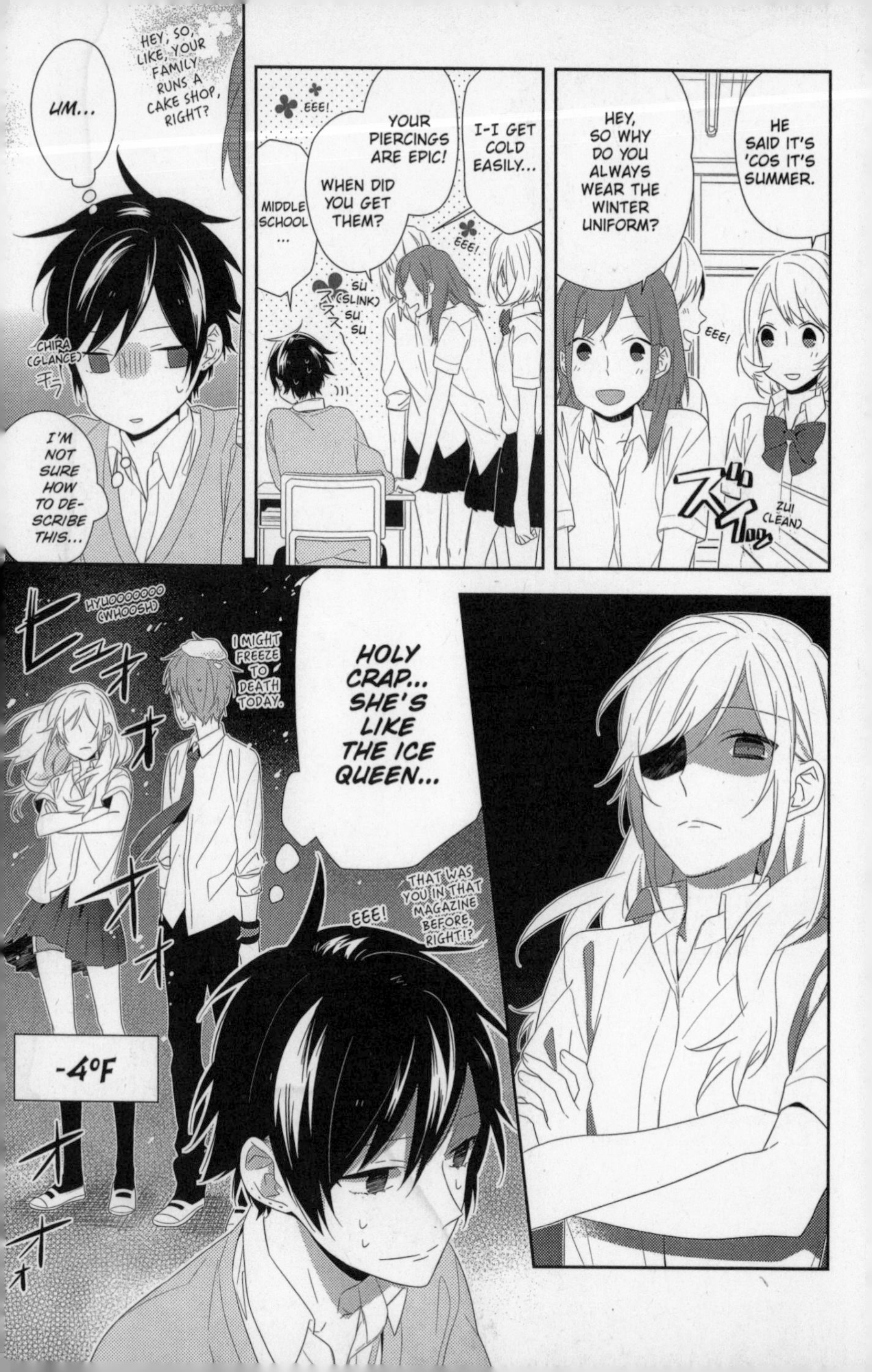
HE SAID IT'S 'COS IT'S SUMMER.
HEY, SO WHY DO YOU ALWAYS WEAR THE WINTER UNIFORM?
EEE!
ZUI (LEAN)
I-I GET COLD EASILY...
EEE!
YOUR PIERCINGS ARE EPIC!
WHEN DID YOU GET THEM?
EEE!
MIDDLE SCHOOL...
SU (SLINK) SU SU
HEY, SO, LIKE, YOUR FAMILY RUNS A CAKE SHOP, RIGHT?
UM...
CHIRA (GLANCE)
I'M NOT SURE HOW TO DESCRIBE THIS...
THAT WAS YOU IN THAT MAGAZINE BEFORE, RIGHT!?
EEE!
HOLY CRAP... SHE'S LIKE THE ICE QUEEN...
HYUOOOOOOO (WHOOSH)
I MIGHT FREEZE TO DEATH TODAY.
-4°F

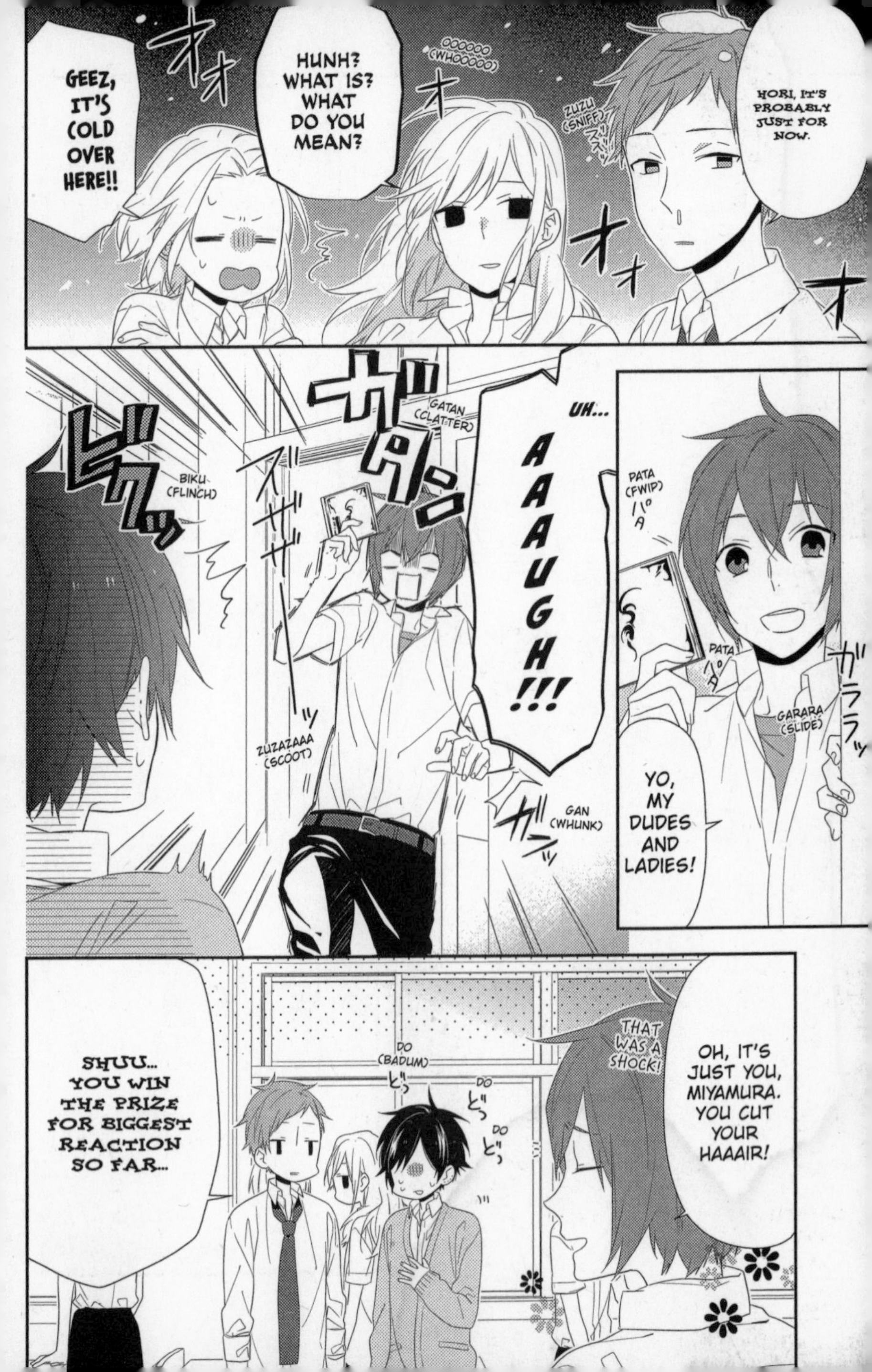
HORI, IT'S PROBABLY JUST FOR NOW.
OOOOOO (WHOOOOOO)
HUNH? WHAT IS? WHAT DO YOU MEAN?
ZUZU (SNIFF)
GEEZ, IT'S COLD OVER HERE!!
PATA (FWIP)
PATA
GARARA (SLIDE)
YO, MY DUDES AND LADIES!
UH...
AAAAUGH!!!
GATAN (CLATTER)
BIKU (FLINCH)
GAN (WHUNK)
ZUZAZAAA (SCOOT)
OH, IT'S JUST YOU, MIYAMURA. YOU CUT YOUR HAAAIR!
THAT WAS A SHOCK!
DO (BADUM)
DO
DO
SHUU... YOU WIN THE PRIZE FOR BIGGEST REACTION SO FAR...

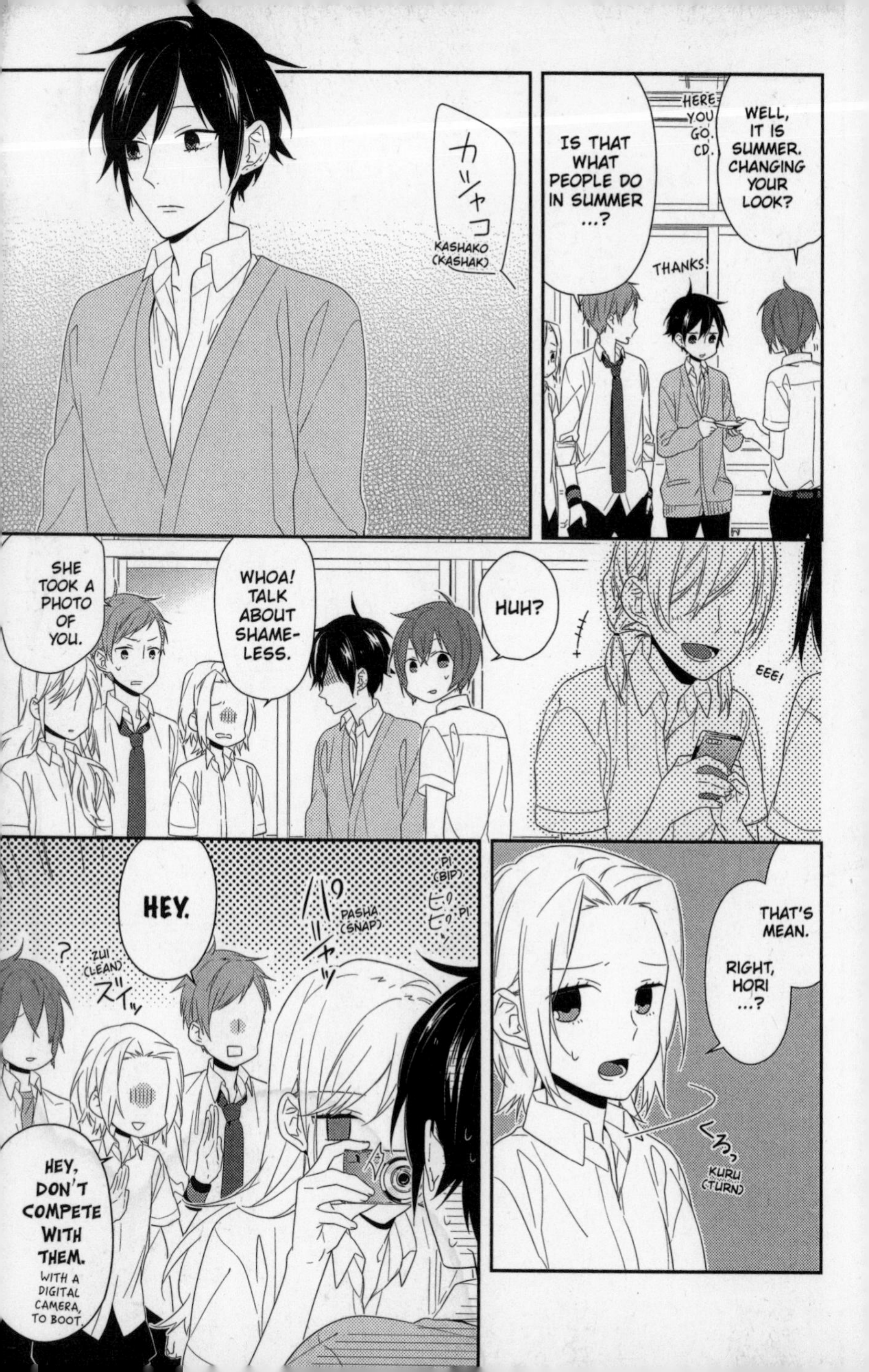
WELL, IT IS SUMMER. CHANGING YOUR LOOK?
HERE YOU GO. CD.
THANKS!
IS THAT WHAT PEOPLE DO IN SUMMER ...?
カシャコ
KASHAKO (KASHAK)
HUH?
EEE!
WHOA! TALK ABOUT SHAME-LESS.
SHE TOOK A PHOTO OF YOU.
THAT'S MEAN.
RIGHT, HORI ...?
くるっ
KURU (TURN)
ピピッ
PI (BIP) PI
パシャッ
PASHA (SNAP)
HEY.
ズイッ
ZUI (LEAN)
?
HEY, DON'T COMPETE WITH THEM.
WITH A DIGITAL CAMERA, TO BOOT.

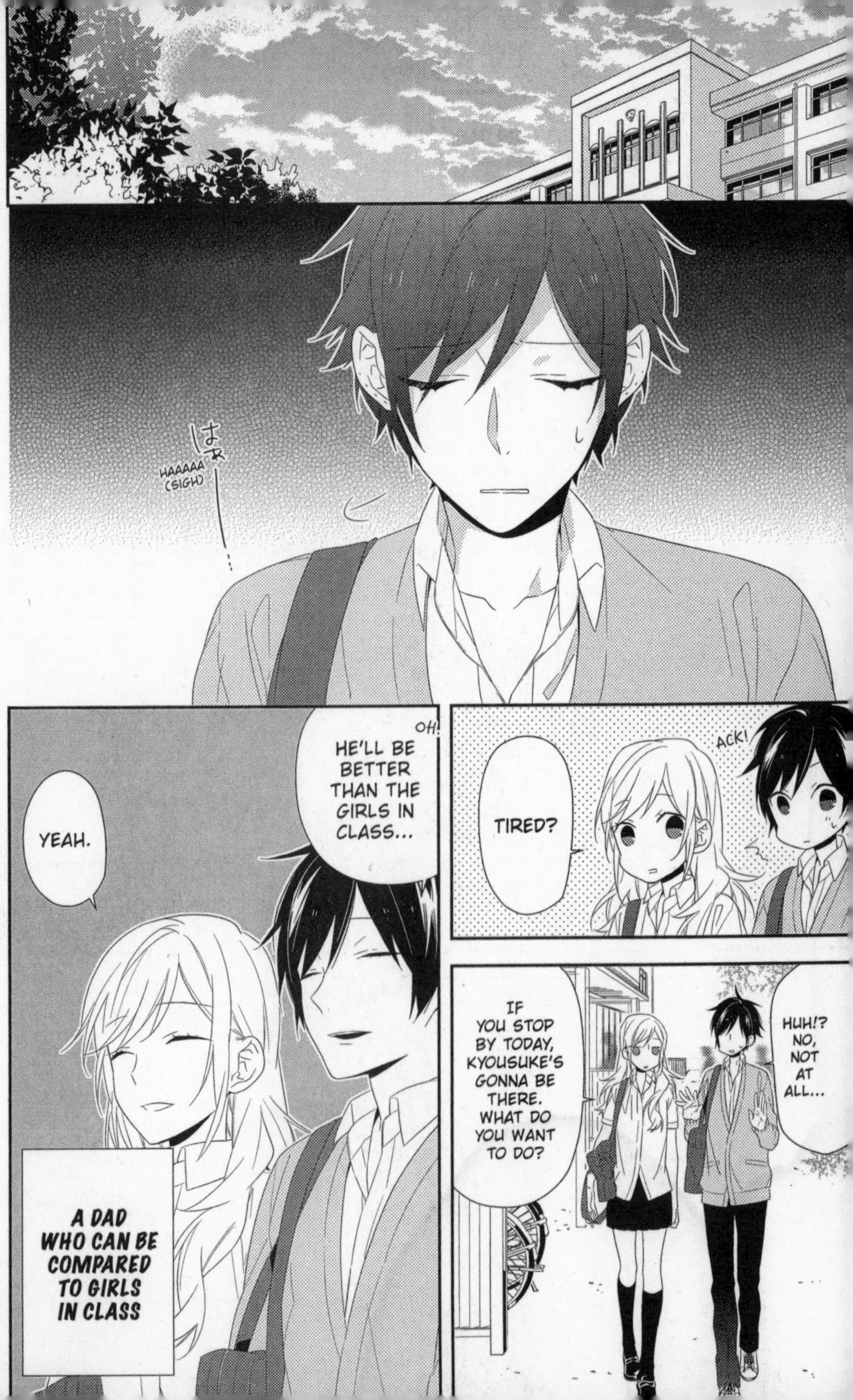
はぁ
HAAAAA (SIGH)
ACK!
TIRED?
HUH!? NO, NOT AT ALL...
IF YOU STOP BY TODAY, KYOUSUKE'S GONNA BE THERE. WHAT DO YOU WANT TO DO?
OH!
HE'LL BE BETTER THAN THE GIRLS IN CLASS...
YEAH.
A DAD WHO CAN BE COMPARED TO GIRLS IN CLASS

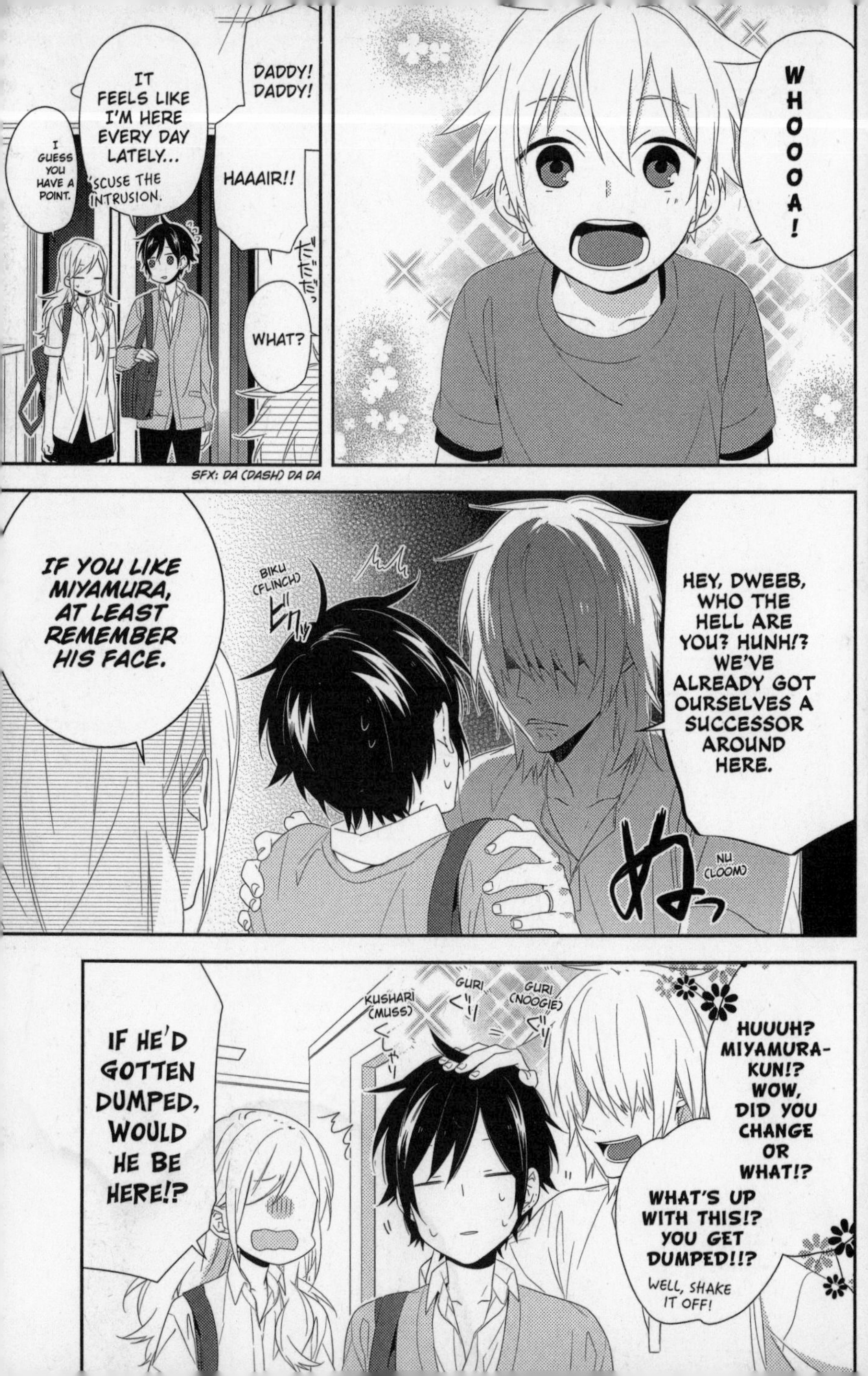
WHOOOA!
DADDY! DADDY!
HAAAIR!!
WHAT?
IT FEELS LIKE I'M HERE EVERY DAY LATELY...
'SCUSE THE INTRUSION.
I GUESS YOU HAVE A POINT.
SFX: DA (DASH) DA DA
HEY, DWEEB, WHO THE HELL ARE YOU? HUNH!? WE'VE ALREADY GOT OURSELVES A SUCCESSOR AROUND HERE.
NU (LOOM)
BIKU (FLINCH)
IF YOU LIKE MIYAMURA, AT LEAST REMEMBER HIS FACE.
HUUUH? MIYAMURA-KUN!? WOW, DID YOU CHANGE OR WHAT!?
WHAT'S UP WITH THIS!? YOU GET DUMPED!!?
WELL, SHAKE IT OFF!
GURI
GURI (NOOGIE)
KUSHARI (MUSS)
IF HE'D GOTTEN DUMPED, WOULD HE BE HERE!?

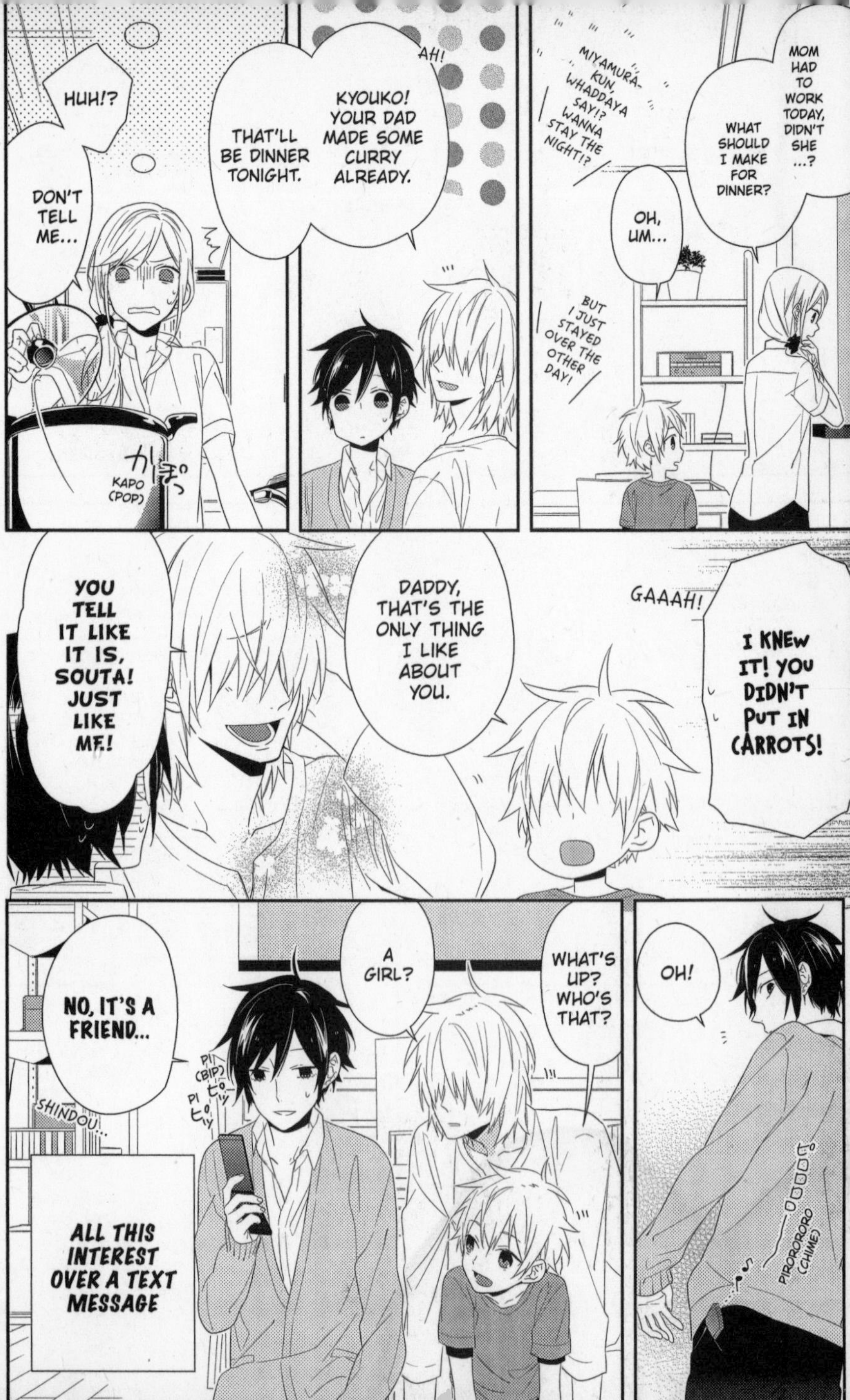
MOM HAD TO WORK TODAY, DIDN'T SHE ...?
WHAT SHOULD I MAKE FOR DINNER?
OH, UM...
MIYAMURA-KUN, WHADDAYA SAY!? WANNA STAY THE NIGHT!?
BUT I JUST STAYED OVER THE OTHER DAY!
AH!
KYOUKO! YOUR DAD MADE SOME CURRY ALREADY.
THAT'LL BE DINNER TONIGHT.
HUH!?
DON'T TELL ME...
KAPO (POP)
GAAAH!
I KNEW IT! YOU DIDN'T PUT IN CARROTS!
DADDY, THAT'S THE ONLY THING I LIKE ABOUT YOU.
YOU TELL IT LIKE IT IS, SOUTA! JUST LIKE ME!
OH!
PIROROROR (CHIME)
WHAT'S UP? WHO'S THAT?
A GIRL?
NO, IT'S A FRIEND...
PI (BIP) PI
SHINDOU...
ALL THIS INTEREST OVER A TEXT MESSAGE

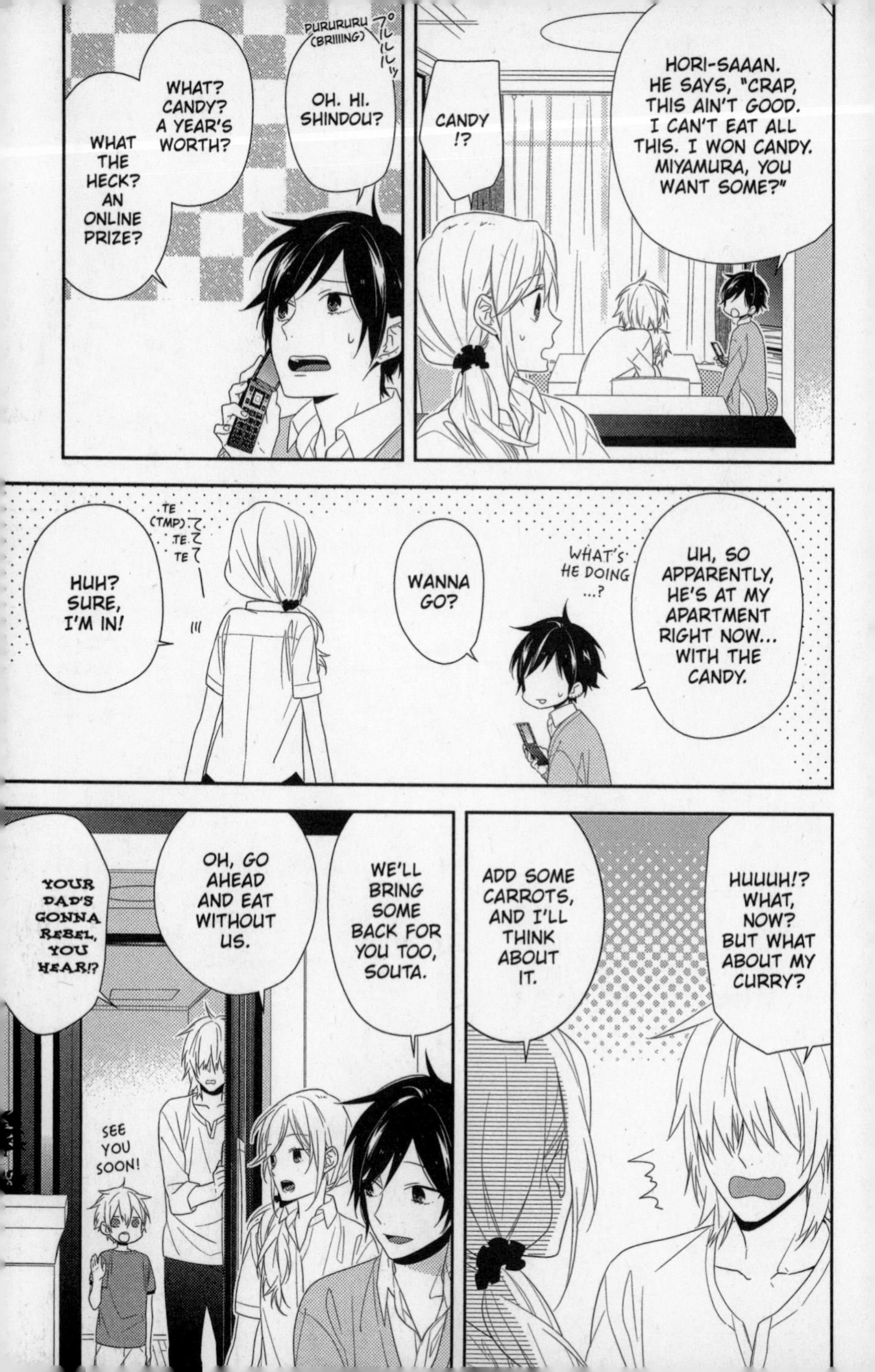
HORI-SAAAN. HE SAYS, "CRAP, THIS AIN'T GOOD. I CAN'T EAT ALL THIS. I WON CANDY. MIYAMURA, YOU WANT SOME?"
CANDY !?
PURURURU (BRIIIING)
プルルルッ
OH. HI. SHINDOU?
WHAT? CANDY? A YEAR'S WORTH?
WHAT THE HECK? AN ONLINE PRIZE?
UH, SO APPARENTLY, HE'S AT MY APARTMENT RIGHT NOW... WITH THE CANDY.
WHAT'S HE DOING ...?
WANNA GO?
TE (TMP) TE TE
HUH? SURE, I'M IN!
HUUUH!? WHAT, NOW? BUT WHAT ABOUT MY CURRY?
ADD SOME CARROTS, AND I'LL THINK ABOUT IT.
WE'LL BRING SOME BACK FOR YOU TOO, SOUTA.
OH, GO AHEAD AND EAT WITHOUT US.
YOUR DAD'S GONNA REBEL, YOU HEAR!?
SEE YOU SOON!

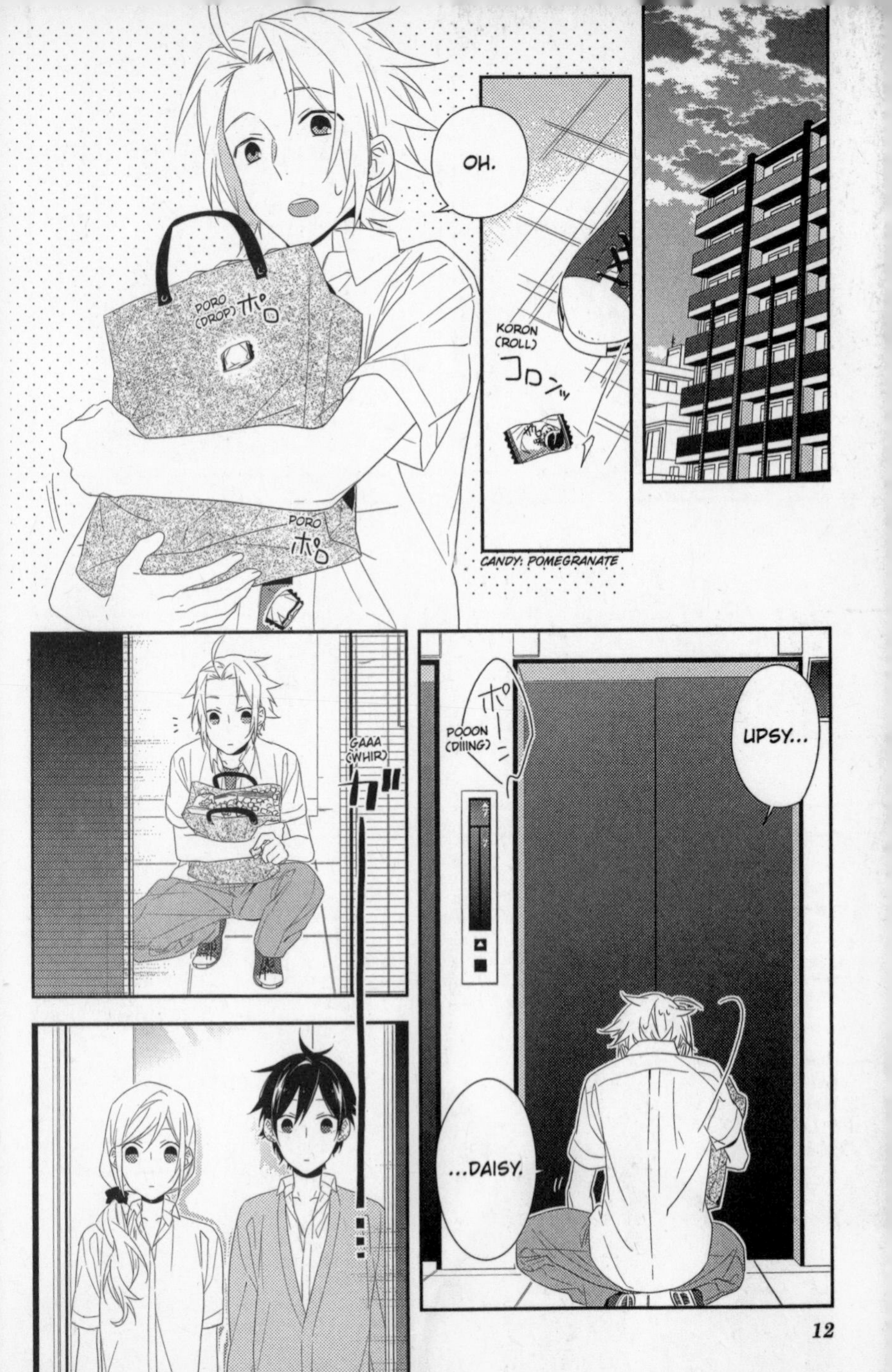
KORON (ROLL)
コロンッ
CANDY: POMEGRANATE
OH.
PORO (DROP) ポロ
PORO ポロ
POOON (DIIING) ポーン
UPSY...
...DAISY.
GAAA (WHIR) ガ

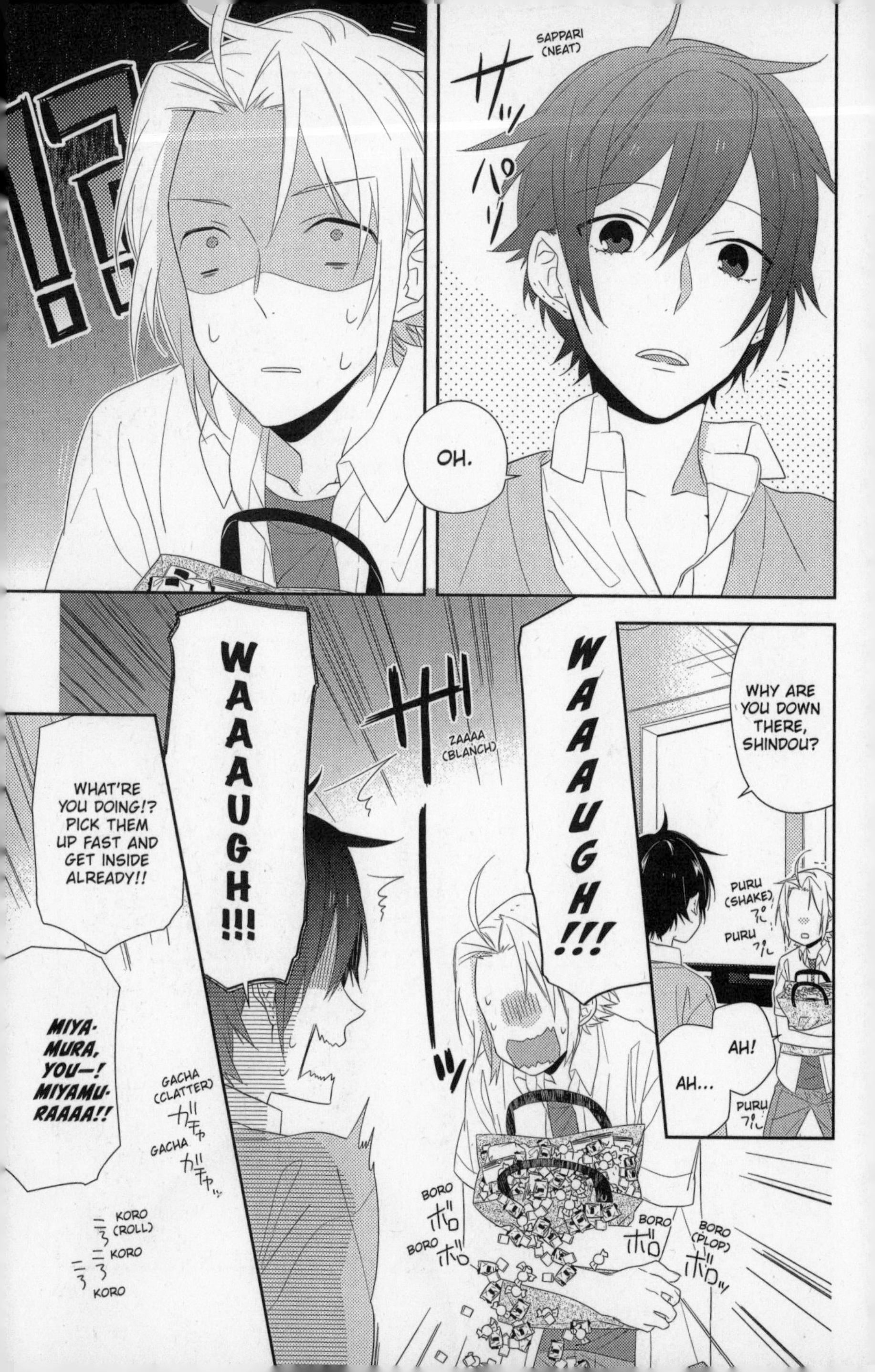
SAPPARI (NEAT)
OH.
WHY ARE YOU DOWN THERE, SHINDOU?
PURU (SHAKE)
PURU
AH!
AH...
PURU
WAAAAUGH!!!
ZAAAA (BLANCH)
BORO (PLOP)
BORO
BORO
BORO
WAAAAUGH!!!
WHAT'RE YOU DOING!? PICK THEM UP FAST AND GET INSIDE ALREADY!!
MIYA-MURA, YOU—! MIYAMU-RAAAA!!
GACHA (CLATTER)
GACHA
KORO (ROLL)
KORO
KORO

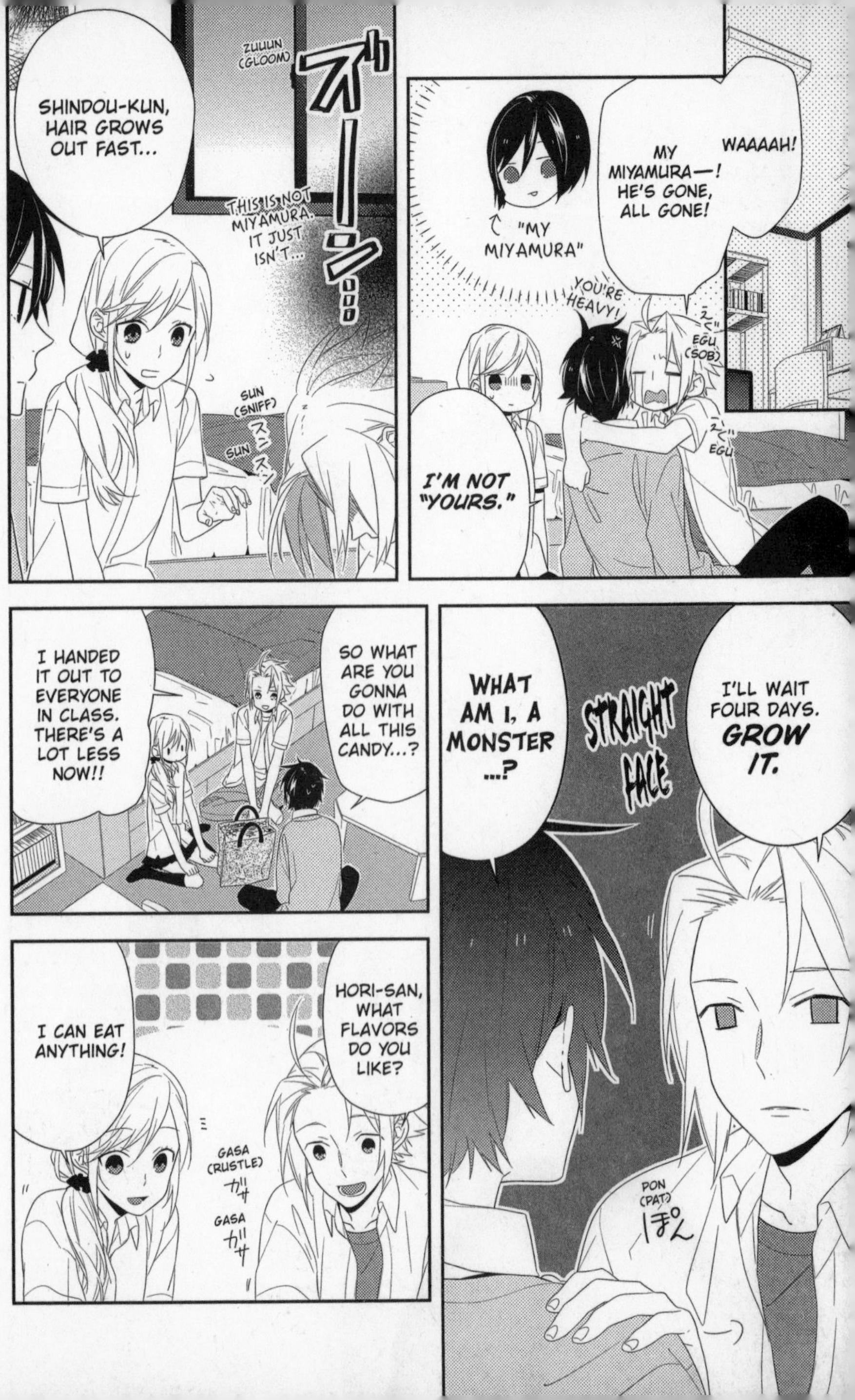
WAAAAH!
MY MIYAMURA—! HE'S GONE, ALL GONE!
"MY MIYAMURA"
YOU'RE HEAVY!
えぐ EGU (SOB)
えぐ EGU
I'M NOT "YOURS."
ZUUUN (GLOOM)
ズーン...
SHINDOU-KUN, HAIR GROWS OUT FAST...
THIS IS NOT MIYAMURA. IT JUST ISN'T...
SUN (SNIFF) スン
SUN スン
I'LL WAIT FOUR DAYS. GROW IT.
STRAIGHT FACE
WHAT AM I, A MONSTER ...?
PON (PAT) ぽん
SO WHAT ARE YOU GONNA DO WITH ALL THIS CANDY...?
I HANDED IT OUT TO EVERYONE IN CLASS. THERE'S A LOT LESS NOW!!
HORI-SAN, WHAT FLAVORS DO YOU LIKE?
GASA (RUSTLE) ガサ
GASA ガサ
I CAN EAT ANYTHING!

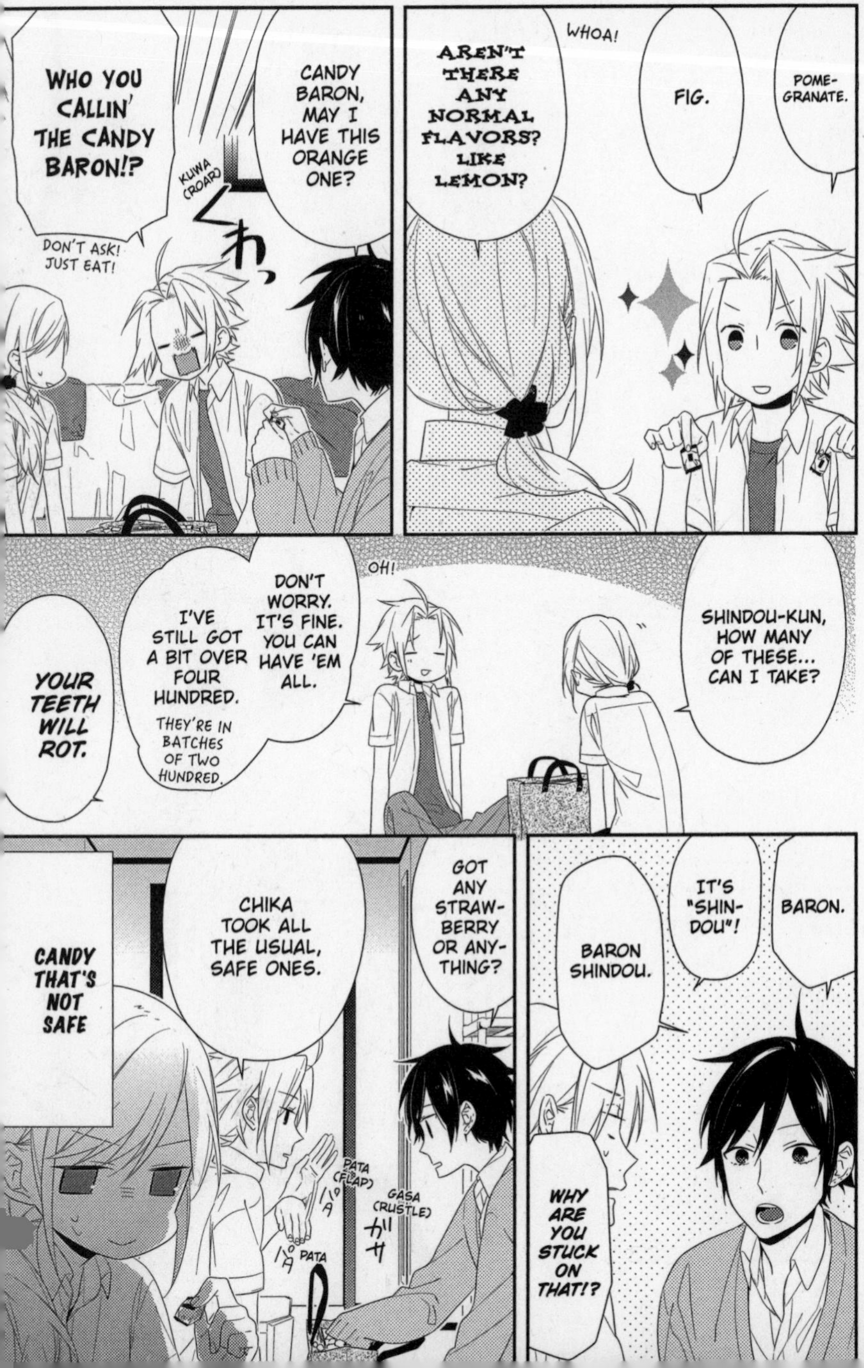
POME-GRANATE.
FIG.
WHOA!
AREN'T THERE ANY NORMAL FLAVORS? LIKE LEMON?
CANDY BARON, MAY I HAVE THIS ORANGE ONE?
KUWA (ROAR)
WHO YOU CALLIN' THE CANDY BARON!?
DON'T ASK! JUST EAT!
SHINDOU-KUN, HOW MANY OF THESE... CAN I TAKE?
OH!
DON'T WORRY. IT'S FINE. YOU CAN HAVE 'EM ALL.
I'VE STILL GOT A BIT OVER FOUR HUNDRED.
THEY'RE IN BATCHES OF TWO HUNDRED.
YOUR TEETH WILL ROT.
BARON.
IT'S "SHIN-DOU"!
BARON SHINDOU.
WHY ARE YOU STUCK ON THAT!?
GOT ANY STRAW-BERRY OR ANY-THING?
CHIKA TOOK ALL THE USUAL, SAFE ONES.
PATA (FLAP)
GASA (RUSTLE)
PATA
CANDY THAT'S NOT SAFE

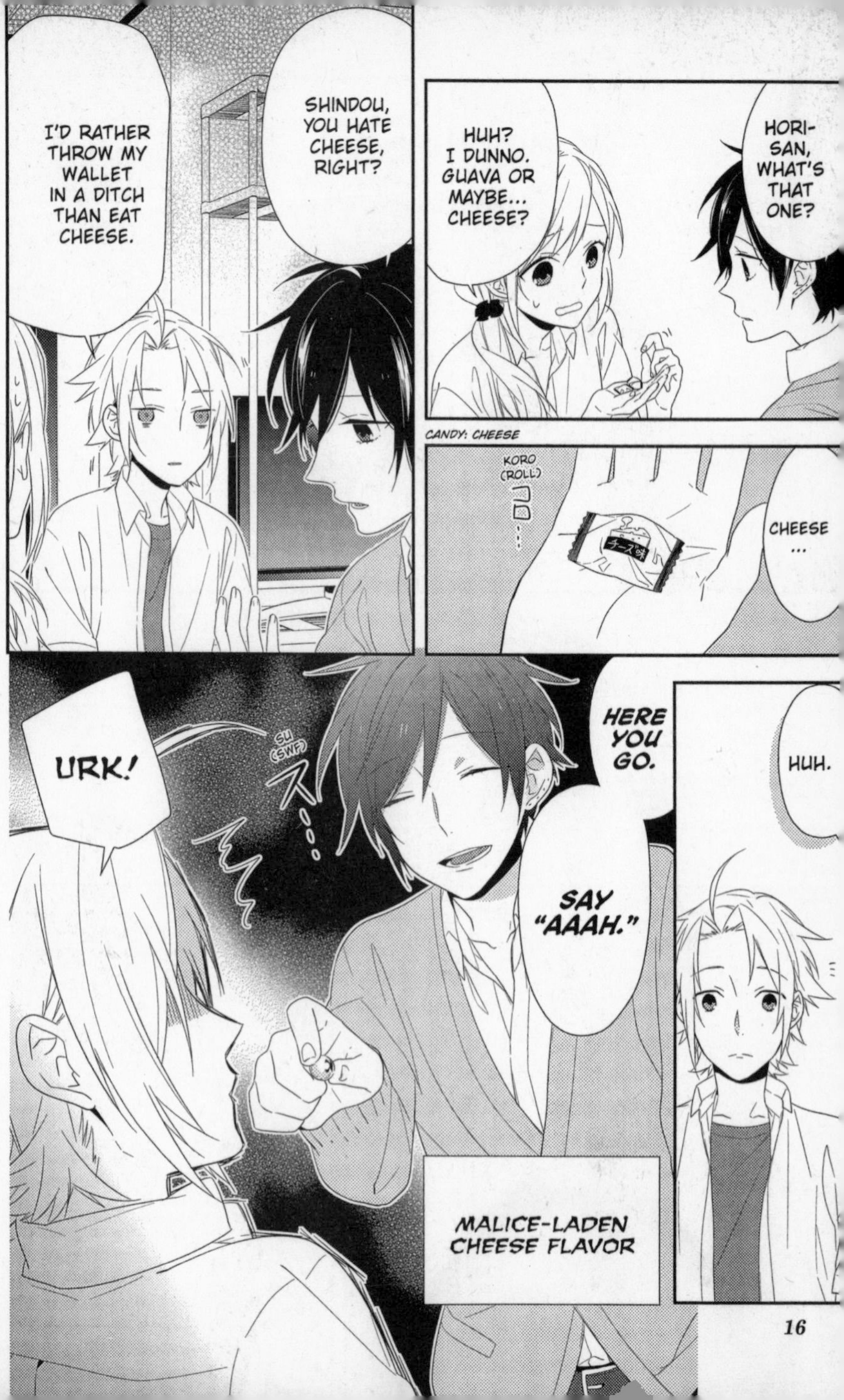
HORI-SAN, WHAT'S THAT ONE?
HUH? I DUNNO. GUAVA OR MAYBE... CHEESE?
CANDY: CHEESE
CHEESE ...
KORO (ROLL)
チーズ味
SHINDOU, YOU HATE CHEESE, RIGHT?
I'D RATHER THROW MY WALLET IN A DITCH THAN EAT CHEESE.
HUH.
HERE YOU GO.
SAY "AAAH."
SU (SWF)
URK!
MALICE-LADEN CHEESE FLAVOR

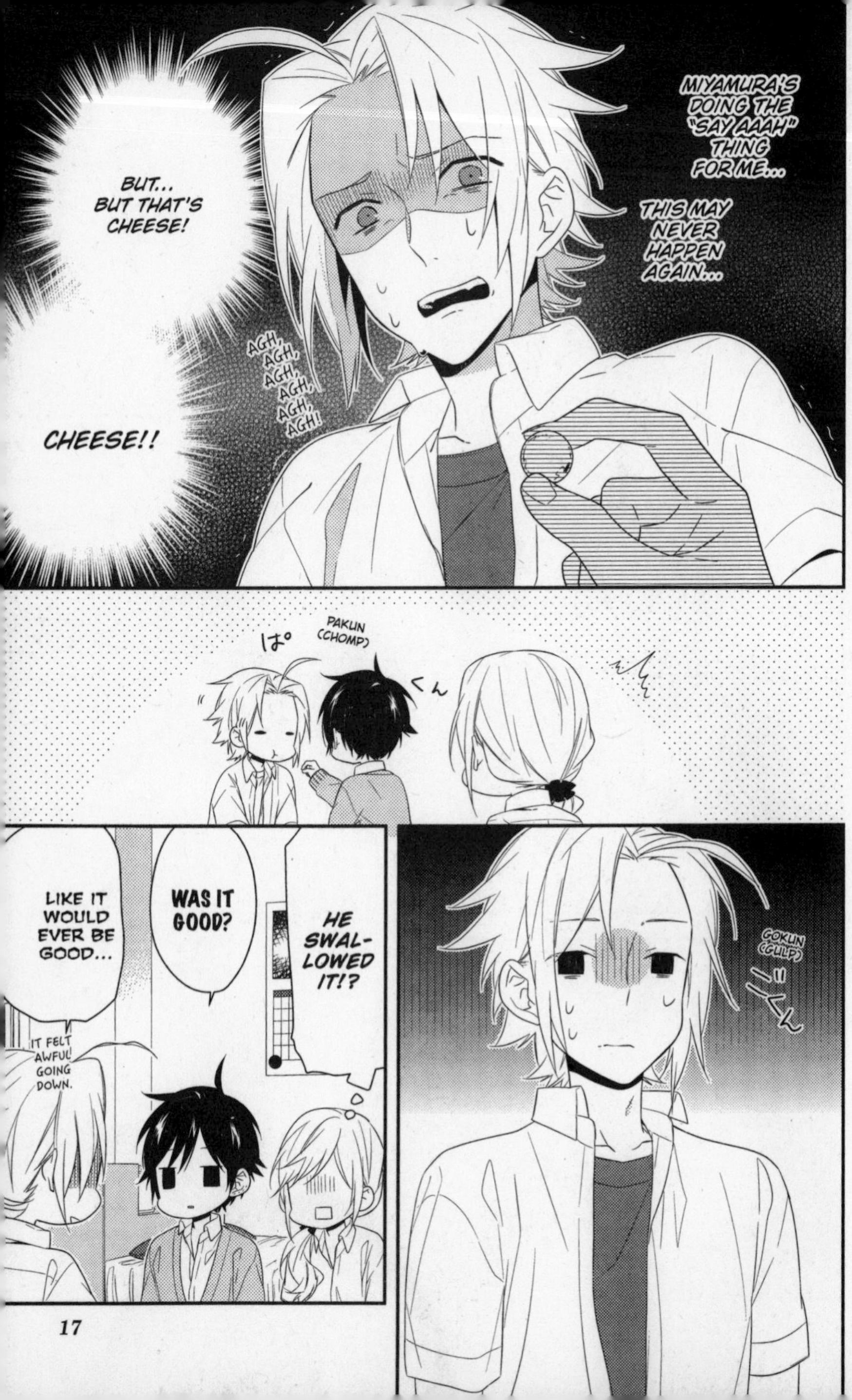
MIYAMURA'S DOING THE "SAY AAAH" THING FOR ME...
THIS MAY NEVER HAPPEN AGAIN...
BUT... BUT THAT'S CHEESE!
AGH, AGH, AGH, AGH, AGH, AGH!
CHEESE!!
ぱ
PAKUN (CHOMP)
くん
GOKUN (GULP)
ごくん
HE SWAL-LOWED IT!?
WAS IT GOOD?
LIKE IT WOULD EVER BE GOOD...
IT FELT AWFUL GOING DOWN.

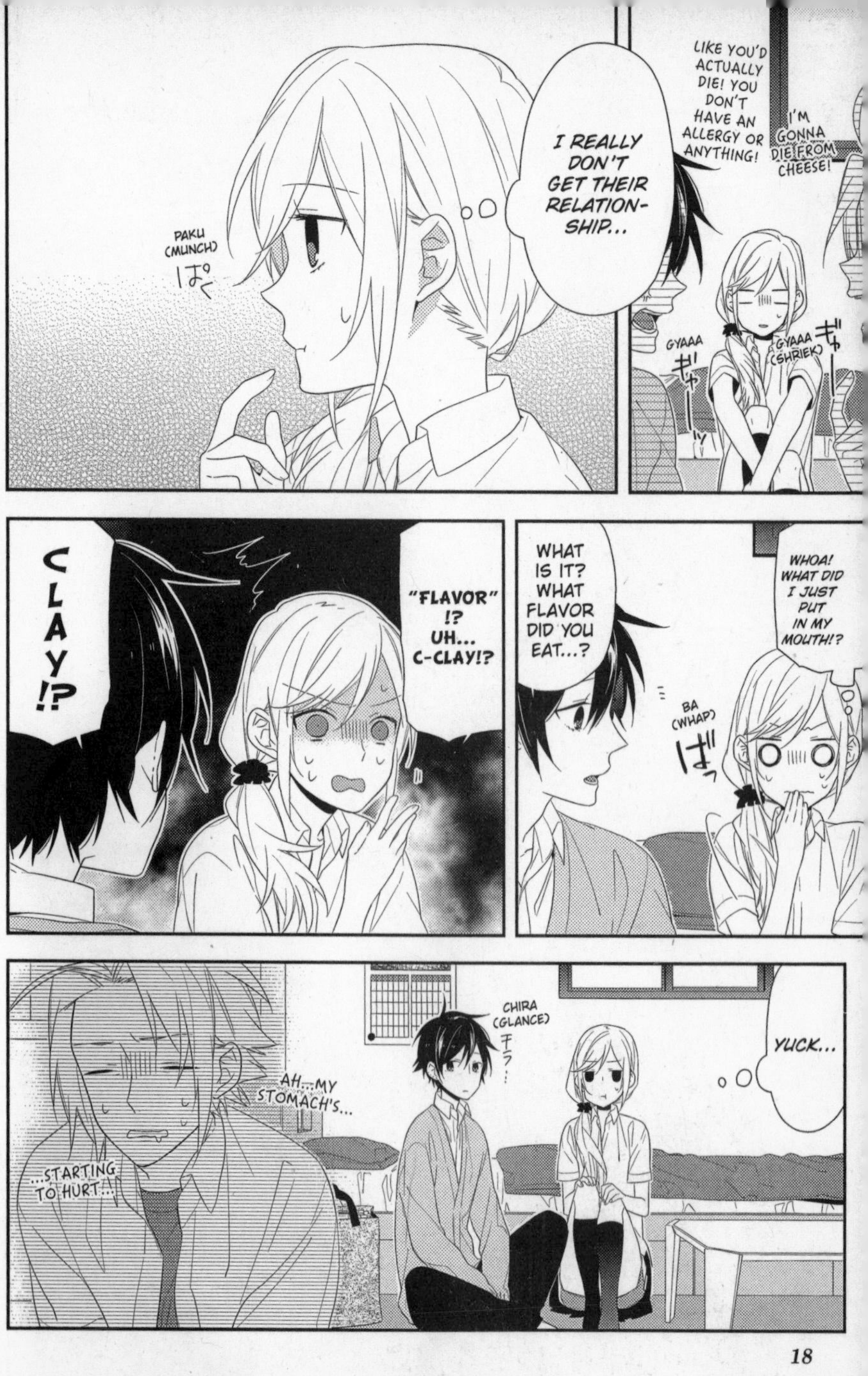
I'M GONNA DIE FROM CHEESE!
LIKE YOU'D ACTUALLY DIE! YOU DON'T HAVE AN ALLERGY OR ANYTHING!
GYAAA (SHRIEK)
ギャー
GYAAA
ギャーッ
I REALLY DON'T GET THEIR RELATION-SHIP...
PAKU (MUNCH)
ぱく
WHOA! WHAT DID I JUST PUT IN MY MOUTH!?
WHAT IS IT? WHAT FLAVOR DID YOU EAT...?
BA (WHAP)
ばっ
"FLAVOR"!? UH... C-CLAY!?
CLAY!?
YUCK...
CHIRA (GLANCE)
チラ...
AH... MY STOMACH'S...
...STARTING TO HURT...

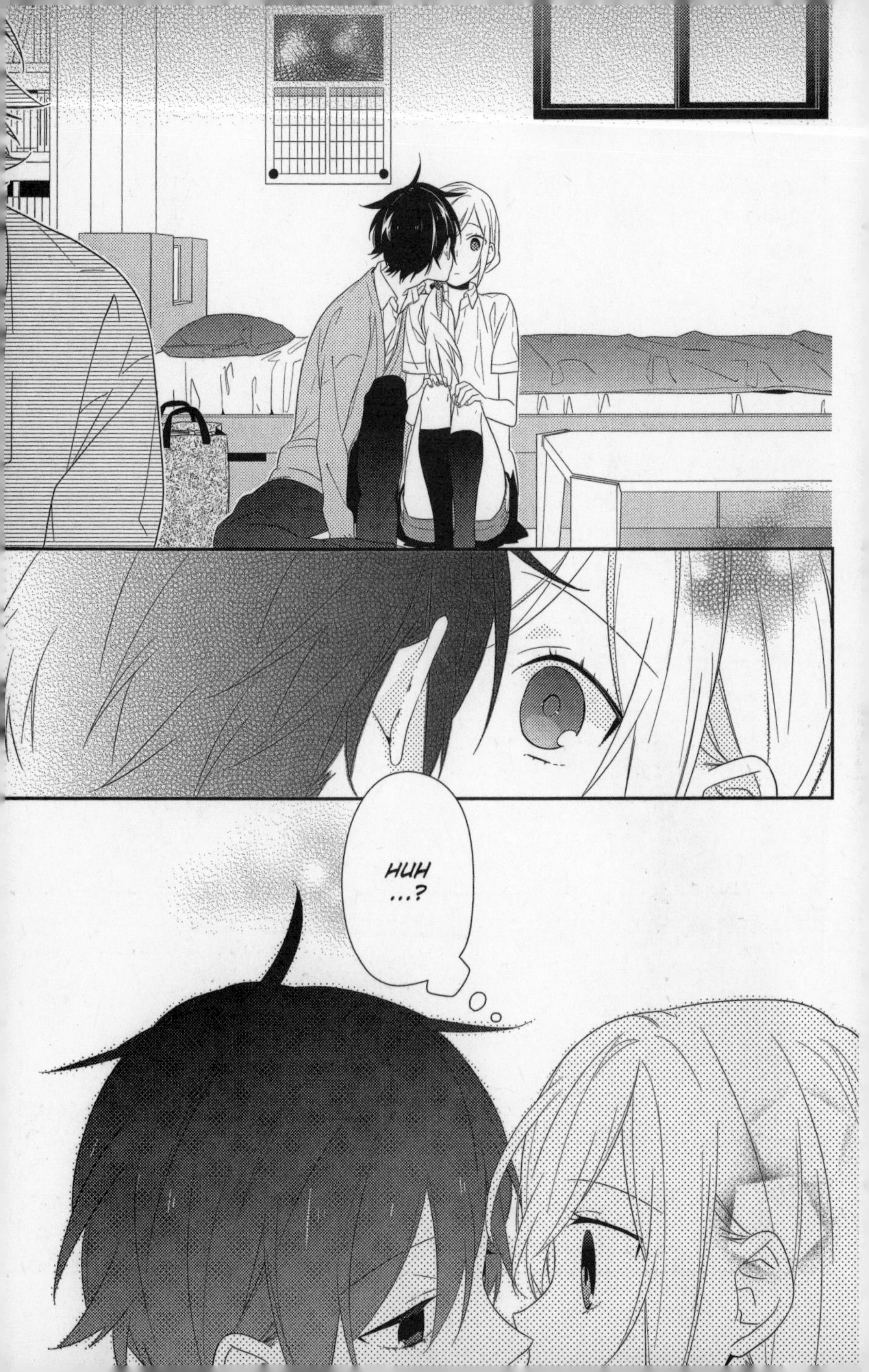
HUH ...?

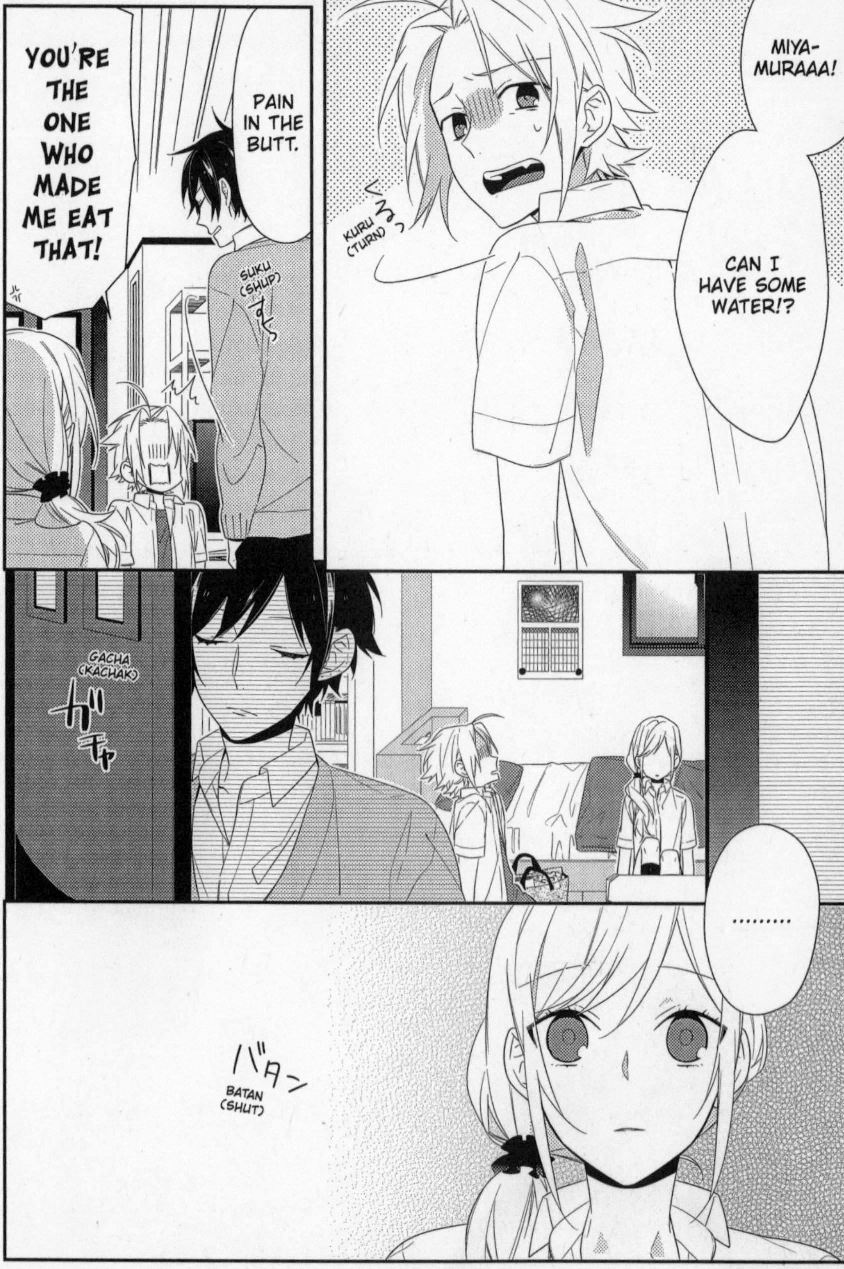
MIYA-MURAAA!
CAN I HAVE SOME WATER!?
KURU (TURN)
PAIN IN THE BUTT.
YOU'RE THE ONE WHO MADE ME EAT THAT!
SUKU (SHUP)
GACHA (KACHAK)
....
BATAN (SHUT)

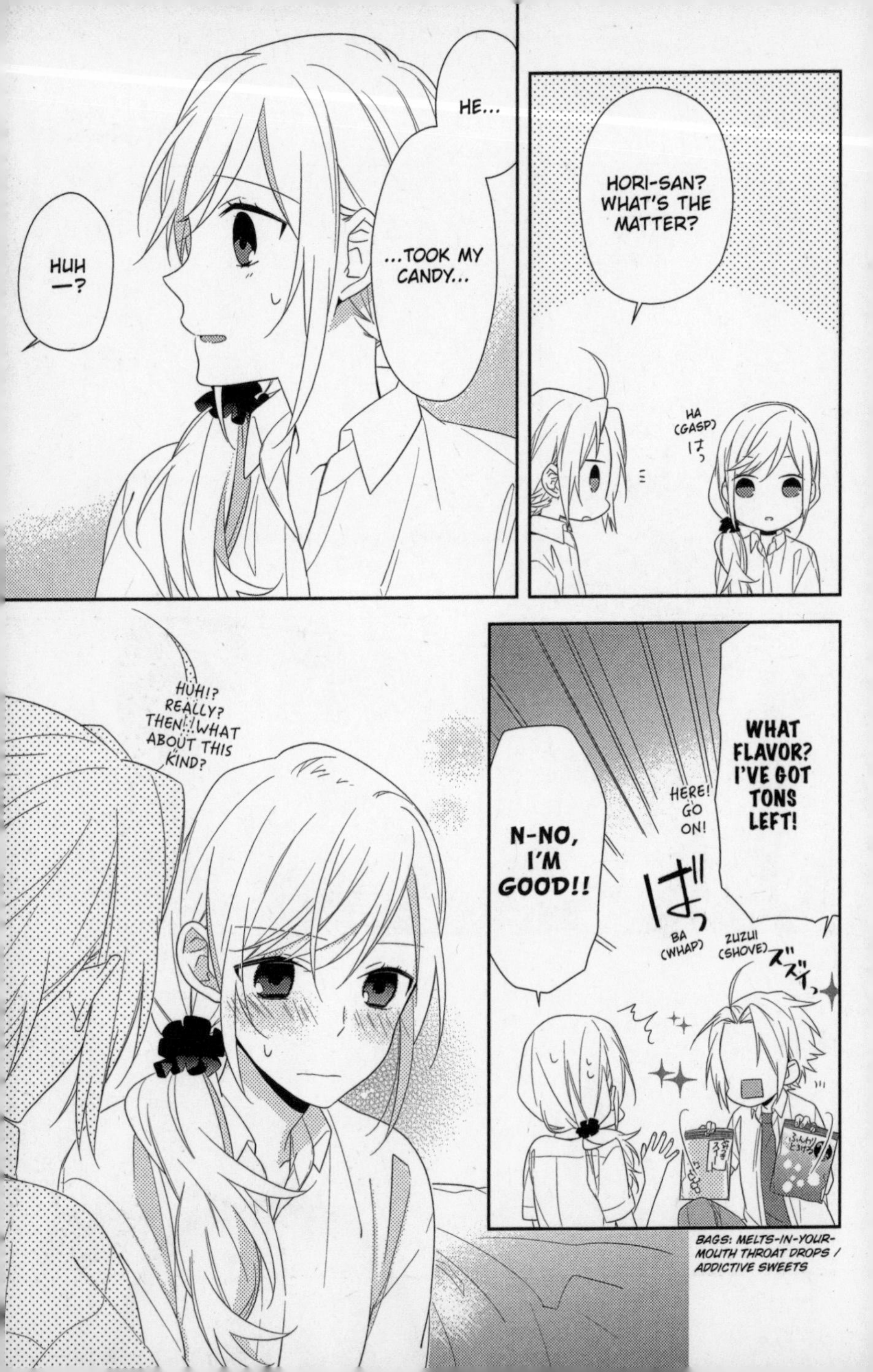
HORI-SAN? WHAT'S THE MATTER?
HA (GASP) はっ
HE...
...TOOK MY CANDY...
HUH —?
WHAT FLAVOR? I'VE GOT TONS LEFT!
HERE! GO ON!
N-NO, I'M GOOD!!
ばっ
BA (WHAP)
ZUZUI (SHOVE) ズズイッ
BAGS: MELTS-IN-YOUR-MOUTH THROAT DROPS / ADDICTIVE SWEETS
HUH!? REALLY? THEN... WHAT ABOUT THIS KIND?

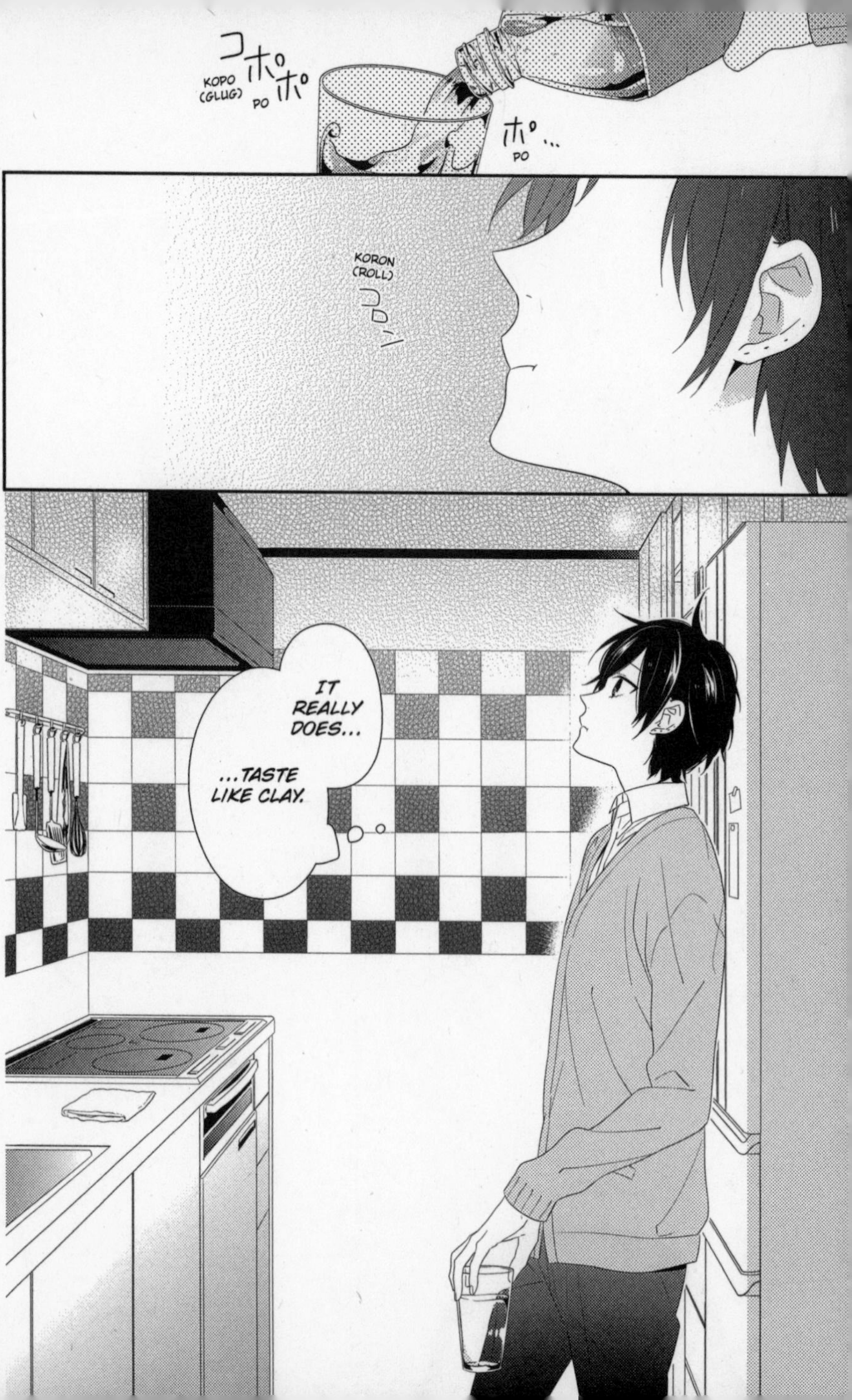

コポポ
KOPO (GLUG)
PO
ポ…
PO
KORON (ROLL)
コロン
IT REALLY DOES… …TASTE LIKE CLAY.

HORIMIYA

HORIMIYA

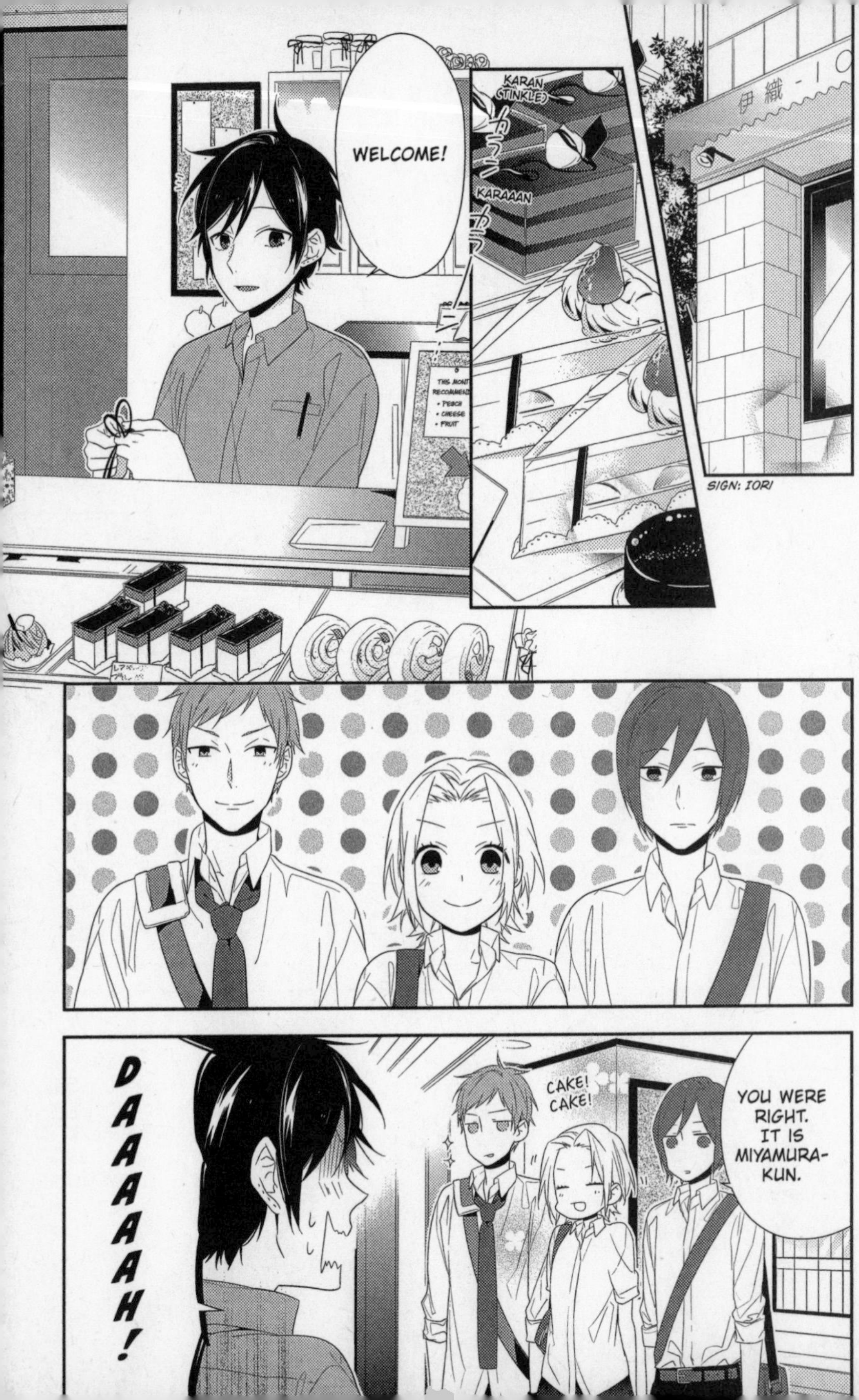
伊織
SIGN: IORI
KARAN (TINKLE)
KARAAAN
WELCOME!
PEACH
CHEESE
FRUIT
YOU WERE RIGHT. IT IS MIYAMURA-KUN.
CAKE! CAKE!
DAAAAAH!

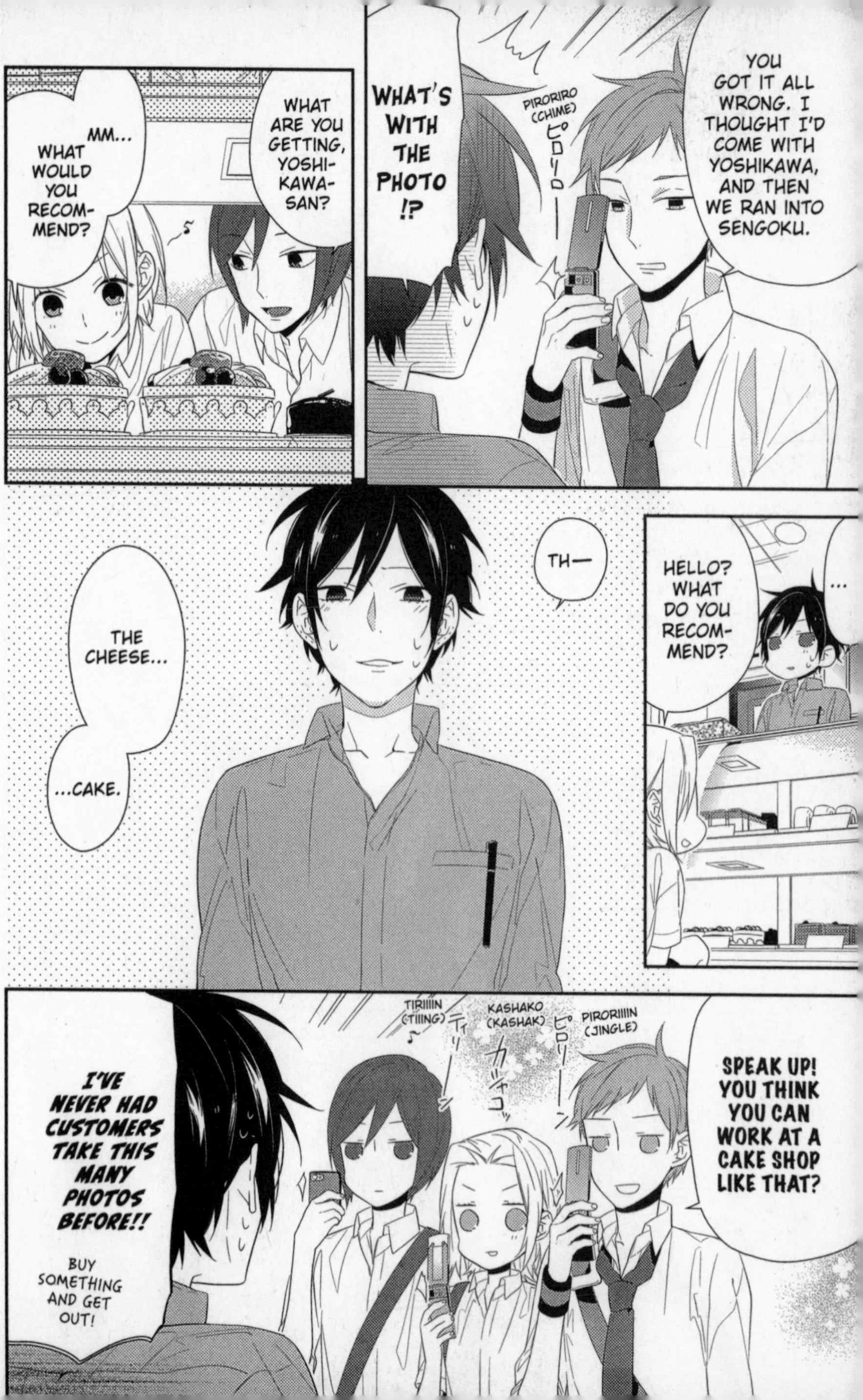
YOU GOT IT ALL WRONG. I THOUGHT I'D COME WITH YOSHIKAWA, AND THEN WE RAN INTO SENGOKU.
PIRORIRO (CHIME)
ピロリロ
WHAT'S WITH THE PHOTO !?
WHAT ARE YOU GETTING, YOSHIKAWA-SAN?
MM... WHAT WOULD YOU RECOMMEND?
...
HELLO? WHAT DO YOU RECOMMEND?
TH—
THE CHEESE...
...CAKE.
SPEAK UP! YOU THINK YOU CAN WORK AT A CAKE SHOP LIKE THAT?
PIRORIIIIN (JINGLE)
ピロリーン
KASHAKO (KASHAK)
カシャコッ
TIRIIIIN (TIIING)
ティリーン
I'VE NEVER HAD CUSTOMERS TAKE THIS MANY PHOTOS BEFORE!!
BUY SOMETHING AND GET OUT!

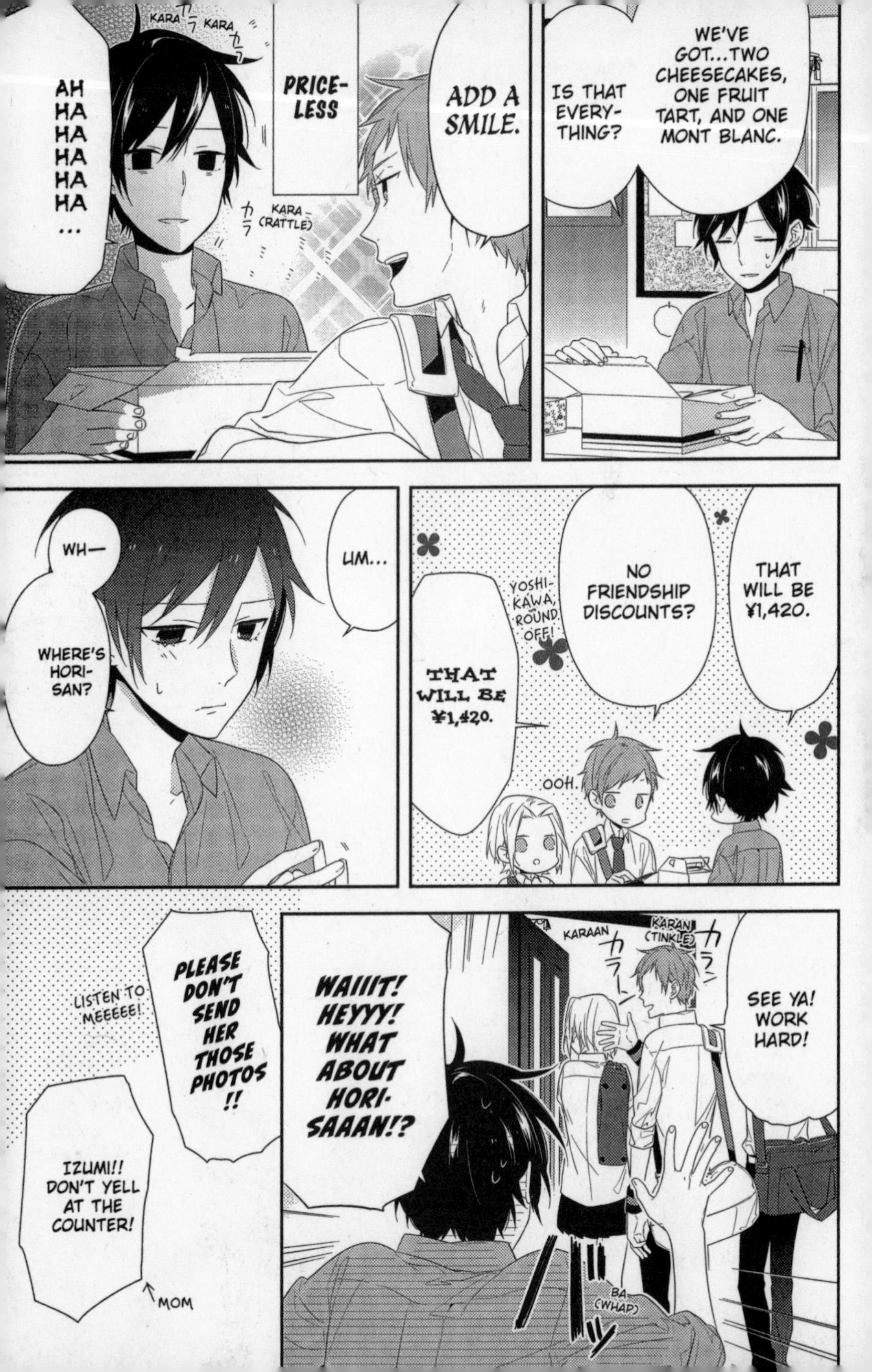
WE'VE GOT...TWO CHEESECAKES, ONE FRUIT TART, AND ONE MONT BLANC.
IS THAT EVERYTHING?
ADD A SMILE.
PRICELESS
KARA KARA
AH HA HA HA HA HA...
KARA (RATTLE)
THAT WILL BE ¥1,420.
NO FRIENDSHIP DISCOUNTS?
YOSHIKAWA, ROUND OFF!
THAT WILL BE ¥1,420.
OOH.
UM...
WH—
WHERE'S HORI-SAN?
SEE YA! WORK HARD!
KARAN (TINKLE)
KARAAN
WAIIIT! HEYYY! WHAT ABOUT HORI-SAAAN!?
BA (WHAP)
PLEASE DON'T SEND HER THOSE PHOTOS!!
LISTEN TO MEEEEEE!
IZUMI!! DON'T YELL AT THE COUNTER!
MOM

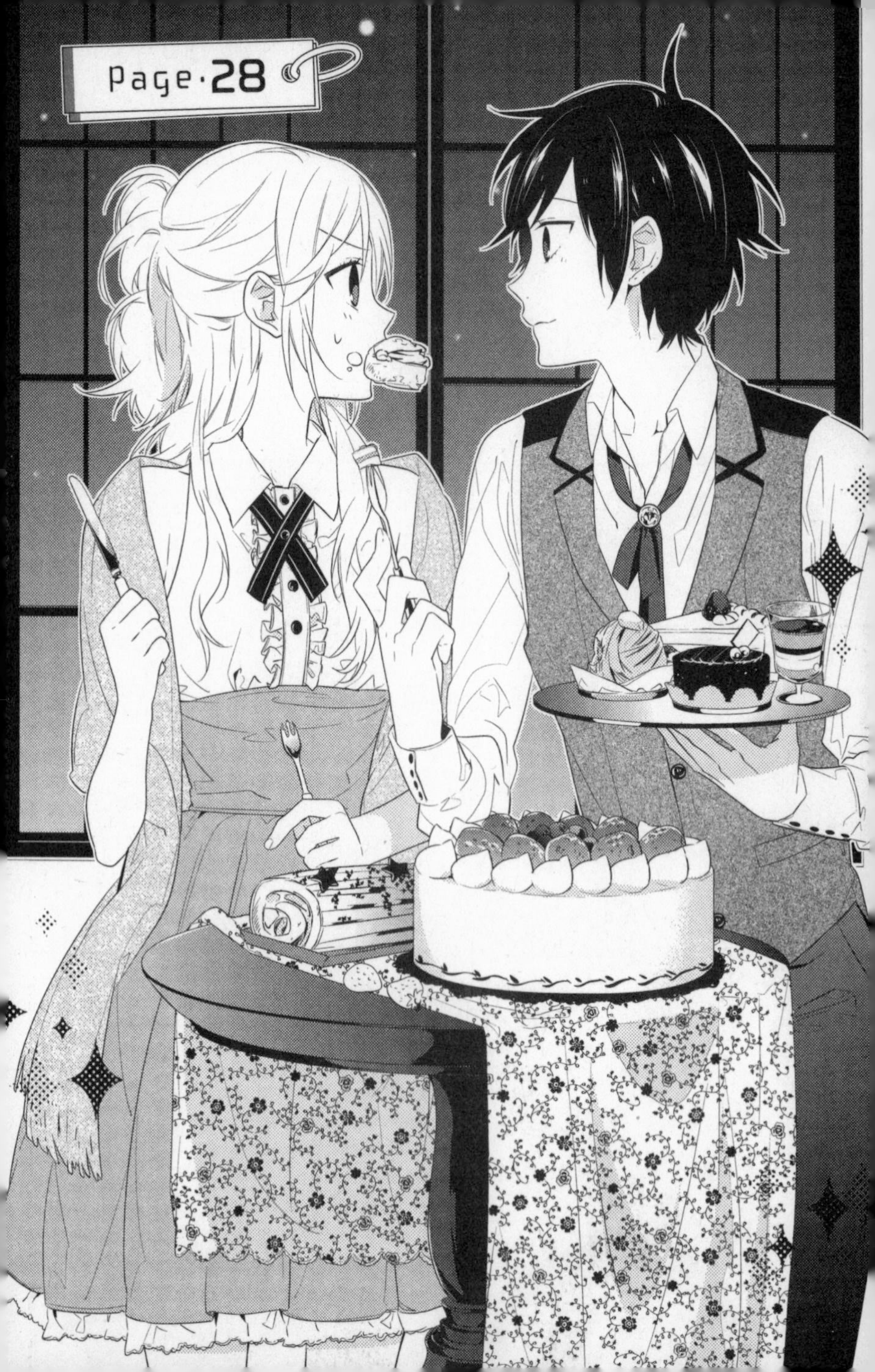
Page·28

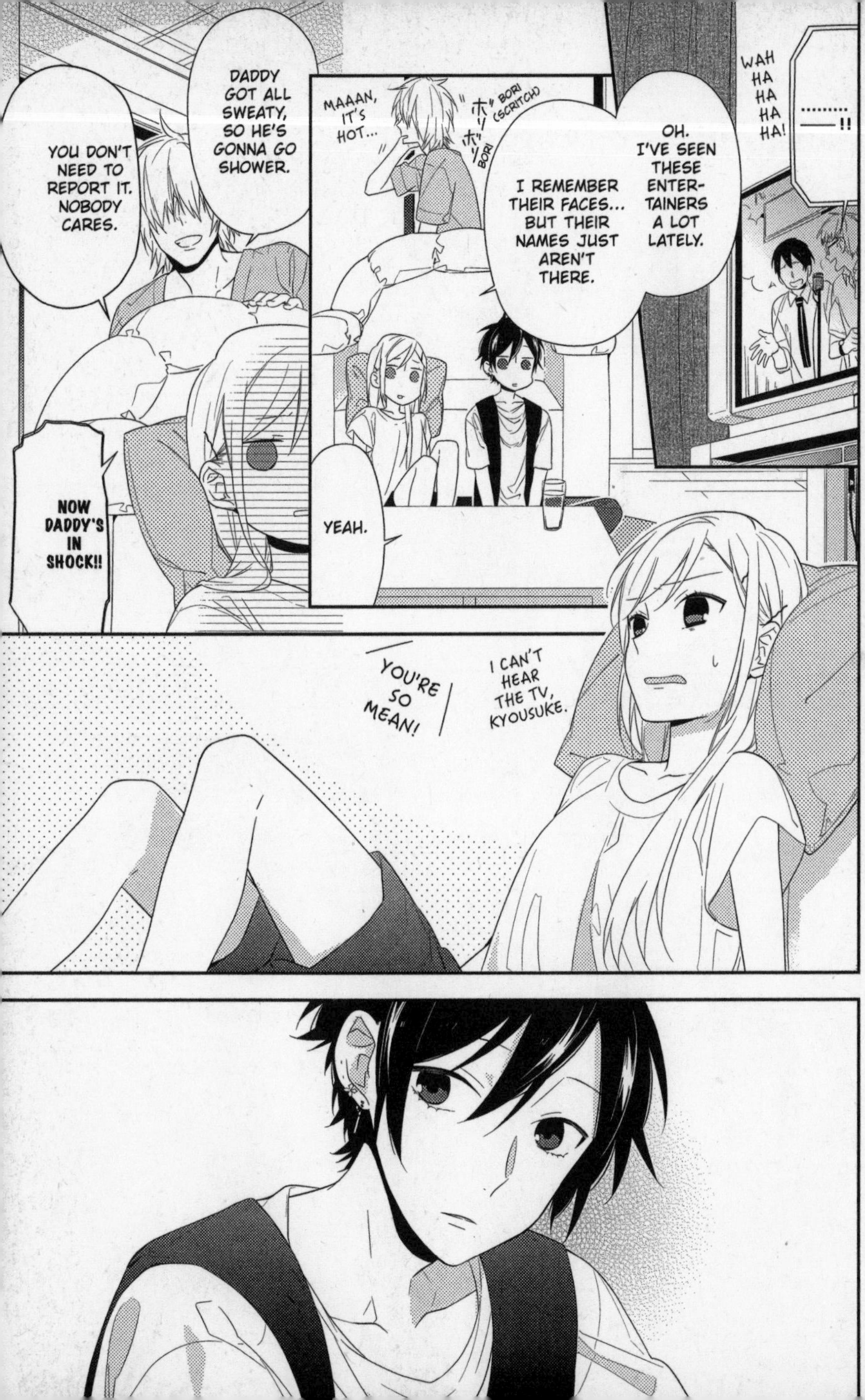
WAH HA HA HA HA!
.... ——!!
OH. I'VE SEEN THESE ENTERTAINERS A LOT LATELY.
I REMEMBER THEIR FACES... BUT THEIR NAMES JUST AREN'T THERE.
MAAAN, IT'S HOT...
ボリ BORI (SCRITCH)
ボリ BORI
YEAH.
DADDY GOT ALL SWEATY, SO HE'S GONNA GO SHOWER.
YOU DON'T NEED TO REPORT IT. NOBODY CARES.
NOW DADDY'S IN SHOCK!!
I CAN'T HEAR THE TV, KYOUSUKE.
YOU'RE SO MEAN!

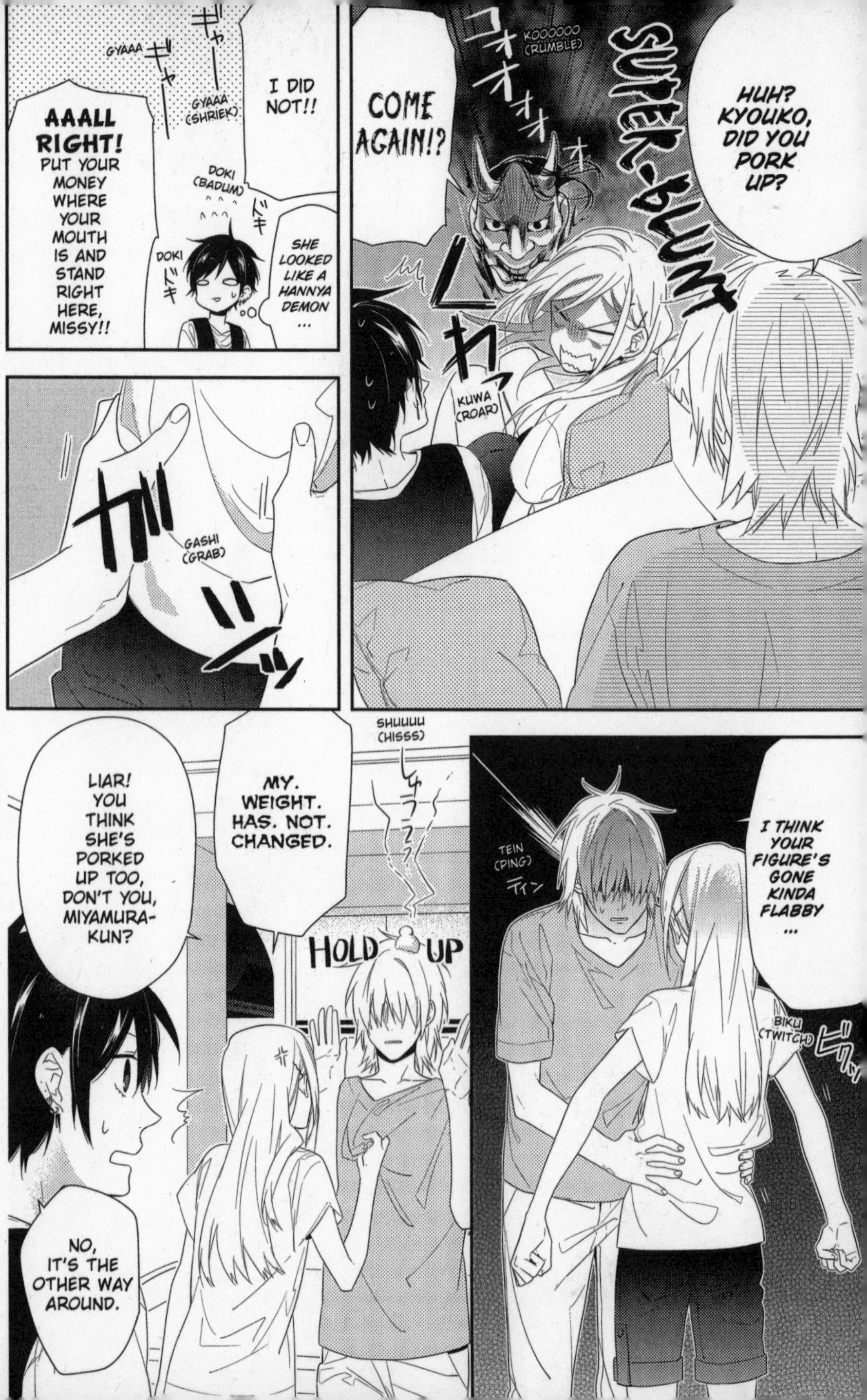
HUH? KYOUKO, DID YOU PORK UP?
SUPER-BLUNT
KOOOOOO (RUMBLE)
COME AGAIN!?
KUWA (ROAR)
I DID NOT!!
GYAAA
GYAAA (SHRIEK)
AAALL RIGHT! PUT YOUR MONEY WHERE YOUR MOUTH IS AND STAND RIGHT HERE, MISSY!!
SHE LOOKED LIKE A HANNYA DEMON...
DOKI (BADUM)
DOKI
GASHI (GRAB)
I THINK YOUR FIGURE'S GONE KINDA FLABBY...
TEIN (PING)
BIKU (TWITCH)
SHUUUU (HISSS)
MY. WEIGHT. HAS. NOT. CHANGED.
HOLD UP
LIAR! YOU THINK SHE'S PORKED UP TOO, DON'T YOU, MIYAMURA-KUN?
NO, IT'S THE OTHER WAY AROUND.

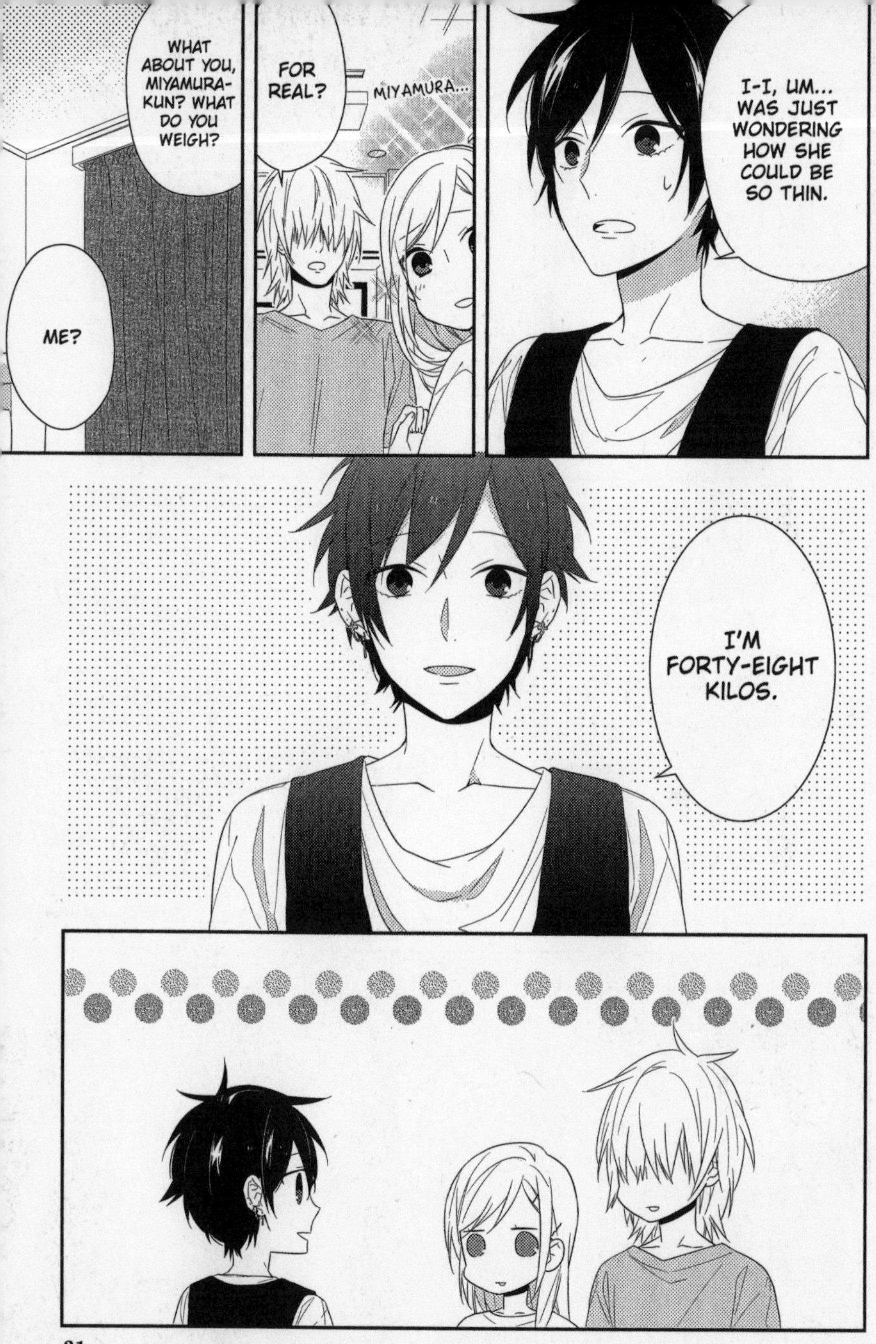
I-I, UM... WAS JUST WONDERING HOW SHE COULD BE SO THIN.
FOR REAL?
MIYAMURA...
WHAT ABOUT YOU, MIYAMURA-KUN? WHAT DO YOU WEIGH?
ME?
I'M FORTY-EIGHT KILOS.

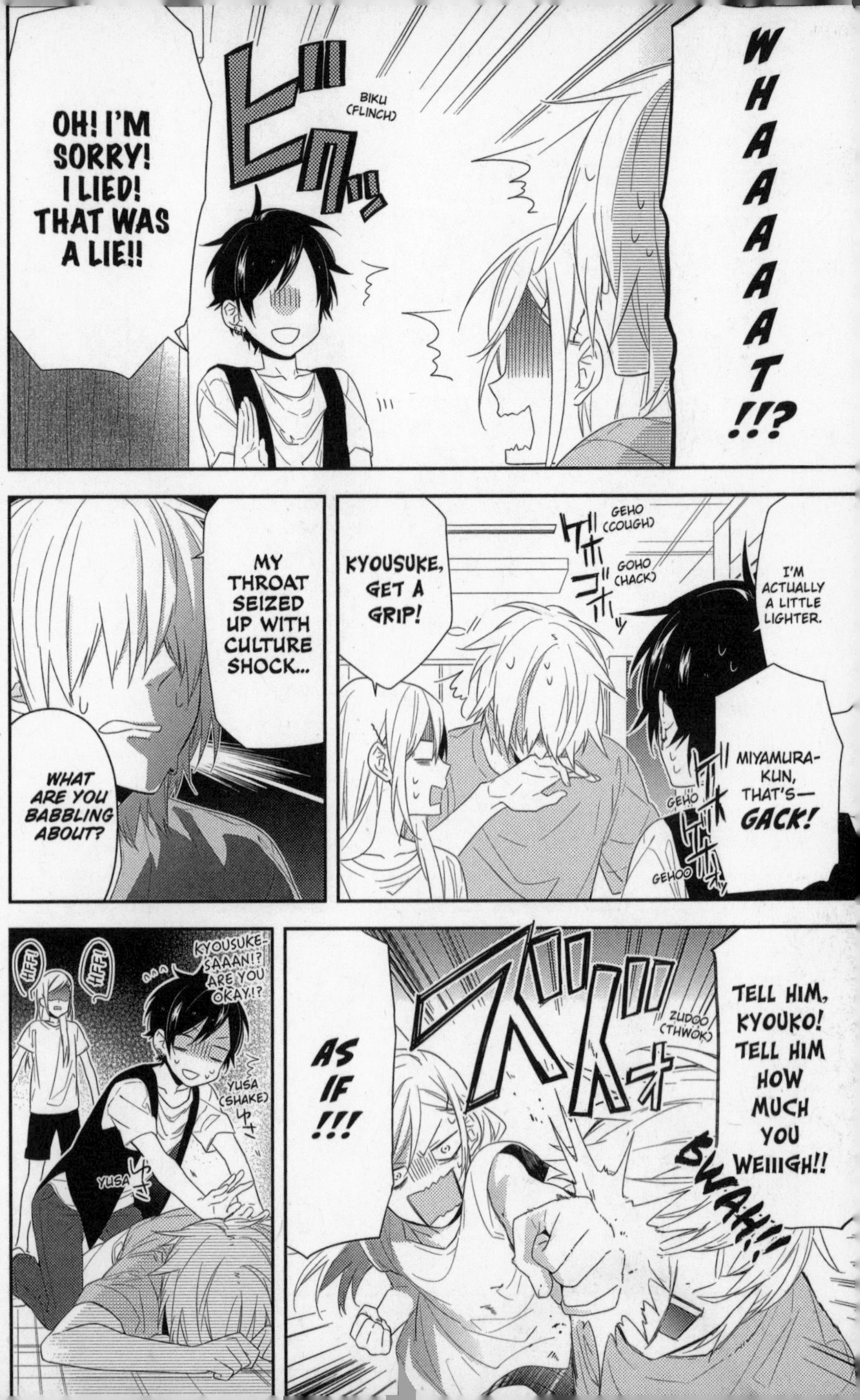
WHAAAAAAT!!?
BIKU (FLINCH)
OH! I'M SORRY! I LIED! THAT WAS A LIE!!
I'M ACTUALLY A LITTLE LIGHTER.
GEHO (COUGH)
GOHO (HACK)
KYOUSUKE, GET A GRIP!
MIYAMURA-KUN, THAT'S—GACK!
GEHO
GEHOO
MY THROAT SEIZED UP WITH CULTURE SHOCK...
WHAT ARE YOU BABBLING ABOUT?
TELL HIM, KYOUKO! TELL HIM HOW MUCH YOU WEIIIGH!!
ZUDOO (THWOK)
AS IF!!!
SWAH!!
KYOUSUKE-SAAAN!? ARE YOU OKAY!?
HFF!
HFF!
YUSA (SHAKE)
YUSA

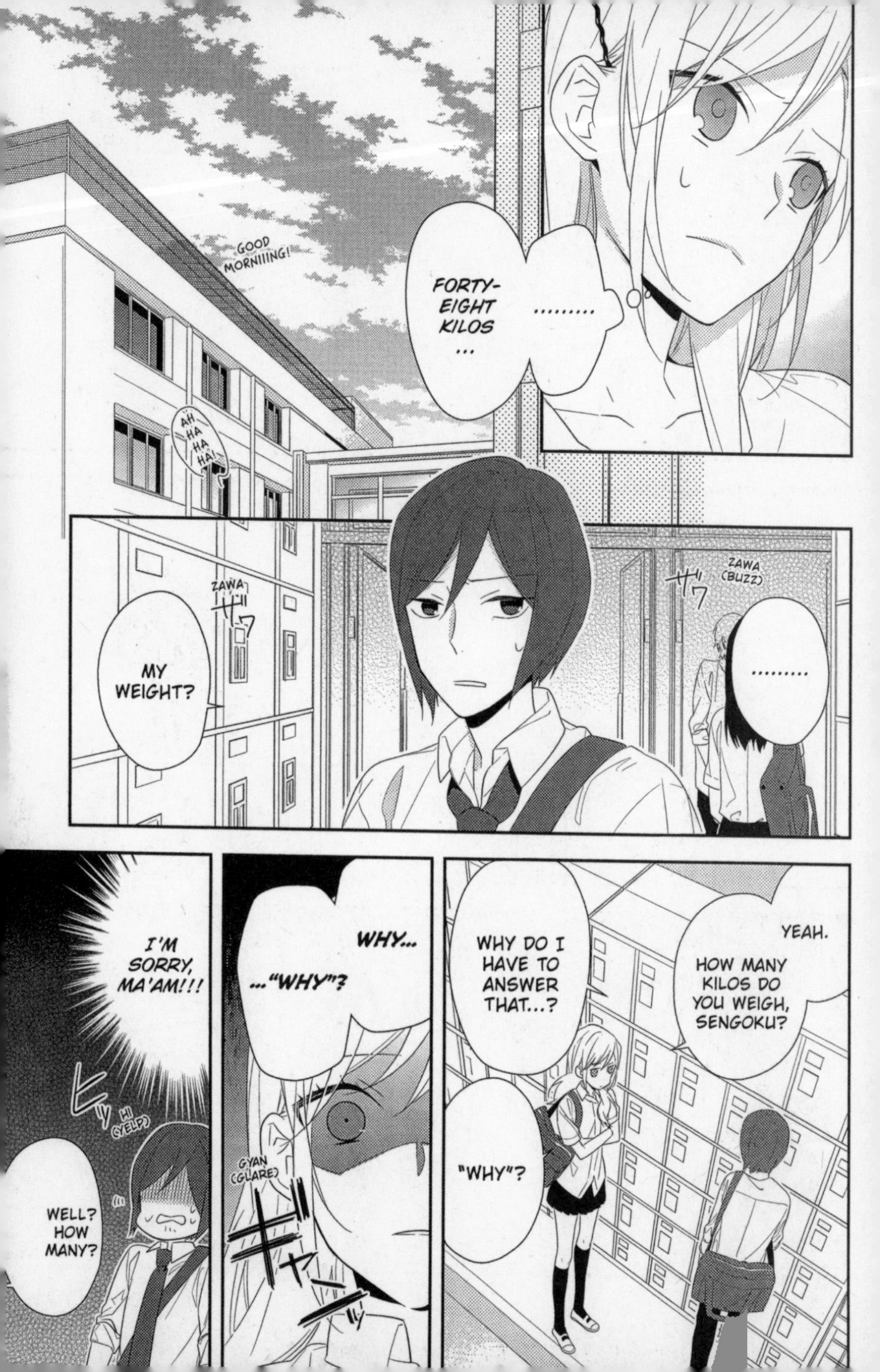
....
FORTY-EIGHT KILOS ...
GOOD MORNIIING!
AH HA HA HA!
ZAWA (BUZZ)
....
ZAWA
MY WEIGHT?
YEAH.
HOW MANY KILOS DO YOU WEIGH, SENGOKU?
WHY DO I HAVE TO ANSWER THAT...?
"WHY"?
WHY...
..."WHY"?
GYAN (GLARE)
I'M SORRY, MA'AM!!!
HI (YELP)
WELL? HOW MANY?

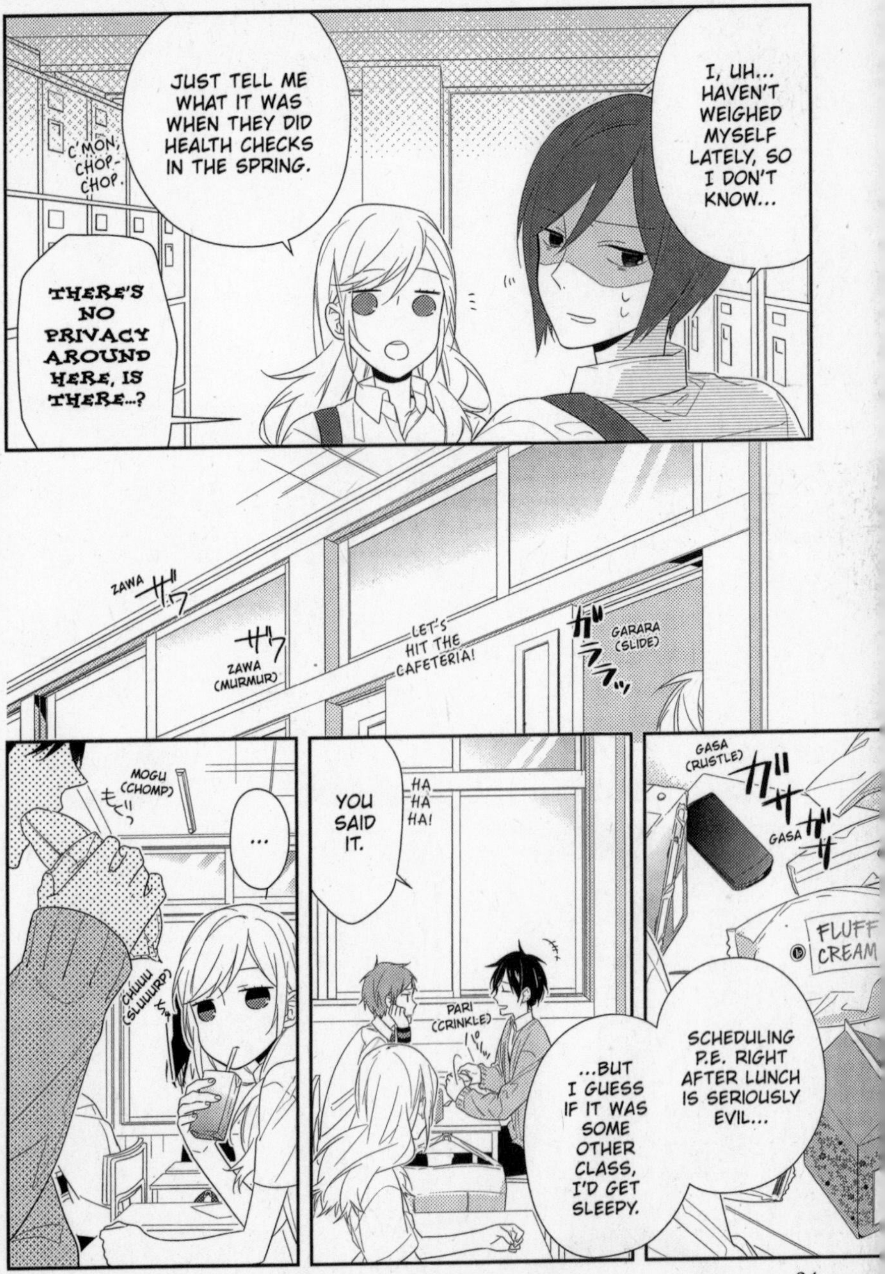
I, UH... HAVEN'T WEIGHED MYSELF LATELY, SO I DON'T KNOW...
JUST TELL ME WHAT IT WAS WHEN THEY DID HEALTH CHECKS IN THE SPRING.
C'MON, CHOP-CHOP.
THERE'S NO PRIVACY AROUND HERE, IS THERE...?
GARARA (SLIDE)
LET'S HIT THE CAFETERIA!
ZAWA (MURMUR)
ZAWA
GASA (RUSTLE)
GASA
FLUFF CREAM
SCHEDULING P.E. RIGHT AFTER LUNCH IS SERIOUSLY EVIL...
...BUT I GUESS IF IT WAS SOME OTHER CLASS, I'D GET SLEEPY.
HA HA HA!
YOU SAID IT.
PARI (CRINKLE)
MOGU (CHOMP)
...
CHUUU (SLUUURP)

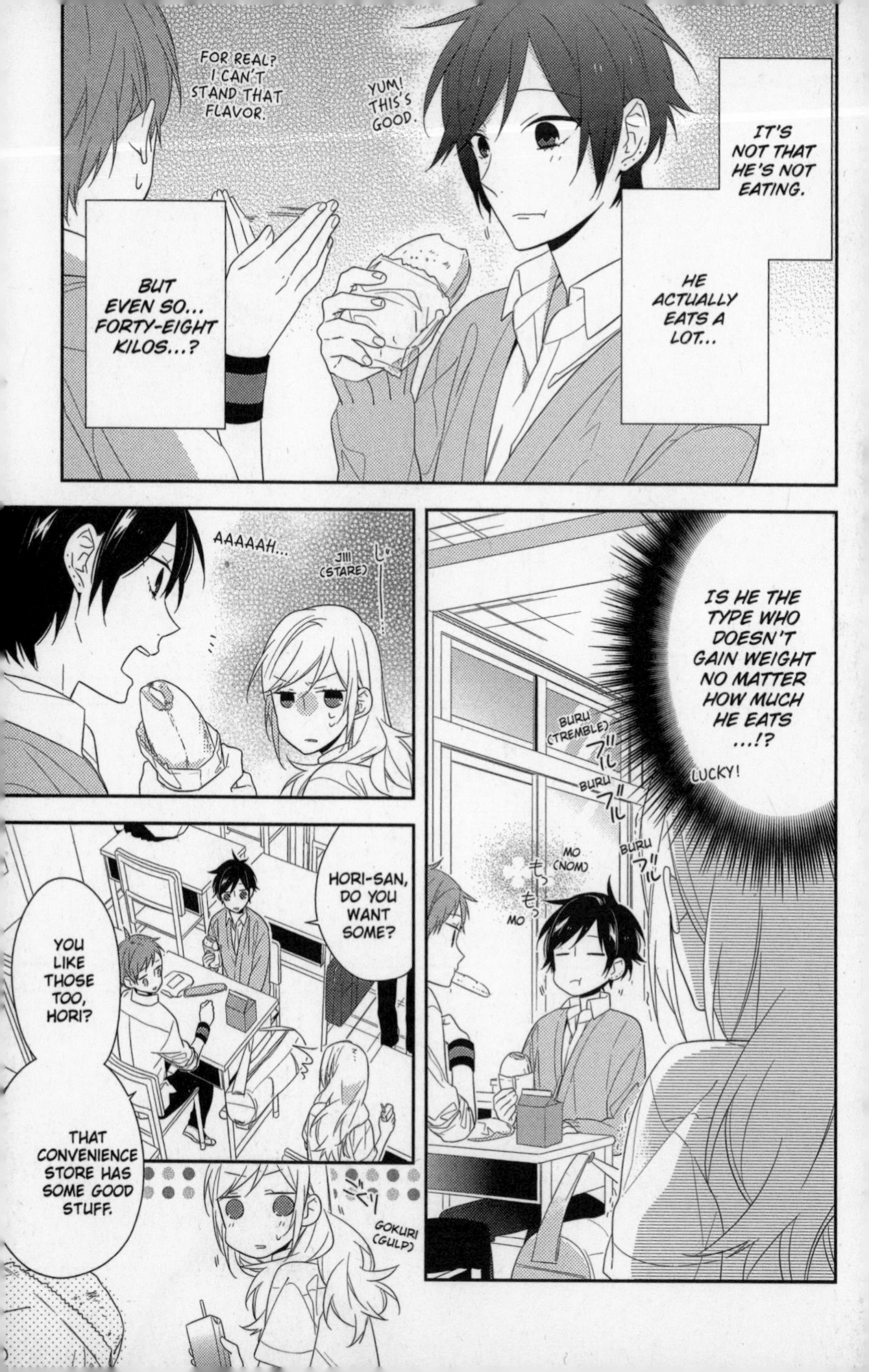
IT'S NOT THAT HE'S NOT EATING.
HE ACTUALLY EATS A LOT...
YUM! THIS'S GOOD.
FOR REAL? I CAN'T STAND THAT FLAVOR.
BUT EVEN SO... FORTY-EIGHT KILOS...?
IS HE THE TYPE WHO DOESN'T GAIN WEIGHT NO MATTER HOW MUCH HE EATS ...!?
LUCKY!
BURU (TREMBLE) ブル
BURU ブル
BURU ブル
MO (NOM) もっ
MO もっ
AAAAAH...
JIII (STARE) じー
HORI-SAN, DO YOU WANT SOME?
YOU LIKE THOSE TOO, HORI?
THAT CONVENIENCE STORE HAS SOME GOOD STUFF.
GOKURI (GULP) ごくり

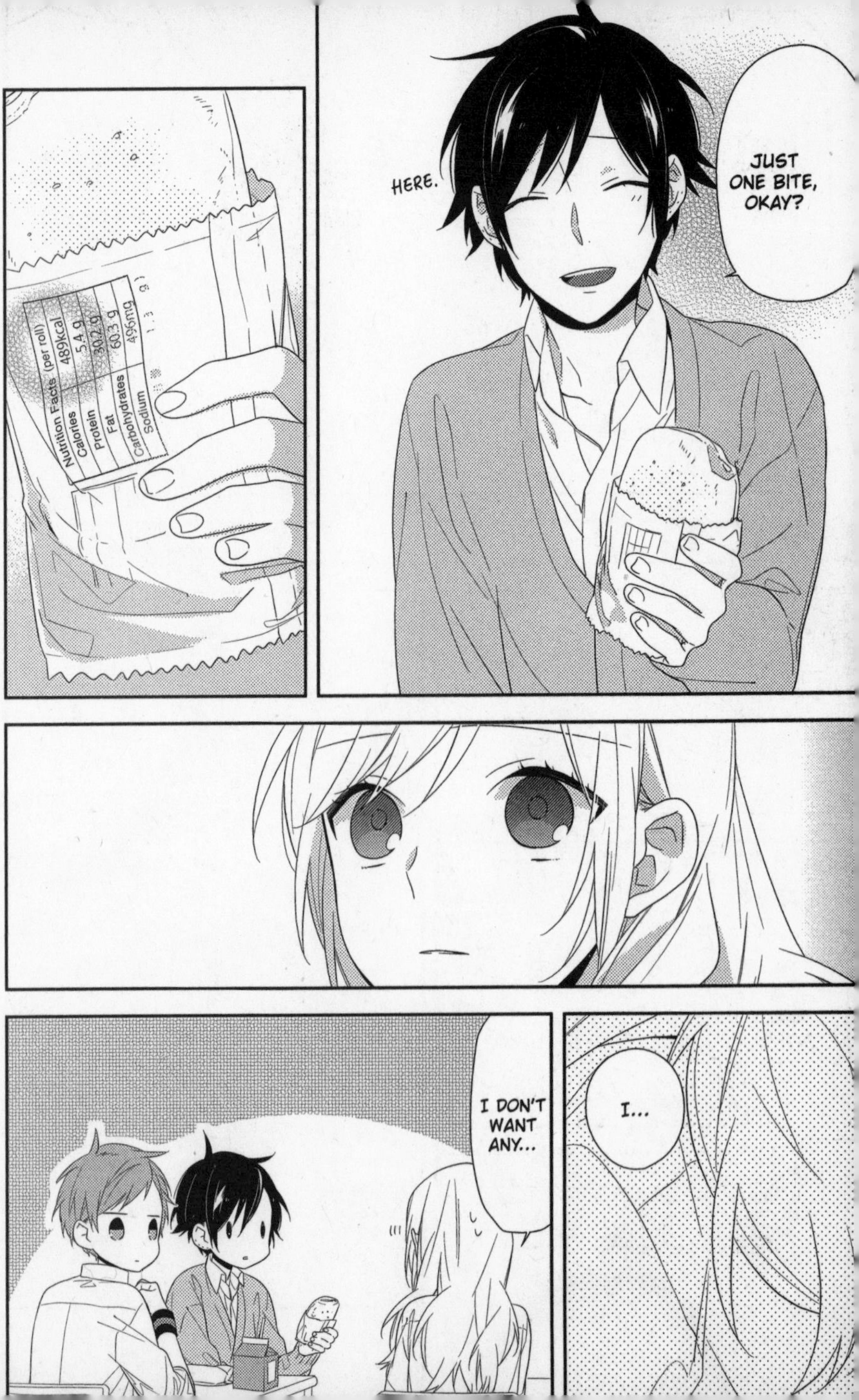
JUST ONE BITE, OKAY?
HERE.
Nutrition Facts (per roll)
Calories 489kcal
Protein 5.4 g
Fat 30.2 g
Carbohydrates 60.3 g
Sodium 496mg
I...
I DON'T WANT ANY...

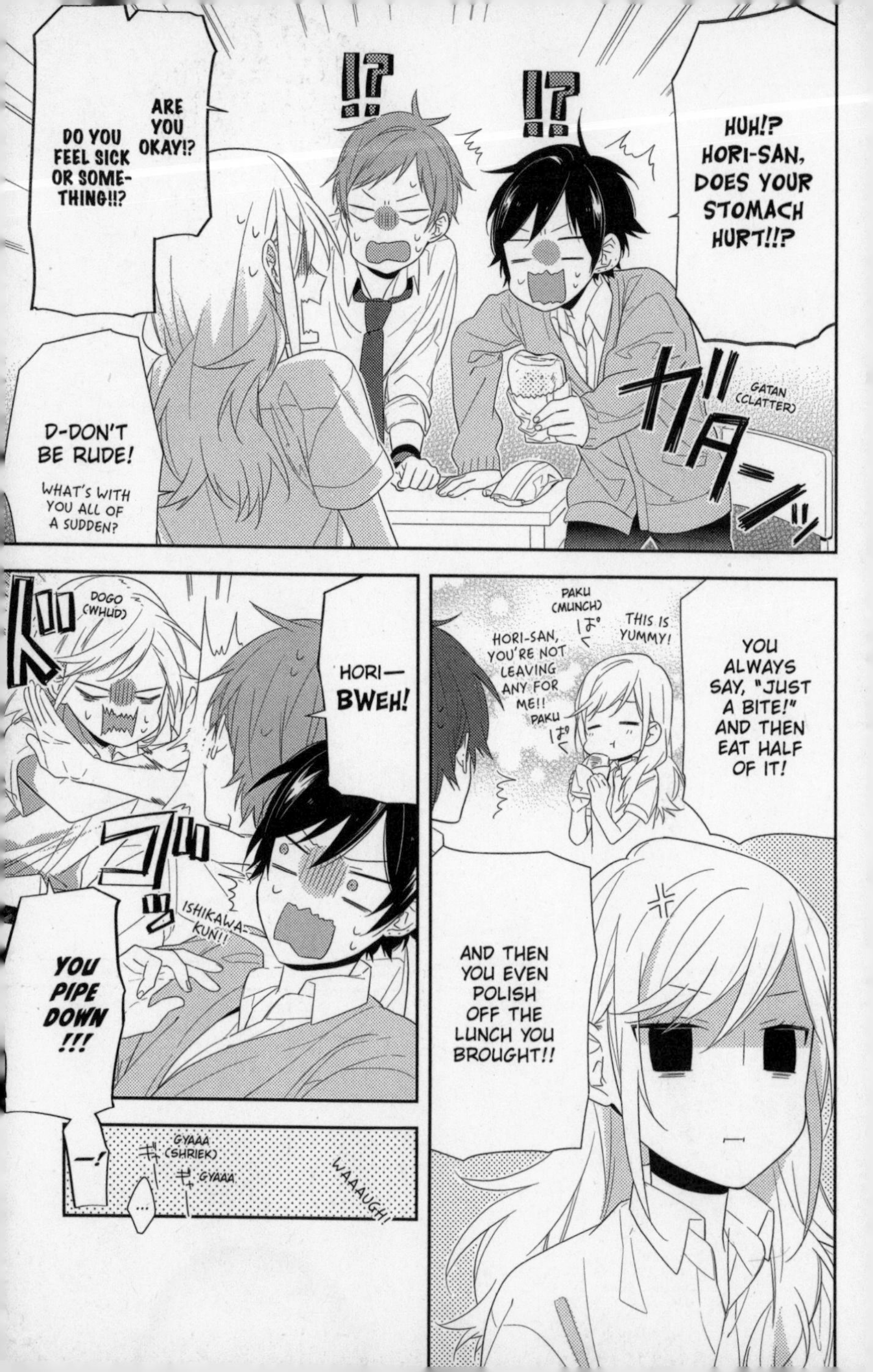

HUH!? HORI-SAN, DOES YOUR STOMACH HURT!!?
!?
!?
GATAN (CLATTER)
ARE YOU OKAY!?
DO YOU FEEL SICK OR SOMETHING!!?
D-DON'T BE RUDE!
WHAT'S WITH YOU ALL OF A SUDDEN?
YOU ALWAYS SAY, "JUST A BITE!" AND THEN EAT HALF OF IT!
PAKU (MUNCH)
THIS IS YUMMY!
HORI-SAN, YOU'RE NOT LEAVING ANY FOR ME!!
PAKU
AND THEN YOU EVEN POLISH OFF THE LUNCH YOU BROUGHT!!
HORI— BWEH!
DOGO (WHUD)
ISHIKAWA-KUN!!
YOU PIPE DOWN!!!
—!
...
GYAAA (SHRIEK)
GYAAA
WAAAUGH!

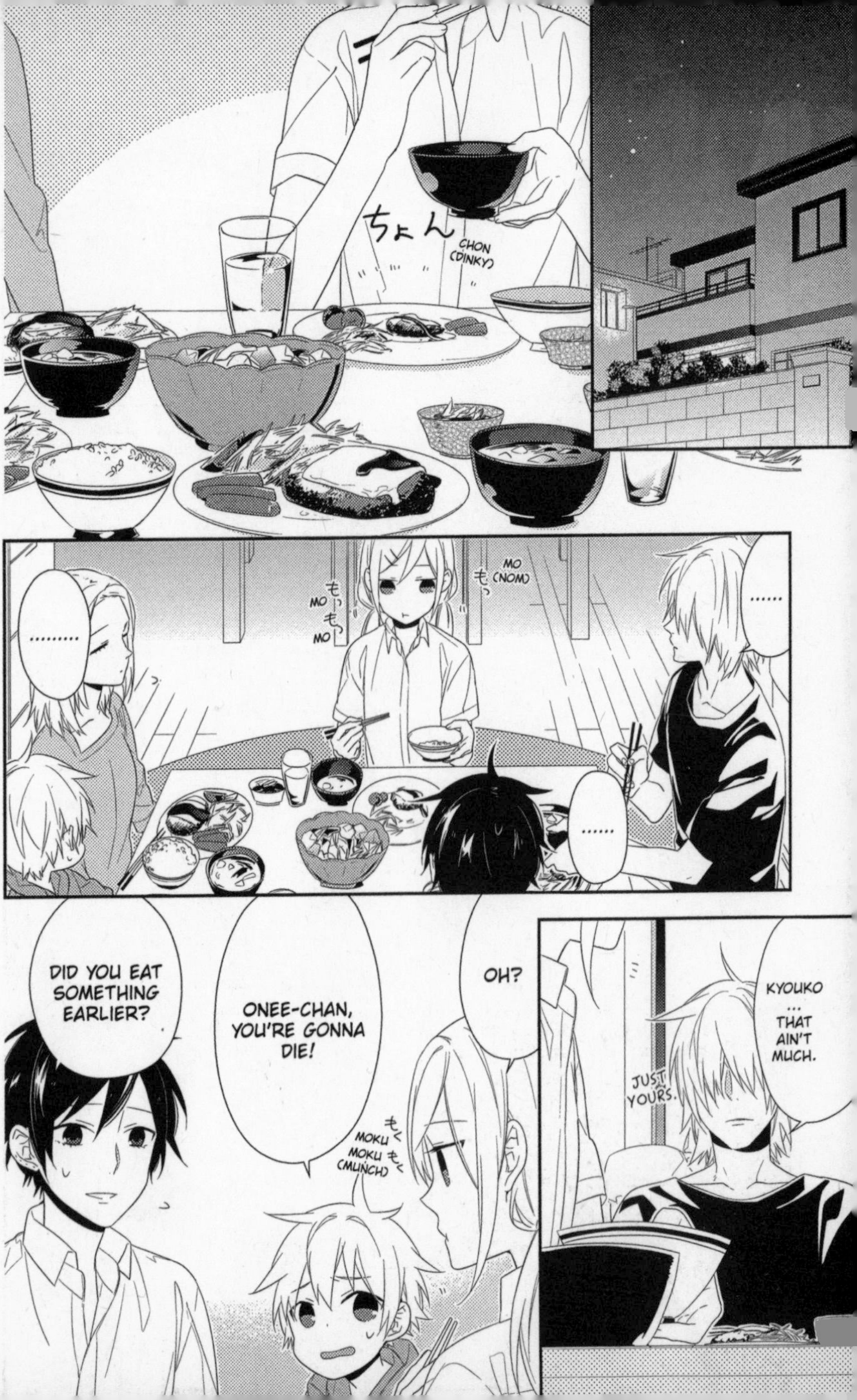
ちょん
CHON (DINKY)
......
もっ
MO (NOM)
もっもっ
MO MO
....
....
KYOUKO ... THAT AIN'T MUCH.
JUST YOURS.
OH?
ONEE-CHAN, YOU'RE GONNA DIE!
もくもく
MOKU MOKU (MUNCH)
DID YOU EAT SOMETHING EARLIER?

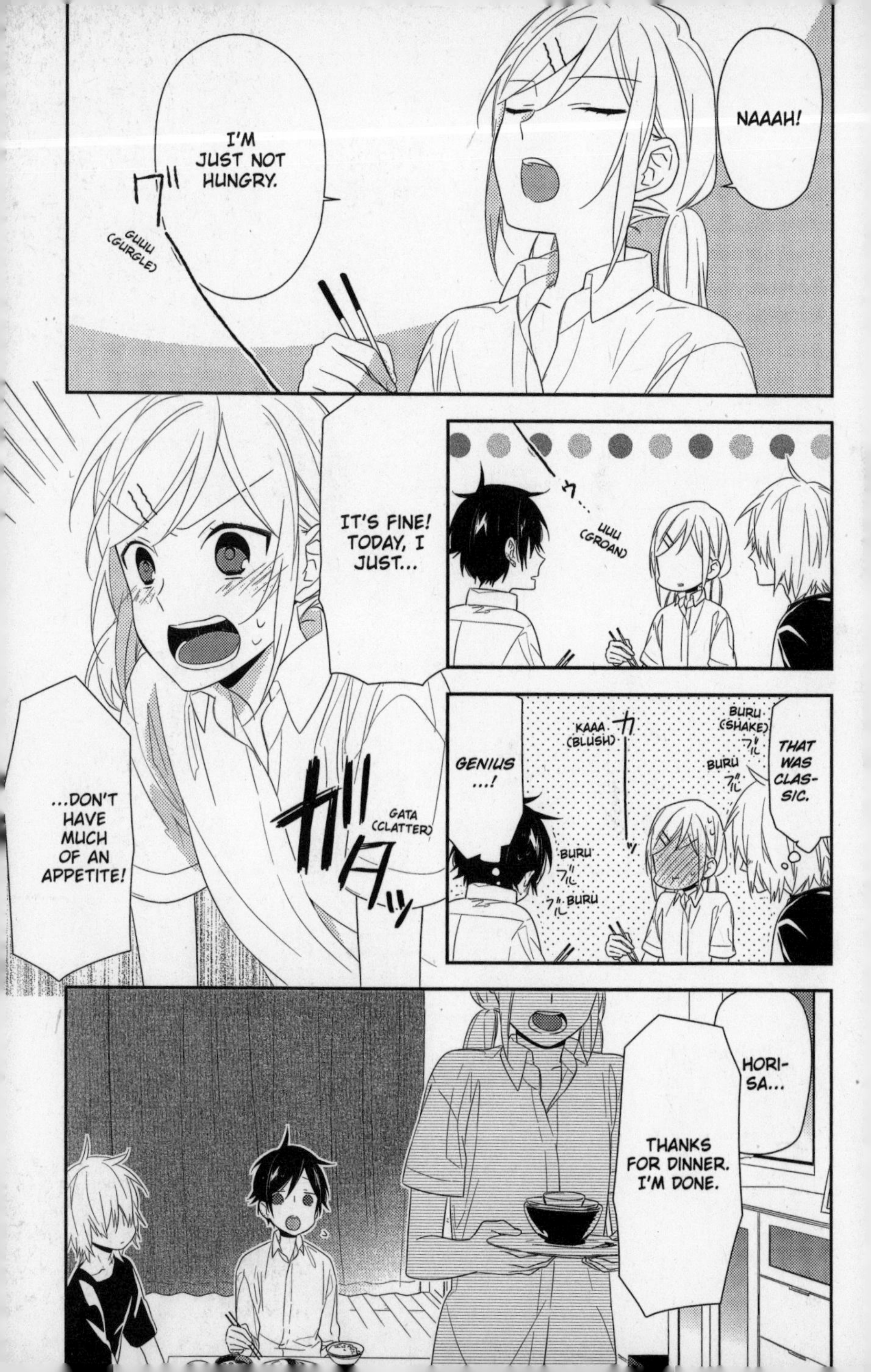
NAAAH!
I'M JUST NOT HUNGRY.
GUUU (GURGLE)
UUU (GROAN)
THAT WAS CLAS-SIC.
BURU (SHAKE)
BURU
KAAA (BLUSH)
GENIUS ...!
BURU
BURU
IT'S FINE! TODAY, I JUST...
GATA (CLATTER)
...DON'T HAVE MUCH OF AN APPETITE!
HORI-SA...
THANKS FOR DINNER. I'M DONE.

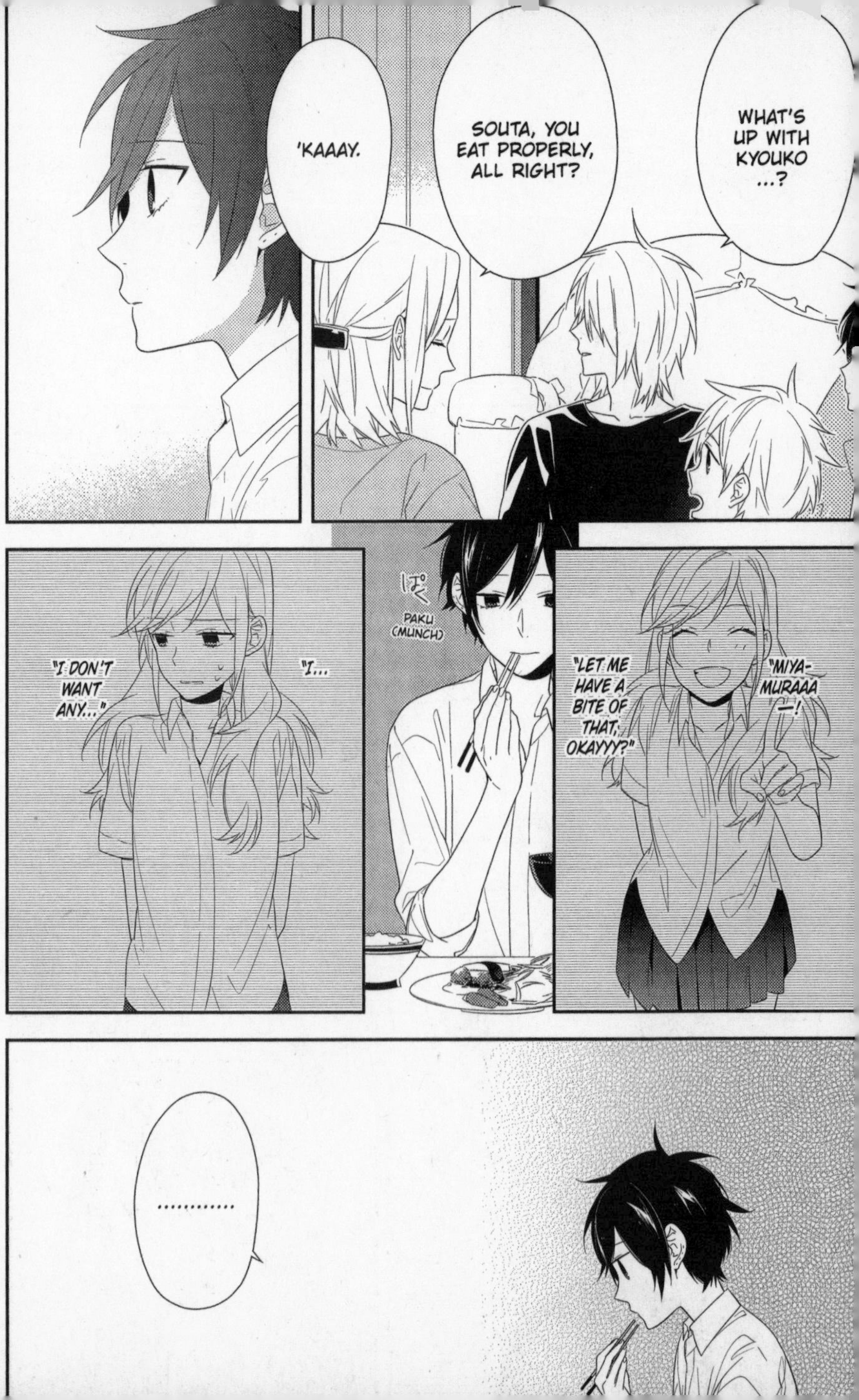
WHAT'S UP WITH KYOUKO ...?
SOUTA, YOU EAT PROPERLY, ALL RIGHT?
'KAAAY.
"MIYA-MURAAA—!
"LET ME HAVE A BITE OF THAT, OKAYYY?"
ぱく
PAKU (MUNCH)
"I...
"I DON'T WANT ANY..."
....

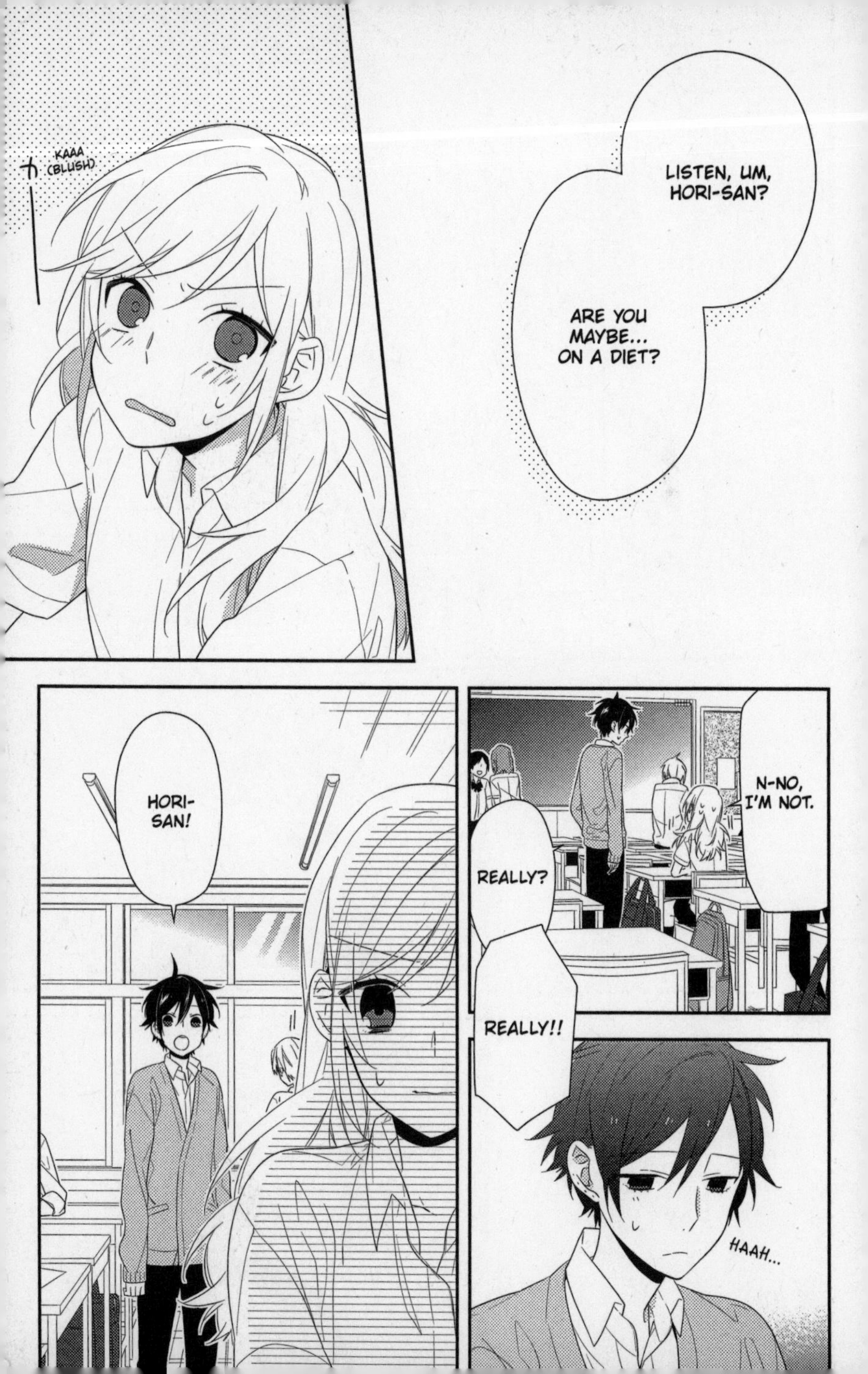

LISTEN, UM, HORI-SAN?
ARE YOU MAYBE... ON A DIET?
カ
KAAA (BLUSH)
N-NO, I'M NOT.
REALLY?
REALLY!!
HAAH...
HORI-SAN!

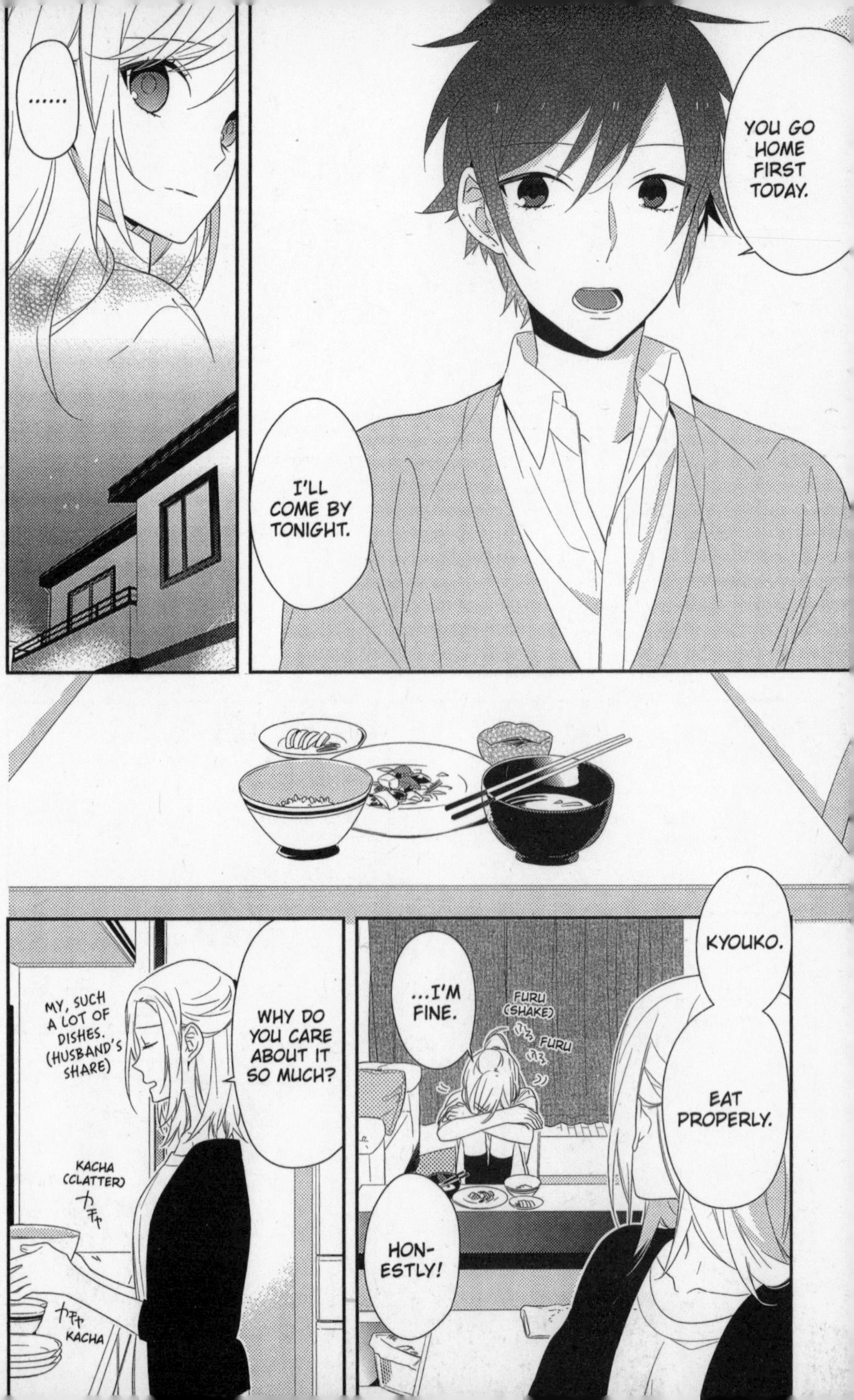
YOU GO HOME FIRST TODAY.
I'LL COME BY TONIGHT.
......
KYOUKO.
EAT PROPERLY.
...I'M FINE.
FURU (SHAKE)
FURU
HON-ESTLY!
WHY DO YOU CARE ABOUT IT SO MUCH?
MY, SUCH A LOT OF DISHES. (HUSBAND'S SHARE)
KACHA (CLATTER)
KACHA

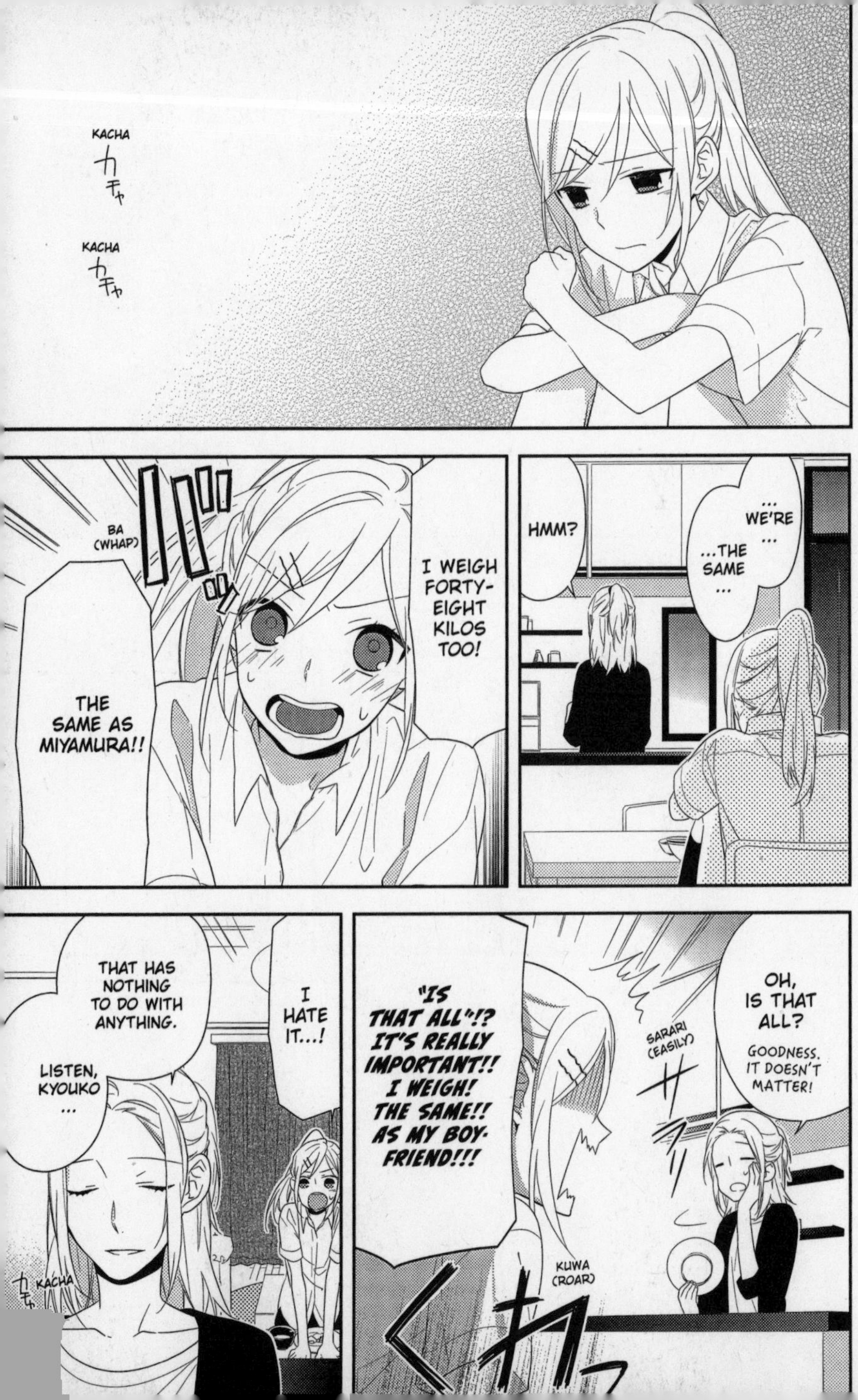
KACHA
KACHA
... WE'RE ...
...THE SAME ...
HMM?
I WEIGH FORTY-EIGHT KILOS TOO!
BA (WHAP)
THE SAME AS MIYAMURA!!
OH, IS THAT ALL?
GOODNESS. IT DOESN'T MATTER!
SARARI (EASILY)
"IS THAT ALL"!? IT'S REALLY IMPORTANT!! I WEIGH! THE SAME!! AS MY BOY-FRIEND!!!
KUWA (ROAR)
I HATE IT...!
THAT HAS NOTHING TO DO WITH ANYTHING.
LISTEN, KYOUKO ...
KACHA

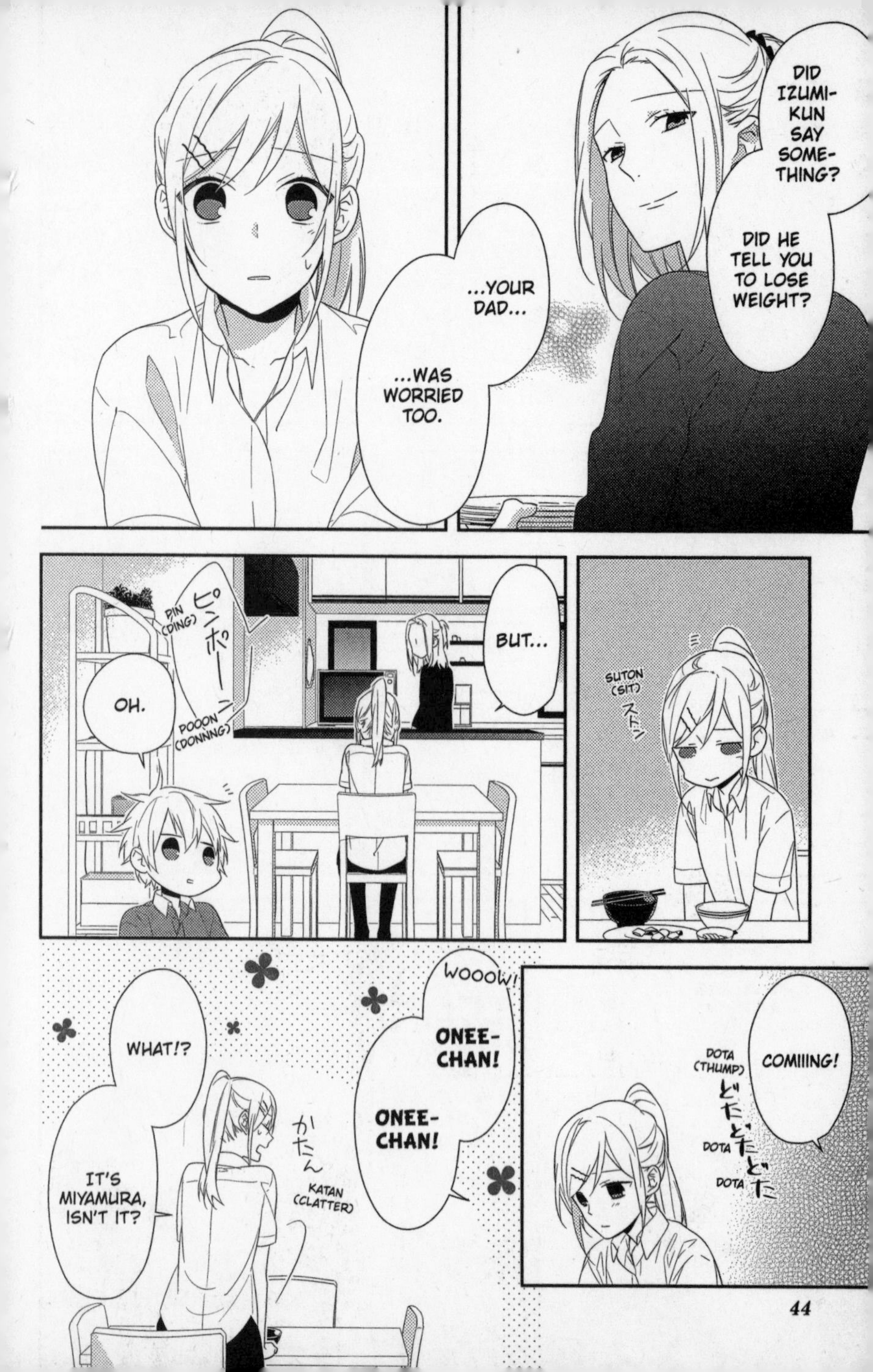
DID IZUMI-KUN SAY SOME-THING?
DID HE TELL YOU TO LOSE WEIGHT?
...YOUR DAD...
...WAS WORRIED TOO.
SUTON (SIT)
ストン
BUT...
ピンポーン
PIN (DING)
POOON (DONNNG)
OH.
COMIIING!
どたどたどた
DOTA (THUMP)
DOTA
DOTA
WOOOW!
ONEE-CHAN!
ONEE-CHAN!
かたん
KATAN (CLATTER)
WHAT!?
IT'S MIYAMURA, ISN'T IT?

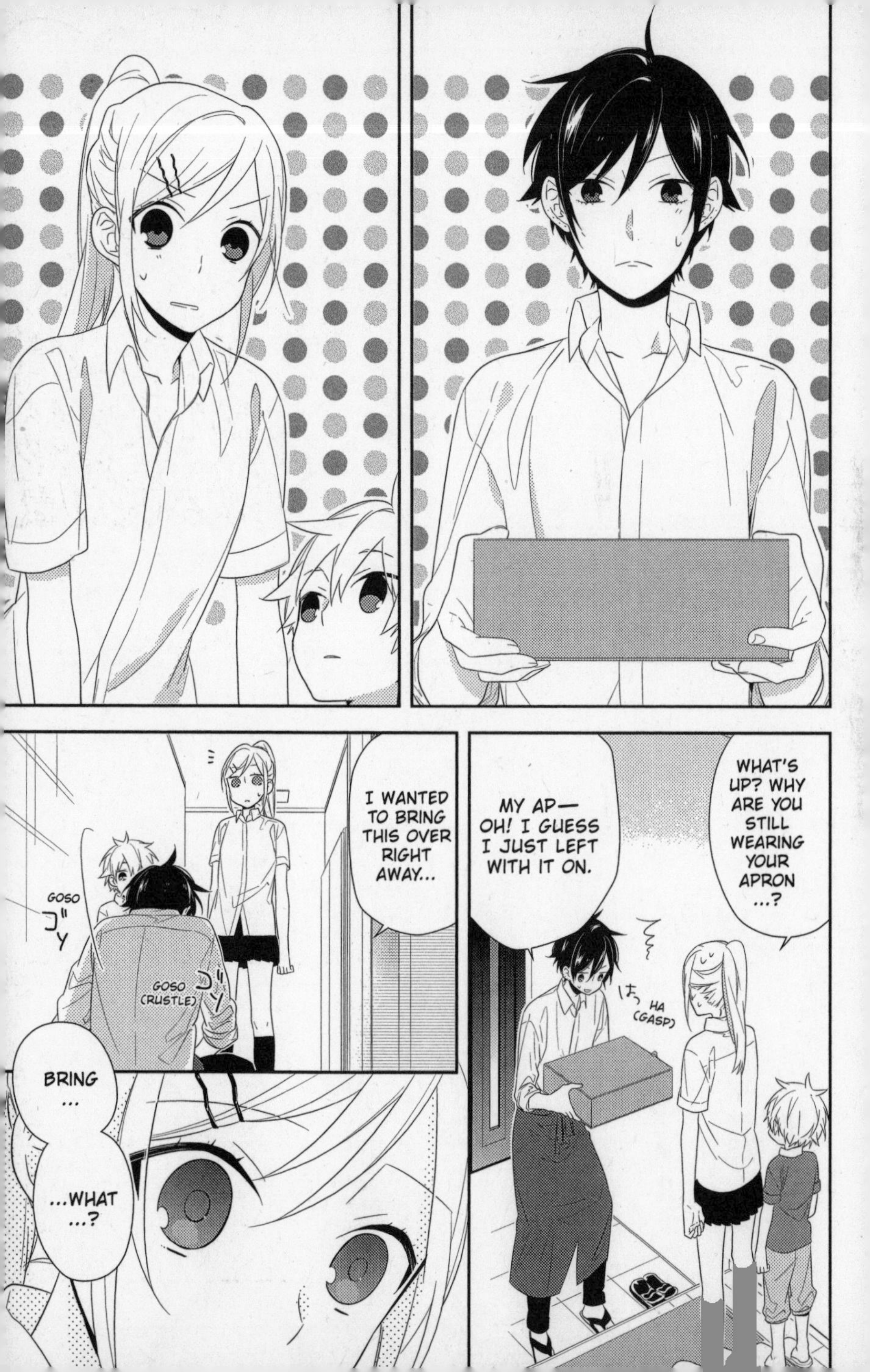
WHAT'S UP? WHY ARE YOU STILL WEARING YOUR APRON ...?
HA (GASP)
MY AP— OH! I GUESS I JUST LEFT WITH IT ON.
I WANTED TO BRING THIS OVER RIGHT AWAY...
GOSO
GOSO (RUSTLE)
BRING ...
...WHAT ...?

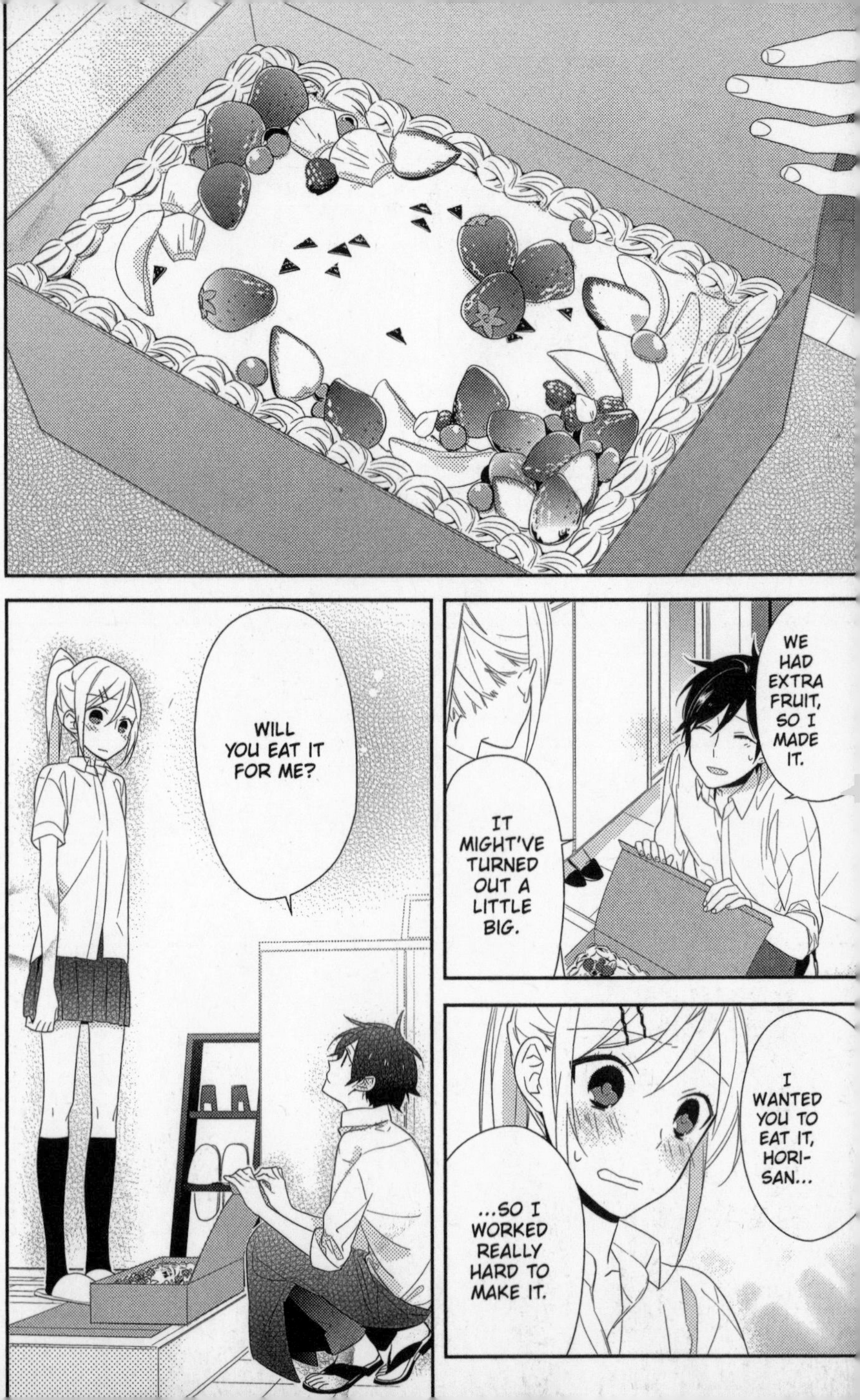
WE HAD EXTRA FRUIT, SO I MADE IT.
IT MIGHT'VE TURNED OUT A LITTLE BIG.
I WANTED YOU TO EAT IT, HORI-SAN...
...SO I WORKED REALLY HARD TO MAKE IT.
WILL YOU EAT IT FOR ME?

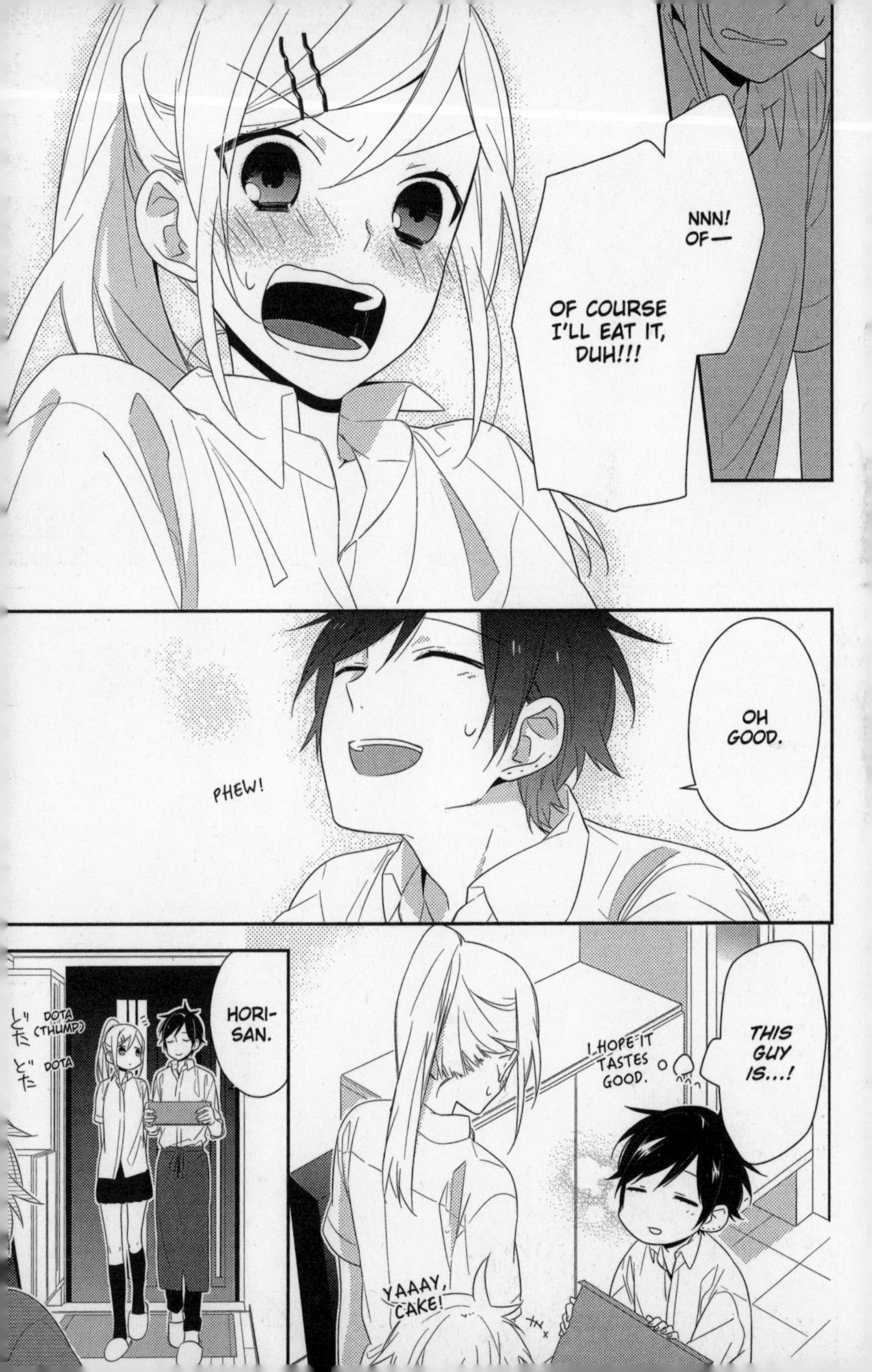
NNN! OF—
OF COURSE I'LL EAT IT, DUH!!!
OH GOOD.
PHEW!
THIS GUY IS...!
I HOPE IT TASTES GOOD.
YAAAY, CAKE!
HORI-SAN.
どた どた
DOTA (THUMP) DOTA

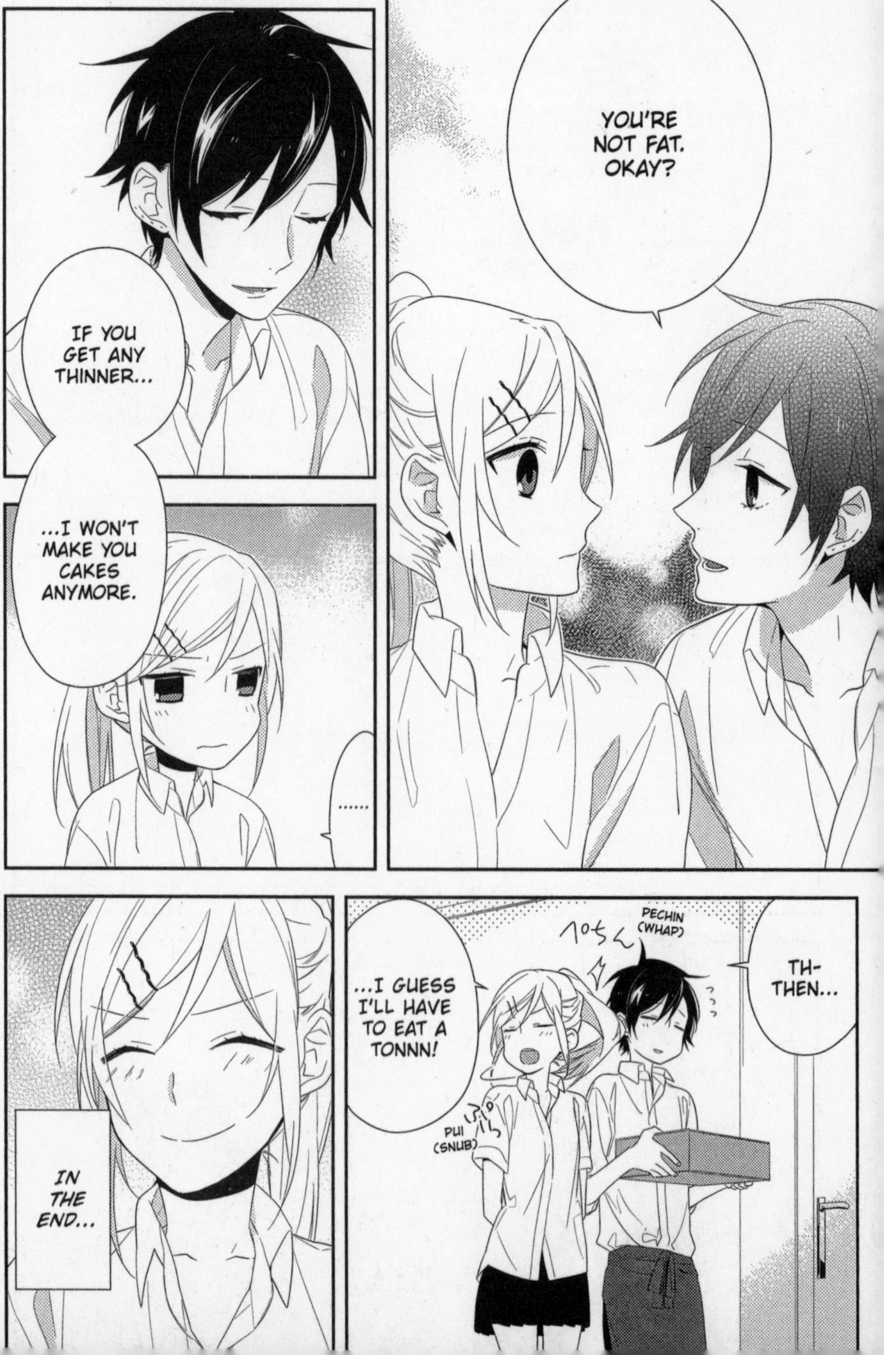
YOU'RE NOT FAT. OKAY?
IF YOU GET ANY THINNER...
...I WON'T MAKE YOU CAKES ANYMORE.
......
TH- THEN...
PECHIN (WHAP)
...I GUESS I'LL HAVE TO EAT A TONNN!
PUI (SNUB)
IN THE END...

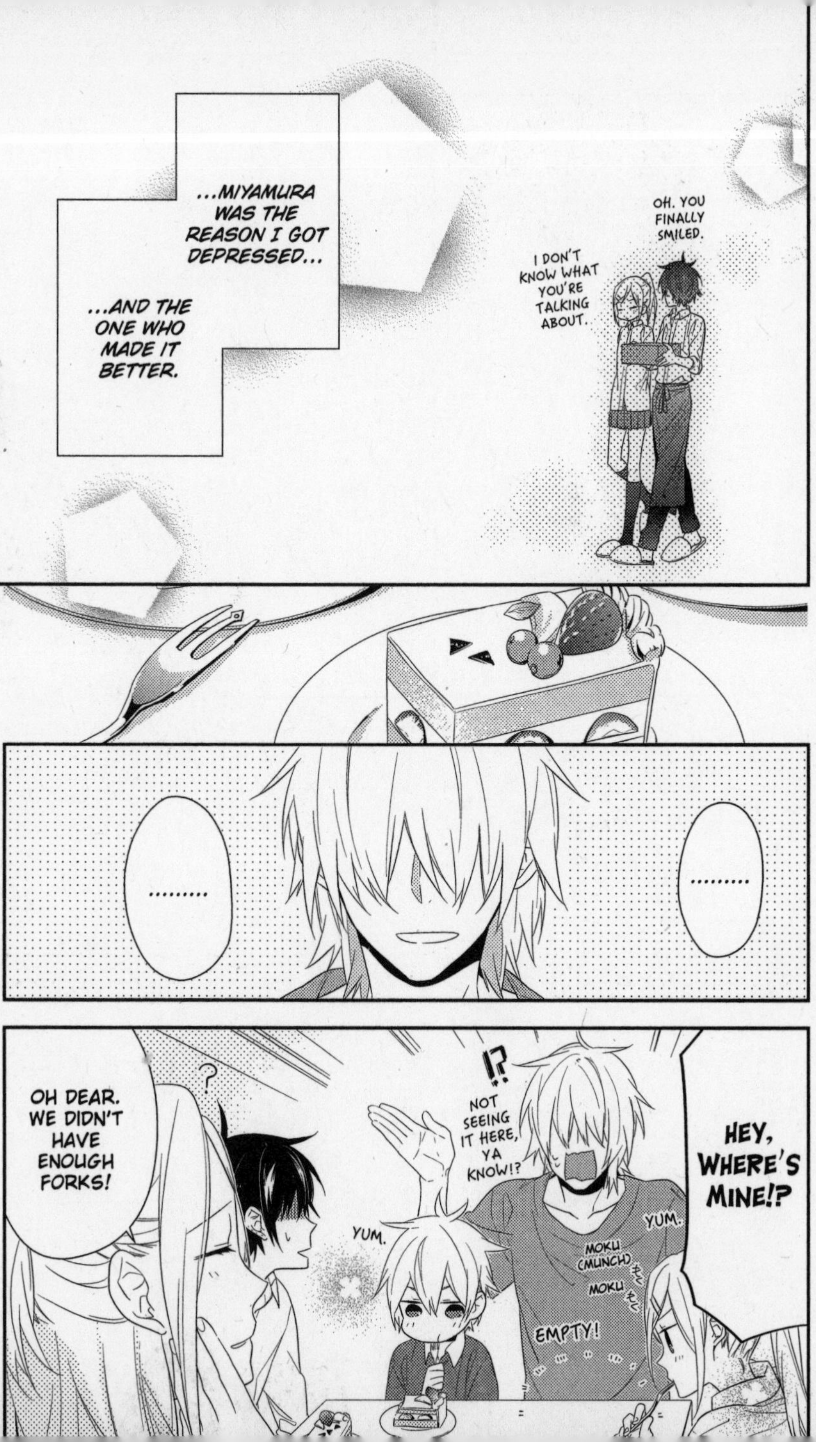
OH. YOU FINALLY SMILED.
I DON'T KNOW WHAT YOU'RE TALKING ABOUT.
...MIYAMURA WAS THE REASON I GOT DEPRESSED...
...AND THE ONE WHO MADE IT BETTER.
....
....
HEY, WHERE'S MINE!?
!?
NOT SEEING IT HERE, YA KNOW!?
YUM.
MOKU (MUNCH) MOKU
EMPTY!
YUM.
?
OH DEAR. WE DIDN'T HAVE ENOUGH FORKS!

HORIMIYA

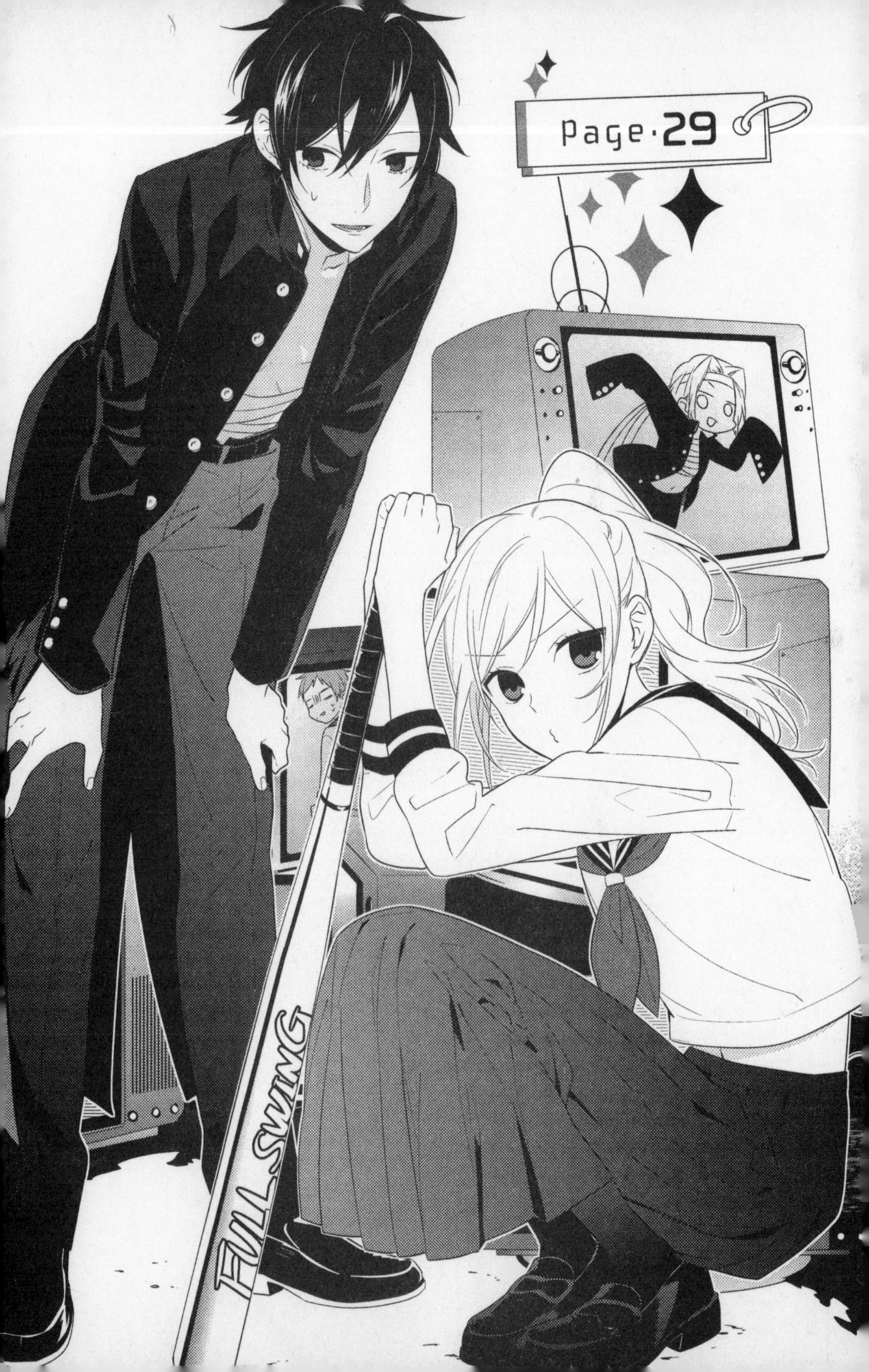
page·29
FULL SWING

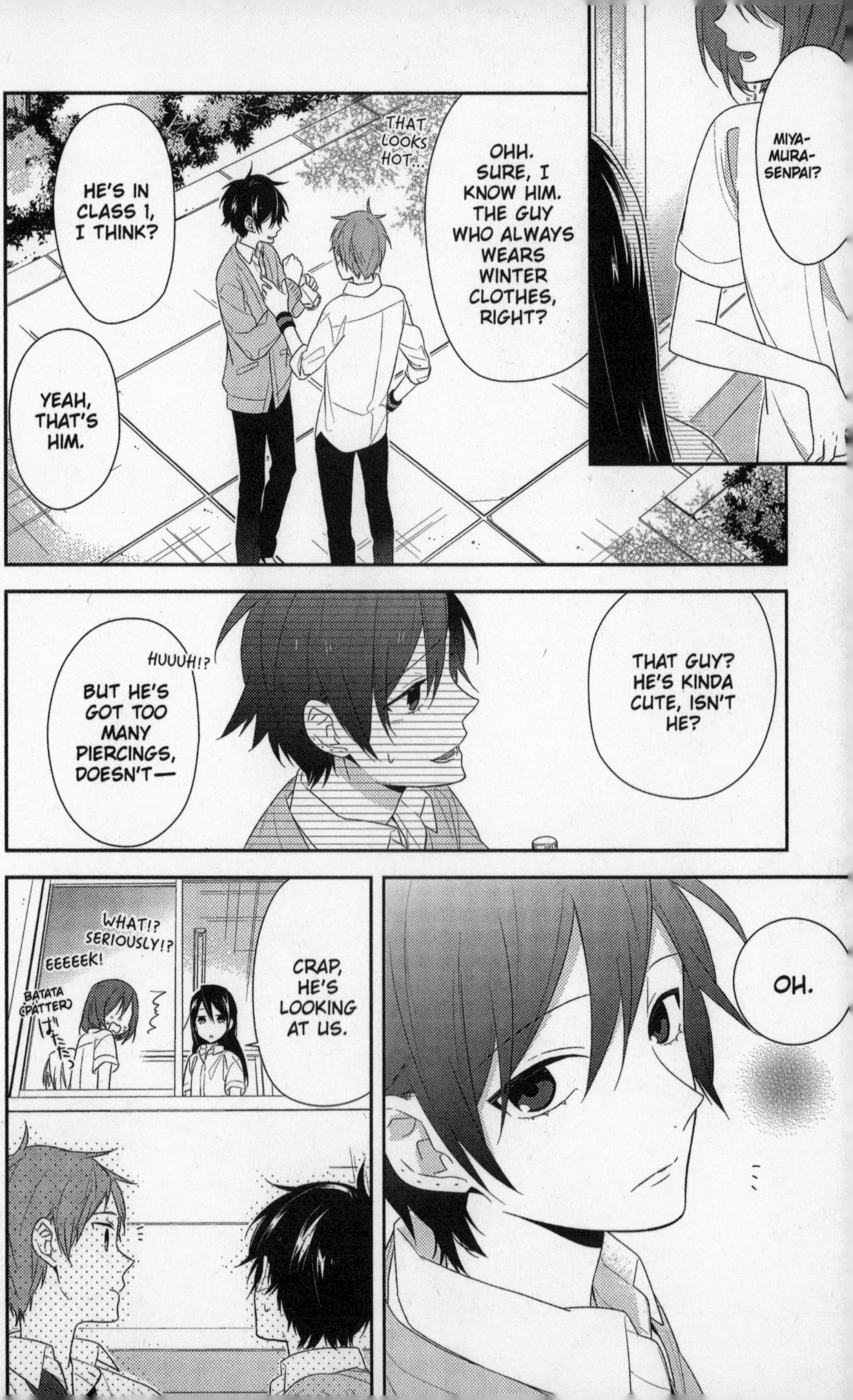
MIYA-MURA-SENPAI?
OHH. SURE, I KNOW HIM. THE GUY WHO ALWAYS WEARS WINTER CLOTHES, RIGHT?
THAT LOOKS HOT...
HE'S IN CLASS 1, I THINK?
YEAH, THAT'S HIM.
THAT GUY? HE'S KINDA CUTE, ISN'T HE?
HUUUH!?
BUT HE'S GOT TOO MANY PIERCINGS, DOESN'T—
OH.
CRAP, HE'S LOOKING AT US.
WHAT!? SERIOUSLY!?
EEEEEK!
BATATA (PATTER)
ばたた

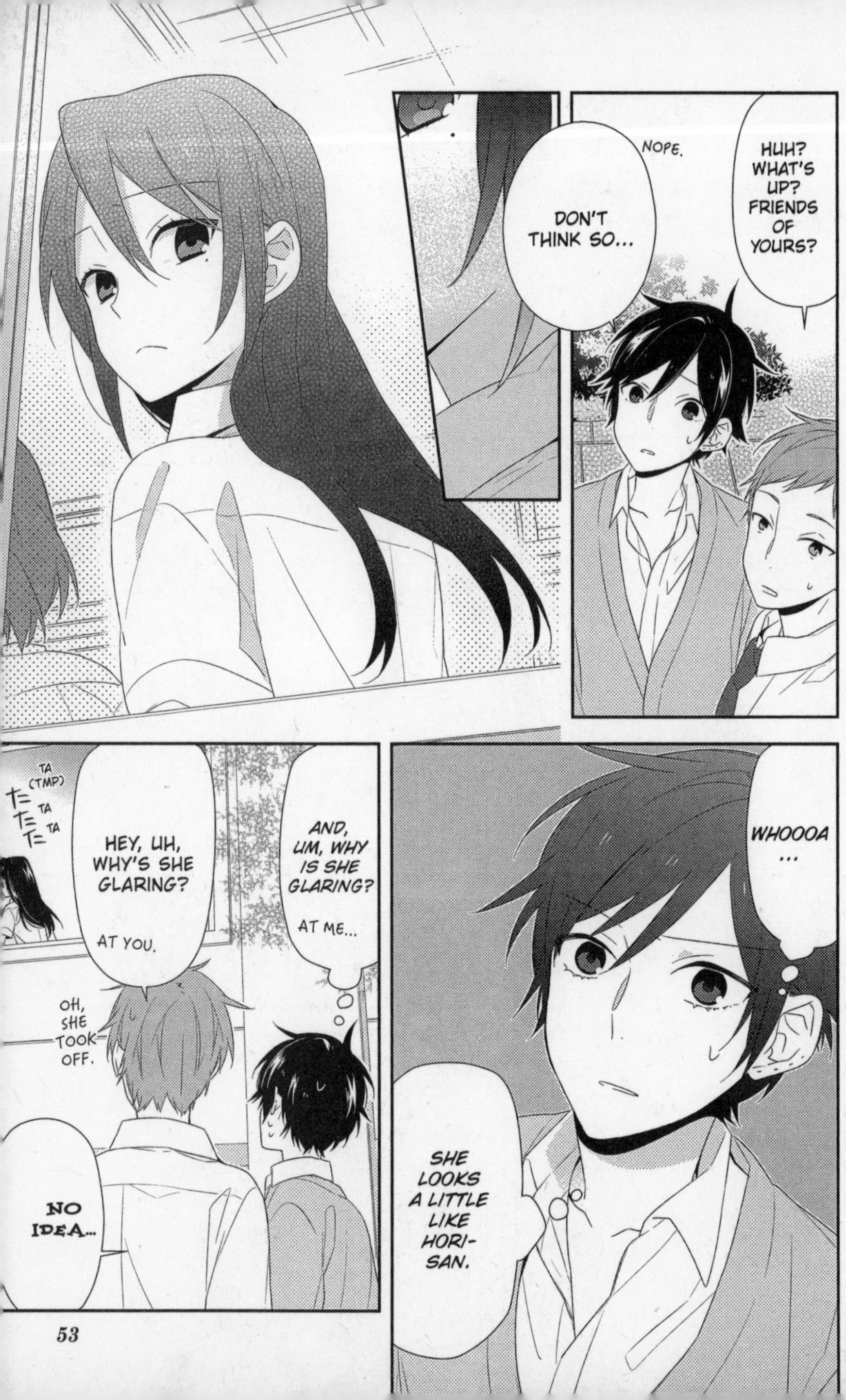
HUH? WHAT'S UP? FRIENDS OF YOURS?
NOPE.
DON'T THINK SO...
WHOOOA...
SHE LOOKS A LITTLE LIKE HORI-SAN.
AND, UM, WHY IS SHE GLARING?
AT ME...
HEY, UH, WHY'S SHE GLARING?
AT YOU.
TA (TMP) TA TA TA
OH, SHE TOOK OFF.
NO IDEA...

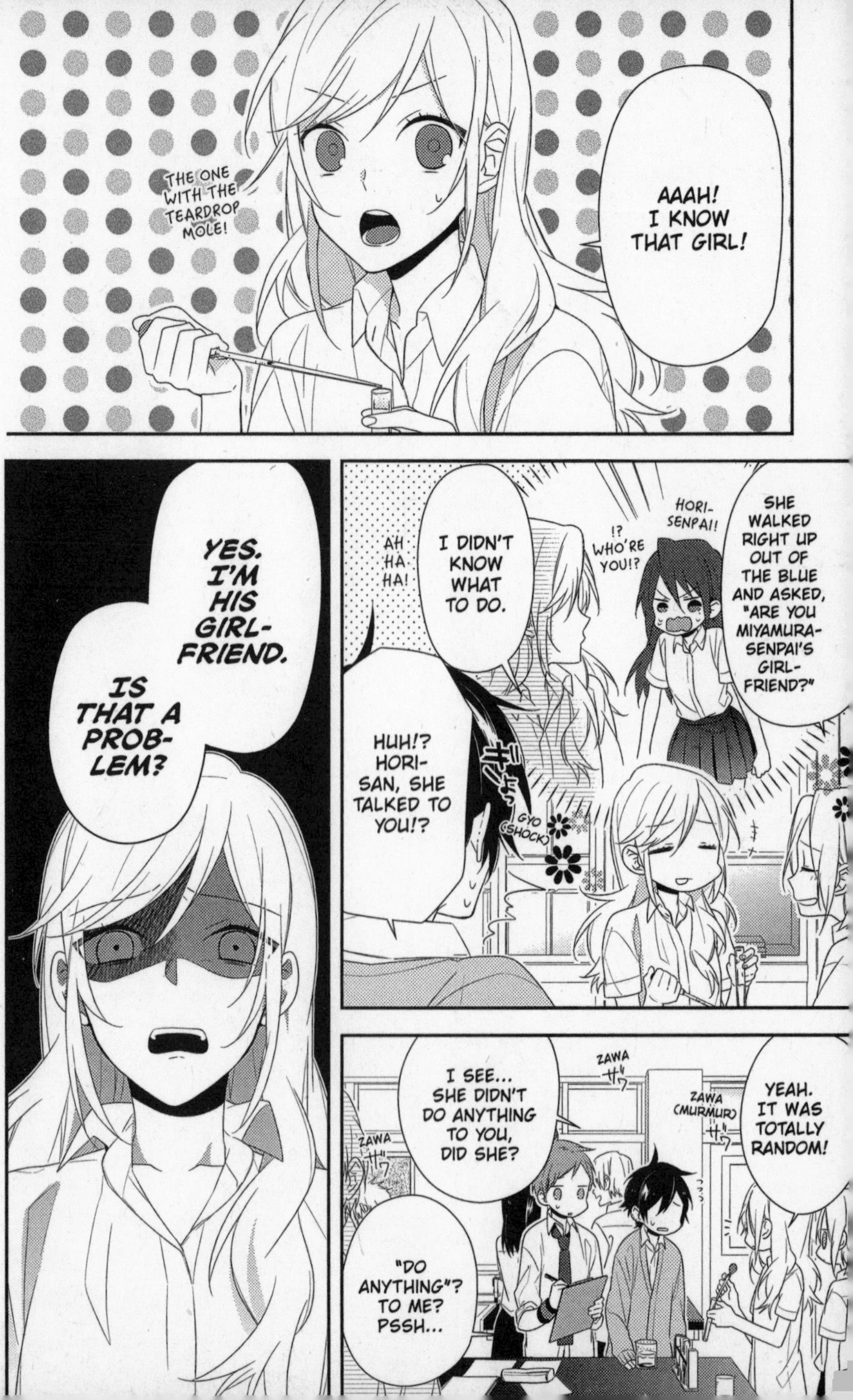
AAAH! I KNOW THAT GIRL!
THE ONE WITH THE TEARDROP MOLE!
SHE WALKED RIGHT UP OUT OF THE BLUE AND ASKED, "ARE YOU MIYAMURA-SENPAI'S GIRL-FRIEND?"
HORI-SENPAI!
!? WHO'RE YOU!?
I DIDN'T KNOW WHAT TO DO.
AH HA HA!
HUH!? HORI-SAN, SHE TALKED TO YOU!?
GYO (SHOCK)
YEAH. IT WAS TOTALLY RANDOM!
ZAWA
ZAWA (MURMUR)
I SEE... SHE DIDN'T DO ANYTHING TO YOU, DID SHE?
ZAWA
"DO ANYTHING"? TO ME? PSSH...
YES. I'M HIS GIRL-FRIEND.
IS THAT A PROB-LEM?

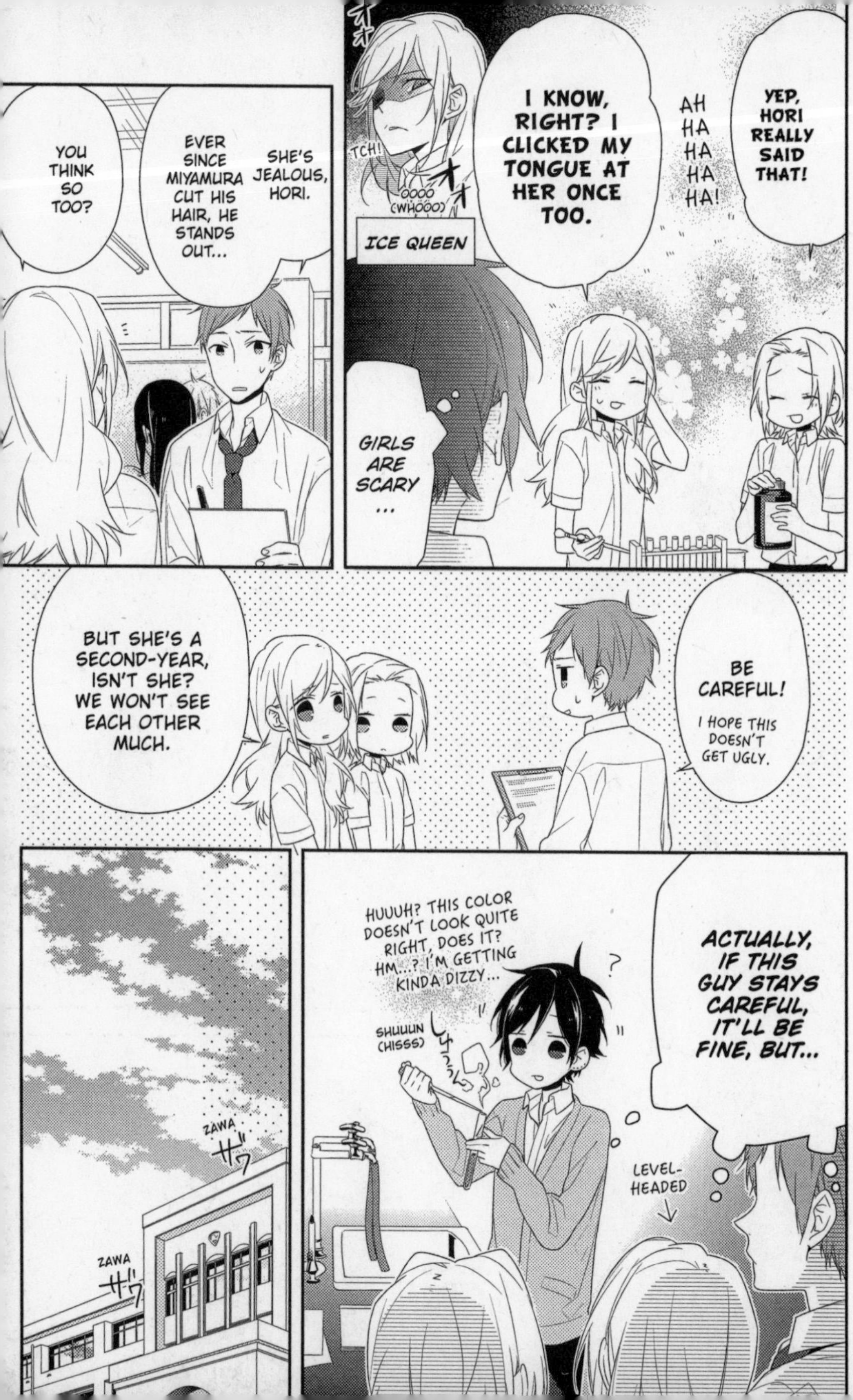
YEP, HORI REALLY SAID THAT!
AH HA HA HA HA!
I KNOW, RIGHT? I CLICKED MY TONGUE AT HER ONCE TOO.
TCH!
OOOO (WHOOO)
ICE QUEEN
GIRLS ARE SCARY ...
SHE'S JEALOUS, HORI.
EVER SINCE MIYAMURA CUT HIS HAIR, HE STANDS OUT...
YOU THINK SO TOO?
BE CAREFUL!
I HOPE THIS DOESN'T GET UGLY.
BUT SHE'S A SECOND-YEAR, ISN'T SHE? WE WON'T SEE EACH OTHER MUCH.
ACTUALLY, IF THIS GUY STAYS CAREFUL, IT'LL BE FINE, BUT...
LEVEL-HEADED
HUUUH? THIS COLOR DOESN'T LOOK QUITE RIGHT, DOES IT? HM...? I'M GETTING KINDA DIZZY...
SHUUUN (CHISSS)
ZAWA
ZAWA

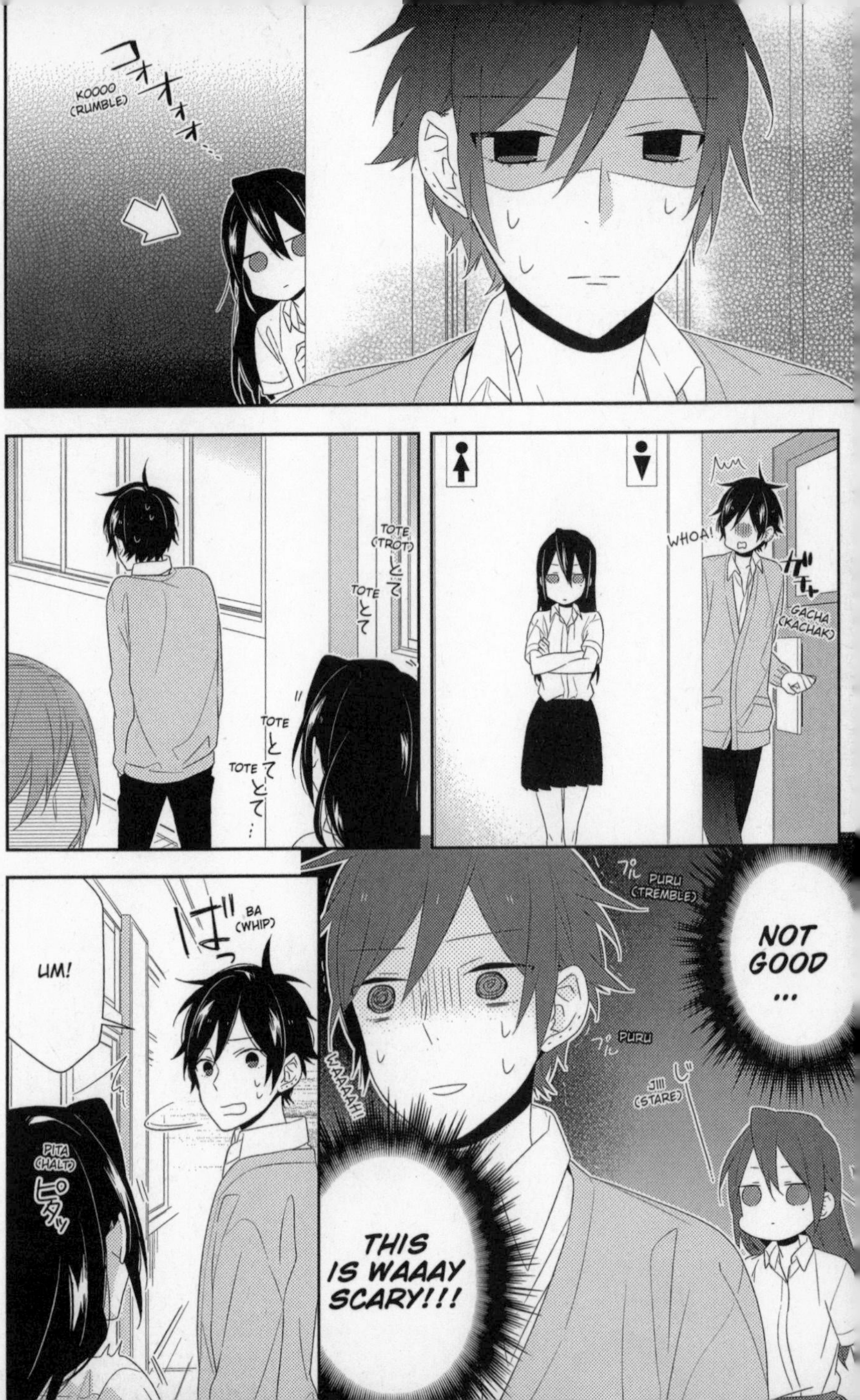

KOOOO (RUMBLE)
コオオオ…
WHOA!
ガチャ
GACHA (KACHAK)
TOTE (TROT)
とて
TOTE
とて
TOTE
とて
TOTE
とて…
プル
PURU (TREMBLE)
NOT GOOD...
プル
PURU
WAAAAH!
じ
JIII (STARE)
THIS IS WAAAY SCARY!!!
ばっ
BA (WHIP)
UM!
PITA (HALT)
ピタッ

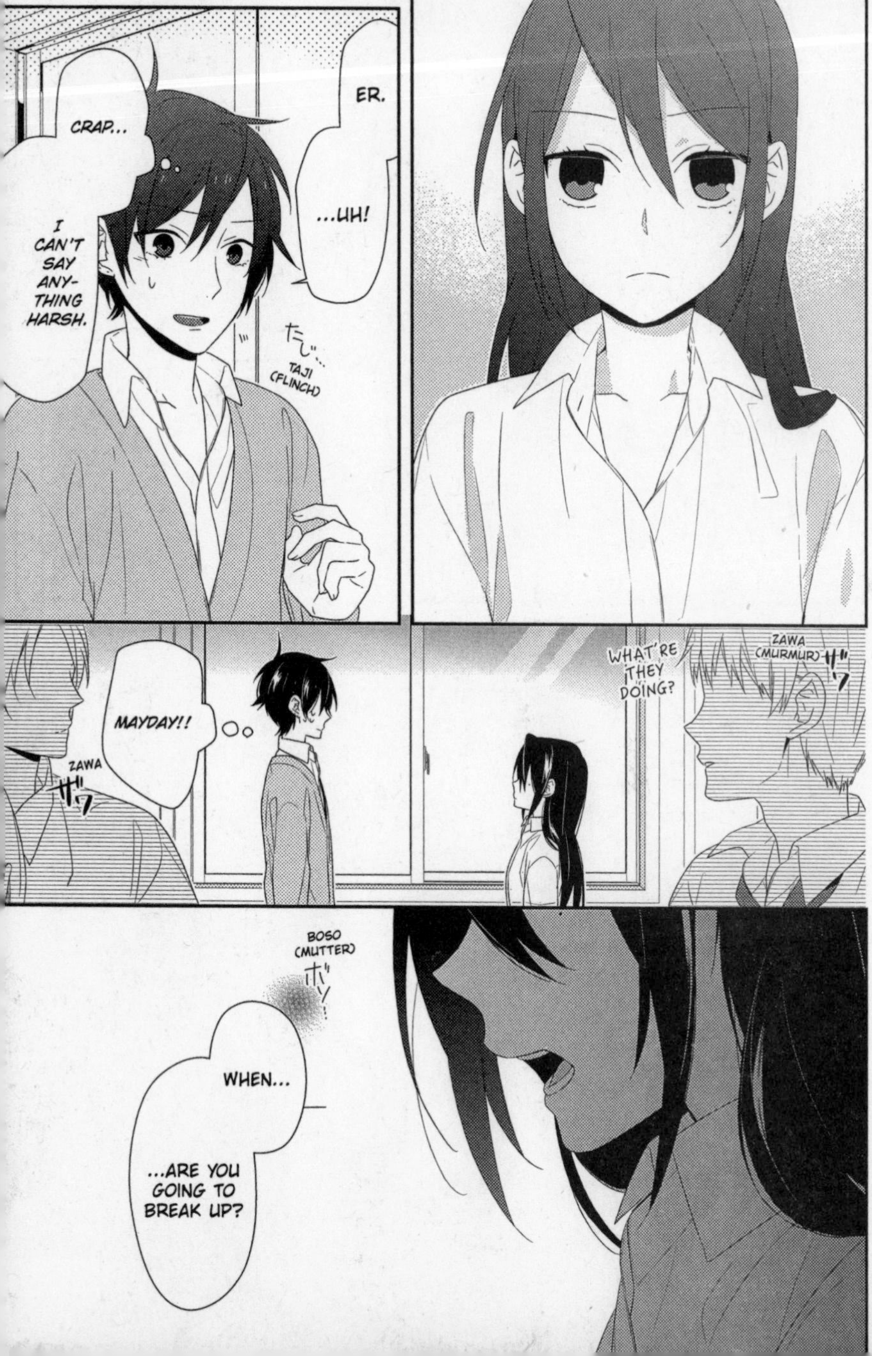
ER.
...UH!
CRAP...
I CAN'T SAY ANY-THING HARSH.
たじ…
TAJI (FLINCH)
ZAWA (MURMUR) ザワ
WHAT'RE THEY DOING?
MAYDAY!!
ZAWA ザワ
BOSO (MUTTER) ボソ…
WHEN...
...ARE YOU GOING TO BREAK UP?

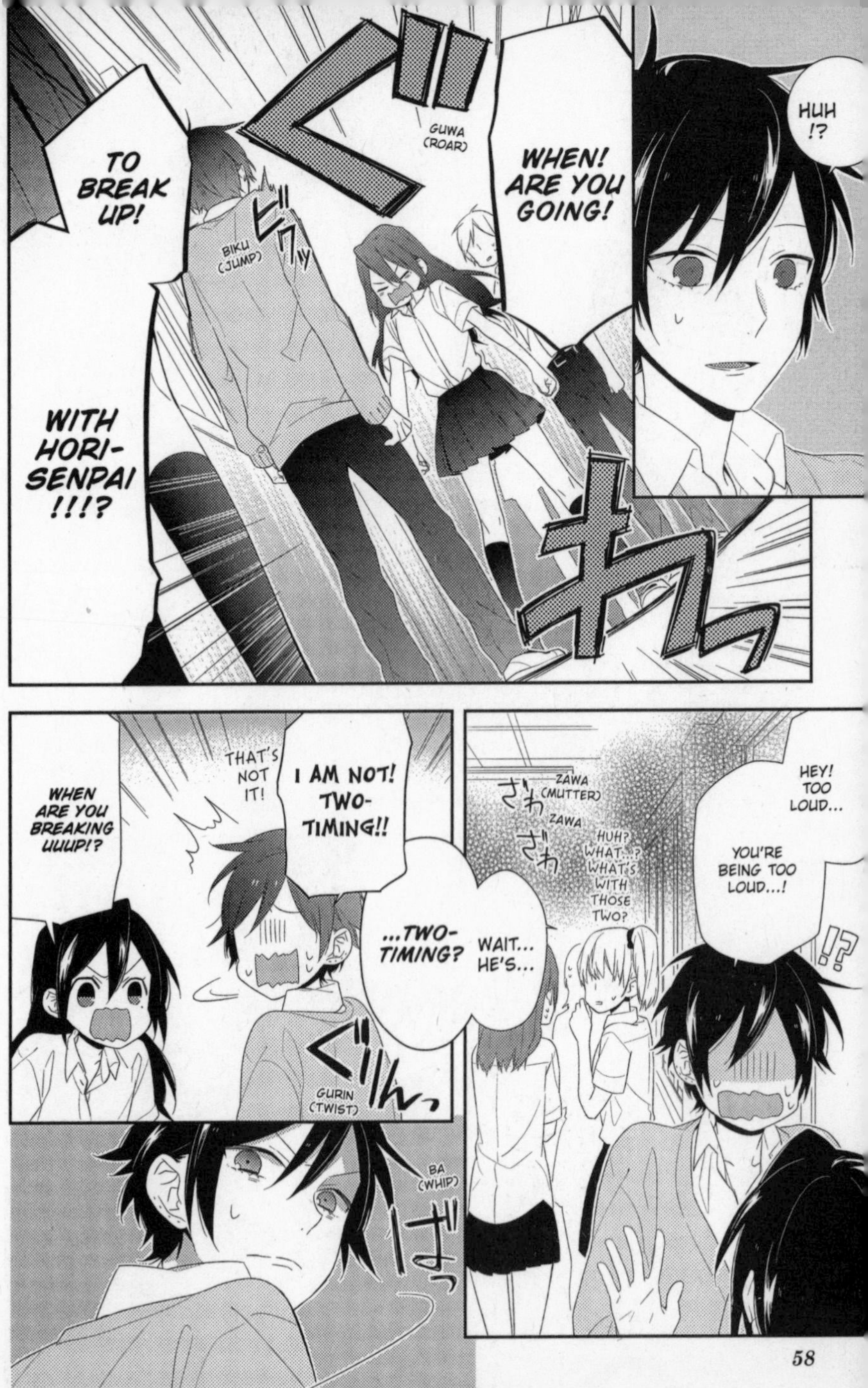
HUH !?
GUWA (ROAR)
WHEN! ARE YOU GOING!
TO BREAK UP!
BIKU (JUMP)
WITH HORI-SENPAI !!!?
HEY! TOO LOUD...
YOU'RE BEING TOO LOUD...!
!?
ZAWA (MUTTER)
ZAWA
HUH? WHAT...? WHAT'S WITH THOSE TWO?
WAIT... HE'S...
I AM NOT! TWO-TIMING!!
THAT'S NOT IT!
WHEN ARE YOU BREAKING UUUP!?
...TWO-TIMING?
GURIN (TWIST)
BA (WHIP)

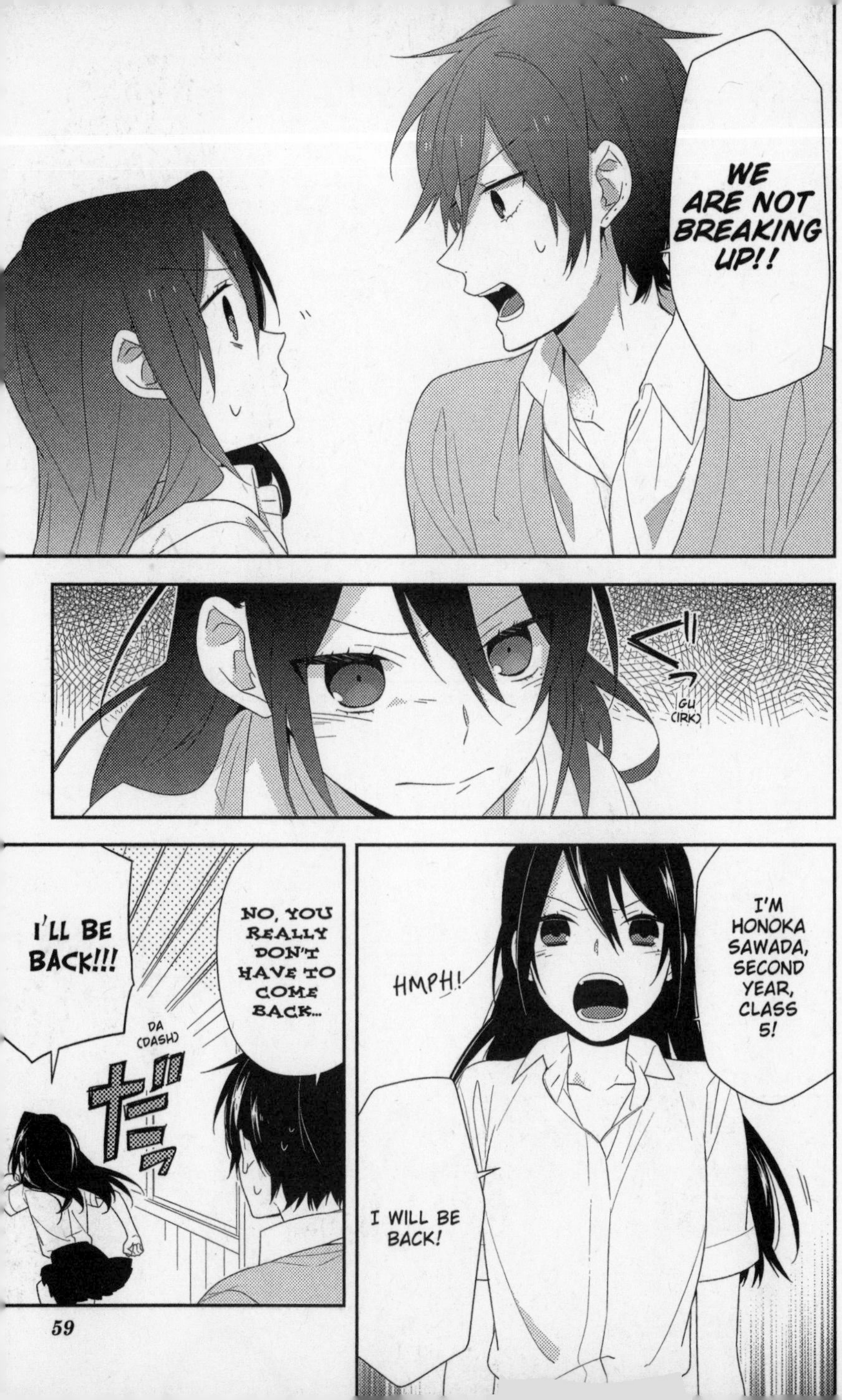
WE ARE NOT BREAKING UP!!
GU (IRK)
I'M HONOKA SAWADA, SECOND YEAR, CLASS 5!
HMPH!
I WILL BE BACK!
NO, YOU REALLY DON'T HAVE TO COME BACK...
I'LL BE BACK!!!
DA (DASH)

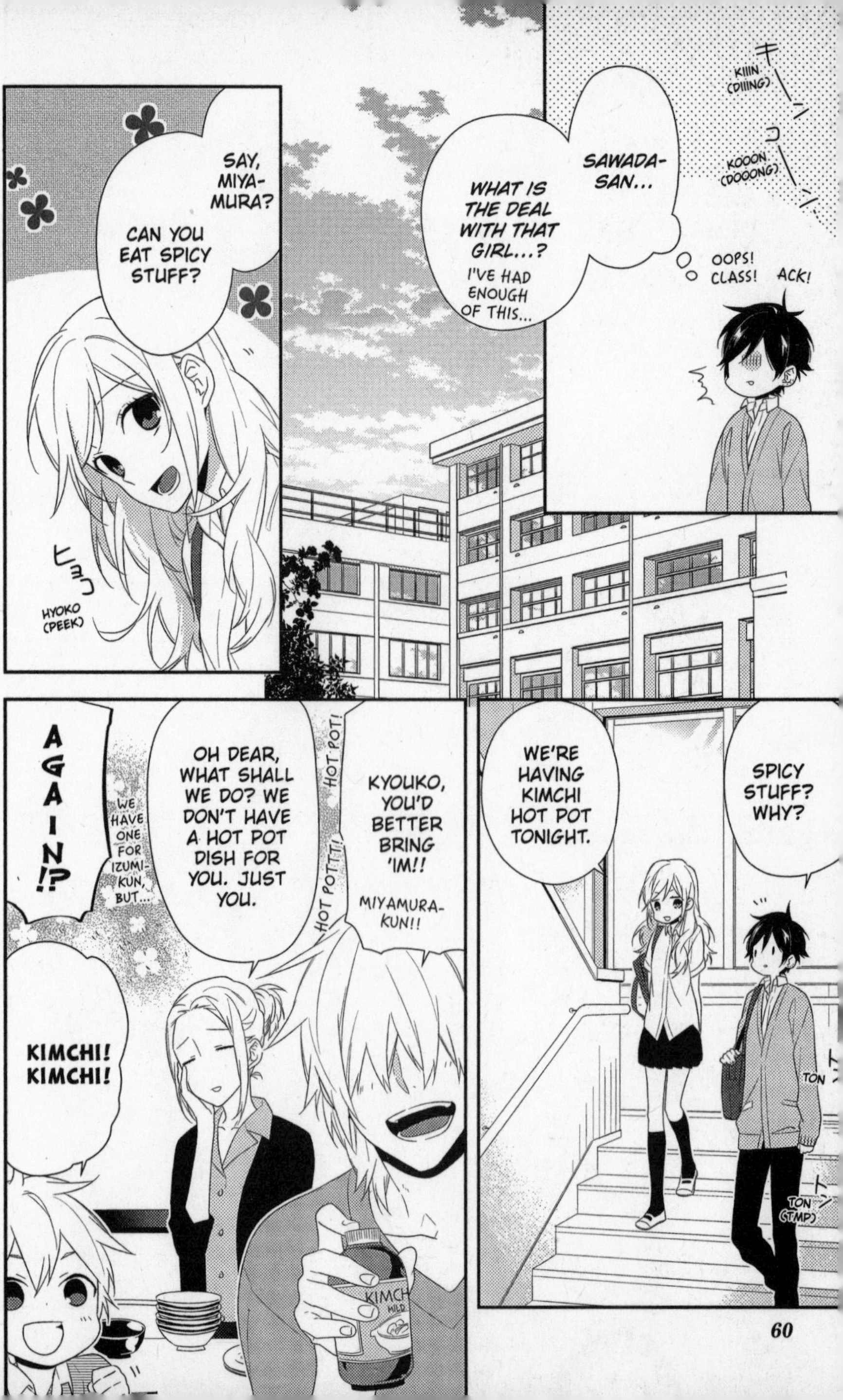
KIIIN (DIIING)
KOOON (DOOONG)
SAWADA-SAN...
WHAT IS THE DEAL WITH THAT GIRL...?
I'VE HAD ENOUGH OF THIS...
ACK!
OOPS! CLASS!
SAY, MIYAMURA?
CAN YOU EAT SPICY STUFF?
HYOKO (PEEK)
SPICY STUFF? WHY?
WE'RE HAVING KIMCHI HOT POT TONIGHT.
TON
TON (TMP)
KYOUKO, YOU'D BETTER BRING 'IM!!
MIYAMURA-KUN!!
HOT POT!
HOT POTTT!
OH DEAR, WHAT SHALL WE DO? WE DON'T HAVE A HOT POT DISH FOR YOU. JUST YOU.
AGAIN!?
WE HAVE ONE FOR IZUMI-KUN, BUT...
KIMCHI! KIMCHI!
KIMCHI MILD

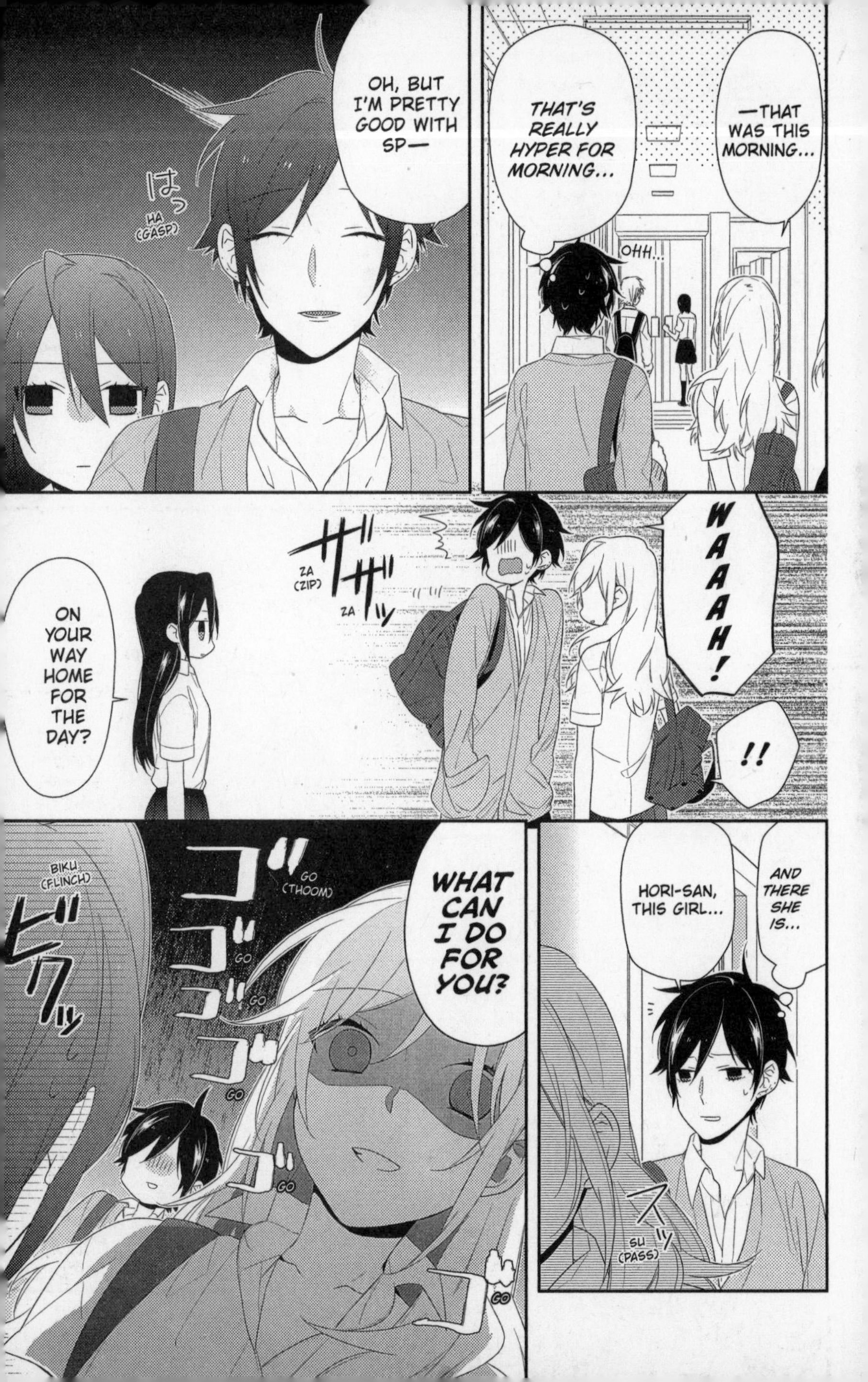
—THAT WAS THIS MORNING...
THAT'S REALLY HYPER FOR MORNING...
OHH...
OH, BUT I'M PRETTY GOOD WITH SP—
はっ
HA (GASP)
WAAAAH!
!!
ザザッ
ZA (ZIP)
ZA
ON YOUR WAY HOME FOR THE DAY?
AND THERE SHE IS...
HORI-SAN, THIS GIRL...
スッ
SU (PASS)
WHAT CAN I DO FOR YOU?
ゴゴゴゴゴ
GO (THOOM)
GO
GO
GO
GO
GO
ビクッ
BIKU (FLINCH)

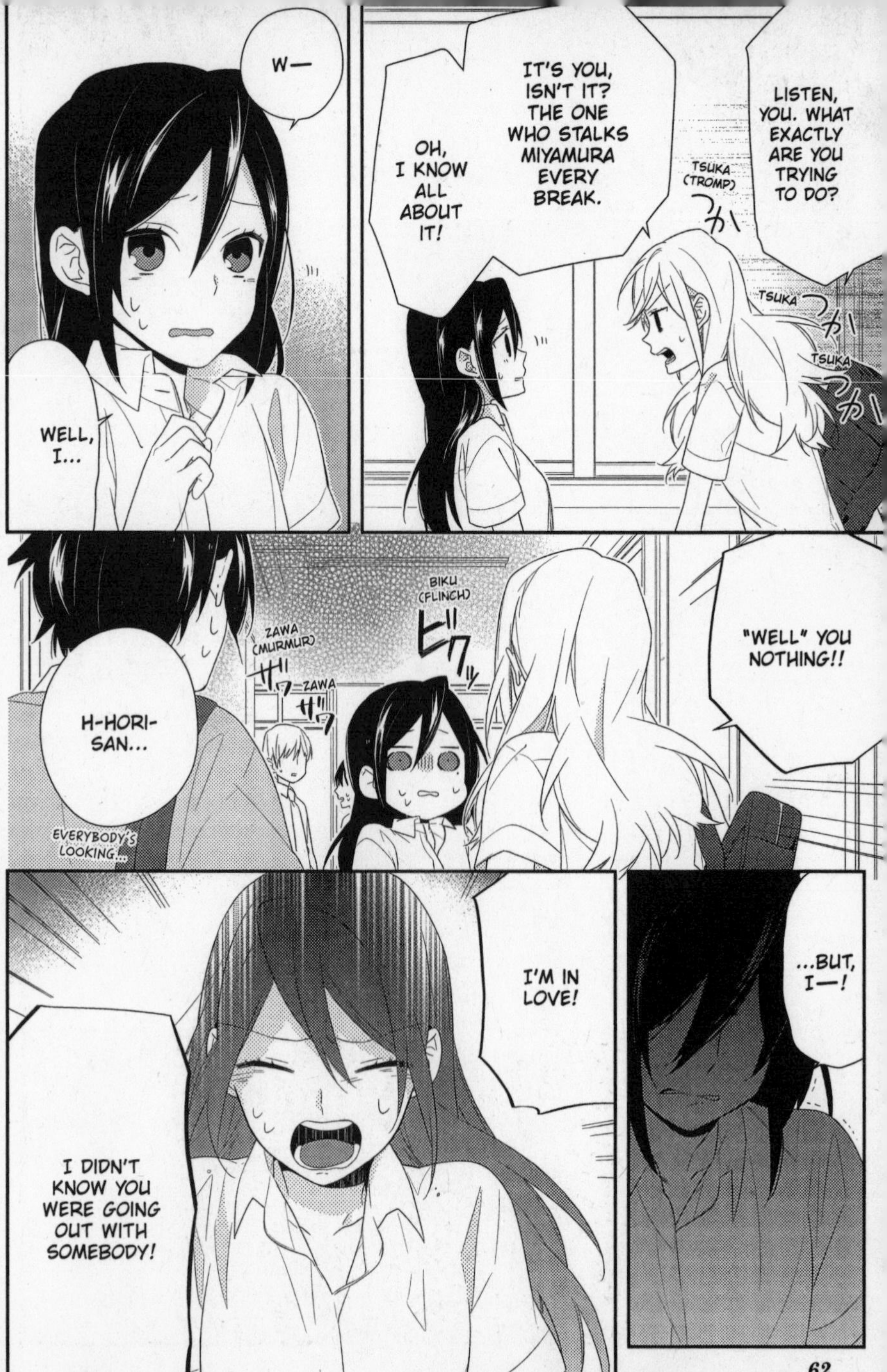
LISTEN, YOU. WHAT EXACTLY ARE YOU TRYING TO DO?
TSUKA つか
TSUKA つか
TSUKA (TROMP) つか
IT'S YOU, ISN'T IT? THE ONE WHO STALKS MIYAMURA EVERY BREAK.
OH, I KNOW ALL ABOUT IT!
W—
WELL, I...
"WELL" YOU NOTHING!!
BIKU (FLINCH) ビクッ
ZAWA (MURMUR) ザワ
ZAWA ザワ
H-HORI-SAN...
EVERYBODY'S LOOKING...
...BUT, I—!
I'M IN LOVE!
I DIDN'T KNOW YOU WERE GOING OUT WITH SOMEBODY!

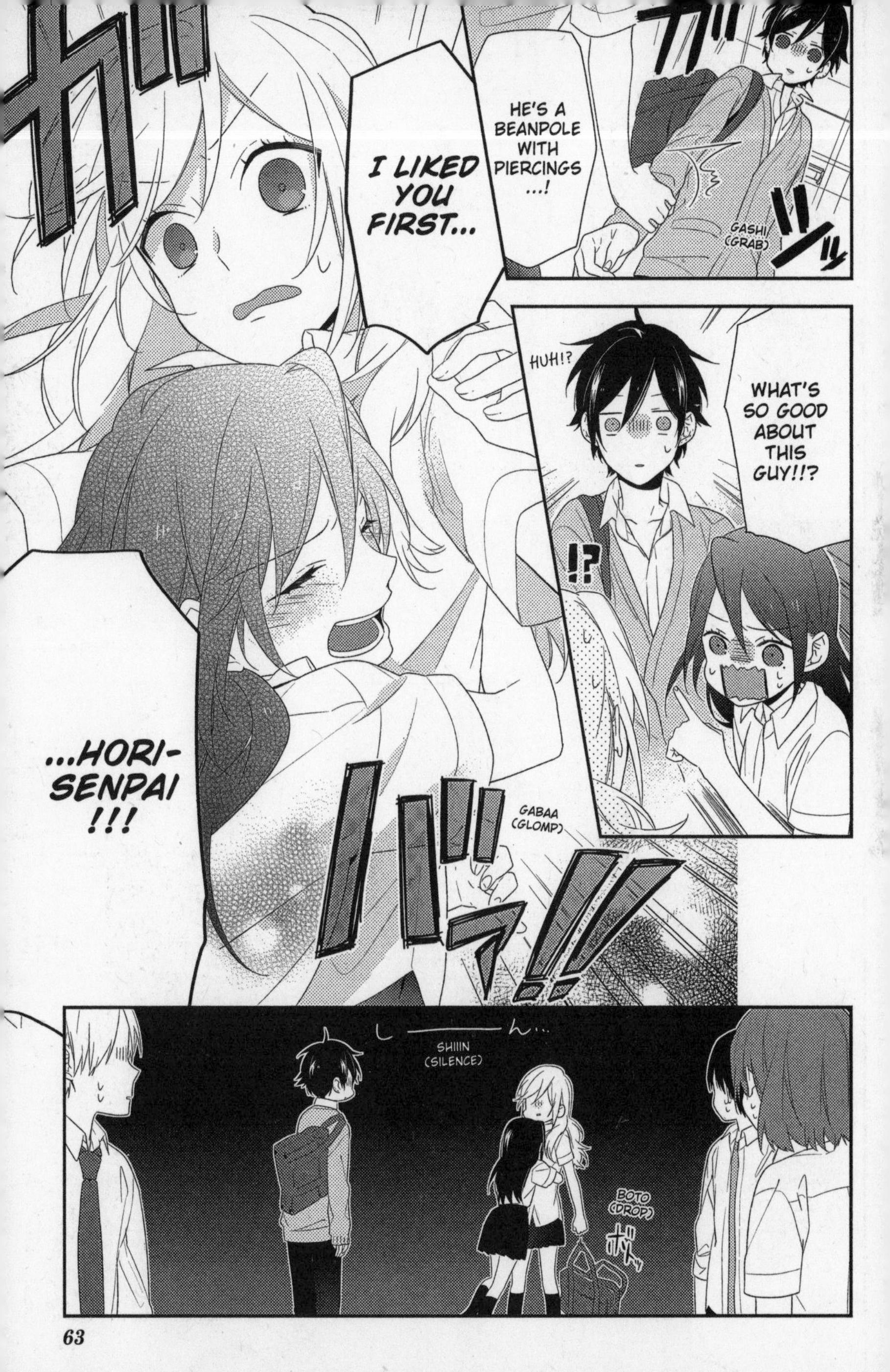
HE'S A BEANPOLE WITH PIERCINGS ...!
GASHI (GRAB)
HUH!?
WHAT'S SO GOOD ABOUT THIS GUY!!?
!?
I LIKED YOU FIRST...
...HORI-SENPAI!!!
GABAA (GLOMP)
SHIIIN (SILENCE)
BOTO (DROP)

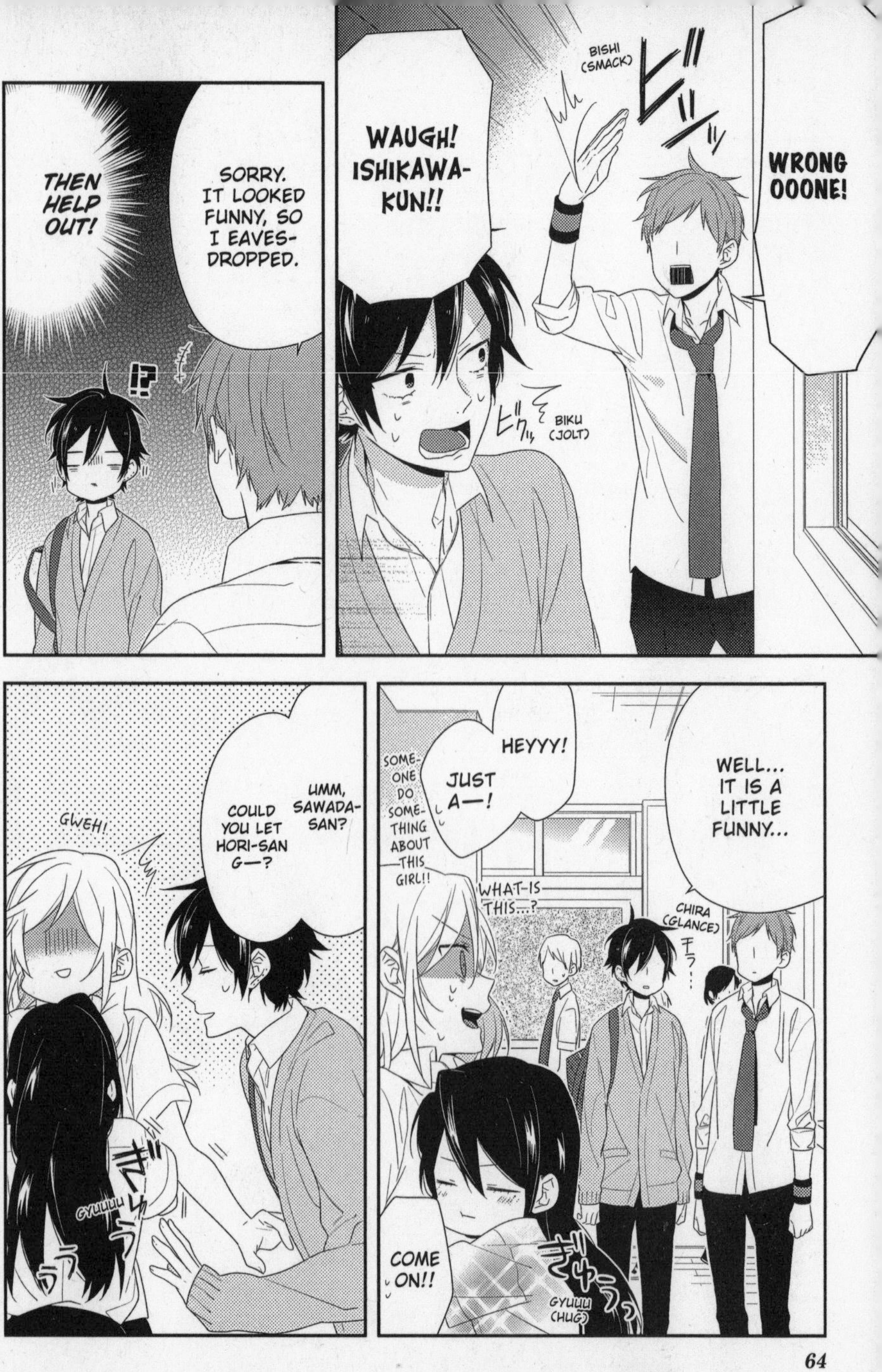
WRONG OOONE!
BISHI (SMACK)
WAUGH! ISHIKAWA-KUN!!
BIKU (JOLT)
SORRY. IT LOOKED FUNNY, SO I EAVES-DROPPED.
THEN HELP OUT!
!?
WELL... IT IS A LITTLE FUNNY...
CHIRA (GLANCE)
HEYYY!
JUST A—!
SOME-ONE DO SOME-THING ABOUT THIS GIRL!!
WHAT-IS THIS...?
COME ON!!
GYUUU (HUG)
UMM, SAWADA-SAN?
COULD YOU LET HORI-SAN G—?
GWEH!
GYUUUU

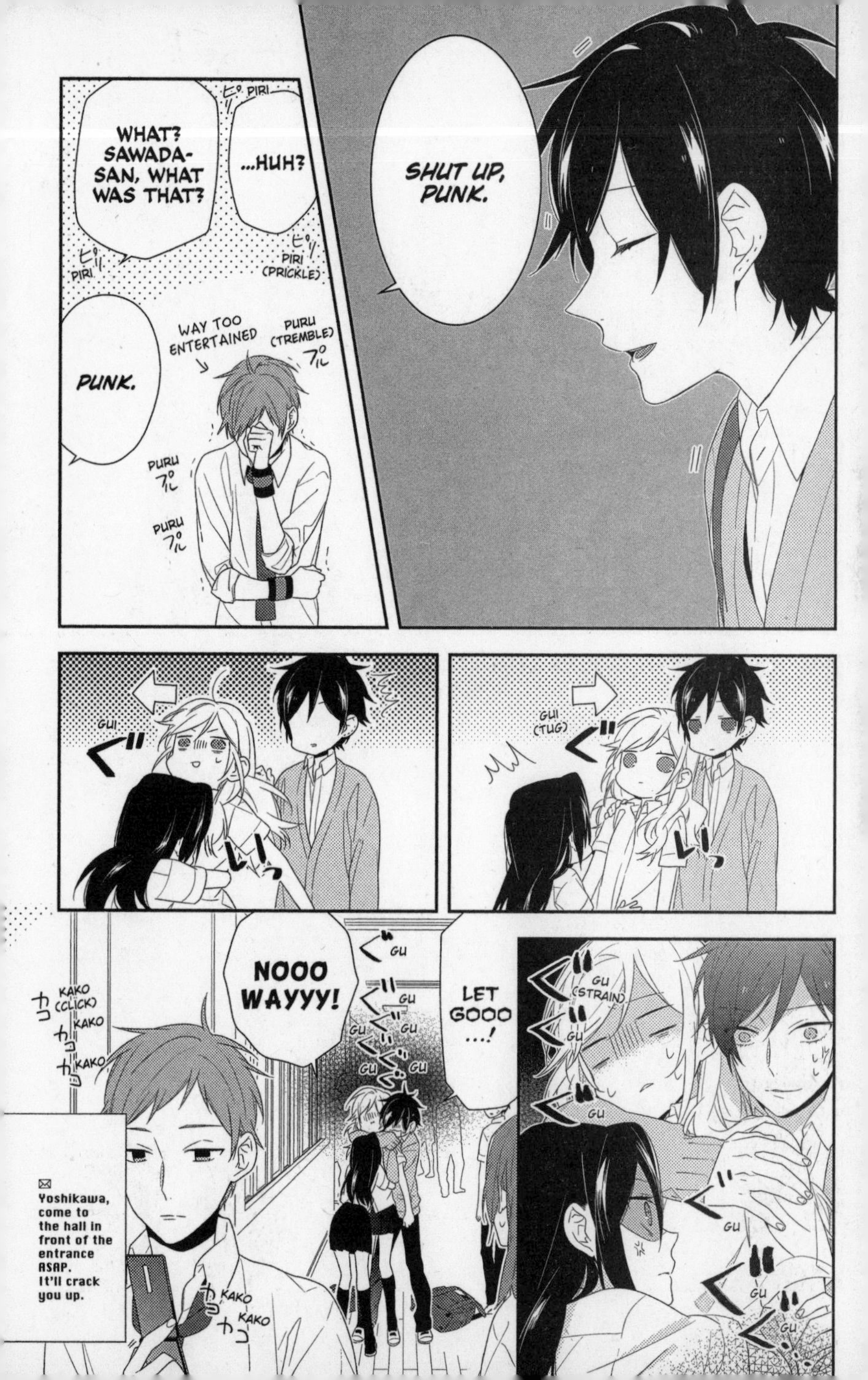
SHUT UP, PUNK.
PIRI
...HUH?
WHAT? SAWADA-SAN, WHAT WAS THAT?
PIRI (PRICKLE)
PIRI
PURU (TREMBLE)
WAY TOO ENTERTAINED
PUNK.
PURU
PURU
GUI (TUG)
GUI
GU (STRAIN)
GU
GU
GU
GU
GU
LET GOOO...!
GU
GU
GU
GU
GU
GU
NOOO WAYYY!
KAKO (CLICK)
KAKO
KAKO
Yoshikawa, come to the hall in front of the entrance ASAP. It'll crack you up.
KAKO
KAKO

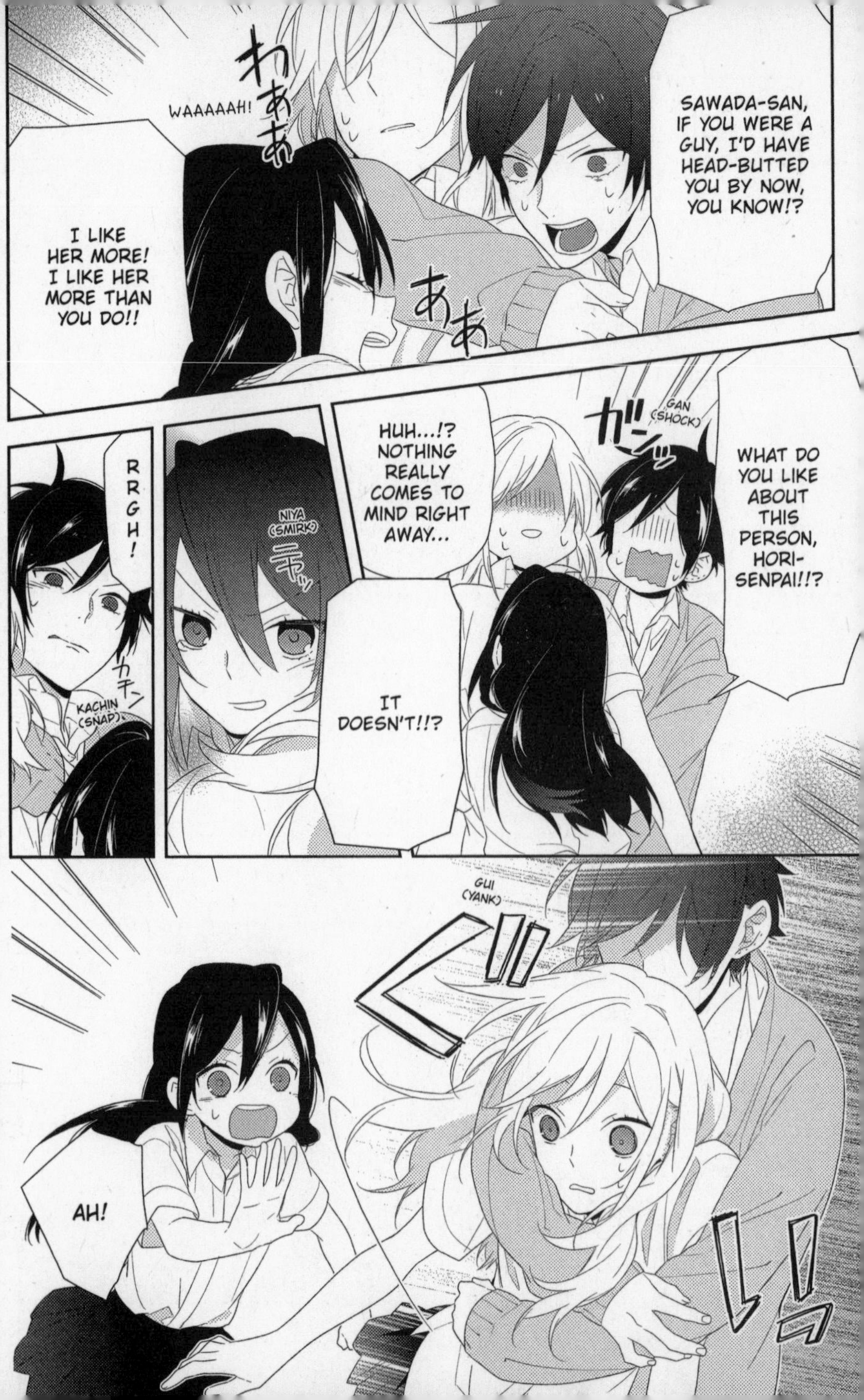
SAWADA-SAN, IF YOU WERE A GUY, I'D HAVE HEAD-BUTTED YOU BY NOW, YOU KNOW!?
わああ
WAAAAAH!
ああ
I LIKE HER MORE! I LIKE HER MORE THAN YOU DO!!
WHAT DO YOU LIKE ABOUT THIS PERSON, HORI-SENPAI!!?
ガーン
GAN (SHOCK)
HUH...!? NOTHING REALLY COMES TO MIND RIGHT AWAY...
IT DOESN'T!!?
ニヤッ
NIYA (SMIRK)
RRGH!
カチン
KACHIN (SNAP)
GUI (YANK)
AH!

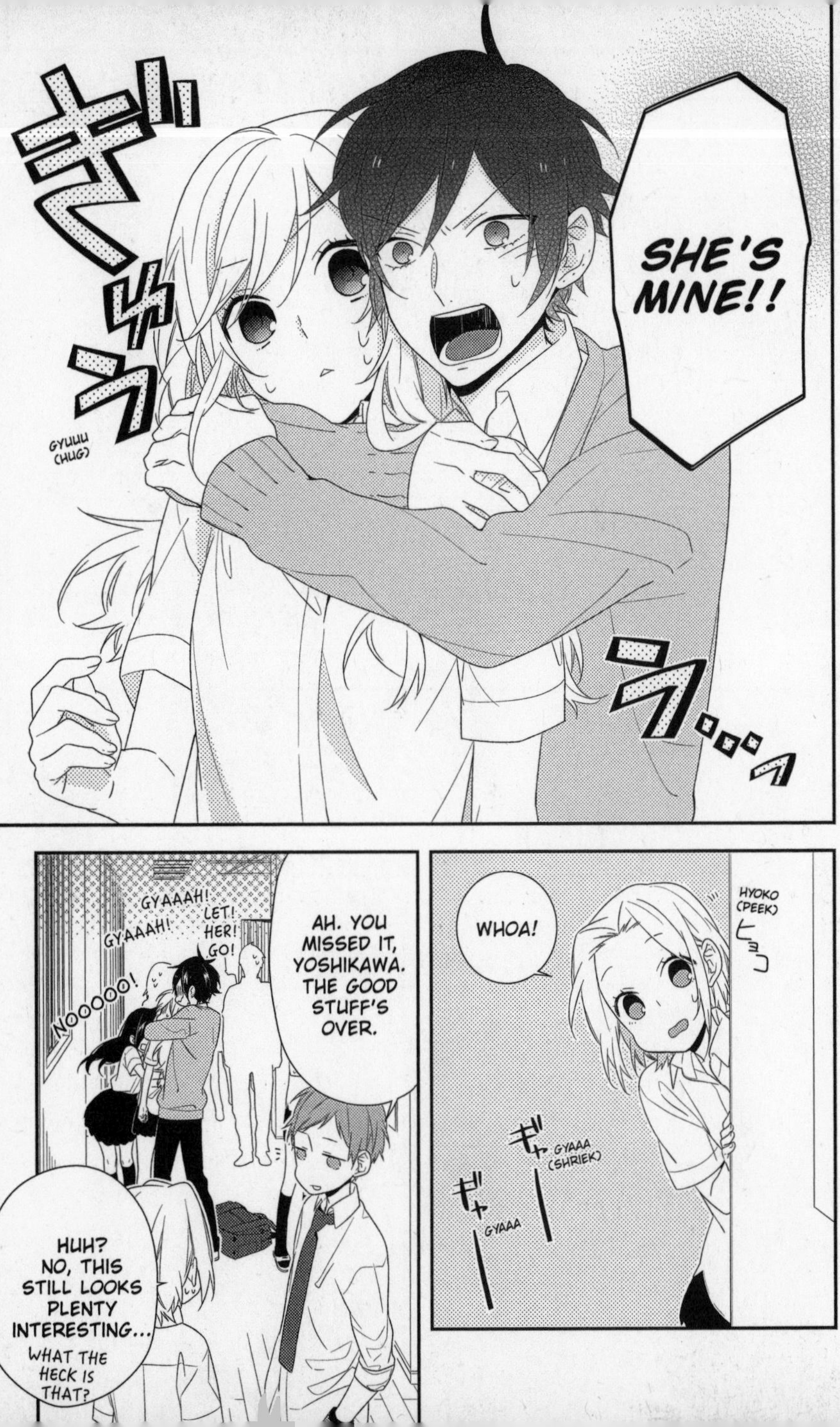
SHE'S MINE!!
GYUUU (HUG)
HYOKO (PEEK)
WHOA!
GYAAA (SHRIEK)
GYAAA
AH. YOU MISSED IT, YOSHIKAWA. THE GOOD STUFF'S OVER.
LET! HER! GO!
GYAAAH!
GYAAAH!
NOOOOO!
HUH? NO, THIS STILL LOOKS PLENTY INTERESTING...
WHAT THE HECK IS THAT?

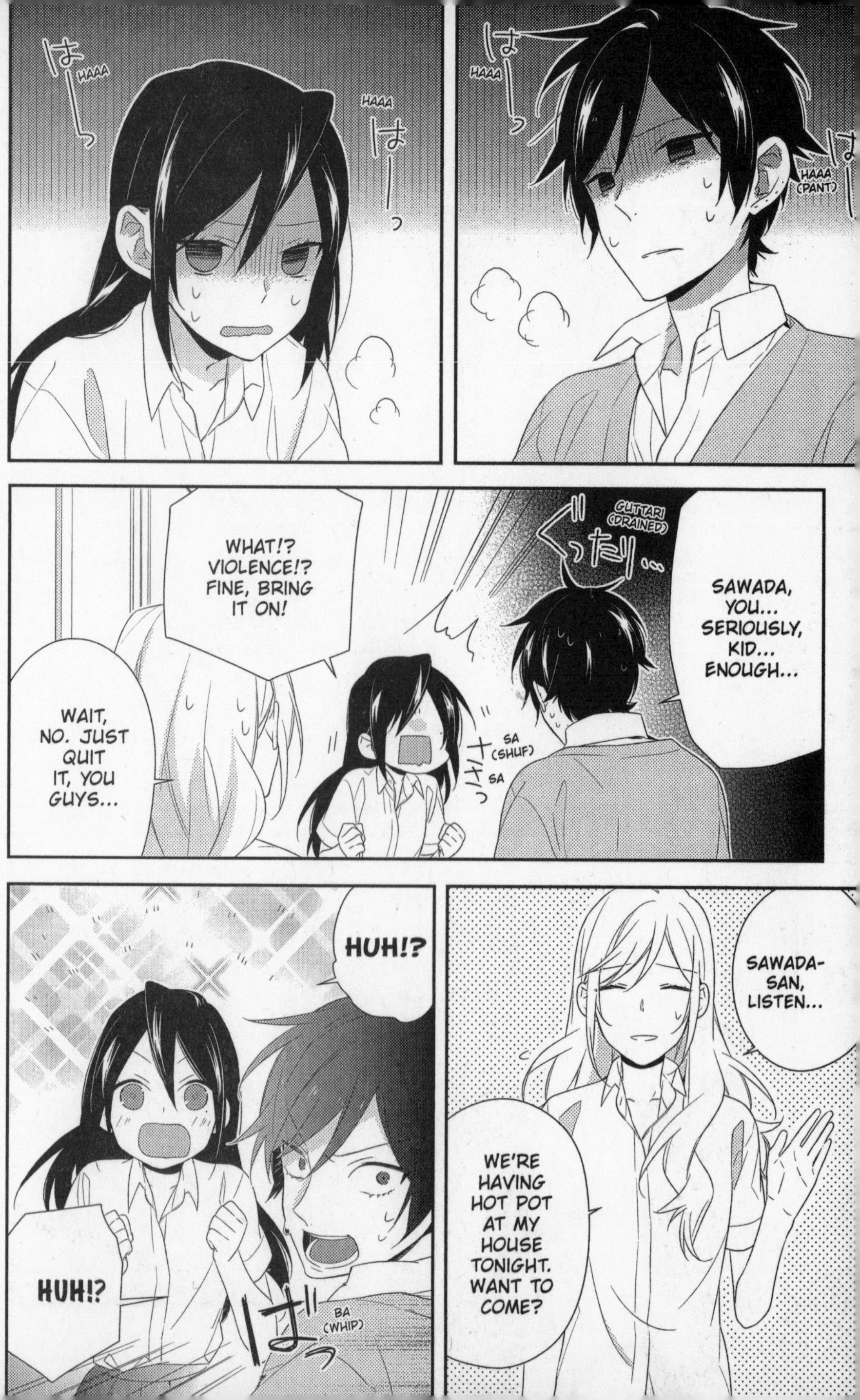
はーっ
HAAA
はーっ
HAAA (PANT)
はーっ
HAAA
はーっ
HAAA
ぐったり…
GUTTARI (DRAINED)
SAWADA, YOU... SERIOUSLY, KID... ENOUGH...
WHAT!? VIOLENCE!? FINE, BRING IT ON!
サッ
SA (SHUF)
サッ
SA
WAIT, NO. JUST QUIT IT, YOU GUYS...
SAWADA-SAN, LISTEN...
WE'RE HAVING HOT POT AT MY HOUSE TONIGHT. WANT TO COME?
HUH!?
ばっ
BA (WHIP)
HUH!?

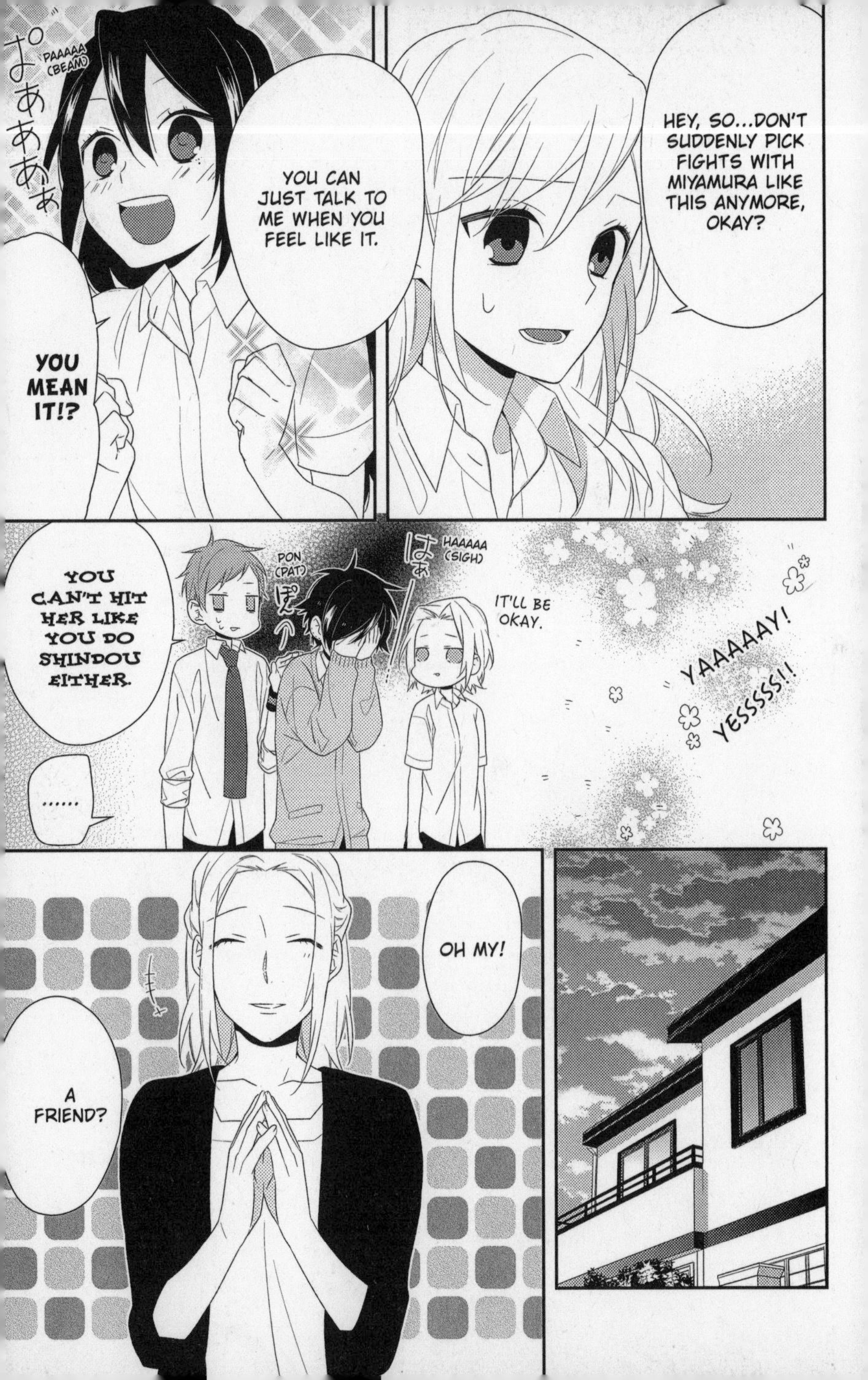
HEY, SO...DON'T SUDDENLY PICK FIGHTS WITH MIYAMURA LIKE THIS ANYMORE, OKAY?
ぱあああぁ
PAAAAAA (BEAM)
YOU CAN JUST TALK TO ME WHEN YOU FEEL LIKE IT.
YOU MEAN IT!?
YAAAAAY!
YESSSSS!!
IT'LL BE OKAY.
はぁー
HAAAAA (SIGH)
ぽん
PON (PAT)
YOU CAN'T HIT HER LIKE YOU DO SHINDOU EITHER.
......
OH MY!
A FRIEND?

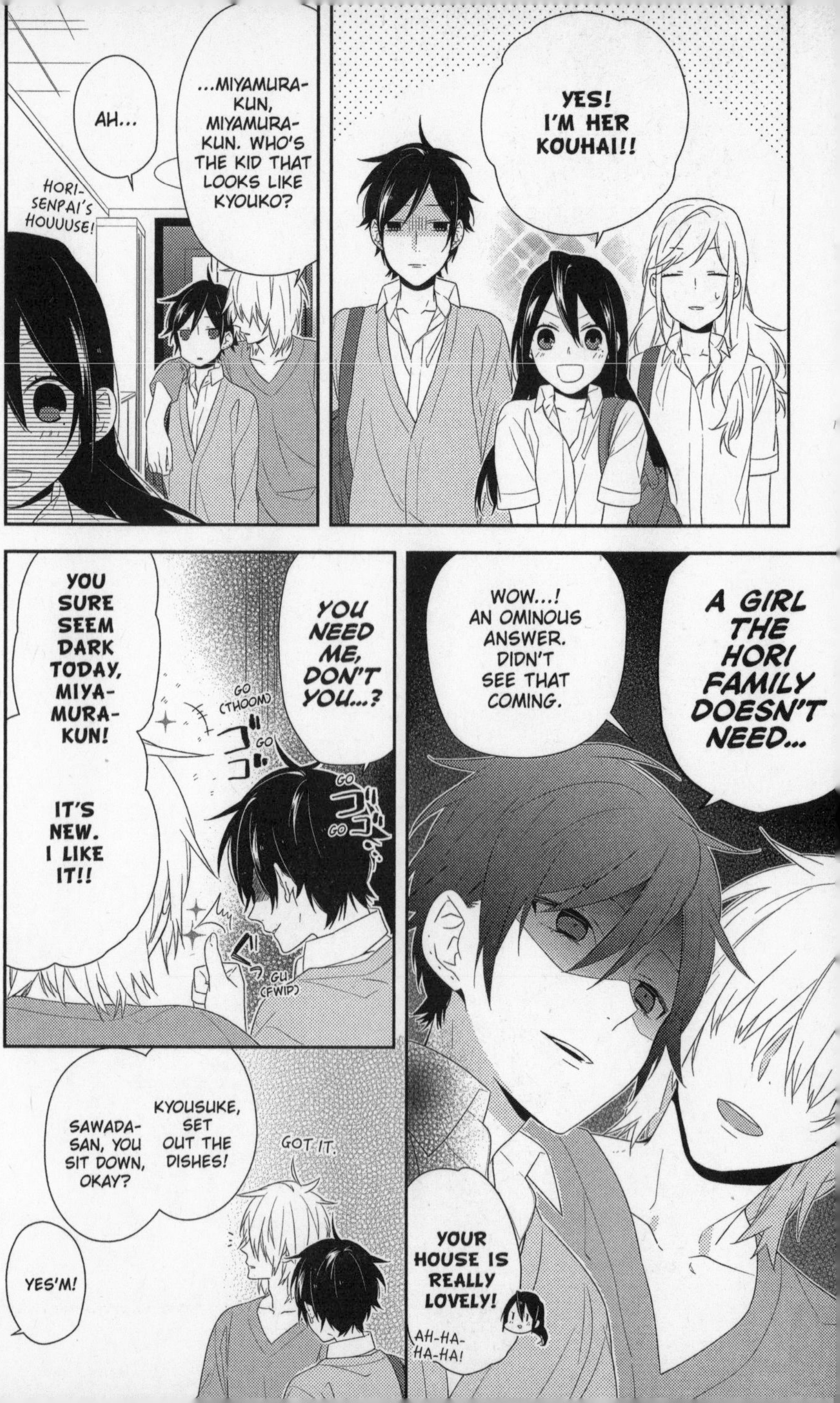
YES! I'M HER KOUHAI!!
...MIYAMURA-KUN, MIYAMURA-KUN. WHO'S THE KID THAT LOOKS LIKE KYOUKO?
AH...
HORI-SENPAI'S HOUUUSE!
A GIRL THE HORI FAMILY DOESN'T NEED...
WOW...! AN OMINOUS ANSWER. DIDN'T SEE THAT COMING.
YOUR HOUSE IS REALLY LOVELY!
AH-HA-HA-HA!
YOU NEED ME, DON'T YOU...?
GO GO GO GO
GO (THOOM)
YOU SURE SEEM DARK TODAY, MIYAMURA-KUN!
IT'S NEW. I LIKE IT!!
GU (FWIP)
KYOUSUKE, SET OUT THE DISHES!
SAWADA-SAN, YOU SIT DOWN, OKAY?
GOT IT.
YES'M!

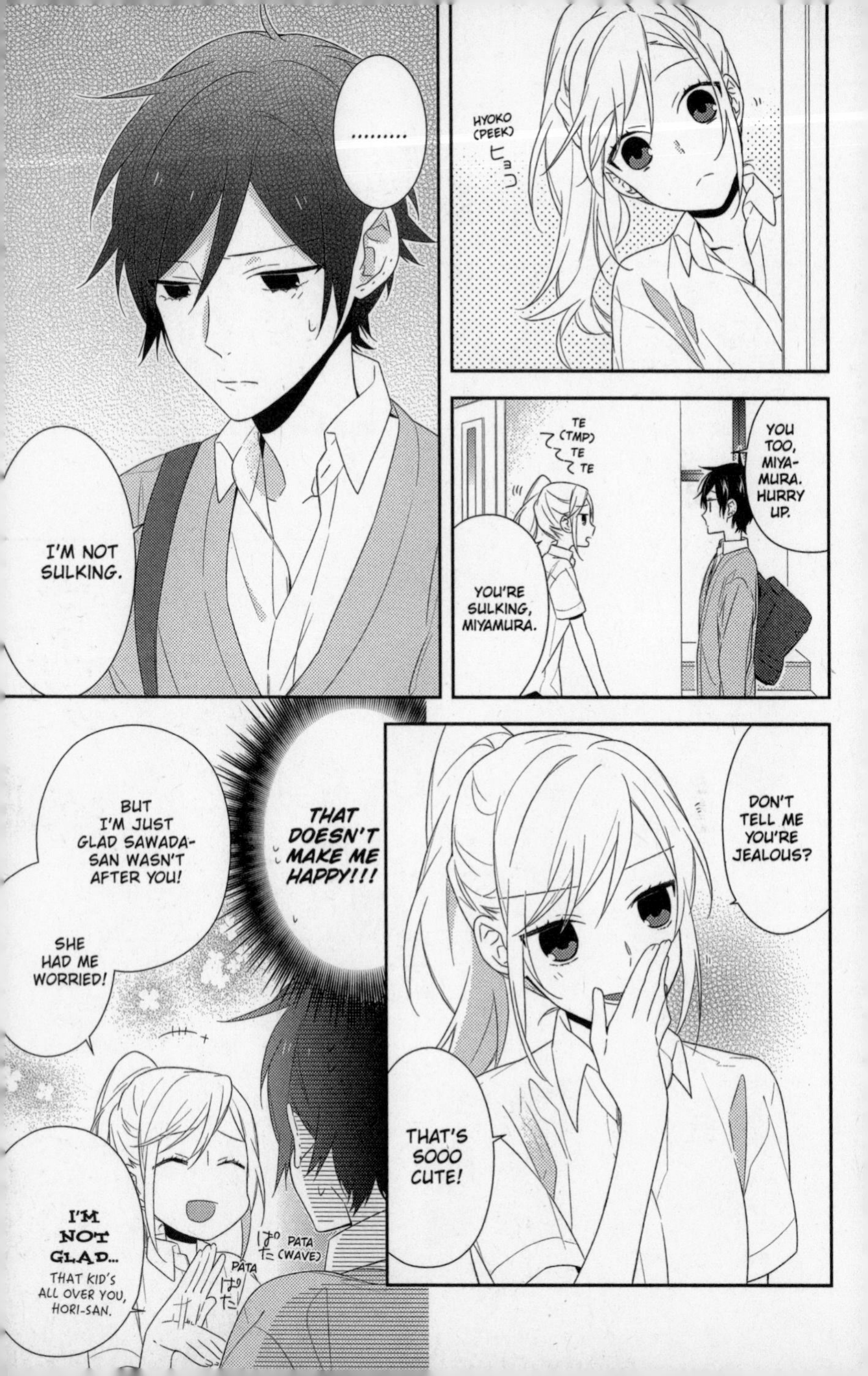
HYOKO (PEEK)
ヒョコ
YOU TOO, MIYAMURA. HURRY UP.
TE (TMP) TE TE
YOU'RE SULKING, MIYAMURA.
....
I'M NOT SULKING.
DON'T TELL ME YOU'RE JEALOUS?
THAT'S SOOO CUTE!
THAT DOESN'T MAKE ME HAPPY!!!
BUT I'M JUST GLAD SAWADA-SAN WASN'T AFTER YOU!
SHE HAD ME WORRIED!
ぱた PATA (WAVE)
PATA ぱた
I'M NOT GLAD... THAT KID'S ALL OVER YOU, HORI-SAN.

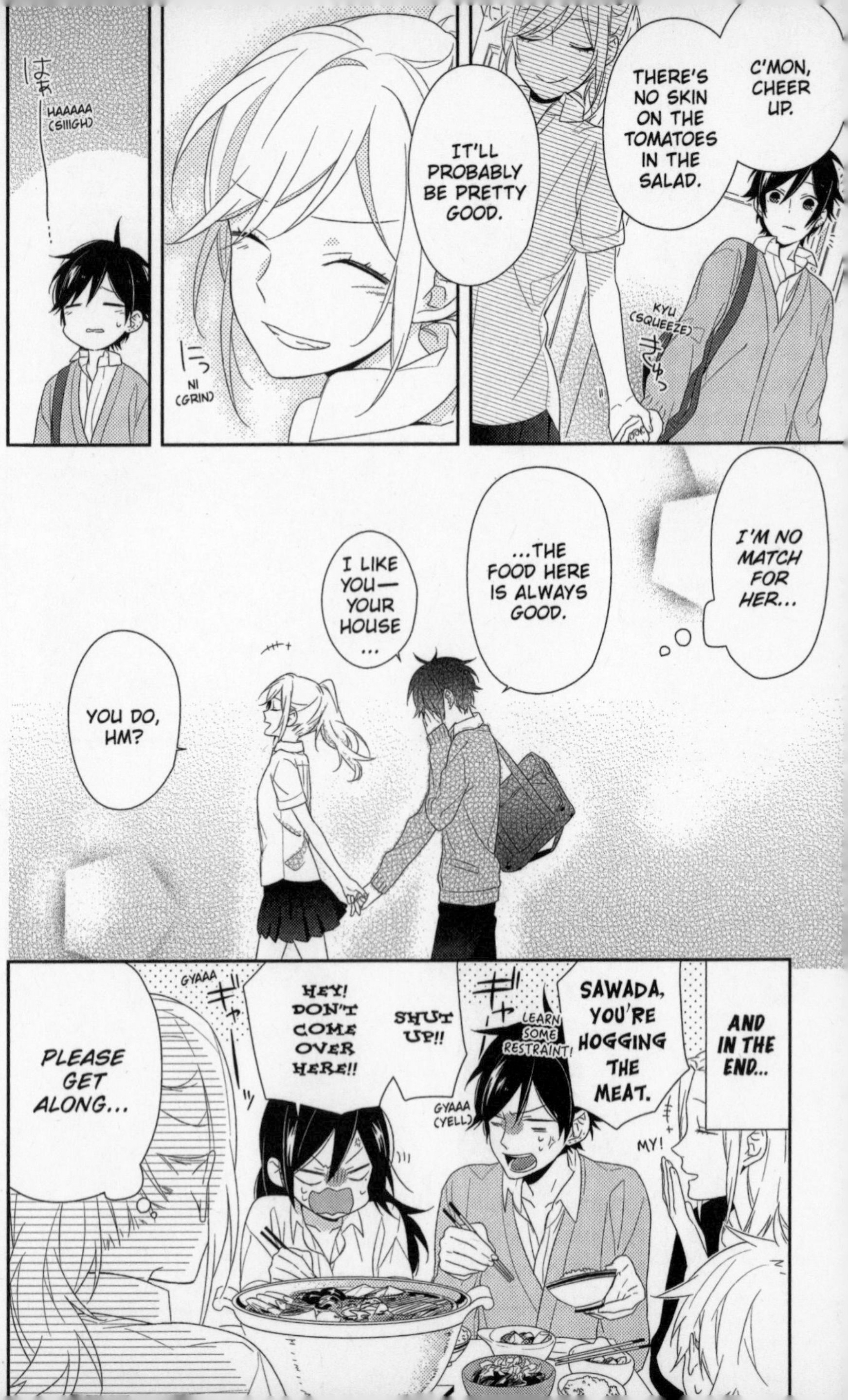
C'MON, CHEER UP.
THERE'S NO SKIN ON THE TOMATOES IN THE SALAD.
KYU (SQUEEZE)
IT'LL PROBABLY BE PRETTY GOOD.
NI (GRIN)
HAAAAA (SIIIGH)
I'M NO MATCH FOR HER...
...THE FOOD HERE IS ALWAYS GOOD.
I LIKE YOU— YOUR HOUSE ...
YOU DO, HM?
AND IN THE END...
MY!
SAWADA, YOU'RE HOGGING THE MEAT.
LEARN SOME RESTRAINT!
GYAAA (YELL)
SHUT UP!!
HEY! DON'T COME OVER HERE!!
GYAAA
PLEASE GET ALONG...

HORIMIYA

HORIMIYA

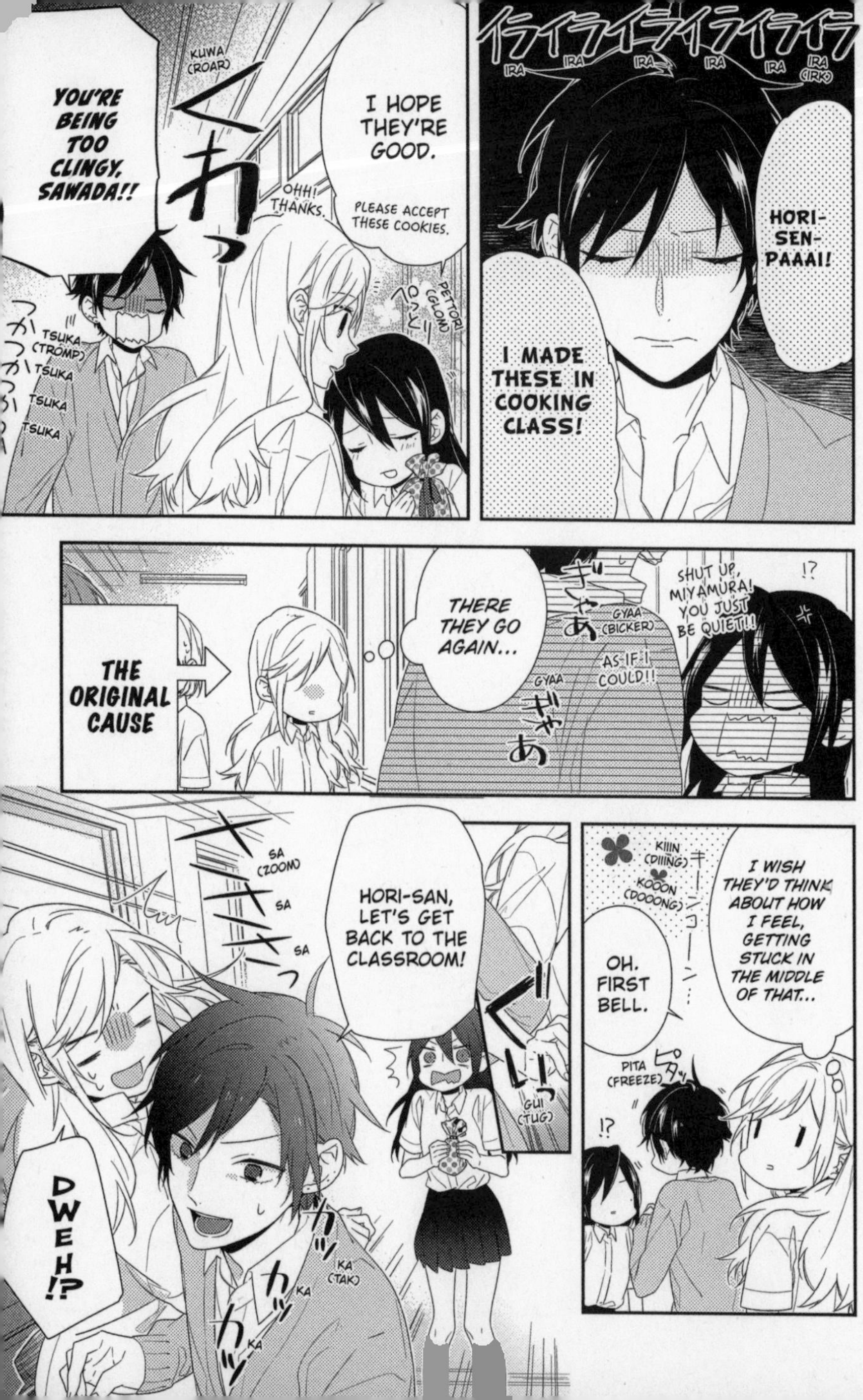
イライライライライライラ
IRA IRA IRA IRA IRA IRA (IRK)
HORI-SEN-PAAAI!
I MADE THESE IN COOKING CLASS!
I HOPE THEY'RE GOOD.
PLEASE ACCEPT THESE COOKIES.
PETTORI (GLOW)
OHH! THANKS.
KUWA (ROAR)
YOU'RE BEING TOO CLINGY, SAWADA!!
TSUKA (TROMP) TSUKA TSUKA TSUKA
!?
SHUT UP, MIYAMURA! YOU JUST BE QUIET!!
GYAA (BICKER)
AS IF I COULD!!
GYAA
THERE THEY GO AGAIN...
THE ORIGINAL CAUSE
I WISH THEY'D THINK ABOUT HOW I FEEL, GETTING STUCK IN THE MIDDLE OF THAT...
KIIIN (DIIING)
KOOON (DOOONG)
OH. FIRST BELL.
PITA (FREEZE)
!?
GUI (TUG)
HORI-SAN, LET'S GET BACK TO THE CLASSROOM!
SA (ZOOM) SA SA
DWEH!?
KA (TAK) KA KA

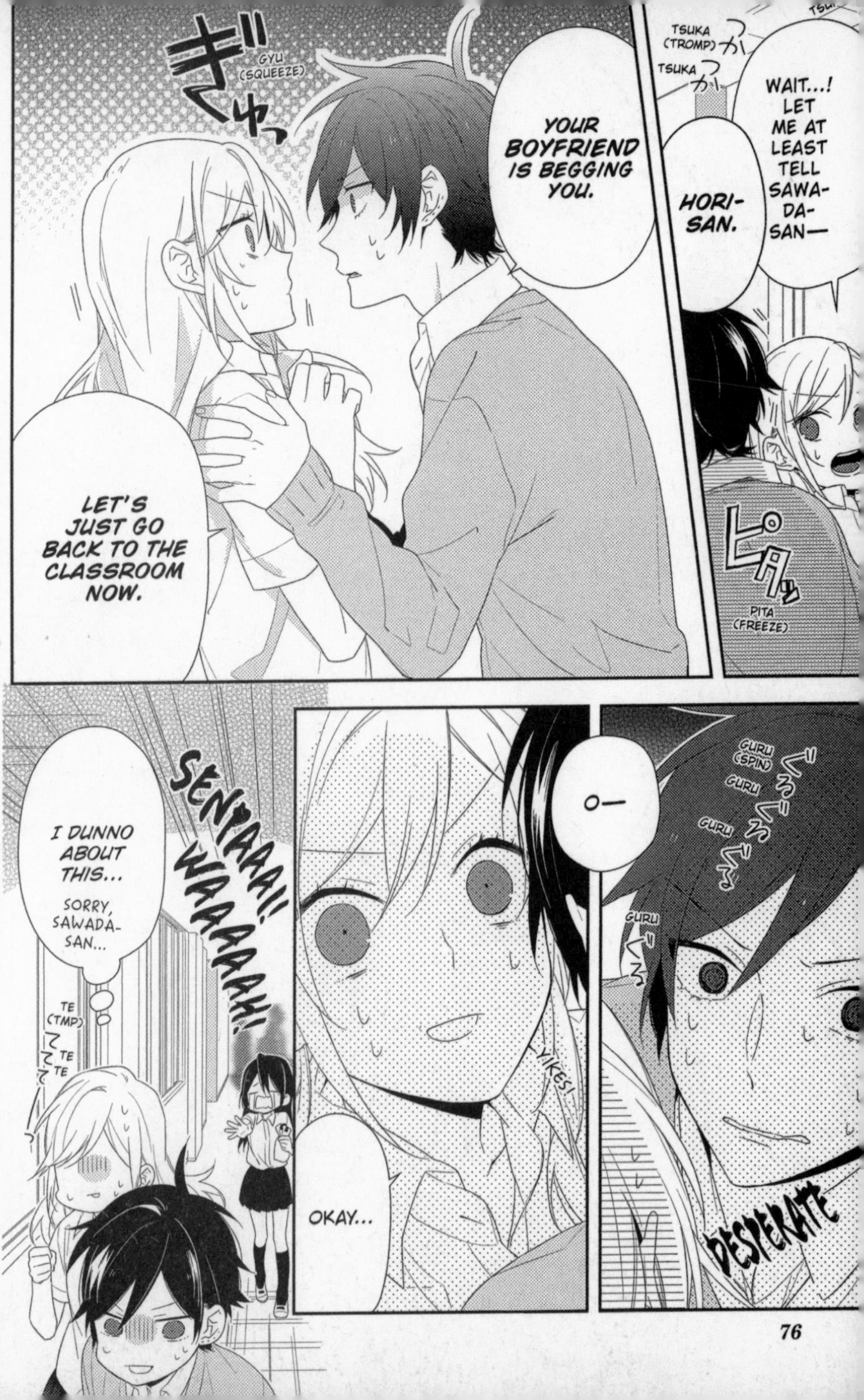
TSU
TSUKA (TROMP)
TSUKA
WAIT...! LET ME AT LEAST TELL SAWA-DA-SAN—
HORI-SAN.
PITA (FREEZE)
YOUR BOYFRIEND IS BEGGING YOU.
GYU (SQUEEZE)
LET'S JUST GO BACK TO THE CLASSROOM NOW.
GURU (SPIN)
GURU
GURU
GURU
DESPERATE
O—
YIKES!
OKAY...
SENPAAAI! WAAAAAAH!
I DUNNO ABOUT THIS...
SORRY, SAWADA-SAN...
TE (TMP)
TE
TE

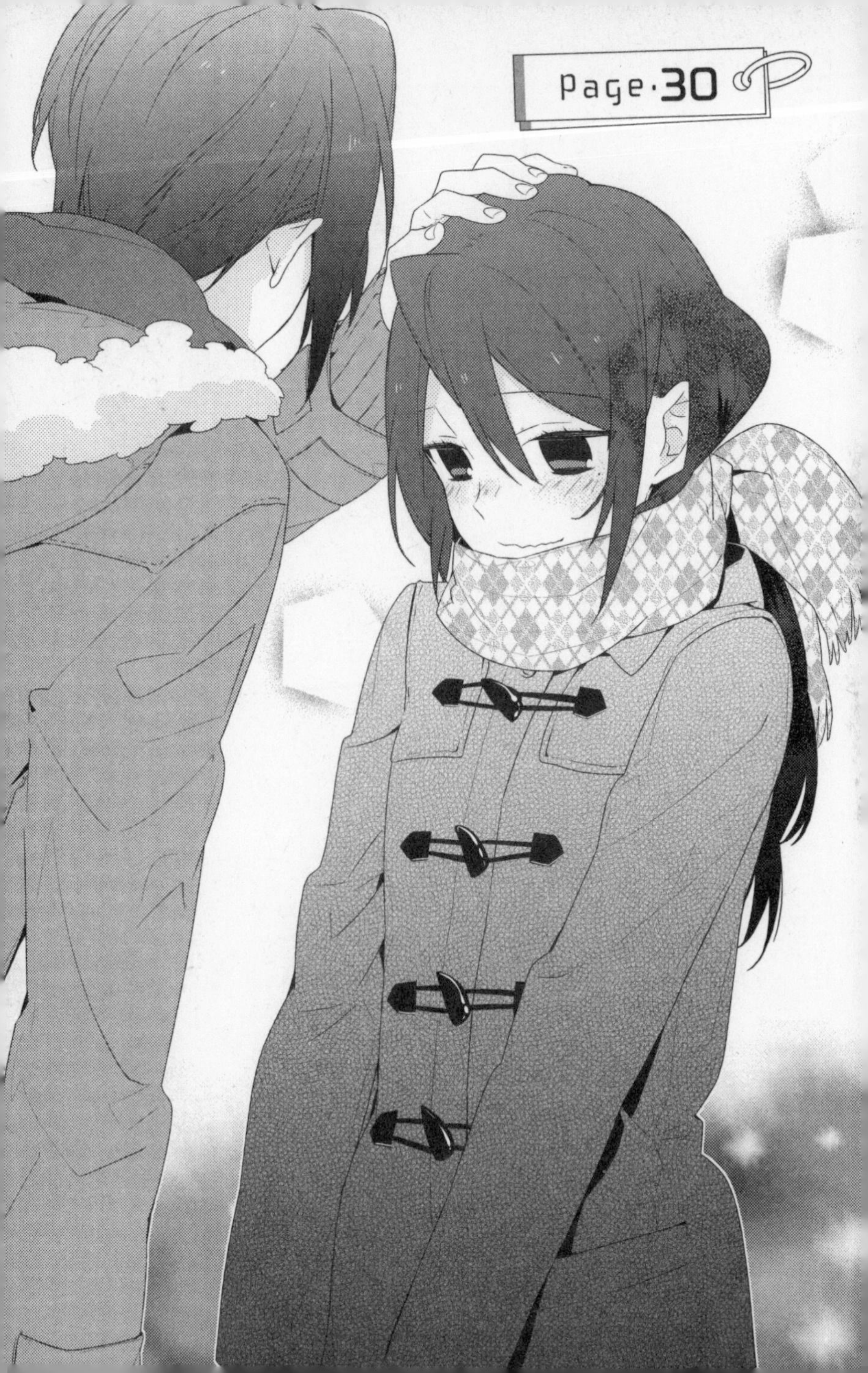
Page·30

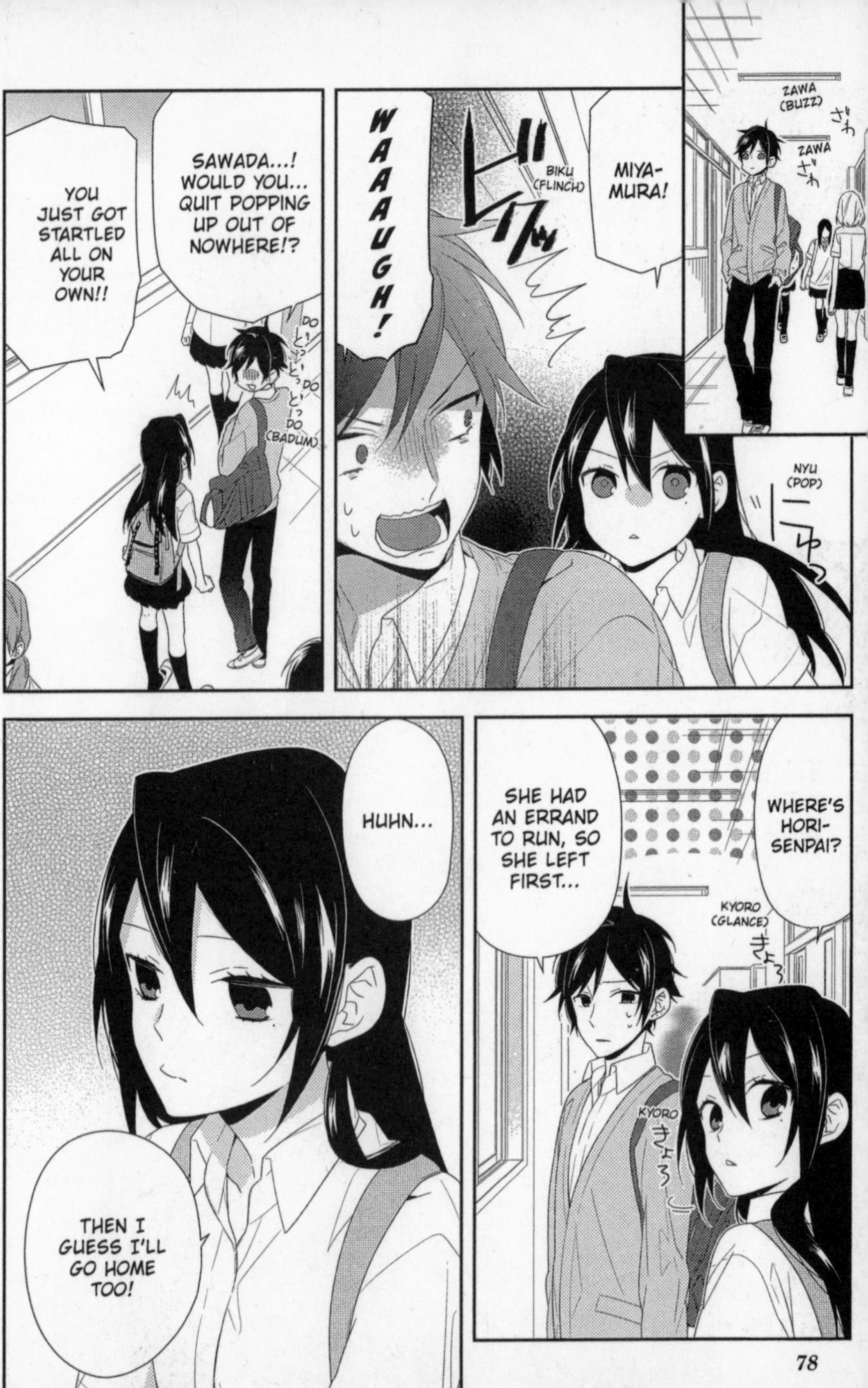
ZAWA (BUZZ)
ZAWA
MIYA-MURA!
BIKU (FLINCH)
NYU (POP)
WAAAAUGH!
SAWADA...! WOULD YOU... QUIT POPPING UP OUT OF NOWHERE!?
DO DO DO (BADUM)
YOU JUST GOT STARTLED ALL ON YOUR OWN!!
WHERE'S HORI-SENPAI?
KYORO (GLANCE)
KYORO
SHE HAD AN ERRAND TO RUN, SO SHE LEFT FIRST...
HUHN...
THEN I GUESS I'LL GO HOME TOO!

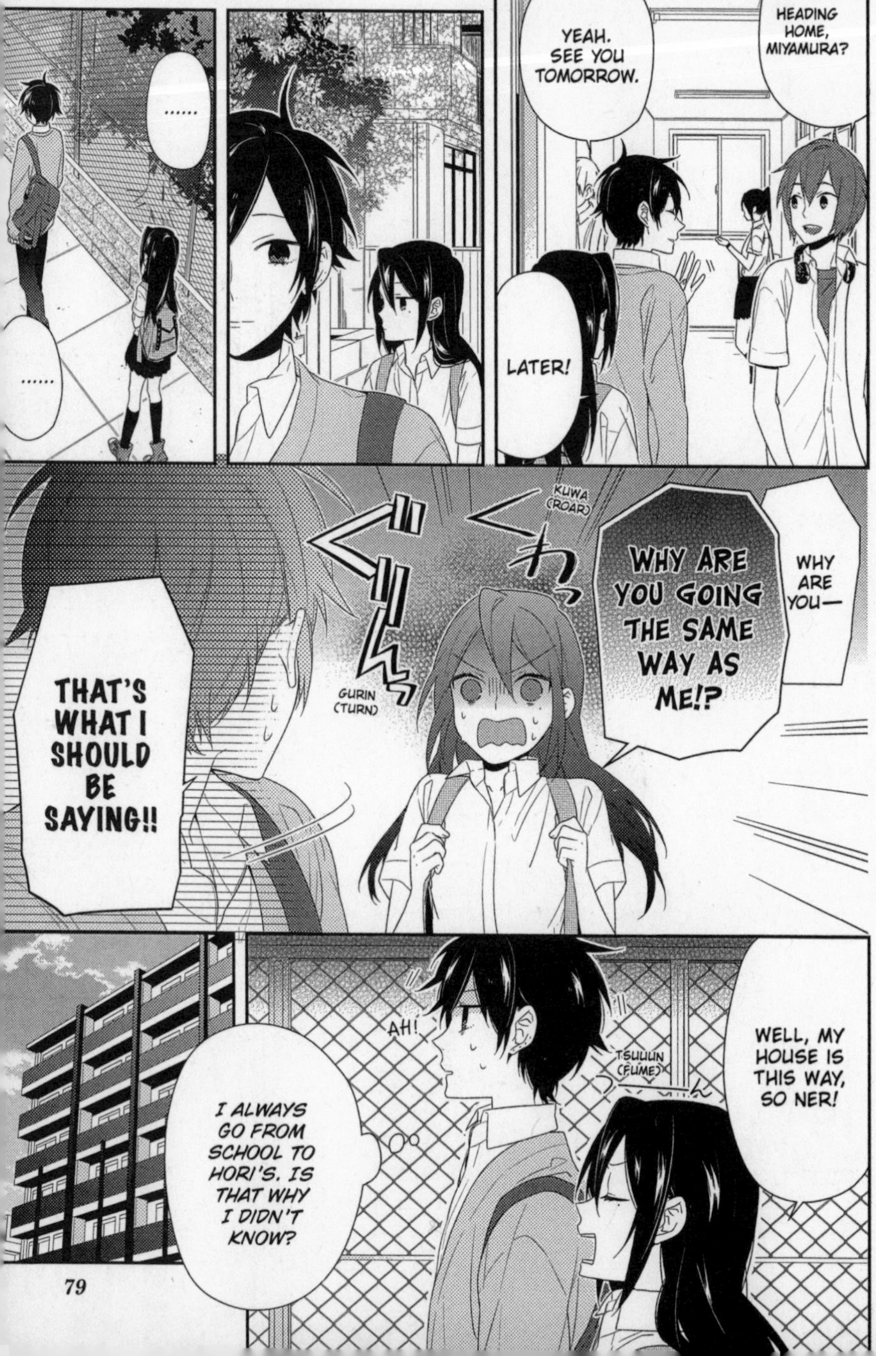
HEADING HOME, MIYAMURA?
YEAH. SEE YOU TOMORROW.
LATER!
......
......
......
WHY ARE YOU—
WHY ARE YOU GOING THE SAME WAY AS ME!?
KUWA (ROAR)
GURIN (TURN)
THAT'S WHAT I SHOULD BE SAYING!!
WELL, MY HOUSE IS THIS WAY, SO NER!
TSUUUN (FUME)
AH!
I ALWAYS GO FROM SCHOOL TO HORI'S. IS THAT WHY I DIDN'T KNOW?

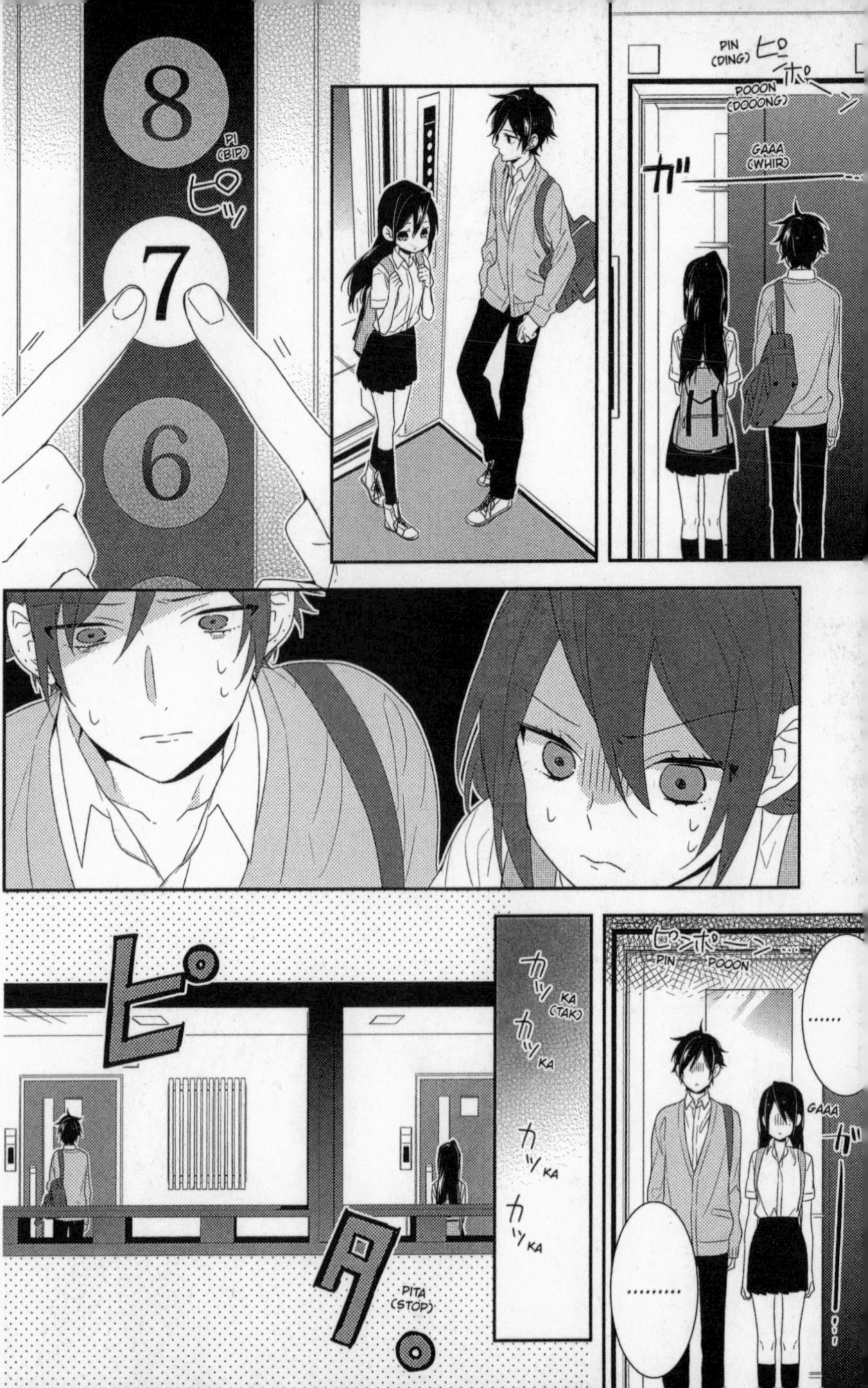

PIN (DING) ピ
POOON (DOOONG) ポーン
GAAA (WHIR) ガ
PI (BIP) ピッ
8
7
6
ピンポーン
PIN POOON
......
....
GAAA ガー
カッ KA (TAK)
カッ KA
カッ KA
カッ KA
ピタ。
PITA (STOP)

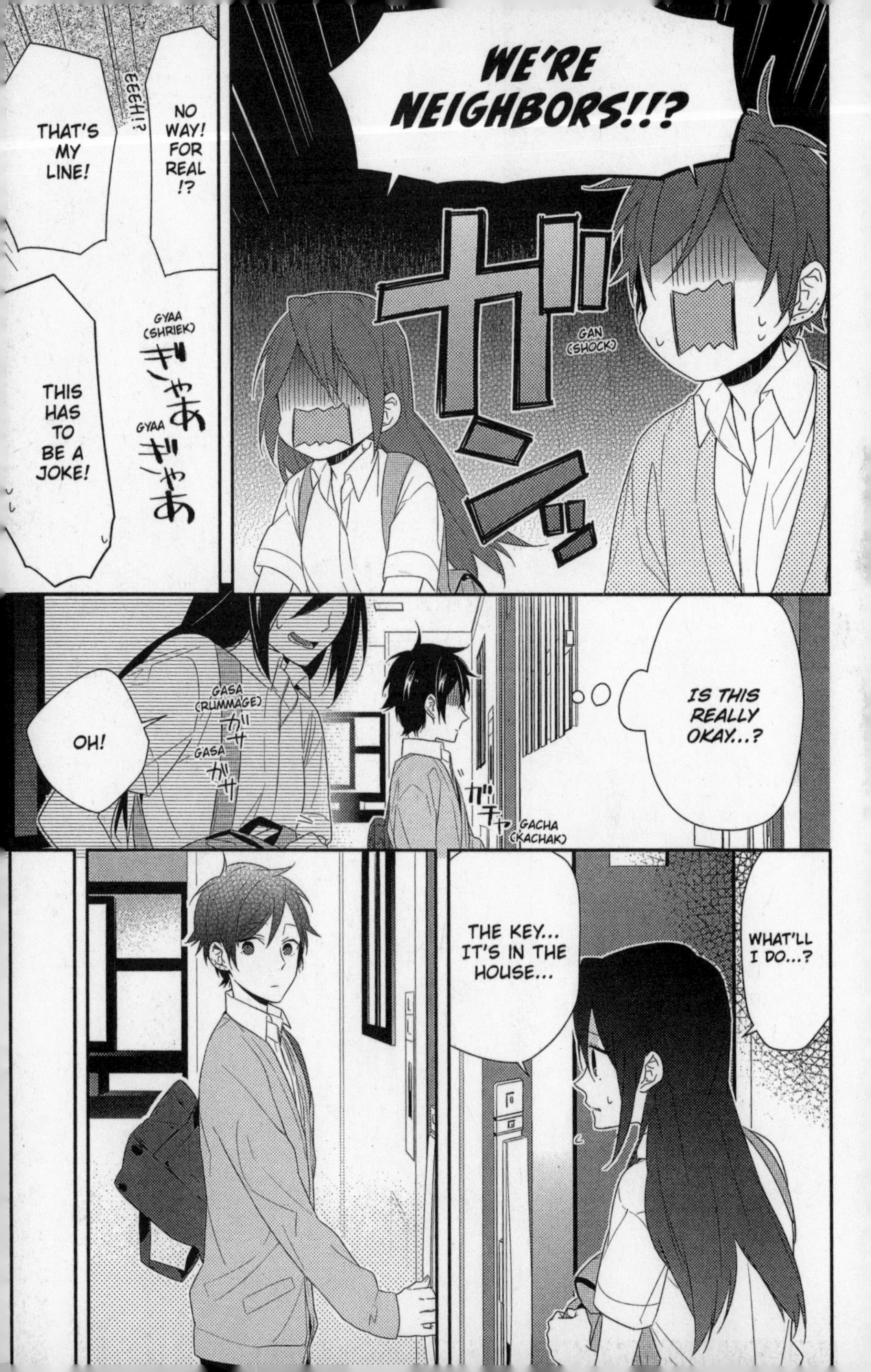
WE'RE NEIGHBORS!!?
ガーン
GAN (SHOCK)
NO WAY! FOR REAL !?
EEEH!!?
THAT'S MY LINE!
GYAA (SHRIEK)
ぎゃあ
GYAA
ぎゃあ
THIS HAS TO BE A JOKE!
IS THIS REALLY OKAY...?
ガチャ
GACHA (KACHAK)
GASA (RUMMAGE)
ガサ
GASA
ガサ
OH!
WHAT'LL I DO...?
THE KEY... IT'S IN THE HOUSE...

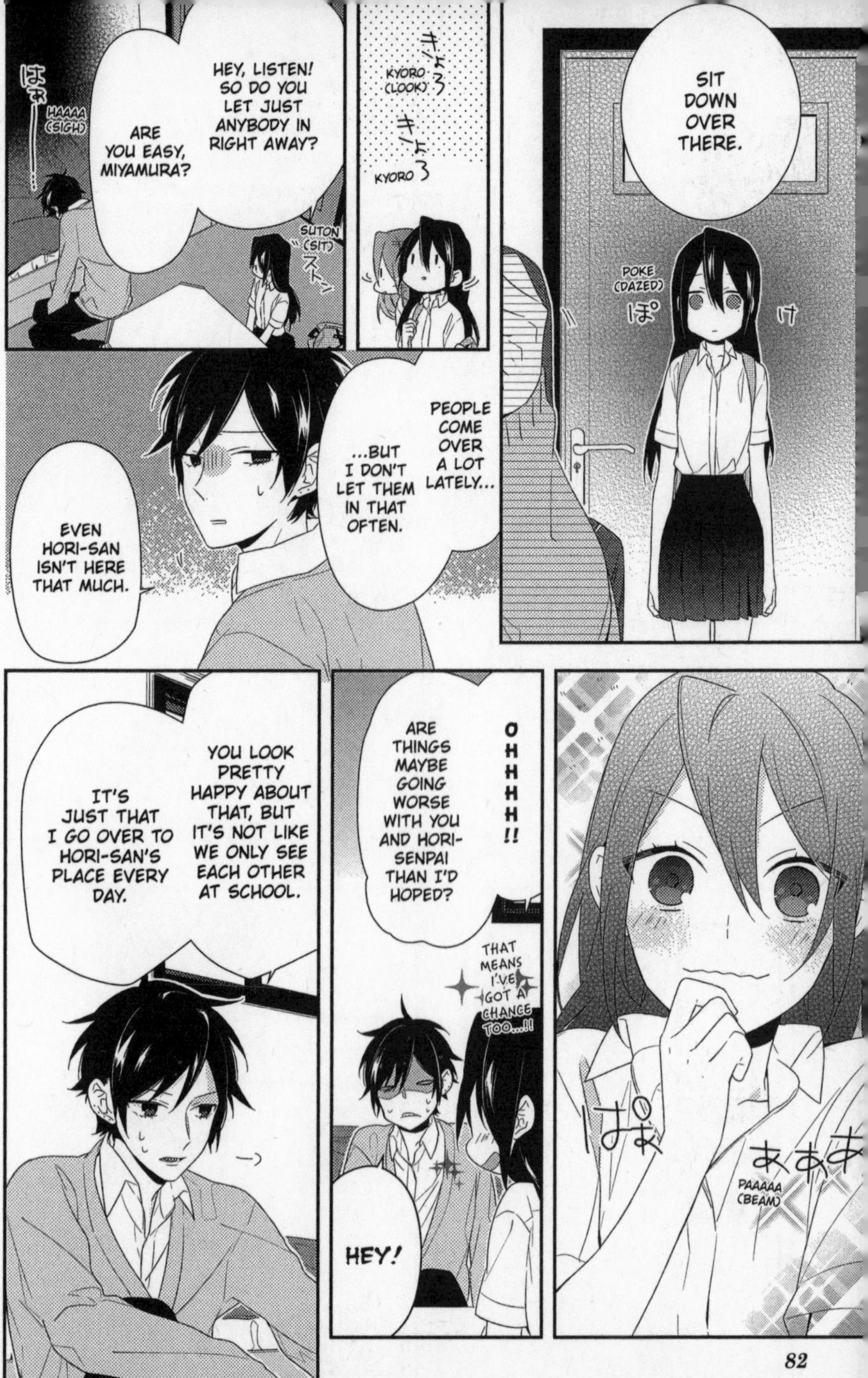
SIT DOWN OVER THERE.
POKE (DAZED)
ぽけ
KYORO (LOOK)
きょろ
きょろ
KYORO
HEY, LISTEN! SO DO YOU LET JUST ANYBODY IN RIGHT AWAY?
ARE YOU EASY, MIYAMURA?
SUTON (SIT)
ストン
HAAAA (SIGH)
PEOPLE COME OVER A LOT LATELY...
...BUT I DON'T LET THEM IN THAT OFTEN.
EVEN HORI-SAN ISN'T HERE THAT MUCH.
PAAAAA (BEAM)
ARE THINGS MAYBE GOING WORSE WITH YOU AND HORI-SENPAI THAN I'D HOPED?
OHHHHH!!
THAT MEANS I'VE GOT A CHANCE TOO...!!
HEY!
YOU LOOK PRETTY HAPPY ABOUT THAT, BUT IT'S NOT LIKE WE ONLY SEE EACH OTHER AT SCHOOL.
IT'S JUST THAT I GO OVER TO HORI-SAN'S PLACE EVERY DAY.

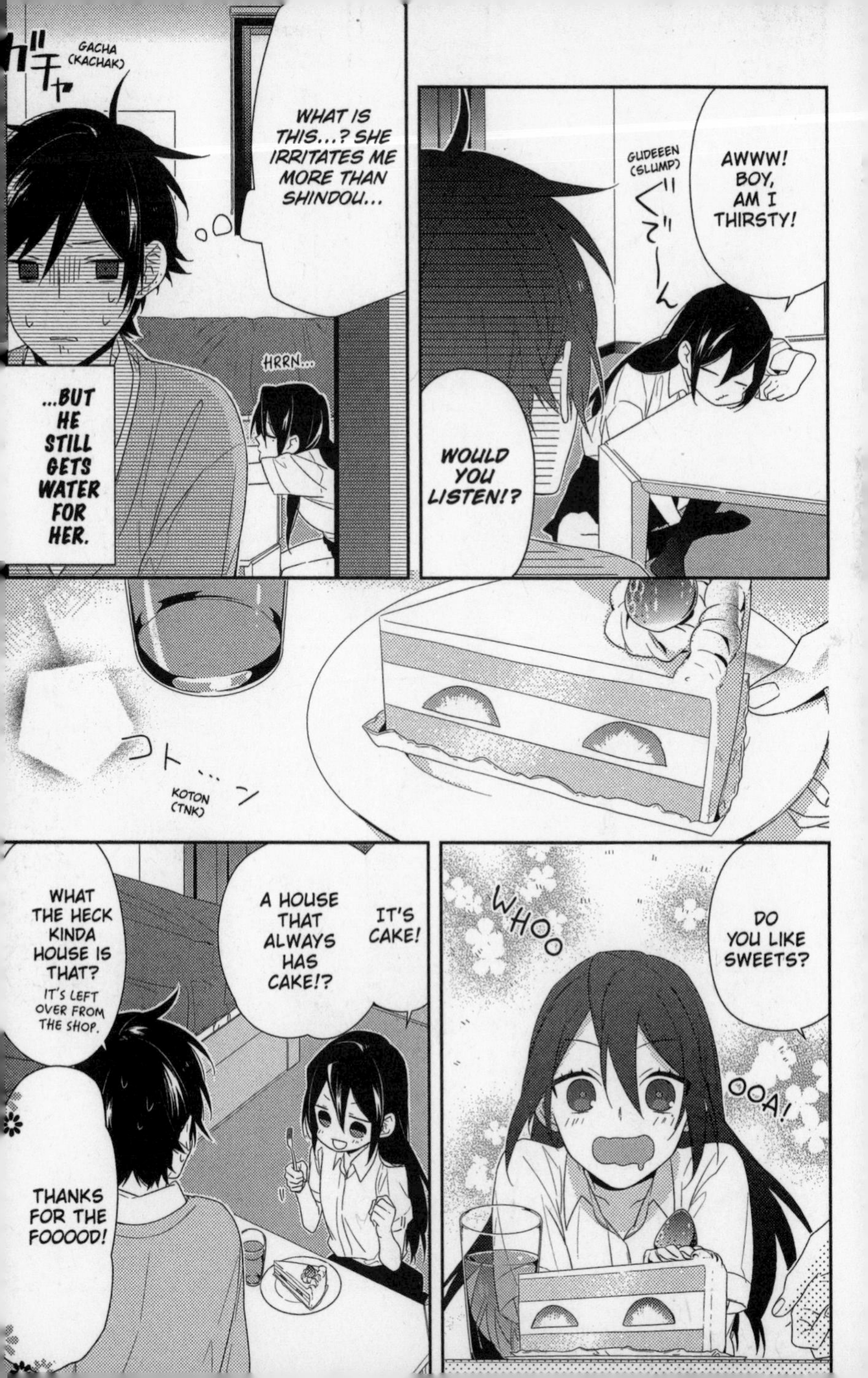
AWWW! BOY, AM I THIRSTY!
GUDEEEN (SLUMP)
WOULD YOU LISTEN!?
GACHA (KACHAK)
WHAT IS THIS...? SHE IRRITATES ME MORE THAN SHINDOU...
HRRN...
...BUT HE STILL GETS WATER FOR HER.
KOTON (TNK)
DO YOU LIKE SWEETS?
WHOO
OOA!
IT'S CAKE!
A HOUSE THAT ALWAYS HAS CAKE!?
WHAT THE HECK KINDA HOUSE IS THAT?
IT'S LEFT OVER FROM THE SHOP.
THANKS FOR THE FOOOOD!

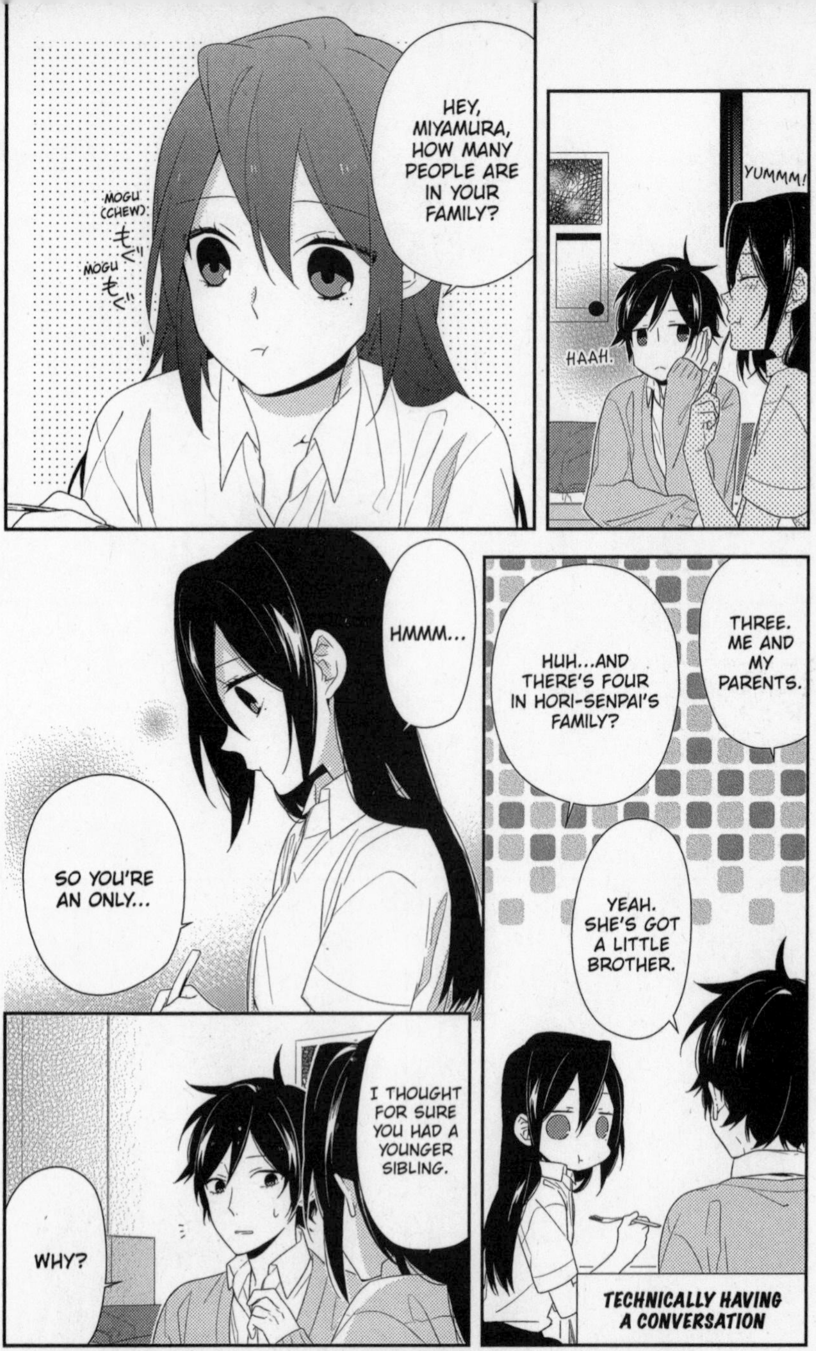
YUMMM!
HAAH.
HEY, MIYAMURA, HOW MANY PEOPLE ARE IN YOUR FAMILY?
MOGU (CHEW) もぐ
MOGU もぐ
THREE. ME AND MY PARENTS.
HUH...AND THERE'S FOUR IN HORI-SENPAI'S FAMILY?
YEAH. SHE'S GOT A LITTLE BROTHER.
TECHNICALLY HAVING A CONVERSATION
HMMM...
SO YOU'RE AN ONLY...
I THOUGHT FOR SURE YOU HAD A YOUNGER SIBLING.
WHY?

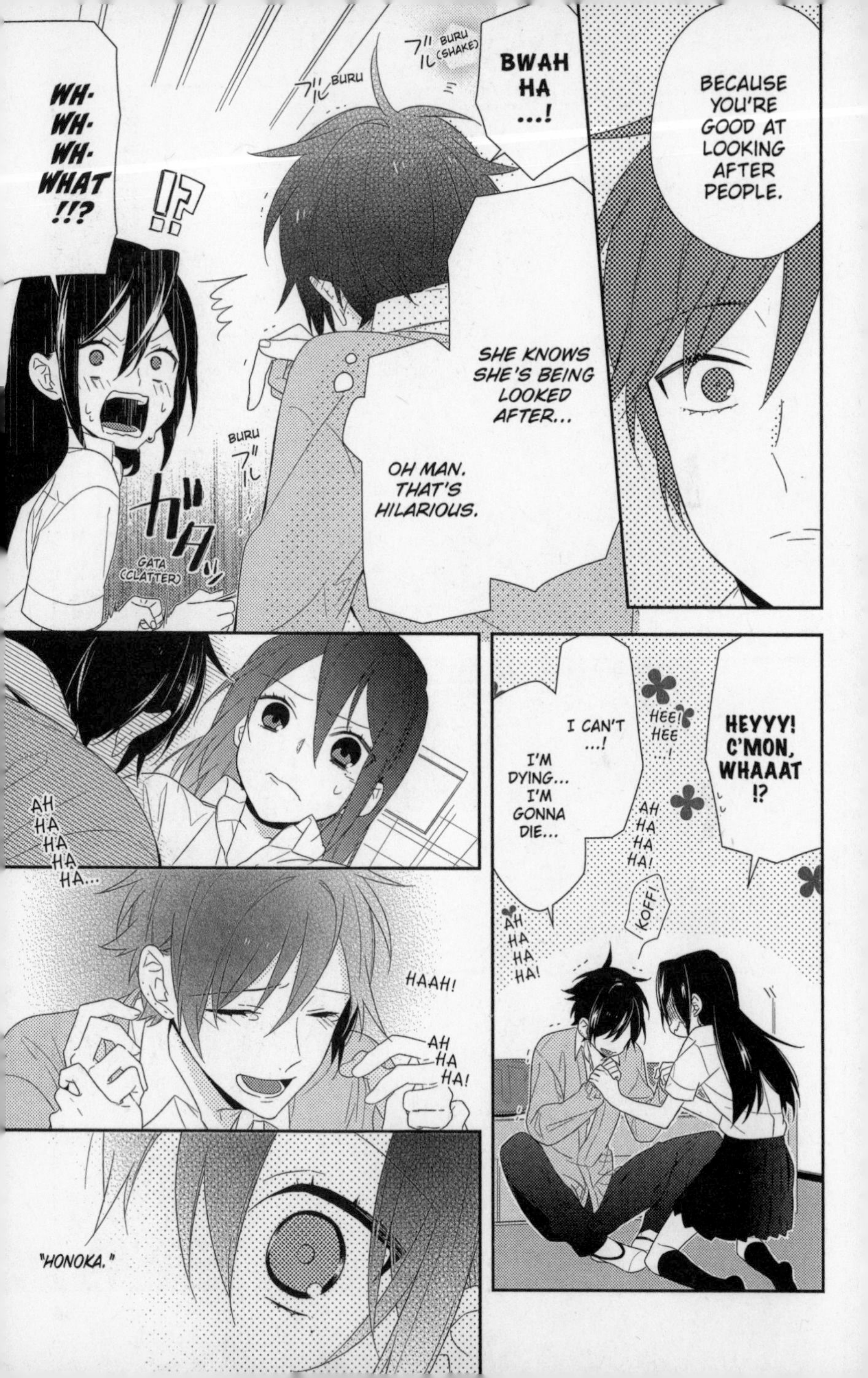
BECAUSE YOU'RE GOOD AT LOOKING AFTER PEOPLE.
BWAH HA ...!
BURU (SHAKE)
BURU
SHE KNOWS SHE'S BEING LOOKED AFTER...
OH MAN. THAT'S HILARIOUS.
WH-WH-WH-WHAT!!?
!!?
BURU
GATA (CLATTER)
HEYYY! C'MON, WHAAAT!?
HEE! HEE ...!
I CAN'T ...!
I'M DYING... I'M GONNA DIE...
AH HA HA HA!
KOFF!
AH HA HA HA!
AH HA HA HA HA...
HAAH!
AH HA HA!
"HONOKA."

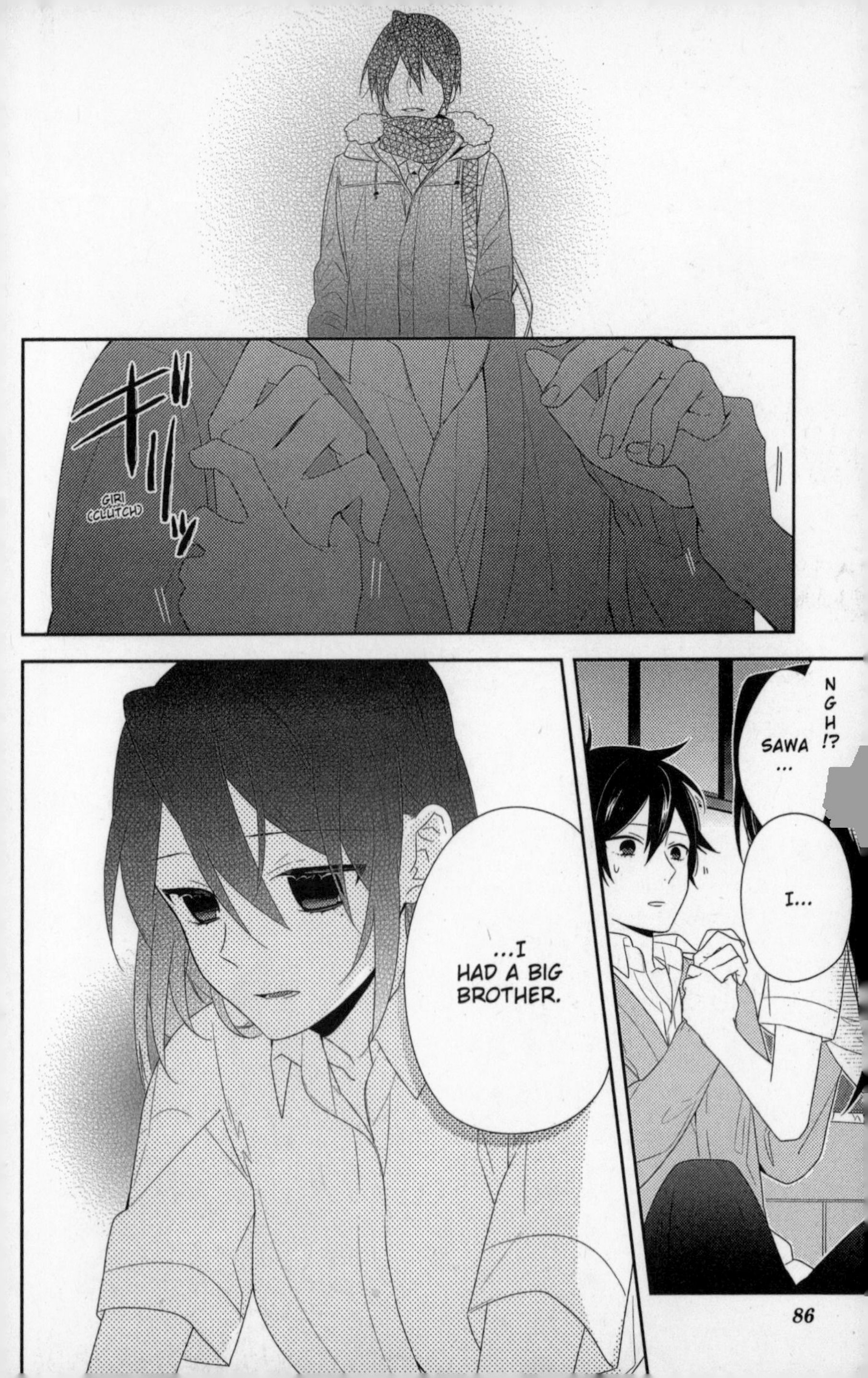
ギリッ
GIRI (CLUTCH)
NGH!?
SAWA...
I...
...I HAD A BIG BROTHER.

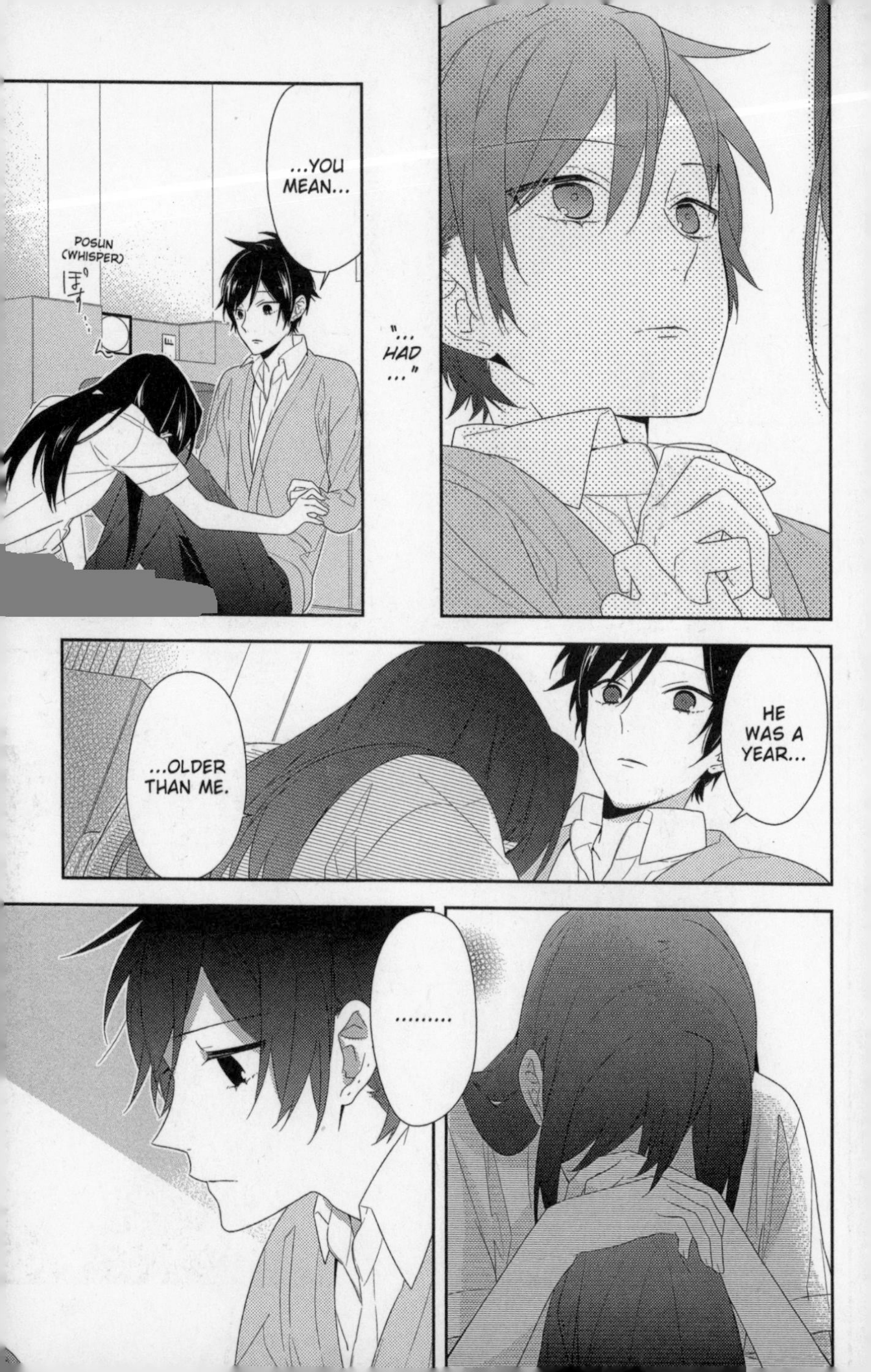
"...HAD..."
...YOU MEAN...
POSUN (WHISPER)
ぽす…
HE WAS A YEAR...
...OLDER THAN ME.
....

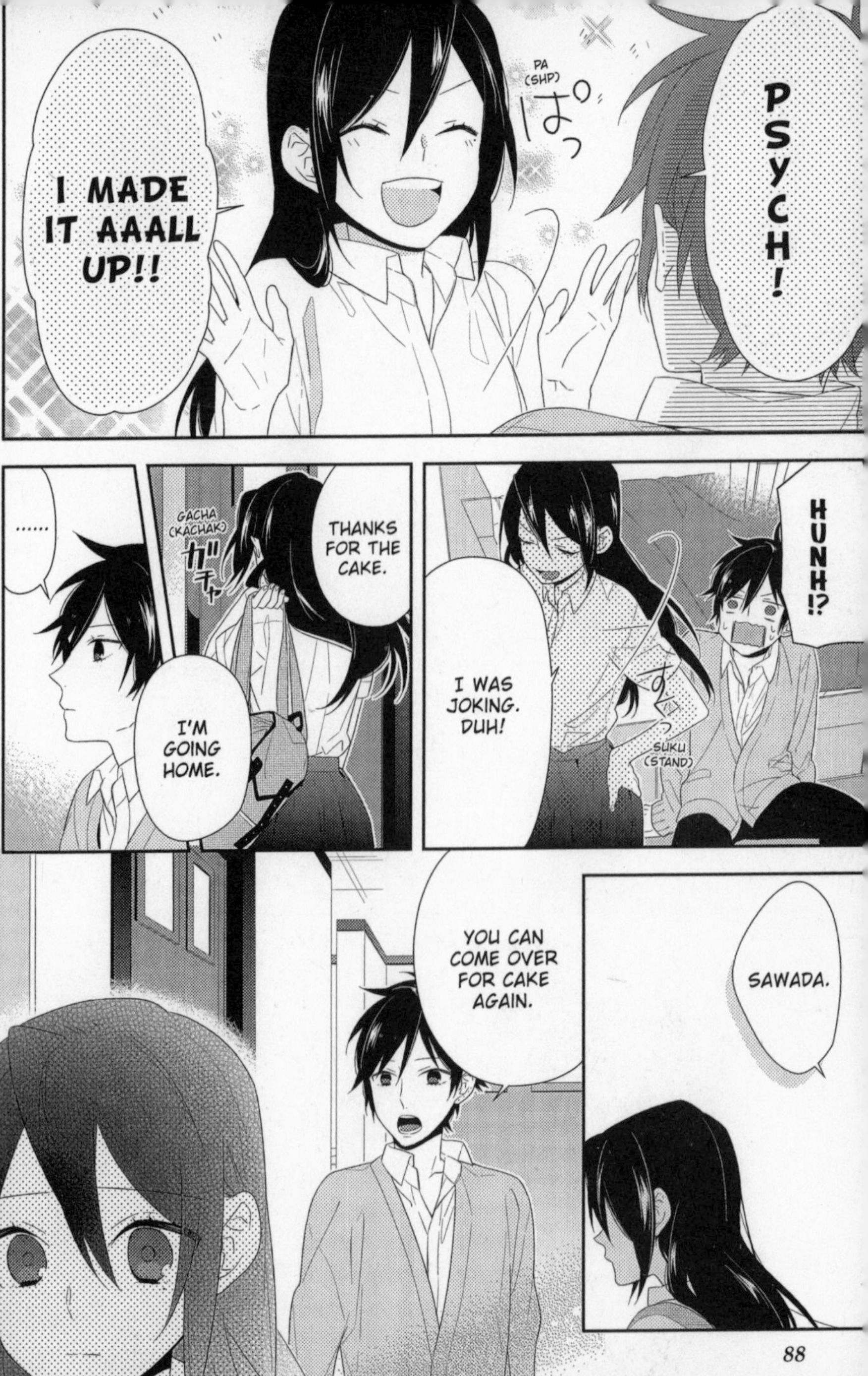
PSYCH!
PA (SHP)
ぱっ
I MADE IT AAALL UP!!
HUNH!?
I WAS JOKING. DUH!
すくっ
SUKU (STAND)
THANKS FOR THE CAKE.
GACHA (KACHAK)
ガチャ
I'M GOING HOME.
......
SAWADA.
YOU CAN COME OVER FOR CAKE AGAIN.

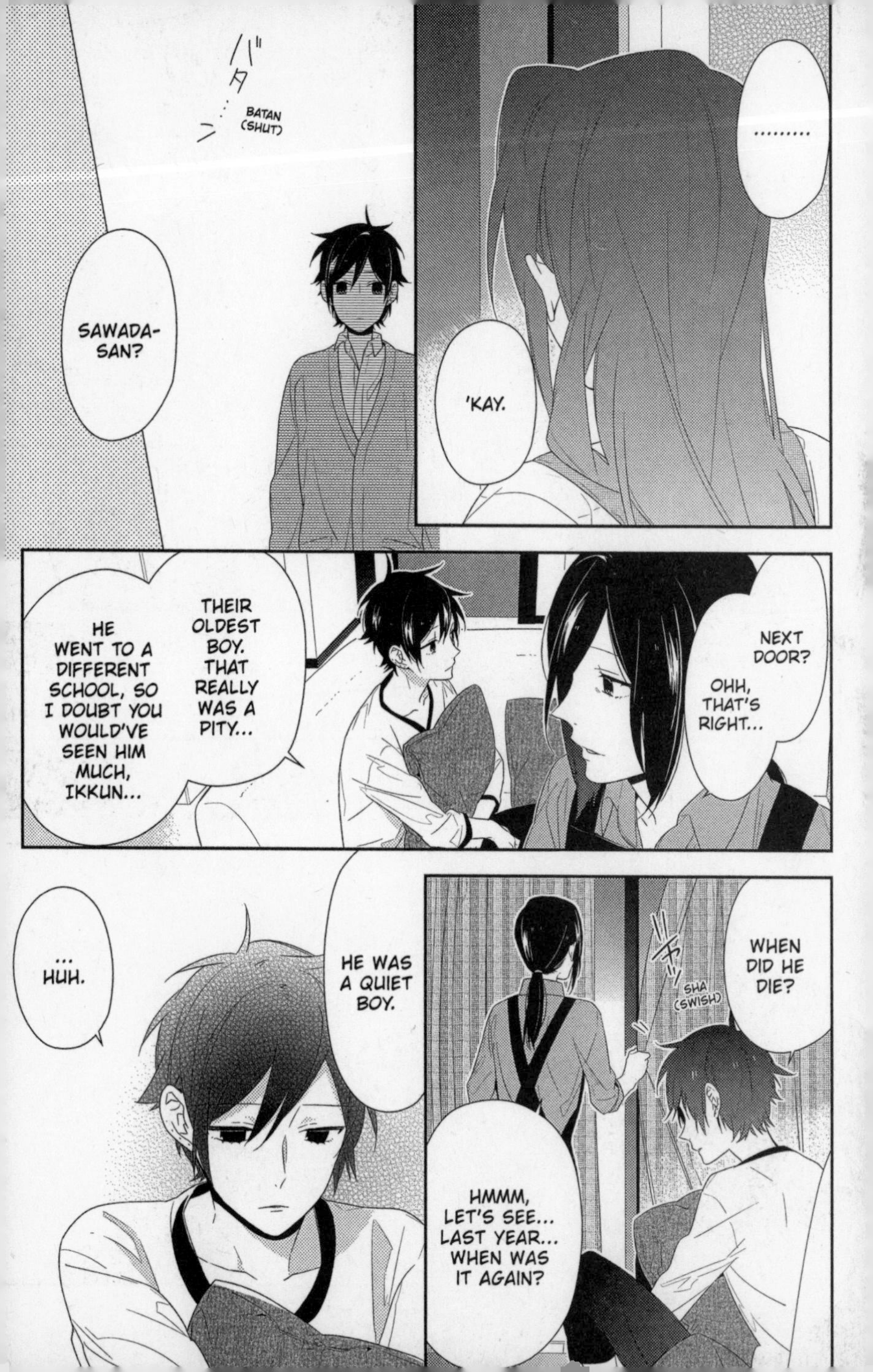
....
'KAY.
BATAN (SHUT)
SAWADA-SAN?
NEXT DOOR? OHH, THAT'S RIGHT...
THEIR OLDEST BOY. THAT REALLY WAS A PITY...
HE WENT TO A DIFFERENT SCHOOL, SO I DOUBT YOU WOULD'VE SEEN HIM MUCH, IKKUN...
WHEN DID HE DIE?
SHA (SWISH)
HMMM, LET'S SEE... LAST YEAR... WHEN WAS IT AGAIN?
HE WAS A QUIET BOY.
... HUH.

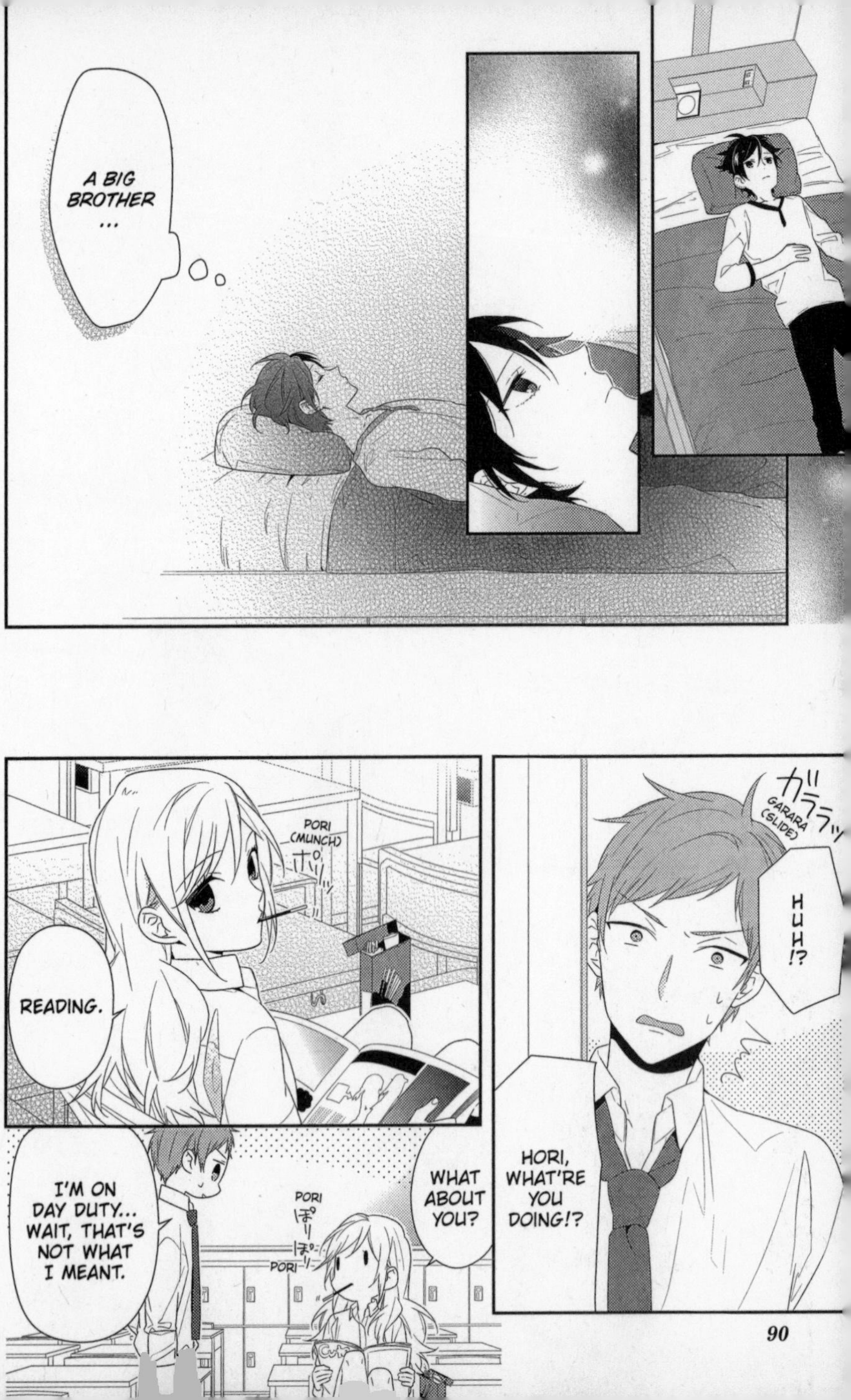
A BIG BROTHER ...
ガララッ
GARARA (SLIDE)
HUH!?
HORI, WHAT'RE YOU DOING!?
ポリッ
PORI (MUNCH)
READING.
WHAT ABOUT YOU?
ぽり
PORI
ぽり
PORI
I'M ON DAY DUTY... WAIT, THAT'S NOT WHAT I MEANT.

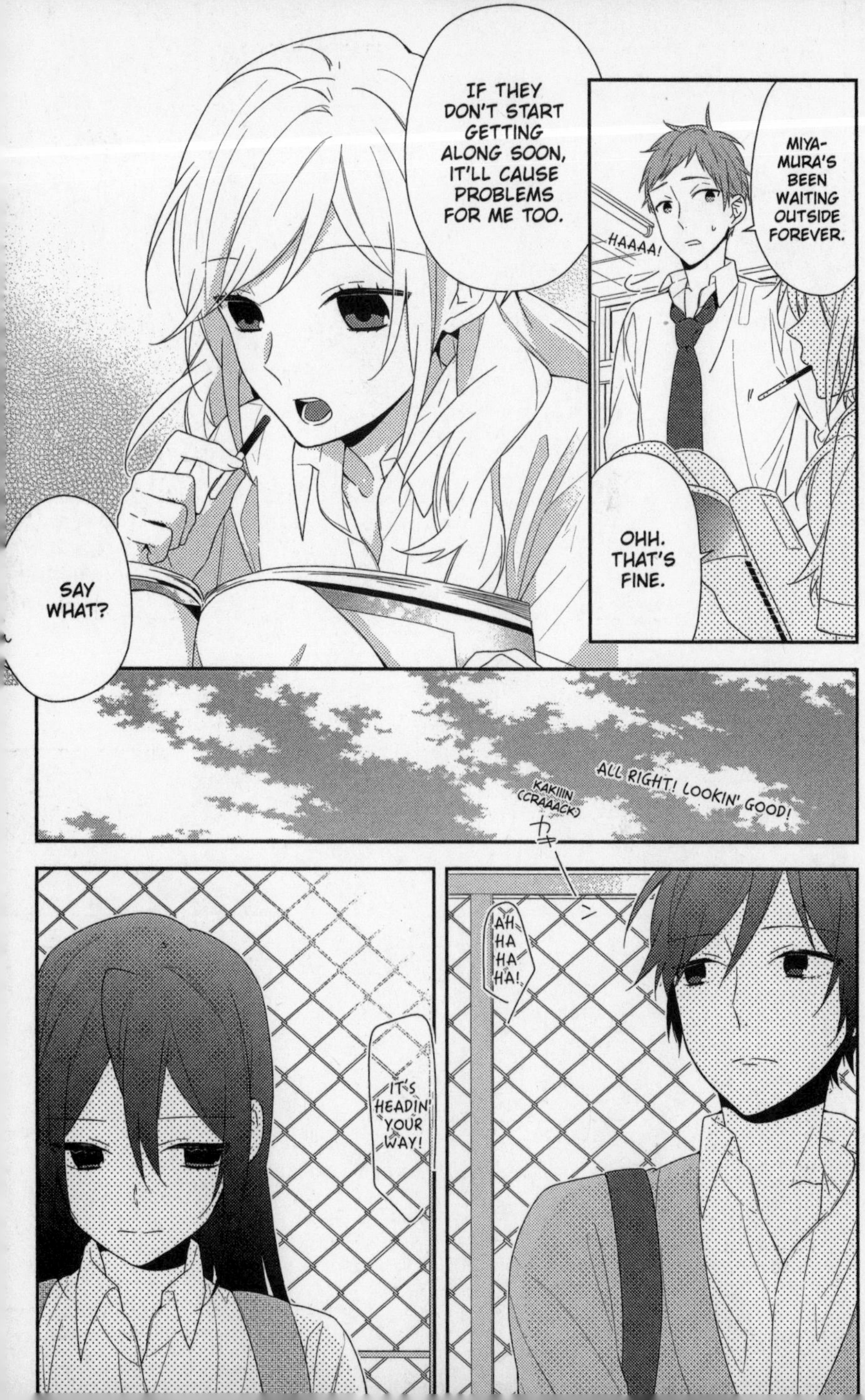
MIYA-MURA'S BEEN WAITING OUTSIDE FOREVER.
HAAAA!
OHH. THAT'S FINE.
IF THEY DON'T START GETTING ALONG SOON, IT'LL CAUSE PROBLEMS FOR ME TOO.
SAY WHAT?
ALL RIGHT! LOOKIN' GOOD!
KAKIIIN (CRAAACK)
AH HA HA HA!
IT'S HEADIN' YOUR WAY!

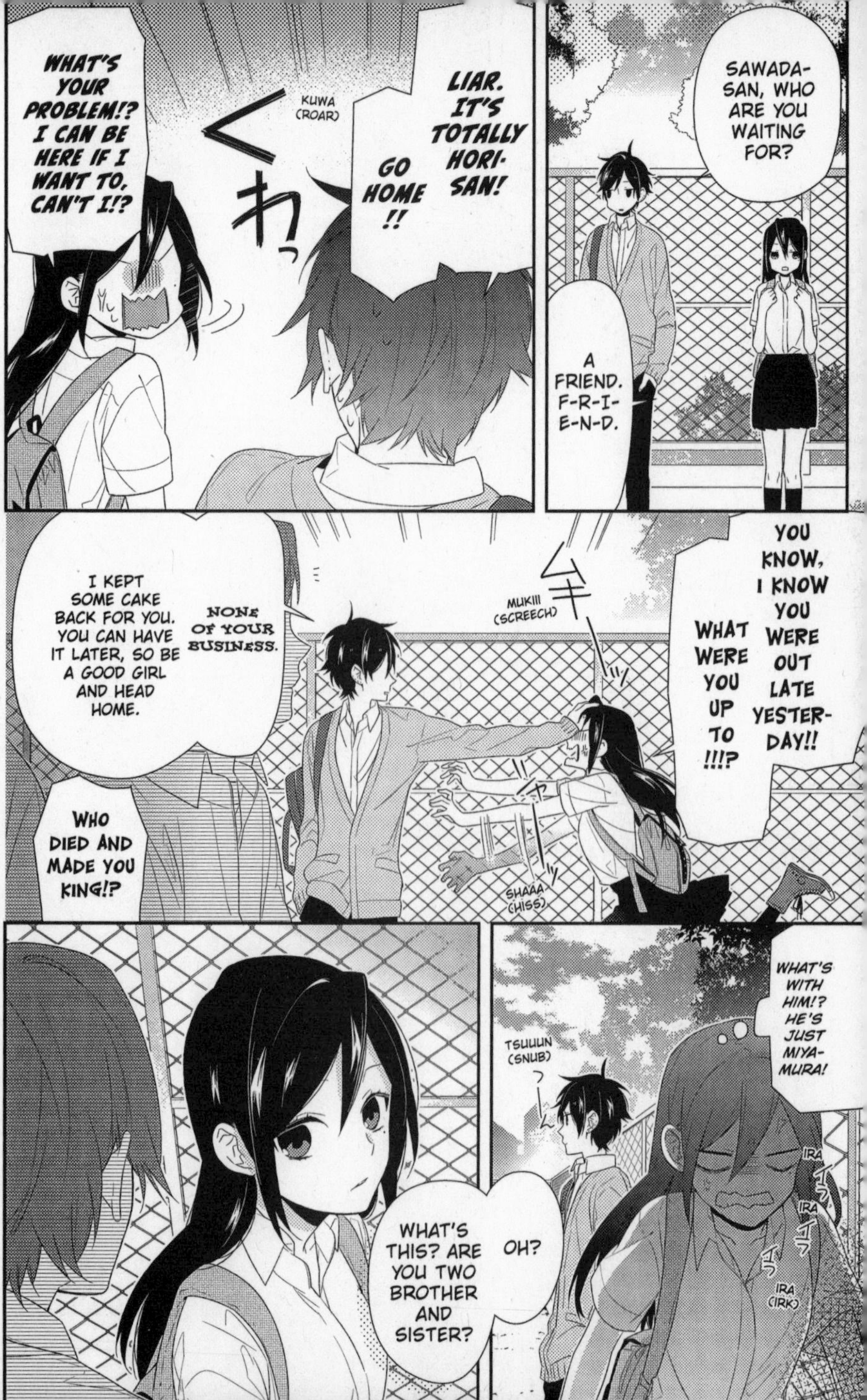
SAWADA-SAN, WHO ARE YOU WAITING FOR?
A FRIEND. F-R-I-E-N-D.
LIAR. IT'S TOTALLY HORI-SAN!
GO HOME!!
KUWA (ROAR)
WHAT'S YOUR PROBLEM!? I CAN BE HERE IF I WANT TO, CAN'T I!?
YOU KNOW, I KNOW YOU WERE OUT LATE YESTERDAY!!
WHAT WERE YOU UP TO !!!?
MUKIII (SCREECH)
NONE OF YOUR BUSINESS.
I KEPT SOME CAKE BACK FOR YOU. YOU CAN HAVE IT LATER, SO BE A GOOD GIRL AND HEAD HOME.
SHAAA (HISS)
WHO DIED AND MADE YOU KING!?
WHAT'S WITH HIM!? HE'S JUST MIYAMURA!
TSUUUN (SNUB)
IRA
IRA
IRA (IRK)
OH?
WHAT'S THIS? ARE YOU TWO BROTHER AND SISTER?

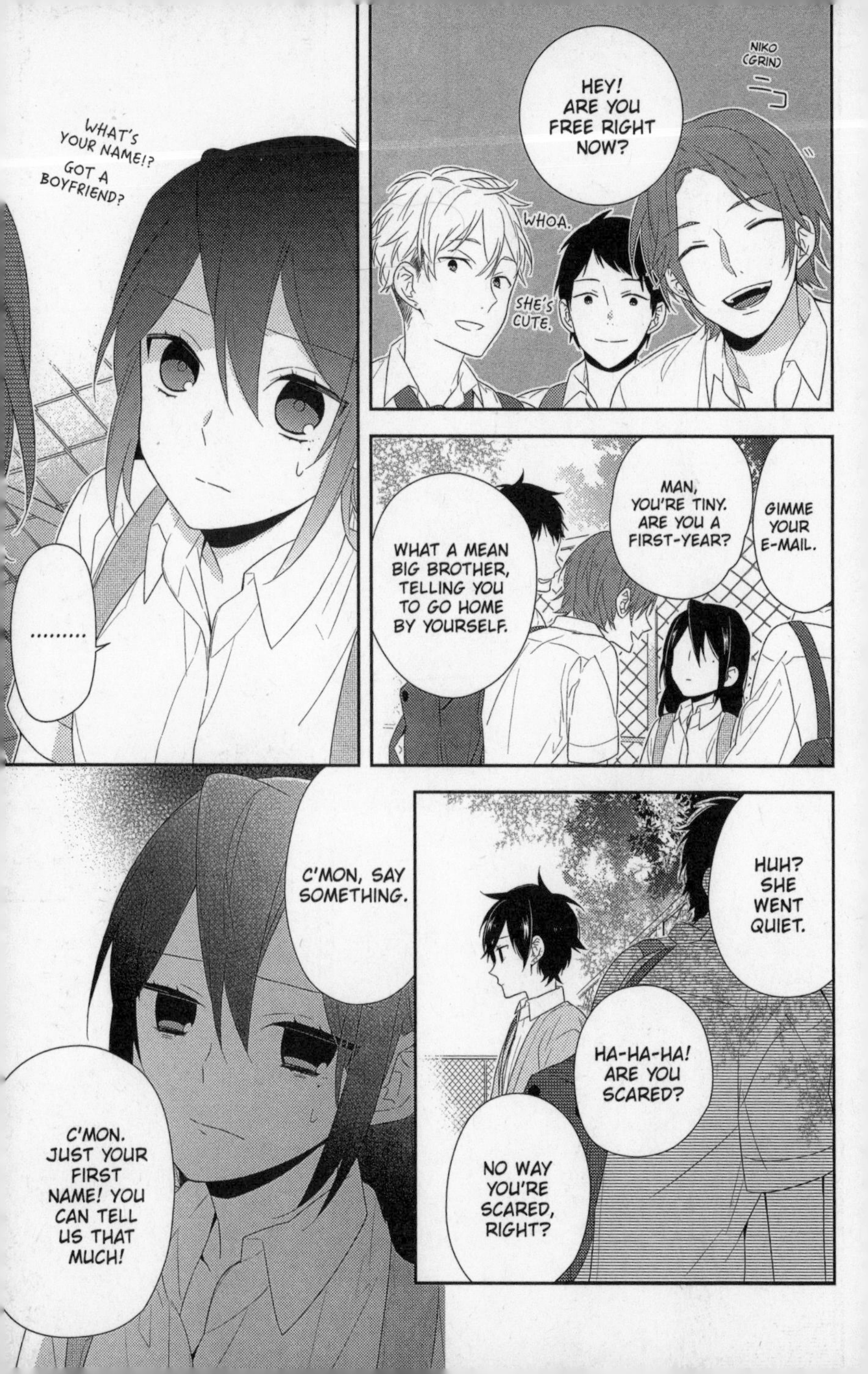
NIKO (GRIN)
HEY! ARE YOU FREE RIGHT NOW?
WHOA.
SHE'S CUTE.
GIMME YOUR E-MAIL.
MAN, YOU'RE TINY. ARE YOU A FIRST-YEAR?
WHAT A MEAN BIG BROTHER, TELLING YOU TO GO HOME BY YOURSELF.
WHAT'S YOUR NAME!?
GOT A BOYFRIEND?
....
HUH? SHE WENT QUIET.
HA-HA-HA! ARE YOU SCARED?
NO WAY YOU'RE SCARED, RIGHT?
C'MON, SAY SOMETHING.
C'MON. JUST YOUR FIRST NAME! YOU CAN TELL US THAT MUCH!

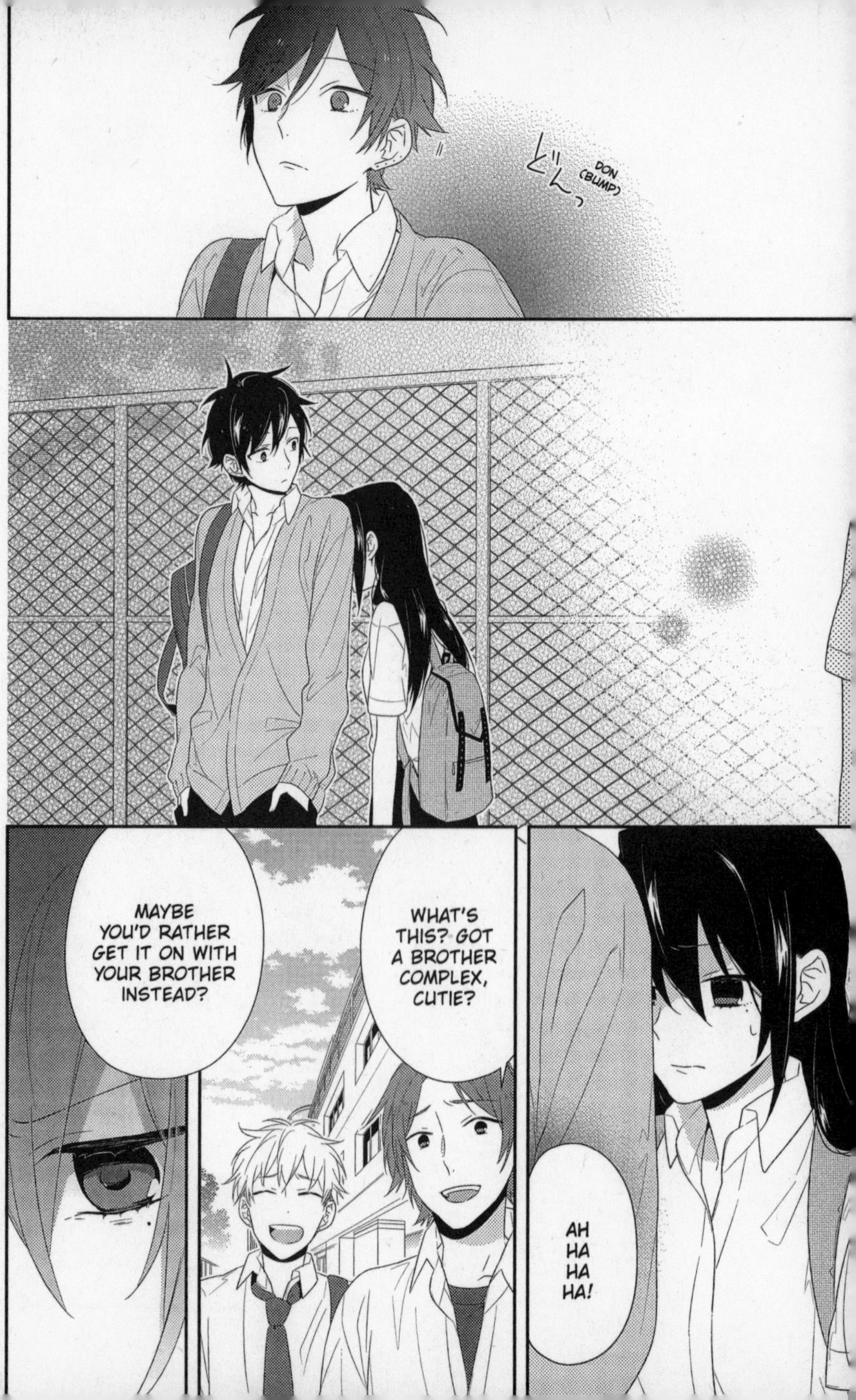
どん
DON (BUMP)
AH HA HA HA!
WHAT'S THIS? GOT A BROTHER COMPLEX, CUTIE?
MAYBE YOU'D RATHER GET IT ON WITH YOUR BROTHER INSTEAD?

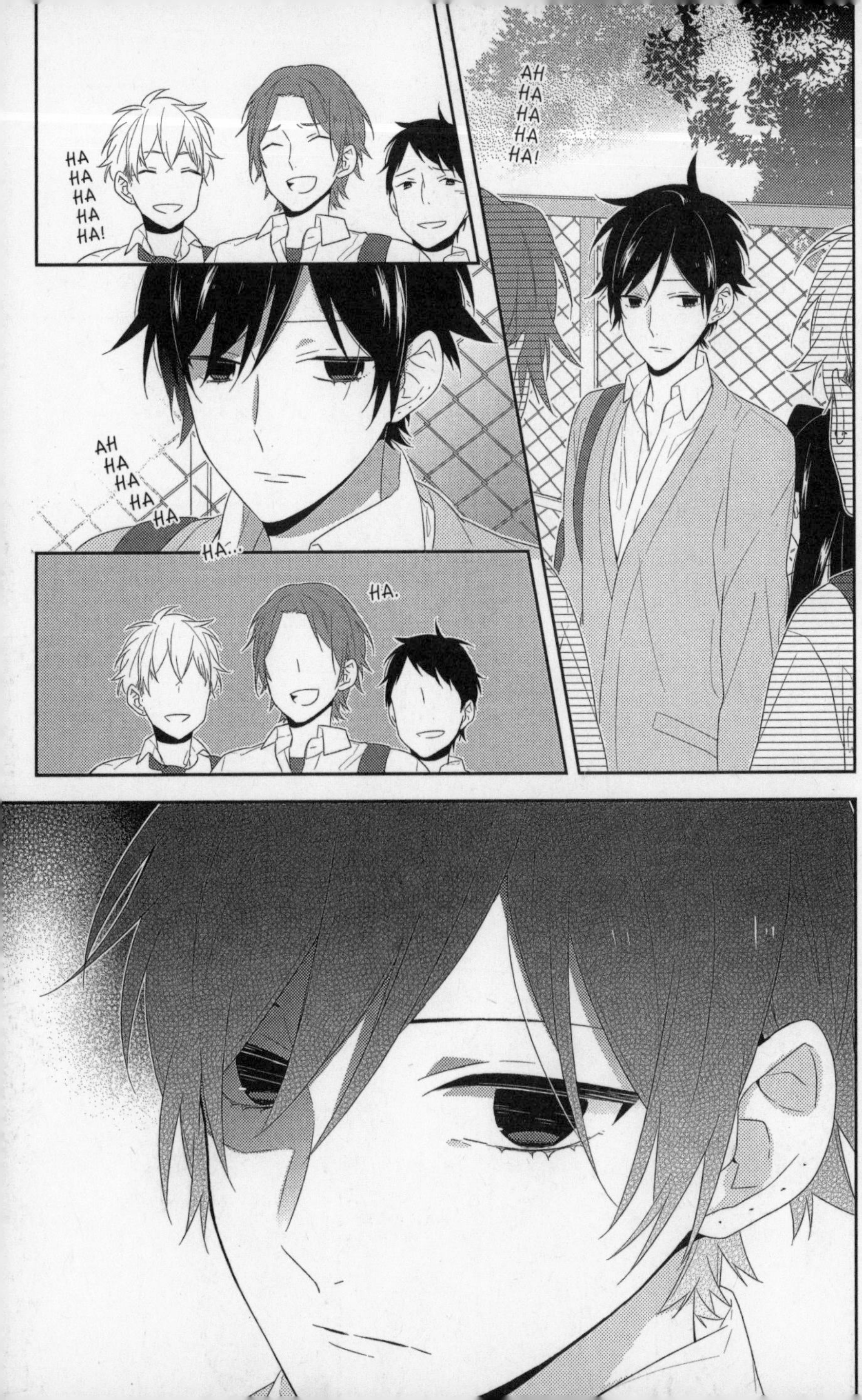
AH HA HA HA HA!
HA HA HA HA HA!
AH HA HA HA HA HA
HA...
HA.

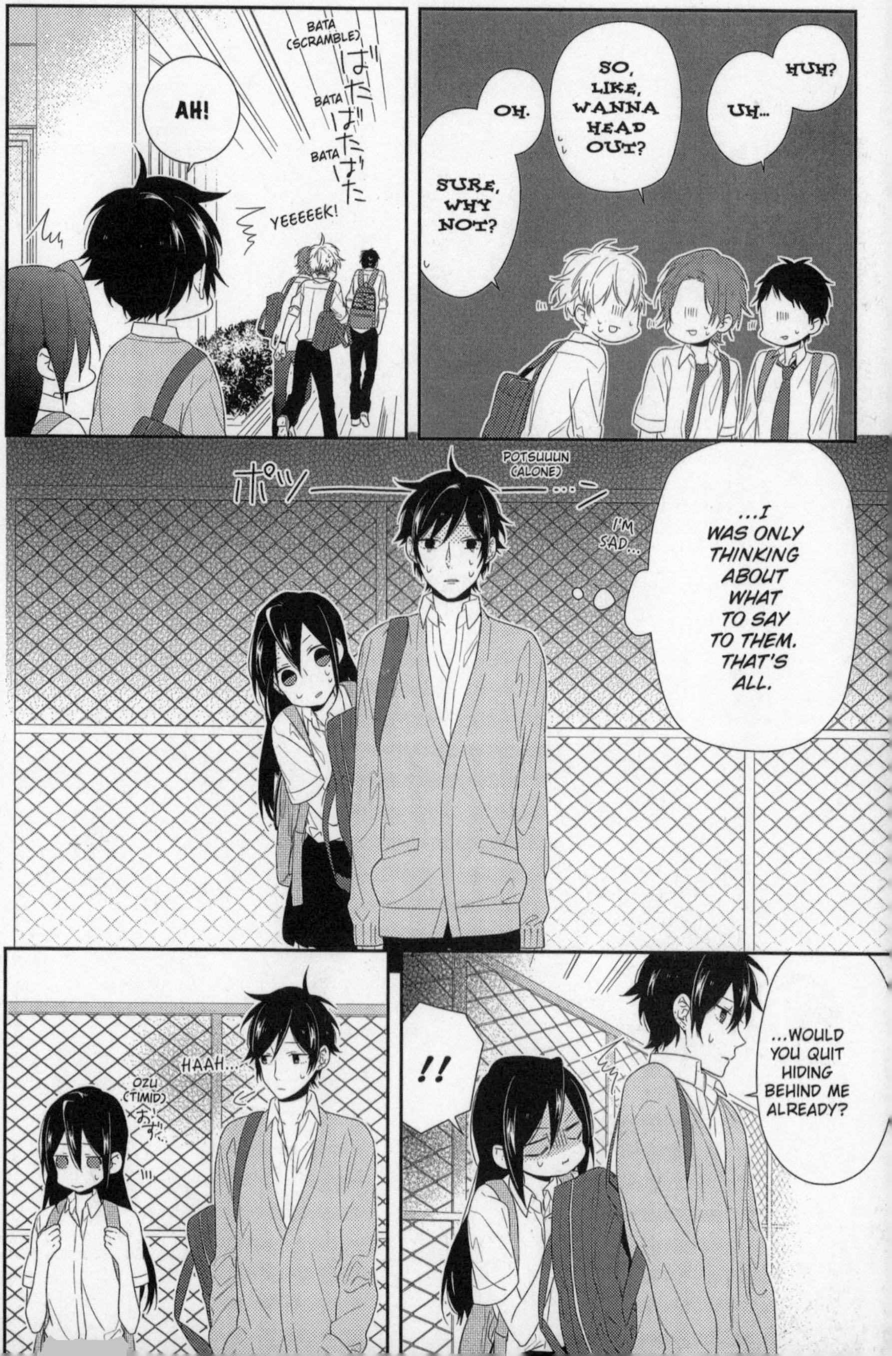
HUH?
UH...
SO, LIKE, WANNA HEAD OUT?
OH.
SURE, WHY NOT?
BATA (SCRAMBLE) ばた
BATA ばた
BATA ばた
AH!
YEEEEEK!
...I WAS ONLY THINKING ABOUT WHAT TO SAY TO THEM. THAT'S ALL.
I'M SAD...
POTSUUUN (ALONE)
ポツーン
...WOULD YOU QUIT HIDING BEHIND ME ALREADY?
!!
HAAH...
OZU (TIMID)
おず おず

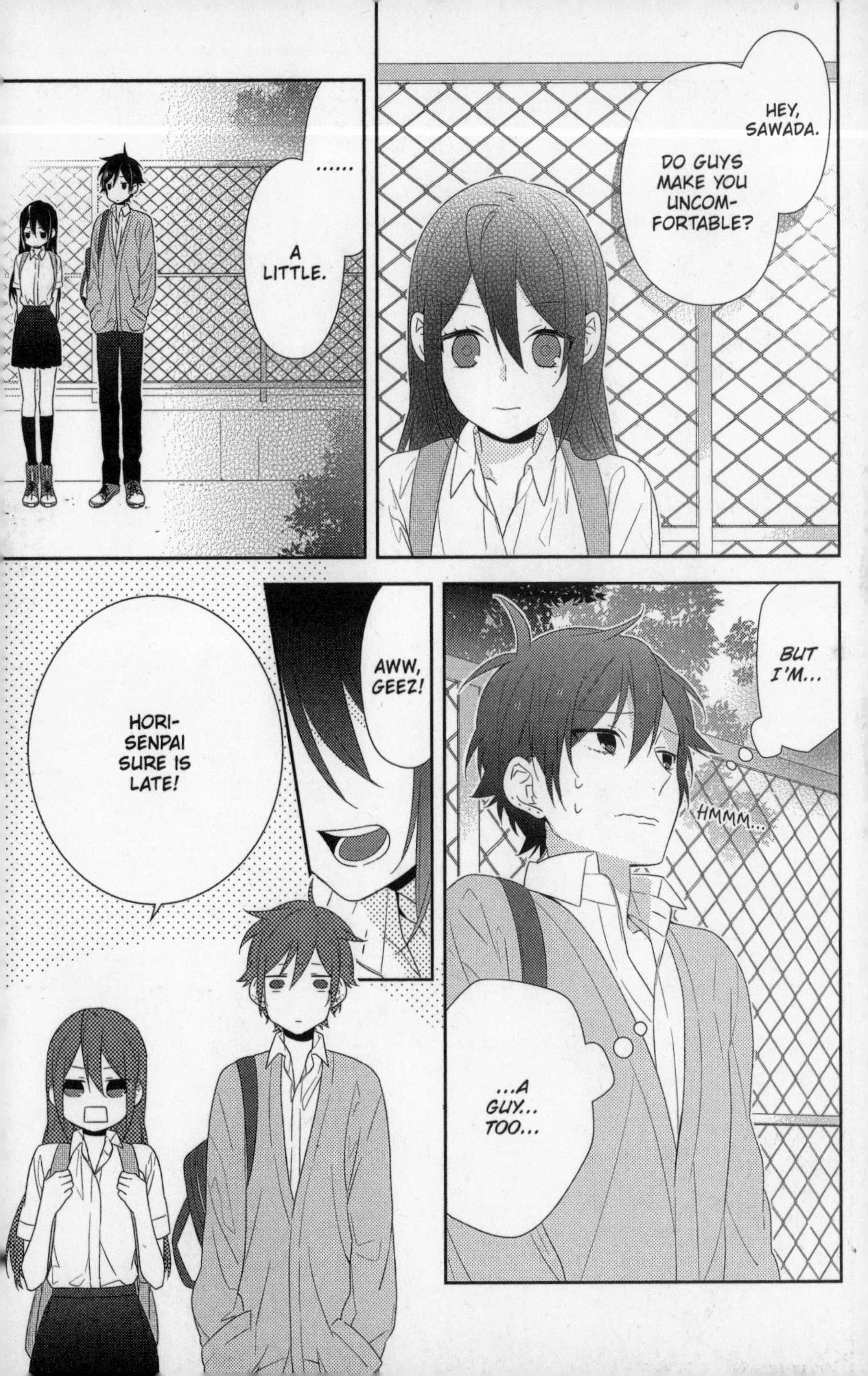
HEY, SAWADA.
DO GUYS MAKE YOU UNCOM-FORTABLE?
......
A LITTLE.
BUT I'M...
HMMM...
...A GUY... TOO...
AWW, GEEZ!
HORI-SENPAI SURE IS LATE!

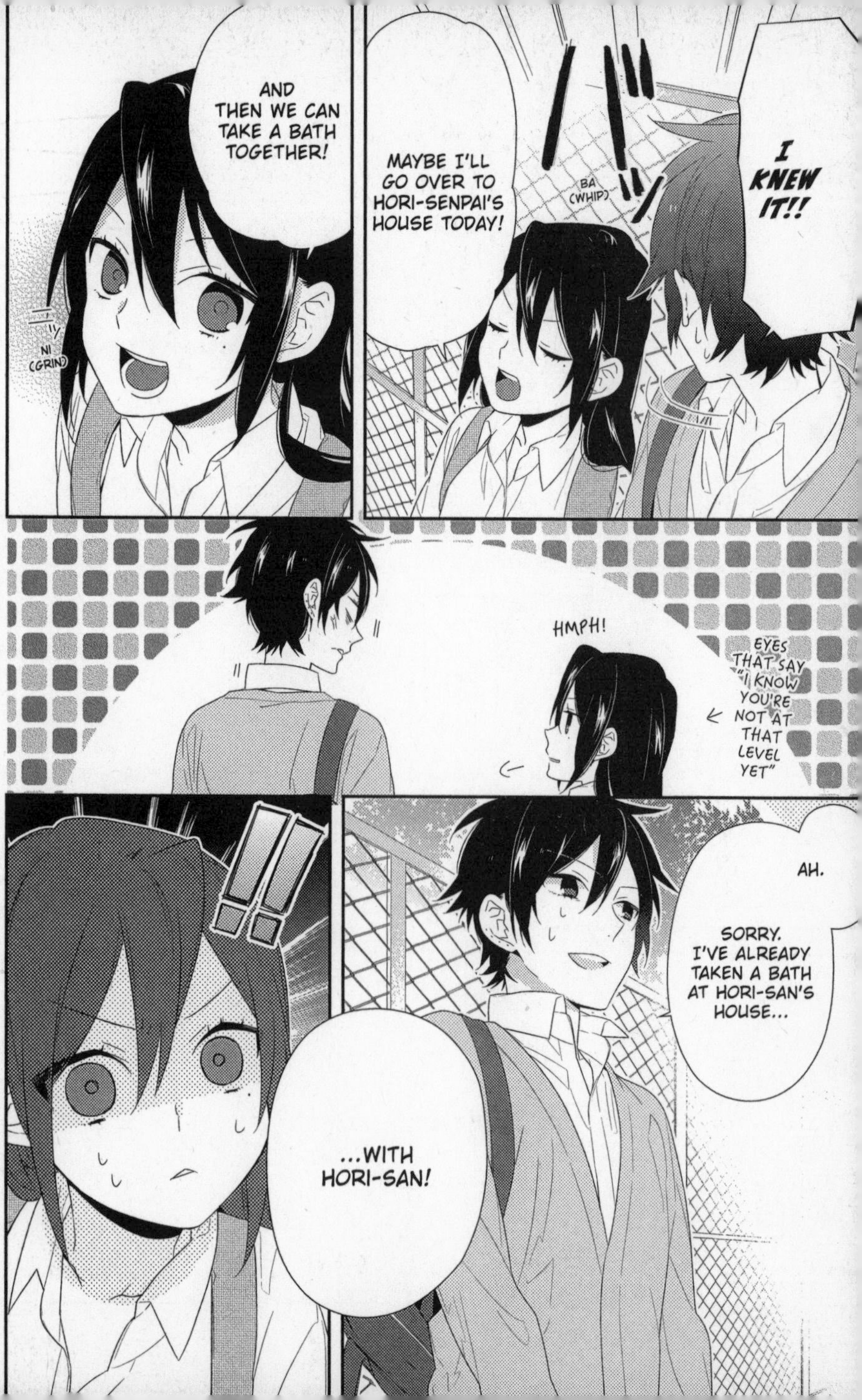
I KNEW IT!!
BA (WHIP)
MAYBE I'LL GO OVER TO HORI-SENPAI'S HOUSE TODAY!
AND THEN WE CAN TAKE A BATH TOGETHER!
NI (GRIN)
EYES THAT SAY "I KNOW YOU'RE NOT AT THAT LEVEL YET"
HMPH!
AH.
SORRY. I'VE ALREADY TAKEN A BATH AT HORI-SAN'S HOUSE...
...WITH HORI-SAN!

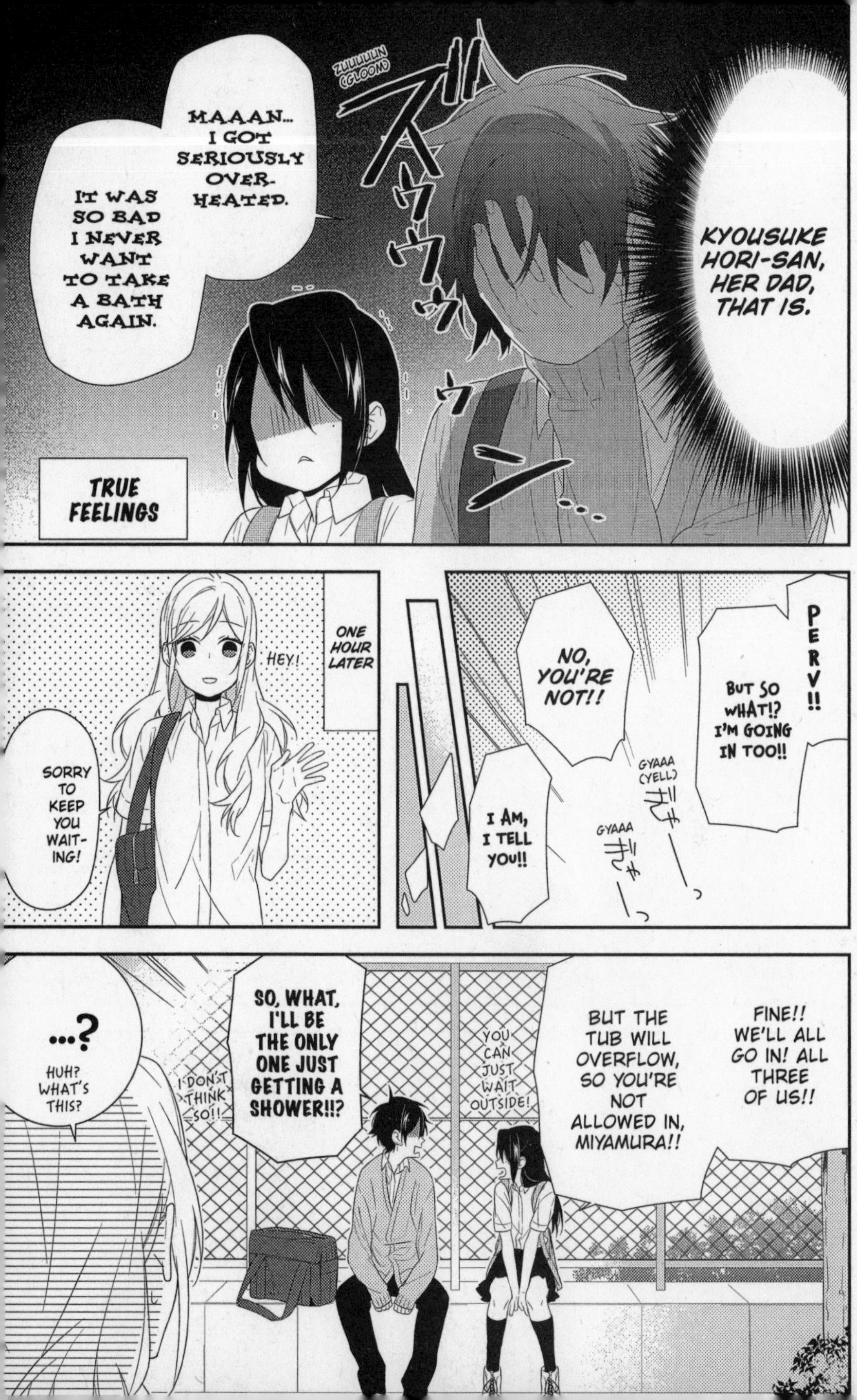
KYOUSUKE HORI-SAN, HER DAD, THAT IS.
ZUUUUUN (GLOOM)
MAAAN... I GOT SERIOUSLY OVER-HEATED.
IT WAS SO BAD I NEVER WANT TO TAKE A BATH AGAIN.
TRUE FEELINGS
PERV!!
BUT SO WHAT!? I'M GOING IN TOO!!
NO, YOU'RE NOT!!
GYAAA (YELL)
GYAAA
I AM, I TELL YOU!!
ONE HOUR LATER
HEY!
SORRY TO KEEP YOU WAIT-ING!
FINE!! WE'LL ALL GO IN! ALL THREE OF US!!
BUT THE TUB WILL OVERFLOW, SO YOU'RE NOT ALLOWED IN, MIYAMURA!!
YOU CAN JUST WAIT OUTSIDE!
SO, WHAT, I'LL BE THE ONLY ONE JUST GETTING A SHOWER!!?
I DON'T THINK SO!!
...?
HUH? WHAT'S THIS?

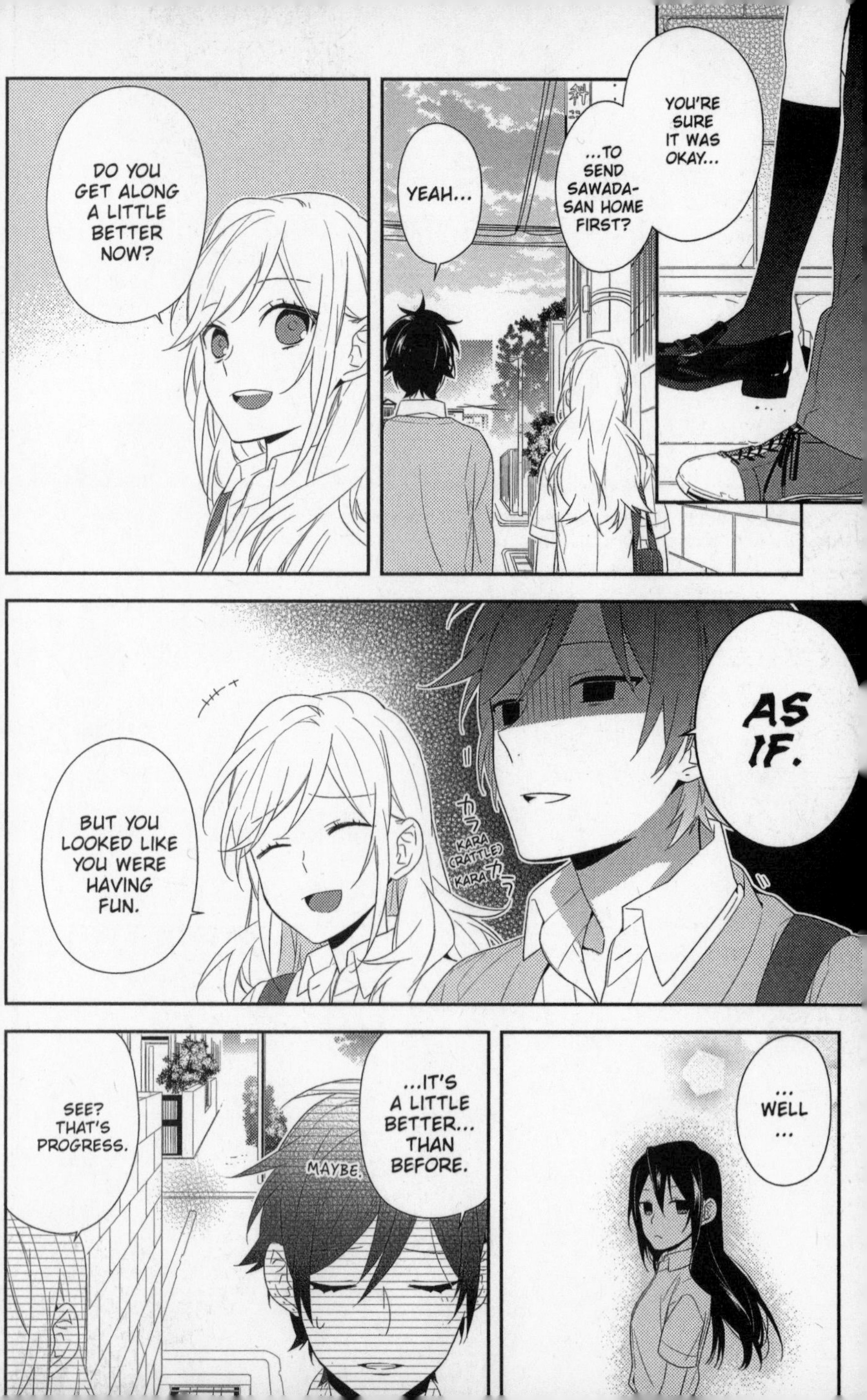
YOU'RE SURE IT WAS OKAY...
...TO SEND SAWADA-SAN HOME FIRST?
YEAH...
DO YOU GET ALONG A LITTLE BETTER NOW?
AS IF.
KARA (RATTLE) KARA
BUT YOU LOOKED LIKE YOU WERE HAVING FUN.
... WELL ...
...IT'S A LITTLE BETTER... THAN BEFORE.
MAYBE.
SEE? THAT'S PROGRESS.

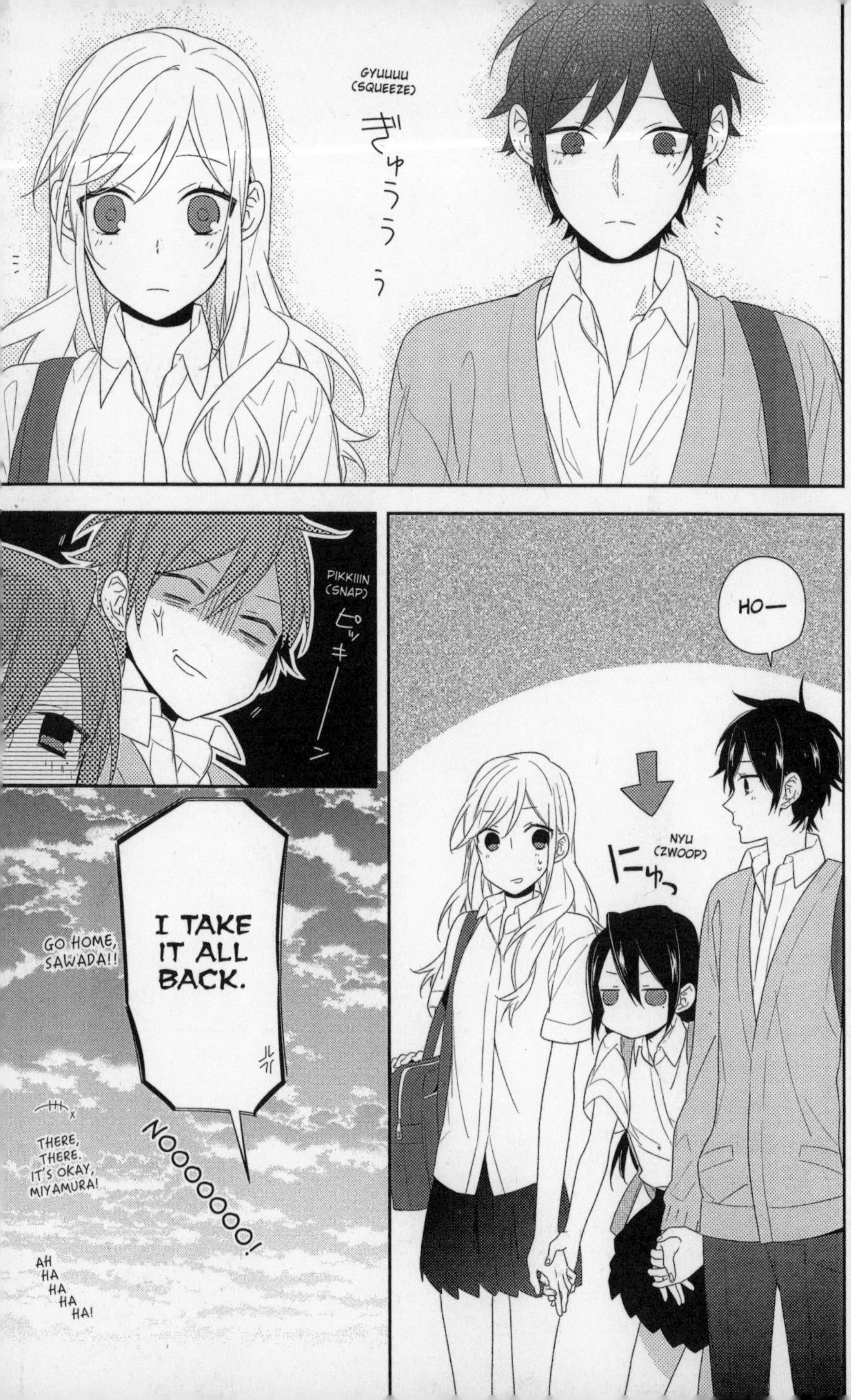
GYUUUU (SQUEEZE)
ぎゅううう
HO—
NYU (ZWOOP)
にゅっ
PIKKIIN (SNAP)
ピッキーン
I TAKE IT ALL BACK.
GO HOME, SAWADA!!
NOOOOOOO!
THERE, THERE. IT'S OKAY, MIYAMURA!
AH HA HA HA HA!

HORIMIYA

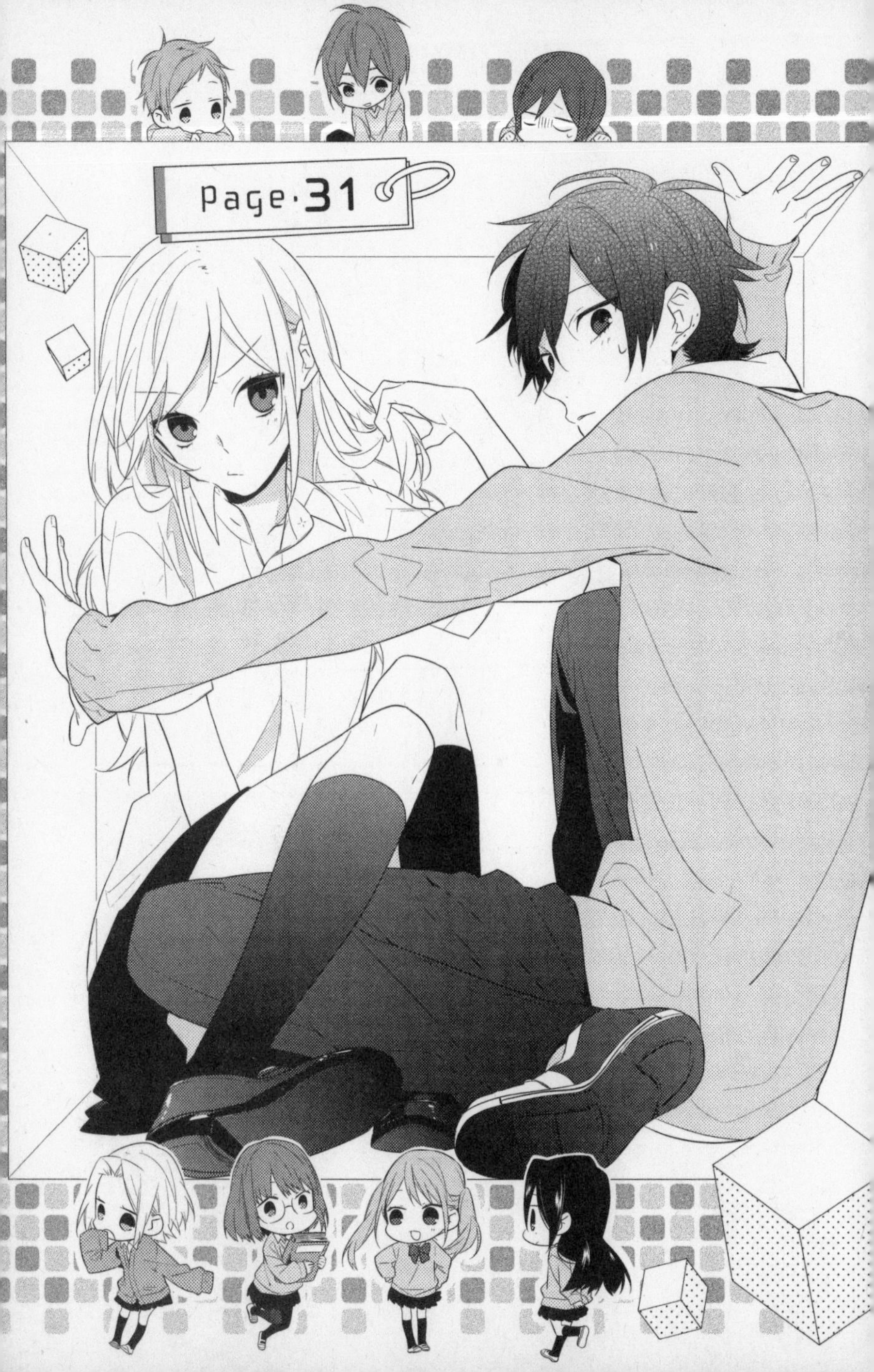
page·31

I'M GONNA DIE.

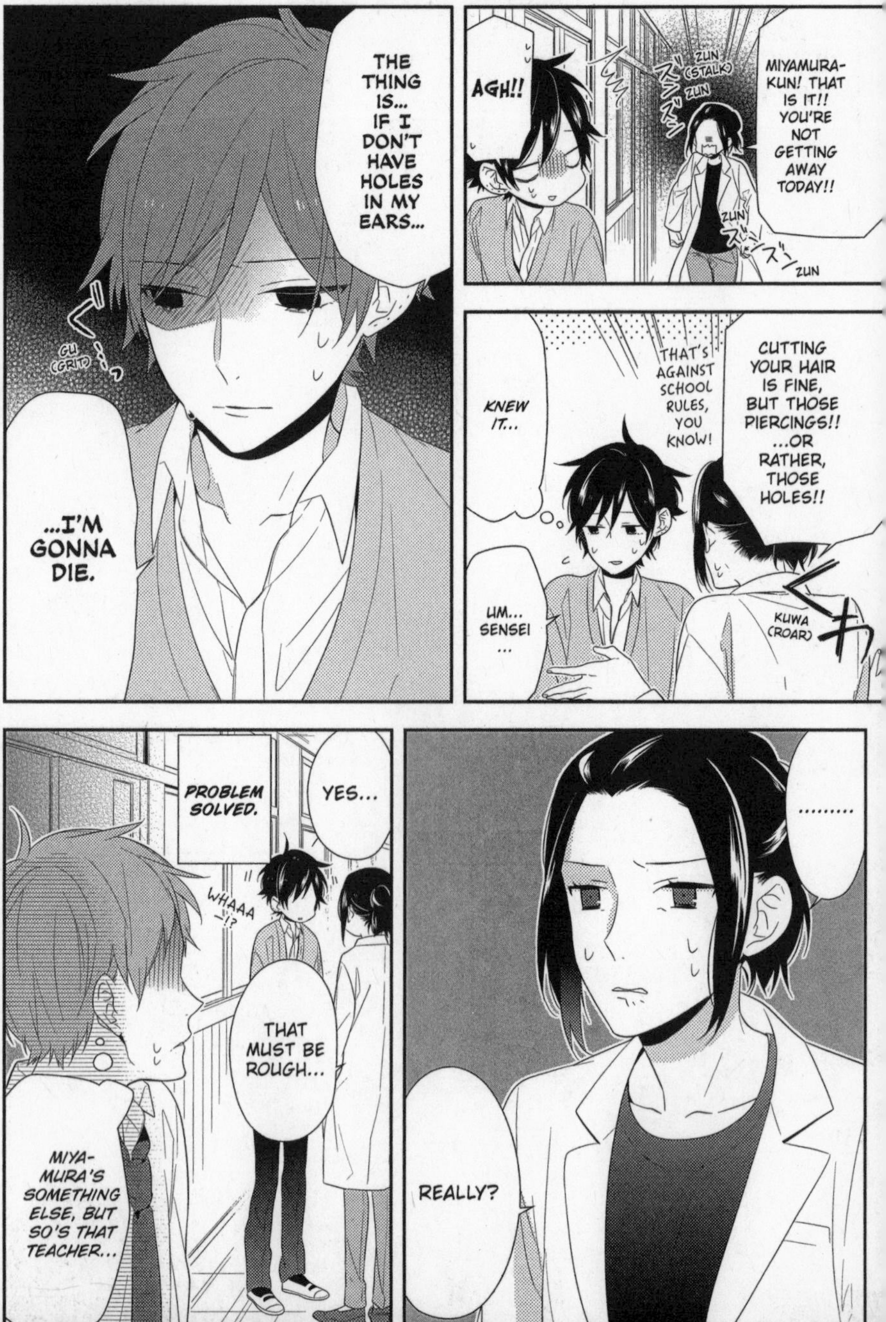
MIYAMURA-KUN! THAT IS IT!! YOU'RE NOT GETTING AWAY TODAY!!
ZUN (STALK) ZUN
AGH!!
ZUN
ZUN
CUTTING YOUR HAIR IS FINE, BUT THOSE PIERCINGS!! ...OR RATHER, THOSE HOLES!!
KUWA (ROAR)
THAT'S AGAINST SCHOOL RULES, YOU KNOW!
KNEW IT...
UM... SENSEI ...
THE THING IS... IF I DON'T HAVE HOLES IN MY EARS...
GU (GRIT)
...I'M GONNA DIE.
....
REALLY?
YES...
PROBLEM SOLVED.
WHAAA-!?
THAT MUST BE ROUGH...
MIYA-MURA'S SOMETHING ELSE, BUT SO'S THAT TEACHER...

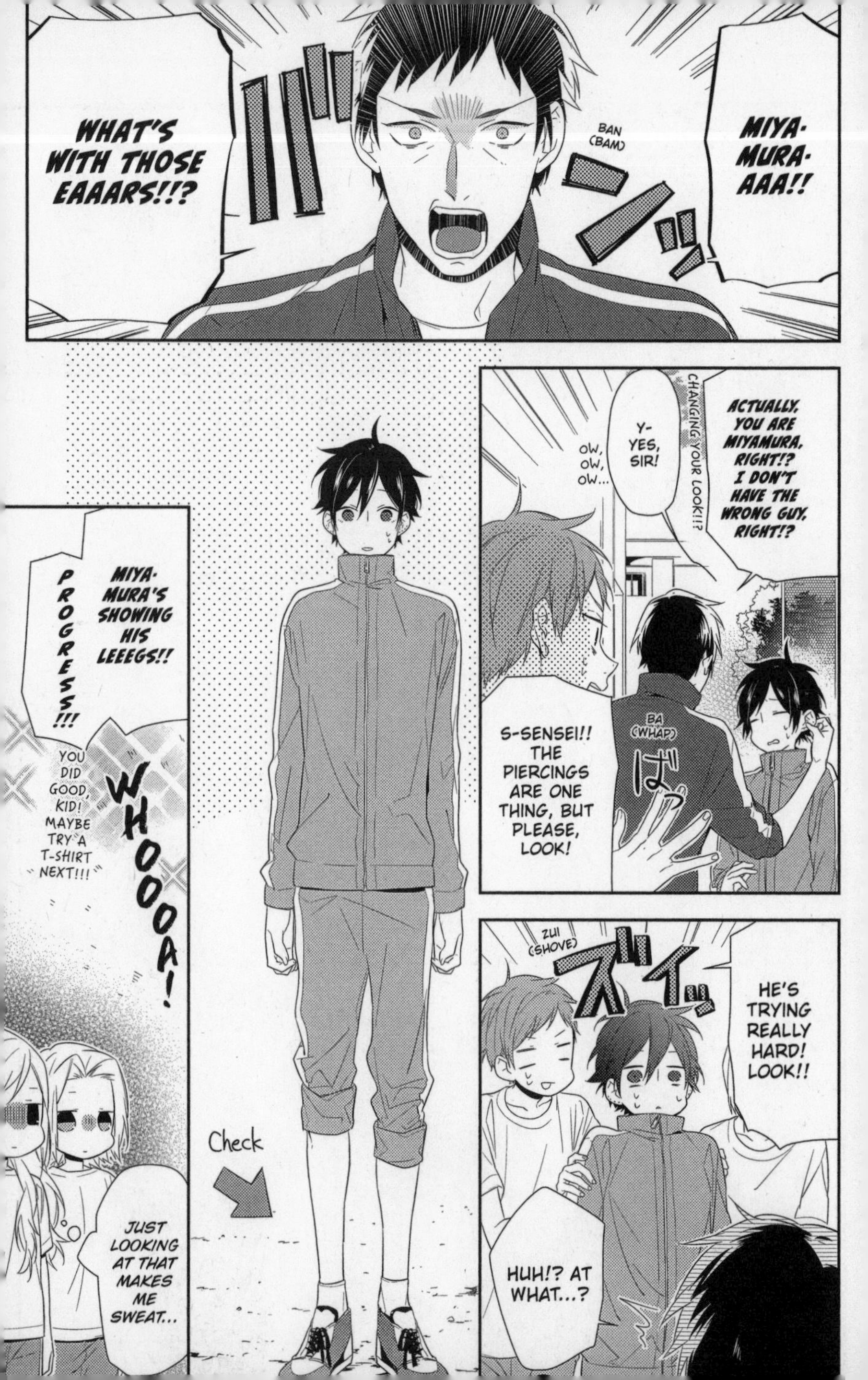
MIYA-MURA-AAA!!
BAN (BAM)
WHAT'S WITH THOSE EAAARS!!?
ACTUALLY, YOU ARE MIYAMURA, RIGHT!? I DON'T HAVE THE WRONG GUY, RIGHT!?
Y-YES, SIR!
CHANGING YOUR LOOK!!?
OW, OW, OW...
BA (WHAP)
S-SENSEI!! THE PIERCINGS ARE ONE THING, BUT PLEASE, LOOK!
ZUI (SHOVE)
HE'S TRYING REALLY HARD! LOOK!!
HUH!? AT WHAT...?
Check
MIYA-MURA'S SHOWING HIS LEEEGS!!
PROGRESS!!!
WHOOOA!
YOU DID GOOD, KID! MAYBE TRY A T-SHIRT NEXT!!!
JUST LOOKING AT THAT MAKES ME SWEAT...

LET'S DANCE...

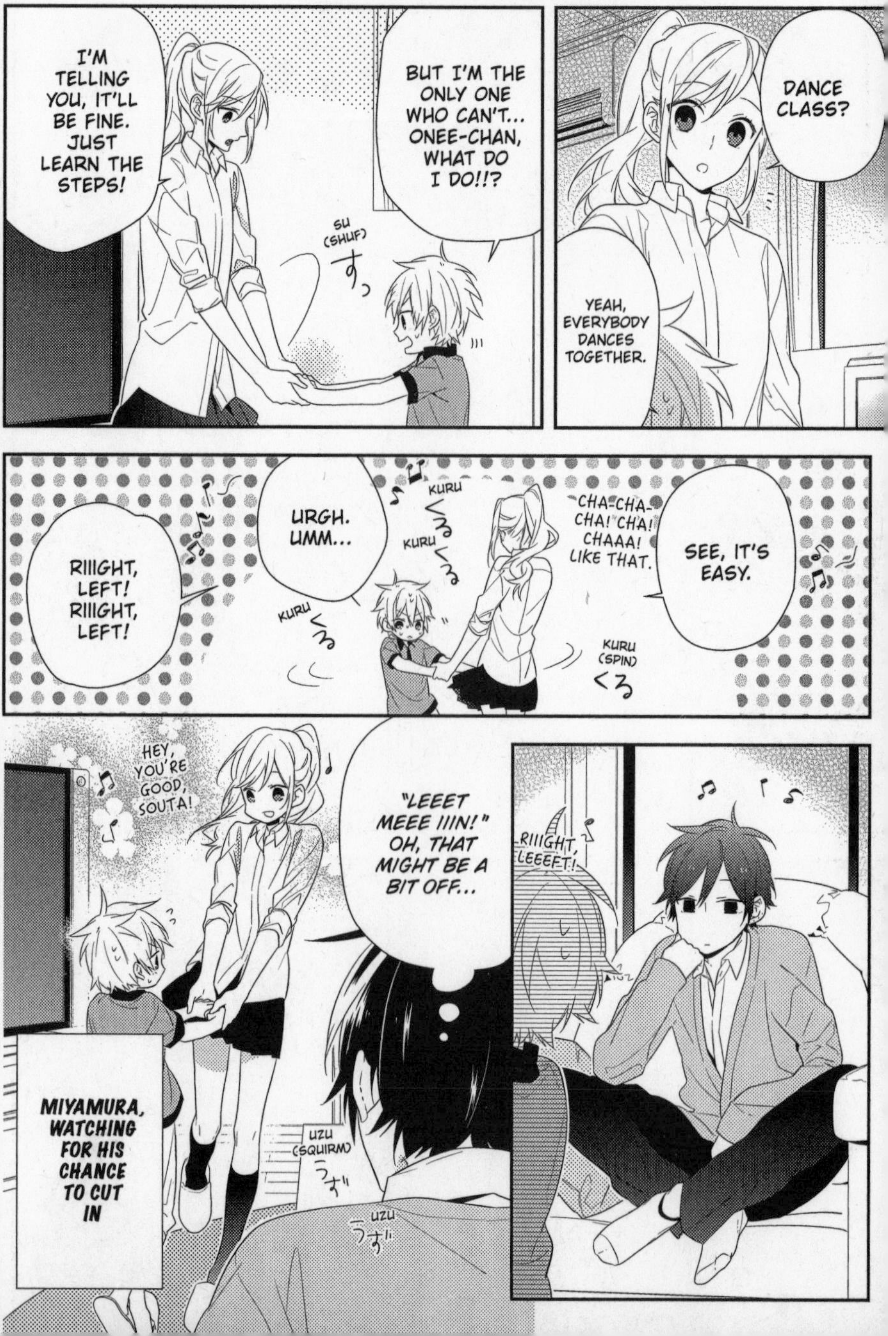

DANCE CLASS?
YEAH, EVERYBODY DANCES TOGETHER.
BUT I'M THE ONLY ONE WHO CAN'T... ONEE-CHAN, WHAT DO I DO!!?
SU (SHUF)
すっ
I'M TELLING YOU, IT'LL BE FINE. JUST LEARN THE STEPS!
SEE, IT'S EASY.
CHA-CHA-CHA! CHA! CHAAA! LIKE THAT.
KURU (SPIN)
くる
KURU
くるくる
KURU
URGH. UMM...
KURU
くる
RIIIGHT, LEFT! RIIIGHT, LEFT!
RIIIGHT, LEEEFT!
"LEEET MEEE IIIN!" OH, THAT MIGHT BE A BIT OFF...
HEY, YOU'RE GOOD, SOUTA!
UZU (SQUIRM)
うず
UZU
うず
MIYAMURA, WATCHING FOR HIS CHANCE TO CUT IN

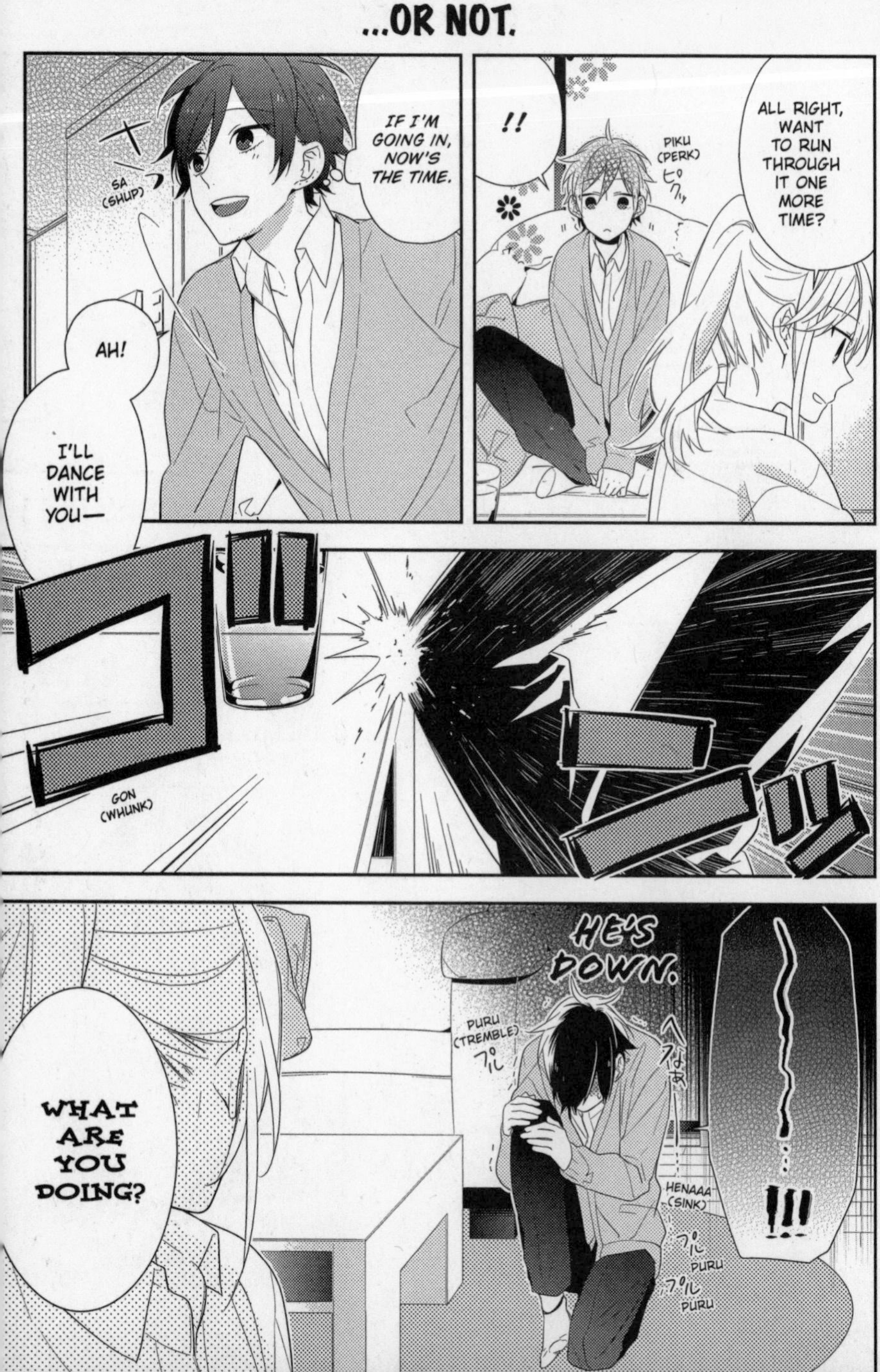
...OR NOT.
ALL RIGHT, WANT TO RUN THROUGH IT ONE MORE TIME?
!!
PIKU (PERK)
ピクッ
IF I'M GOING IN, NOW'S THE TIME.
SA (SHUP)
AH!
I'LL DANCE WITH YOU—
ゴッ
GON (WHUNK)
…!!!
HE'S DOWN.
へなぁ―
HENAAA (SINK)
PURU (TREMBLE)
プル
プル
PURU
プル
PURU
WHAT ARE YOU DOING?

REALLY INTO IT

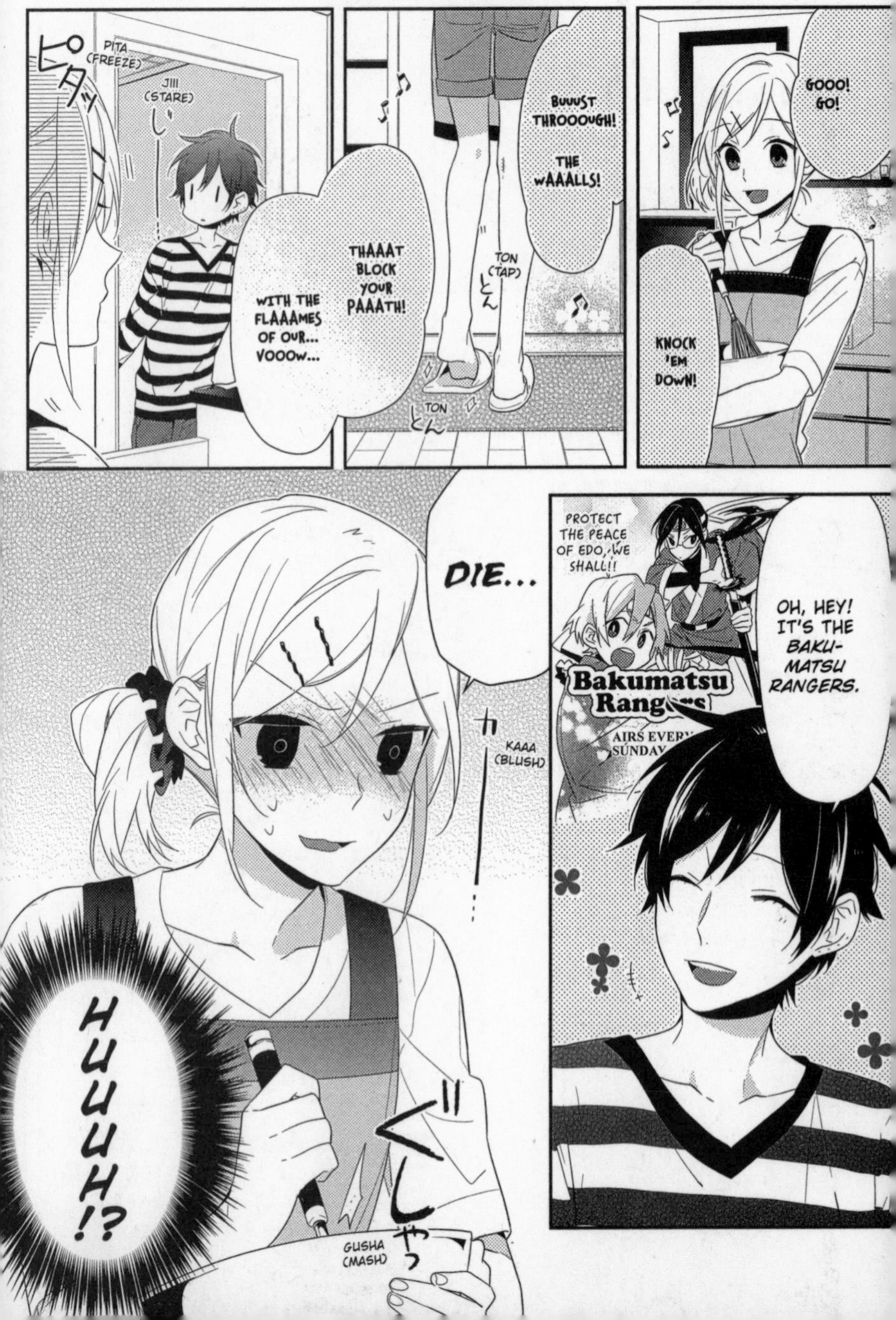

GOOO! GO!
KNOCK 'EM DOWN!
BUUUST THROOOUGH! THE WAAALLS!
TON (TAP)
TON
THAAAT BLOCK YOUR PAAATH!
WITH THE FLAAAMES OF OUR... VOOOW...
PITA (FREEZE)
JIII (STARE)
OH, HEY! IT'S THE BAKU-MATSU RANGERS.
PROTECT THE PEACE OF EDO, WE SHALL!!
Bakumatsu Rangers
DIE...
KAAA (BLUSH)
HUUUH!?
GUSHA (MASH)

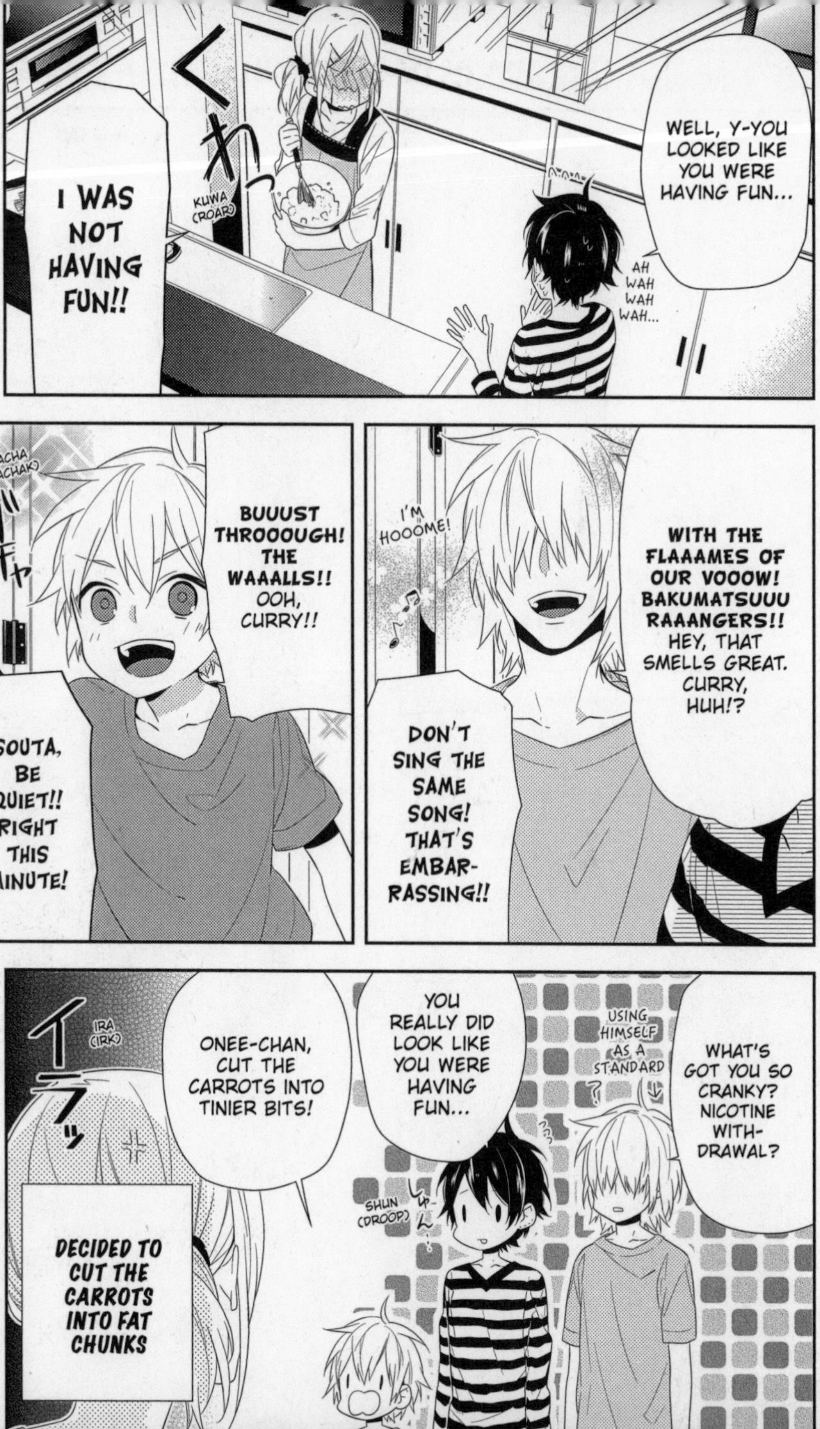
WELL, Y-YOU LOOKED LIKE YOU WERE HAVING FUN...
AH WAH WAH WAH...
KUWA (ROAR)
I WAS NOT HAVING FUN!!
I'M HOOOME!
WITH THE FLAAAMES OF OUR VOOOW! BAKUMATSUUU RAAANGERS!! HEY, THAT SMELLS GREAT. CURRY, HUH!?
DON'T SING THE SAME SONG! THAT'S EMBAR-RASSING!!
GACHA (KACHAK)
ガチャ
BUUUST THROOOUGH! THE WAAALLS!! OOH, CURRY!!
SOUTA, BE QUIET!! RIGHT THIS MINUTE!
WHAT'S GOT YOU SO CRANKY? NICOTINE WITH-DRAWAL?
USING HIMSELF AS A STANDARD
YOU REALLY DID LOOK LIKE YOU WERE HAVING FUN...
ONEE-CHAN, CUT THE CARROTS INTO TINIER BITS!
IRA (IRK)
SHUN (DROOP)
DECIDED TO CUT THE CARROTS INTO FAT CHUNKS

“I'M NOT PREJUDICED LIKE THAT...” (ISHIKAWA)

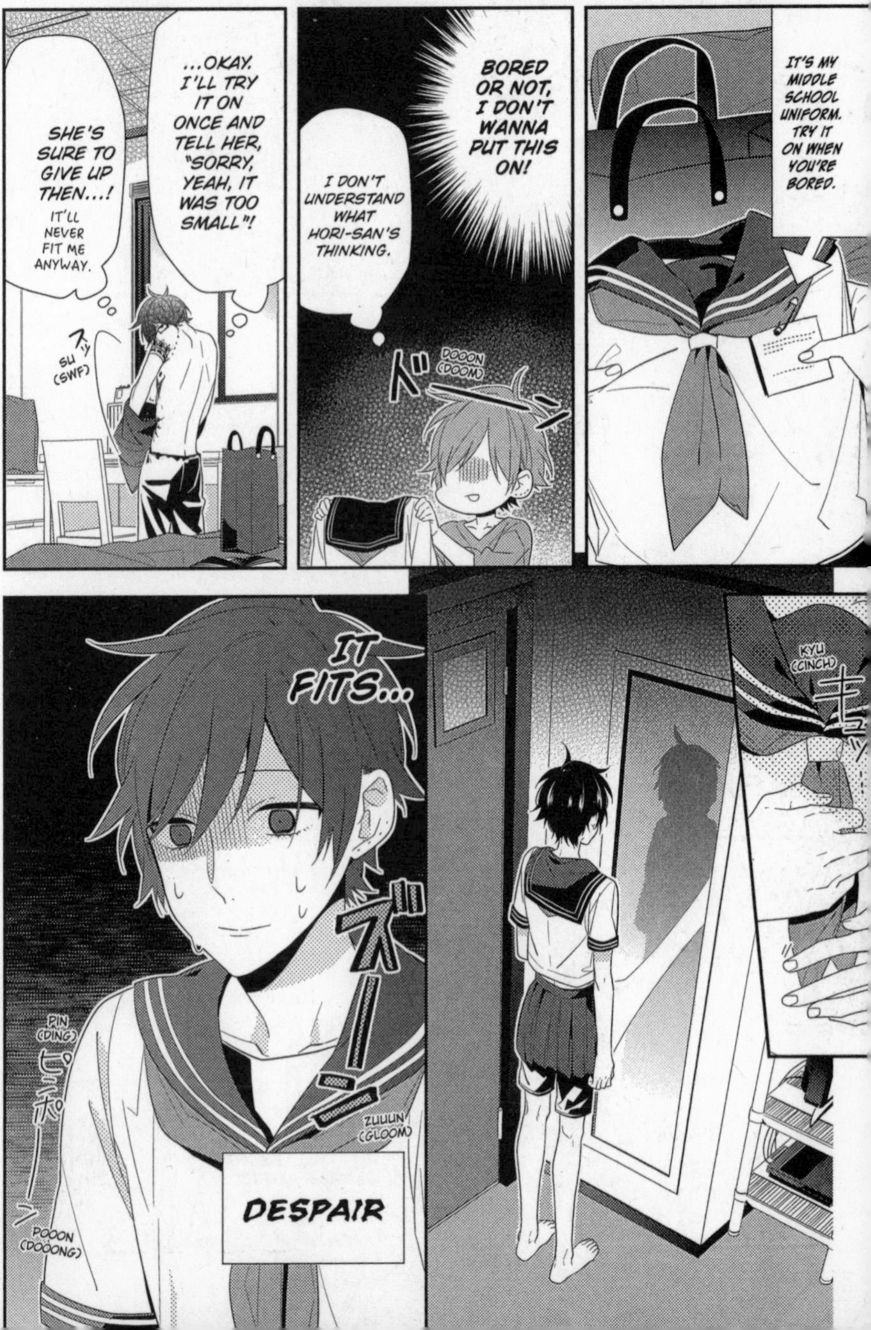
IT'S MY MIDDLE SCHOOL UNIFORM. TRY IT ON WHEN YOU'RE BORED.
BORED OR NOT, I DON'T WANNA PUT THIS ON!
I DON'T UNDERSTAND WHAT HORI-SAN'S THINKING.
DOOON (DOOM)
...OKAY. I'LL TRY IT ON ONCE AND TELL HER, "SORRY, YEAH, IT WAS TOO SMALL"!
SHE'S SURE TO GIVE UP THEN...!
IT'LL NEVER FIT ME ANYWAY.
SU (SWF)
KYU (CINCH)
IT FITS...
ZUUUN (GLOOM)
PIN (DING)
POOON (DOOONG)
DESPAIR

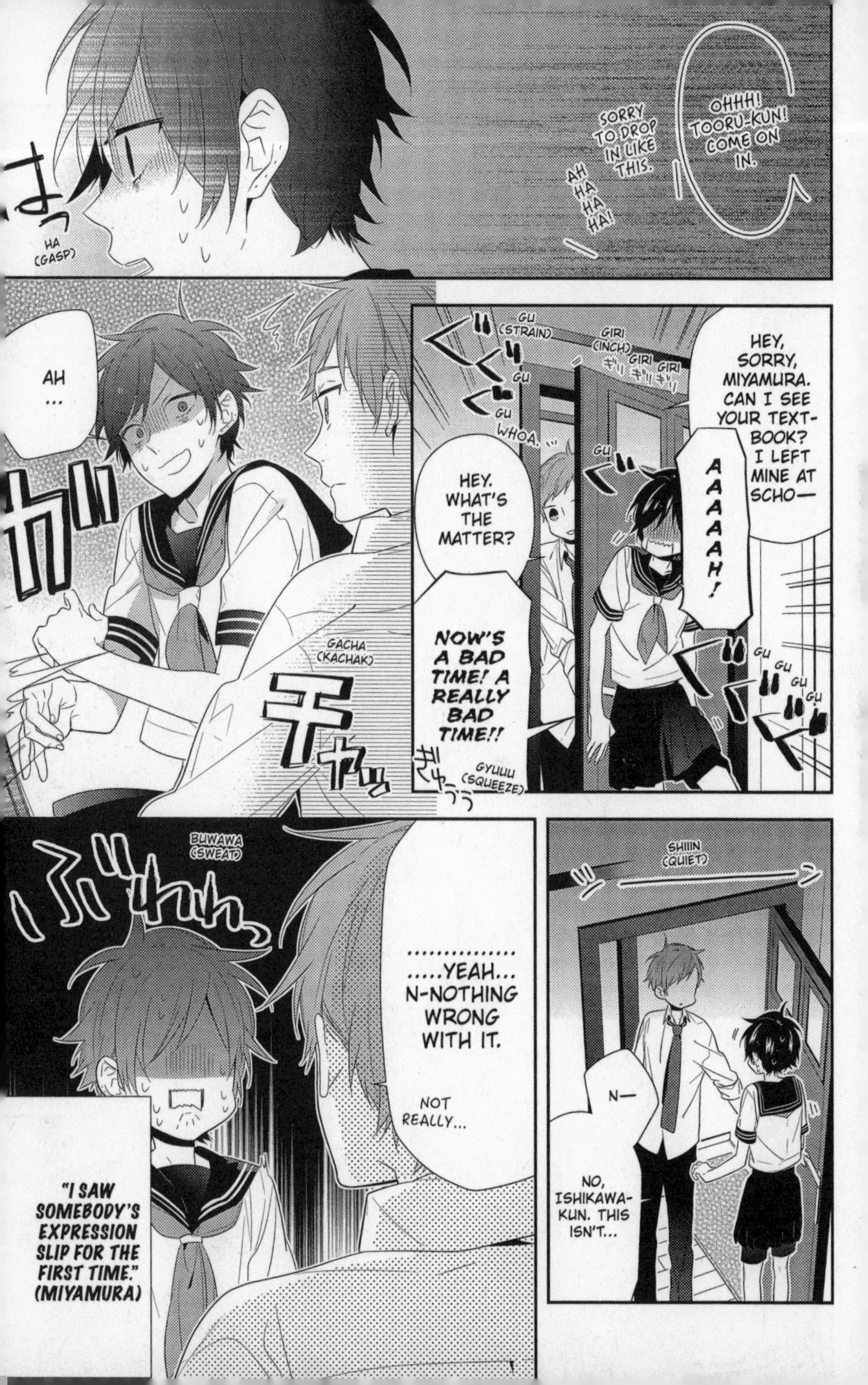
OHHH! TOORU-KUN! COME ON IN.
SORRY TO DROP IN LIKE THIS.
AH HA HA HA!
HA (GASP)
HEY, SORRY, MIYAMURA. CAN I SEE YOUR TEXT-BOOK? I LEFT MINE AT SCHO—
AAAAAAH!
GIRI (INCH) GIRI GIRI
GU (STRAIN) GU GU
GU
WHOA.
HEY. WHAT'S THE MATTER?
GU GU GU GU
NOW'S A BAD TIME! A REALLY BAD TIME!!
GYUUU (SQUEEZE)
GACHA (KACHAK)
AH ...
SHIIN (QUIET)
N—
NO, ISHIKAWA-KUN. THIS ISN'T...
BUWAWA (SWEAT)
....YEAH... N-NOTHING WRONG WITH IT.
NOT REALLY...
"I SAW SOMEBODY'S EXPRESSION SLIP FOR THE FIRST TIME." (MIYAMURA)

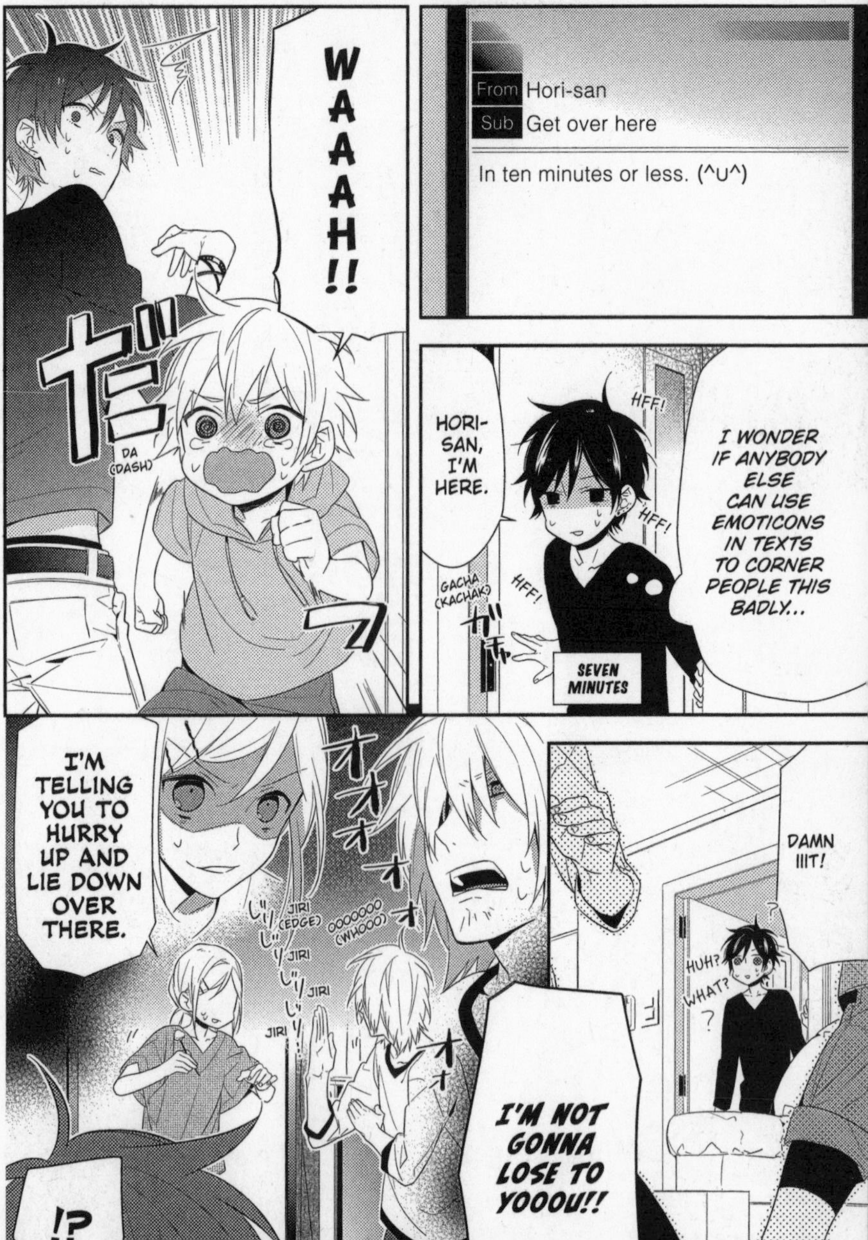
From Hori-san
Sub Get over here
In ten minutes or less. (^U^)
HFF!
I WONDER IF ANYBODY ELSE CAN USE EMOTICONS IN TEXTS TO CORNER PEOPLE THIS BADLY...
HFF!
HORI-SAN, I'M HERE.
HFF!
GACHA (KACHAK)
SEVEN MINUTES
WAAAAH!!
DA (DASH)
DAMN IIIT!
?
HUH? WHAT?
?
I'M NOT GONNA LOSE TO YOOOU!!
OOOOOOO (WHOOO)
JIRI (EDGE)
JIRI
JIRI
JIRI
I'M TELLING YOU TO HURRY UP AND LIE DOWN OVER THERE.
!?

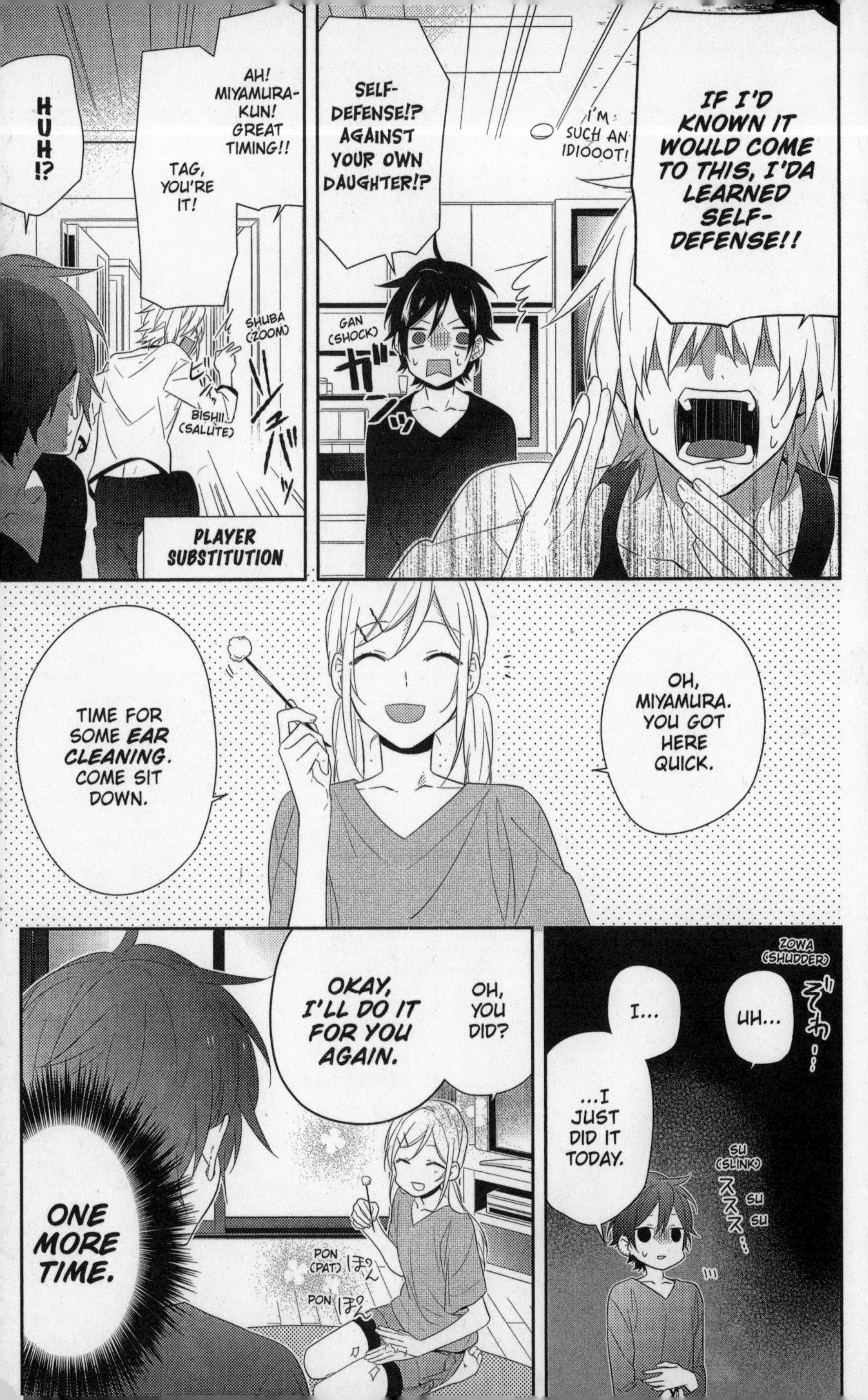
IF I'D KNOWN IT WOULD COME TO THIS, I'DA LEARNED SELF-DEFENSE!!
I'M SUCH AN IDIOOOT!
SELF-DEFENSE!? AGAINST YOUR OWN DAUGHTER!?
GAN (SHOCK)
AH! MIYAMURA-KUN! GREAT TIMING!!
TAG, YOU'RE IT!
HUH!?
SHUBA (ZOOM)
BISHI! (SALUTE)
PLAYER SUBSTITUTION
OH, MIYAMURA. YOU GOT HERE QUICK.
TIME FOR SOME EAR CLEANING. COME SIT DOWN.
ZOWA (SHUDDER)
UH...
I...
...I JUST DID IT TODAY.
SU (SLINK)
SU
SU
OH, YOU DID?
OKAY, I'LL DO IT FOR YOU AGAIN.
PON (PAT)
PON
ONE MORE TIME.

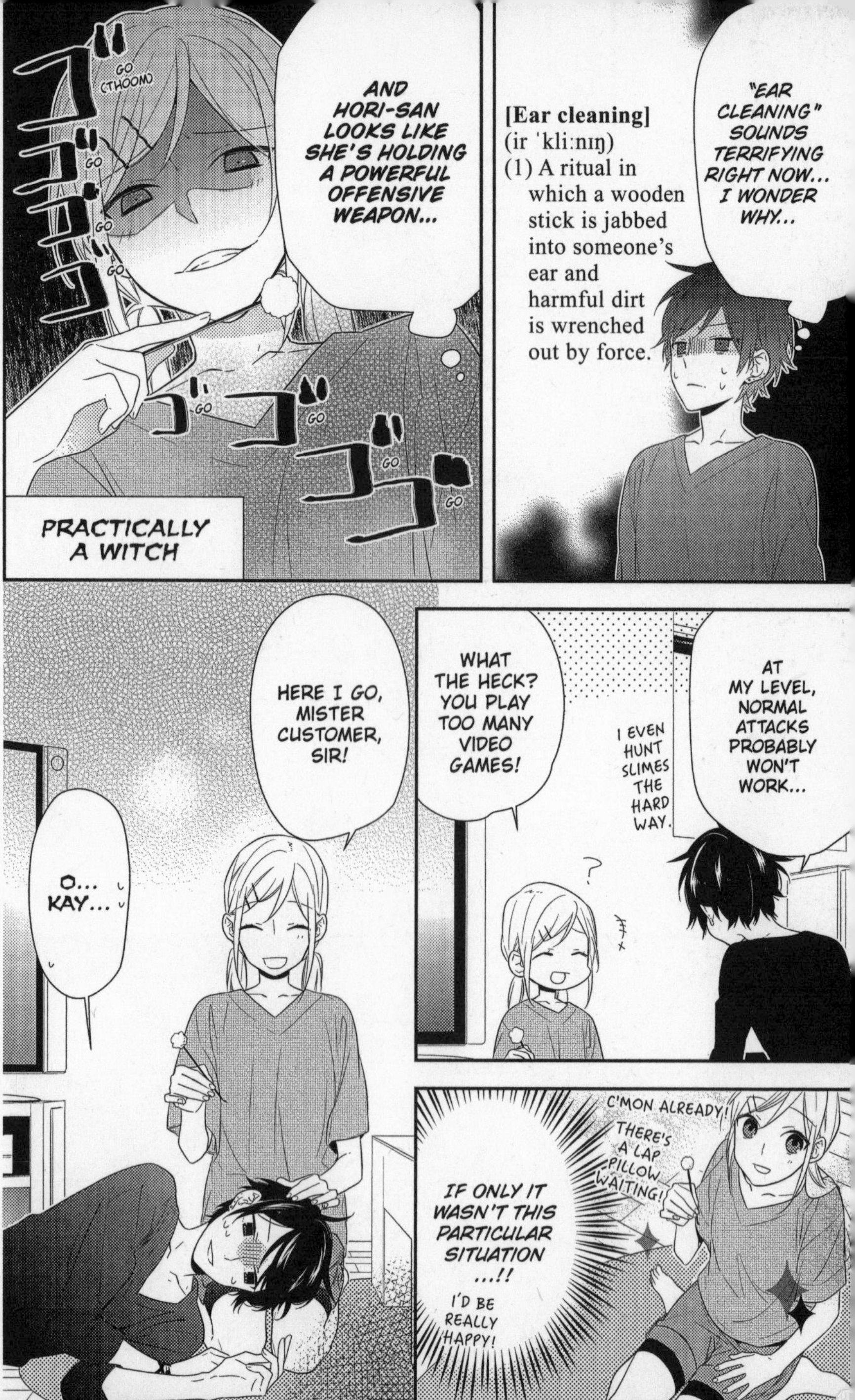
[Ear cleaning]
(ir ˈkliːnɪŋ)
(1) A ritual in which a wooden stick is jabbed into someone's ear and harmful dirt is wrenched out by force.
"EAR CLEANING" SOUNDS TERRIFYING RIGHT NOW... I WONDER WHY...
AND HORI-SAN LOOKS LIKE SHE'S HOLDING A POWERFUL OFFENSIVE WEAPON...
GO (THOOM)
GO
GO
GO
GO
GO
GO
GO
PRACTICALLY A WITCH
AT MY LEVEL, NORMAL ATTACKS PROBABLY WON'T WORK...
I EVEN HUNT SLIMES THE HARD WAY.
WHAT THE HECK? YOU PLAY TOO MANY VIDEO GAMES!
?
C'MON ALREADY! THERE'S A LAP PILLOW WAITING!
IF ONLY IT WASN'T THIS PARTICULAR SITUATION ...!!
I'D BE REALLY HAPPY!
HERE I GO, MISTER CUSTOMER, SIR!
O... KAY...

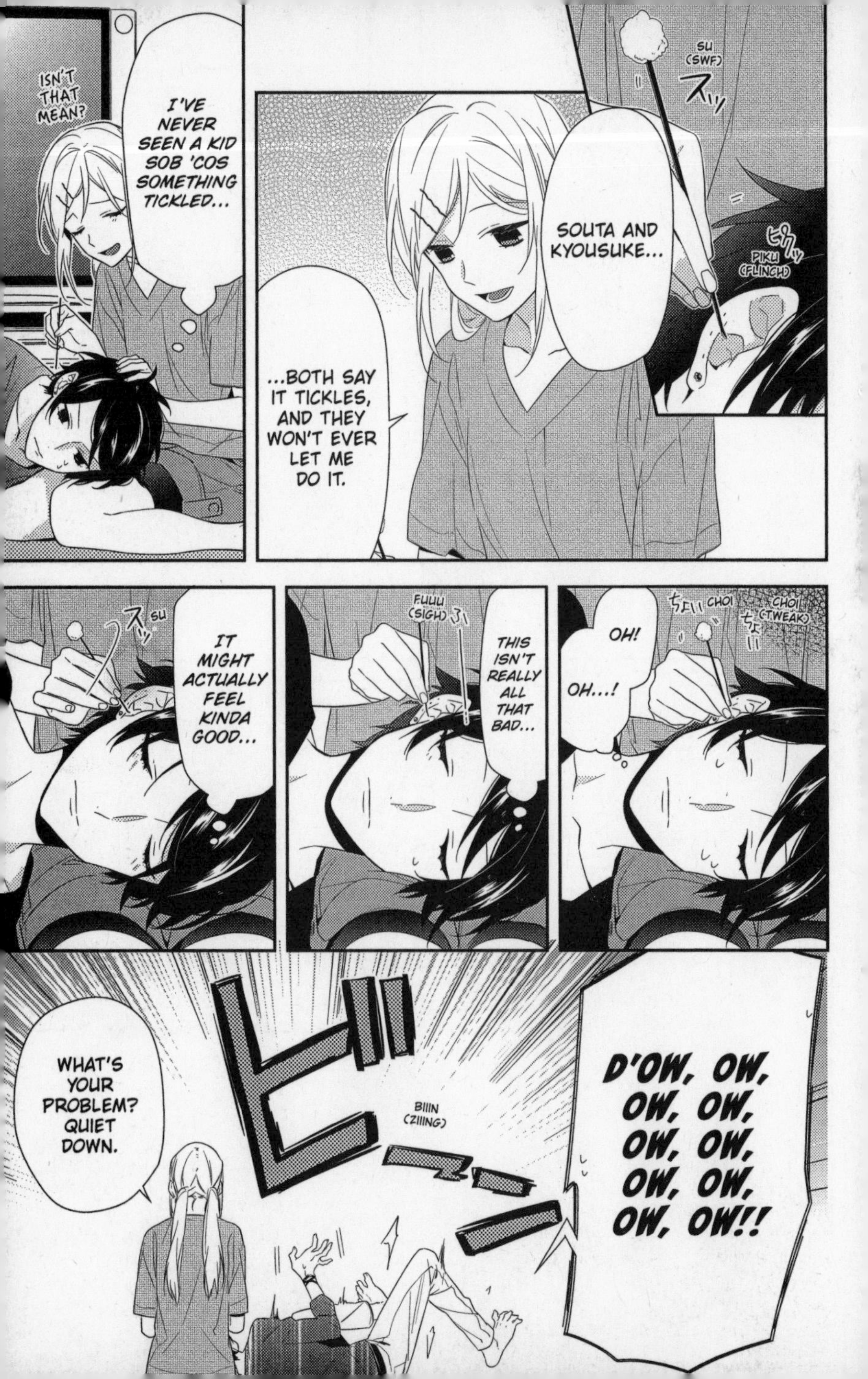
SU (SWF)
PIKU (FLINCH)
SOUTA AND KYOUSUKE...
...BOTH SAY IT TICKLES, AND THEY WON'T EVER LET ME DO IT.
I'VE NEVER SEEN A KID SOB 'COS SOMETHING TICKLED...
ISN'T THAT MEAN?
CHOI
CHOI (TWEAK)
OH!
OH...!
FUUU (SIGH)
THIS ISN'T REALLY ALL THAT BAD...
SU
IT MIGHT ACTUALLY FEEL KINDA GOOD...
D'OW, OW, OW, OW, OW, OW, OW, OW, OW, OW!!
BIIIN (ZIIING)
WHAT'S YOUR PROBLEM? QUIET DOWN.

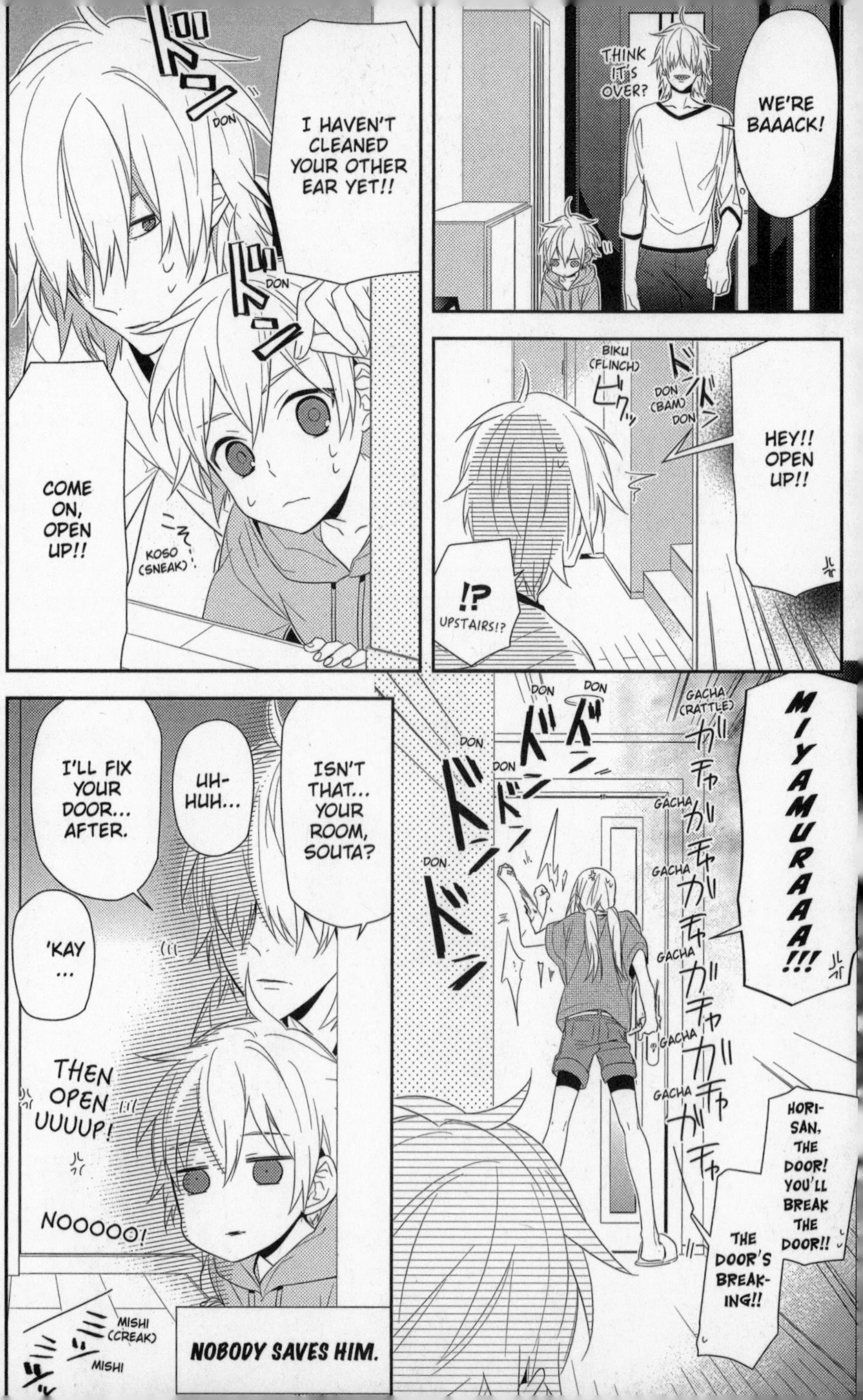
WE'RE BAAACK!
THINK IT'S OVER?
HEY!! OPEN UP!!
DON (BAM) DON
BIKU (FLINCH)
!?
UPSTAIRS!?
I HAVEN'T CLEANED YOUR OTHER EAR YET!!
DON
DON
COME ON, OPEN UP!!
KOSO (SNEAK)
MIYAMURAAAA!!!
GACHA (RATTLE)
GACHA
GACHA
GACHA
GACHA
GACHA
DON
DON
DON
DON
DON
HORI-SAN, THE DOOR! YOU'LL BREAK THE DOOR!!
THE DOOR'S BREAKING!!
ISN'T THAT... YOUR ROOM, SOUTA?
UH-HUH...
I'LL FIX YOUR DOOR... AFTER.
'KAY...
THEN OPEN UUUUP!
NOOOOO!
MISHI (CREAK)
MISHI
NOBODY SAVES HIM.

THE NUMBER OF VICTIMS INCREASES.

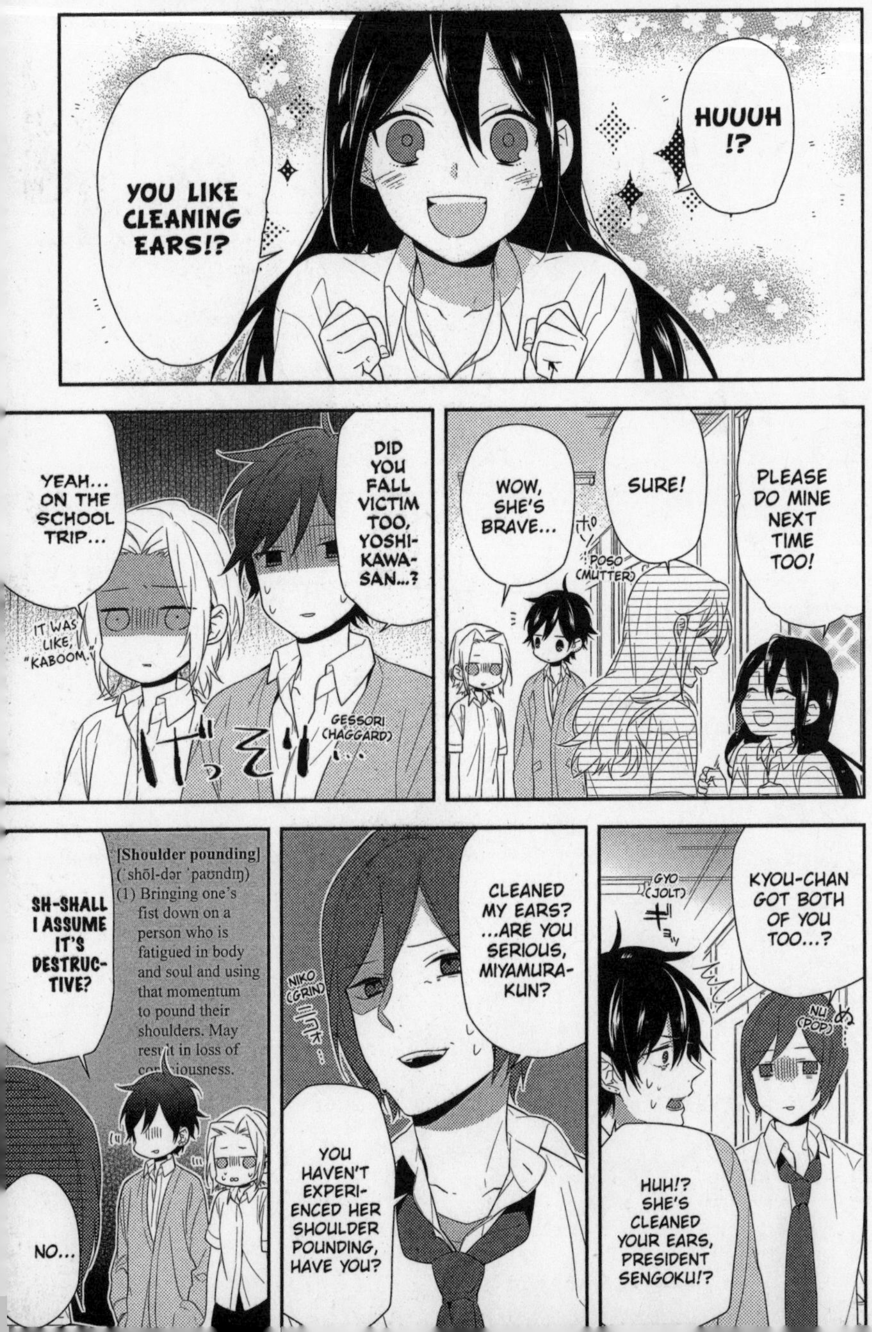
HUUUH!?
YOU LIKE CLEANING EARS!?
PLEASE DO MINE NEXT TIME TOO!
SURE!
WOW, SHE'S BRAVE...
POSO (MUTTER)
DID YOU FALL VICTIM TOO, YOSHIKAWA-SAN...?
YEAH... ON THE SCHOOL TRIP...
IT WAS LIKE, "KABOOM."
GESSORI (HAGGARD)
KYOU-CHAN GOT BOTH OF YOU TOO...?
GYO (JOLT)
NU (POP)
HUH!? SHE'S CLEANED YOUR EARS, PRESIDENT SENGOKU!?
CLEANED MY EARS? ...ARE YOU SERIOUS, MIYAMURA-KUN?
NIKO (GRIN)
YOU HAVEN'T EXPERIENCED HER SHOULDER POUNDING, HAVE YOU?
[Shoulder pounding] (ˈshōl-dər ˈpaʊndɪŋ) (1) Bringing one's fist down on a person who is fatigued in body and soul and using that momentum to pound their shoulders. May result in loss of consciousness.
SH-SHALL I ASSUME IT'S DESTRUCTIVE?
NO...

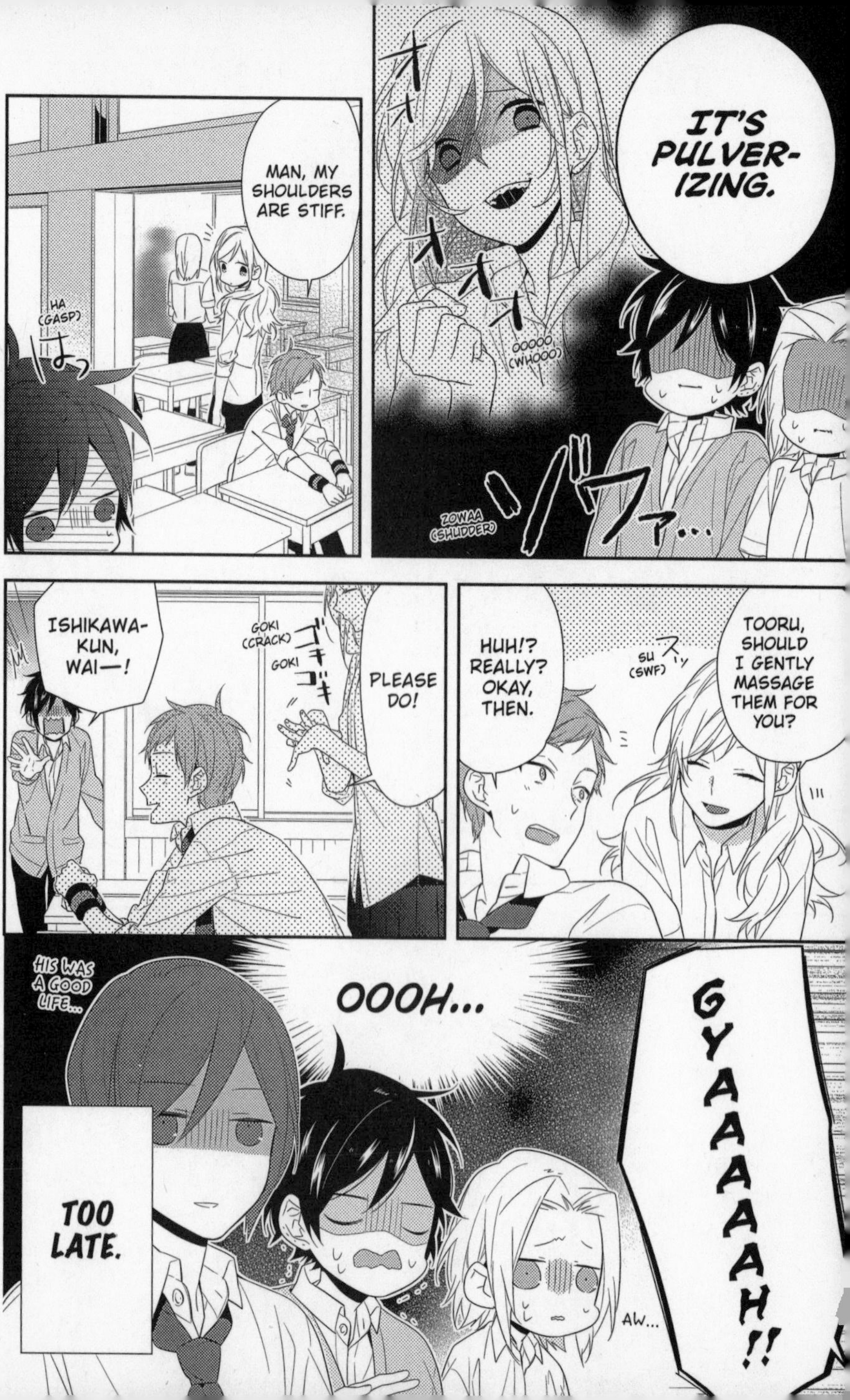
IT'S PULVER-IZING.
OOOOO (WHOOO)
ZOWAA (SHUDDER)
MAN, MY SHOULDERS ARE STIFF.
HA (GASP)
TOORU, SHOULD I GENTLY MASSAGE THEM FOR YOU?
SU (SWF)
HUH!? REALLY? OKAY, THEN.
PLEASE DO!
GOKI (CRACK) GOKI
ISHIKAWA-KUN, WAI—!
GYAAAAAH!!
OOOH...
HIS WAS A GOOD LIFE...
TOO LATE.
AW...

HORIMIYA

HORIMIYA

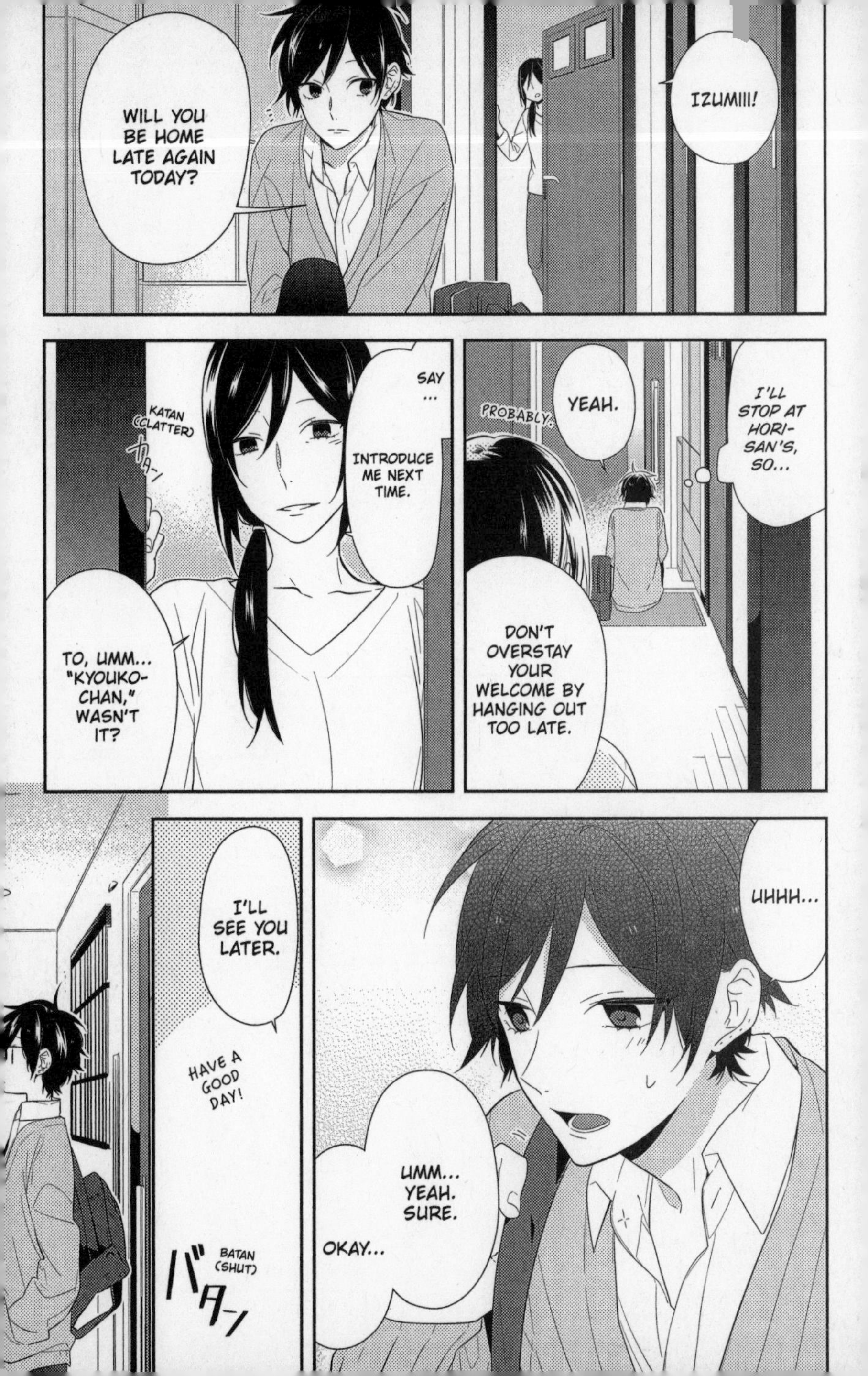
IZUMIII!
WILL YOU BE HOME LATE AGAIN TODAY?
I'LL STOP AT HORI-SAN'S, SO...
YEAH.
PROBABLY.
DON'T OVERSTAY YOUR WELCOME BY HANGING OUT TOO LATE.
SAY ...
INTRODUCE ME NEXT TIME.
KATAN (CLATTER)
TO, UMM... "KYOUKO-CHAN," WASN'T IT?
UHHH...
UMM... YEAH. SURE.
OKAY...
I'LL SEE YOU LATER.
HAVE A GOOD DAY!
BATAN (SHUT)

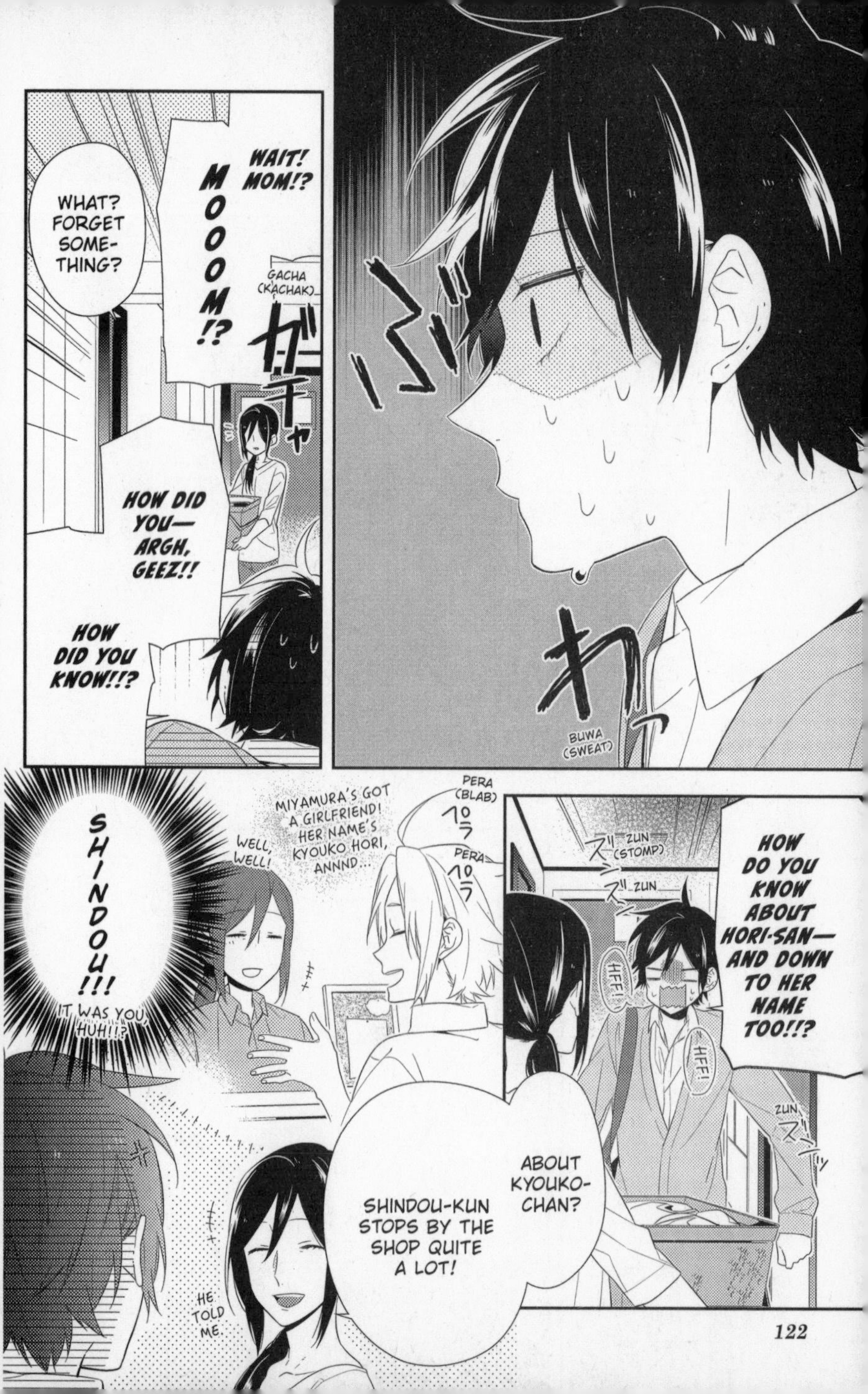
BUWA (SWEAT)
WAIT! MOM!?
MOOOOM!?
GACHA (KACHAK)
WHAT? FORGET SOME-THING?
HOW DID YOU— ARGH, GEEZ!!
HOW DID YOU KNOW!!?
HOW DO YOU KNOW ABOUT HORI-SAN— AND DOWN TO HER NAME TOO!!?
ZUN (STOMP)
ZUN
HFF!
HFF!
ZUN
ABOUT KYOUKO-CHAN?
PERA (BLAB)
PERA
MIYAMURA'S GOT A GIRLFRIEND! HER NAME'S KYOUKO HORI, ANNND...
WELL, WELL!
SHINDOU!!!
IT WAS YOU, HUH!!?
SHINDOU-KUN STOPS BY THE SHOP QUITE A LOT!
HE TOLD ME.

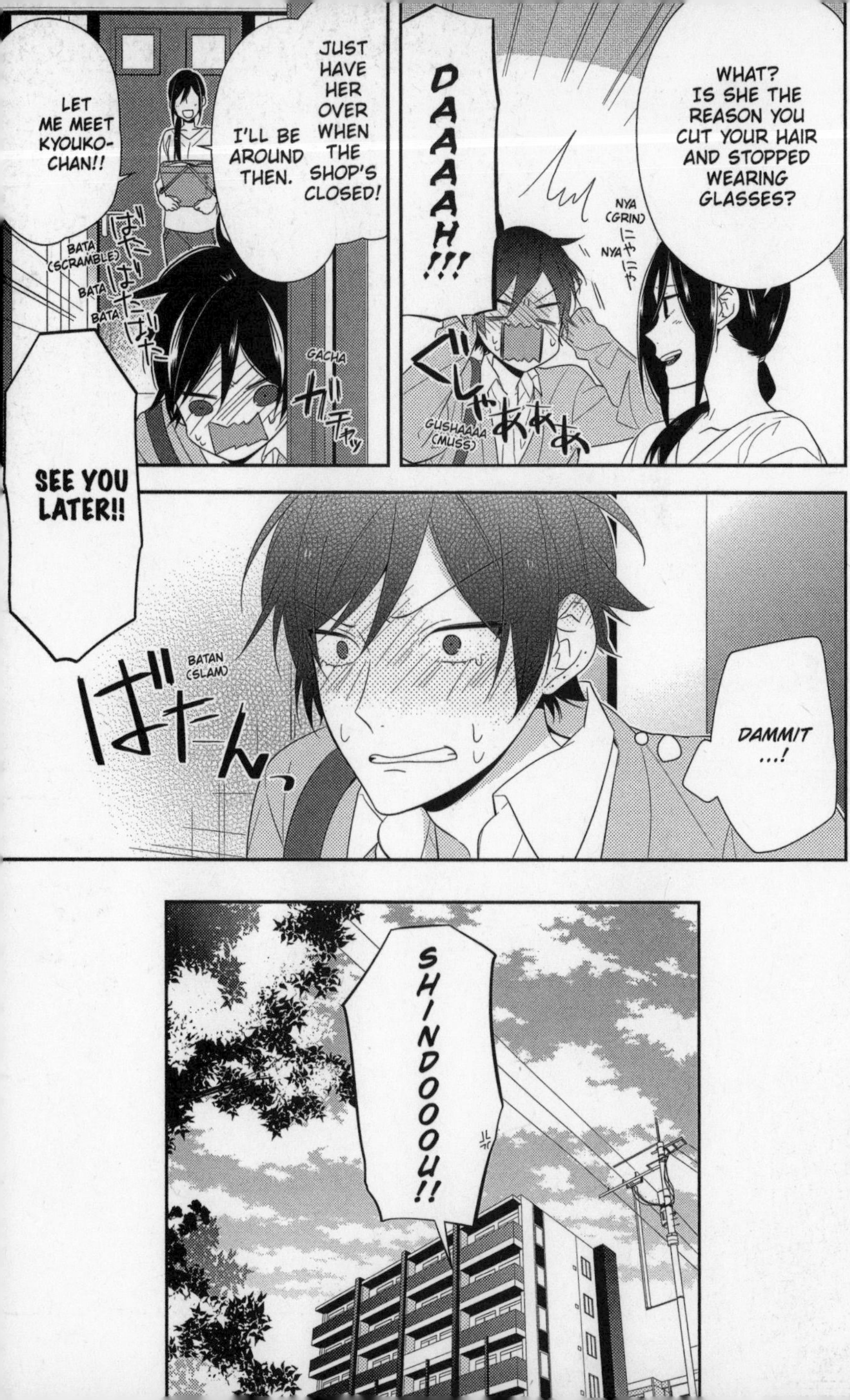
WHAT? IS SHE THE REASON YOU CUT YOUR HAIR AND STOPPED WEARING GLASSES?
NYA (GRIN) にやにや NYA
DAAAAAH!!!
くしゃあああ
GUSHAAAA (MUSS)
JUST HAVE HER OVER WHEN THE SHOP'S CLOSED!
I'LL BE AROUND THEN.
LET ME MEET KYOUKO-CHAN!!
ばたばたばた
BATA (SCRAMBLE) BATA BATA
GACHA
ガチャ
SEE YOU LATER!!
BATAN (SLAM)
ばたん
DAMMIT ...!
SHINDOOOOU!!

Page·32

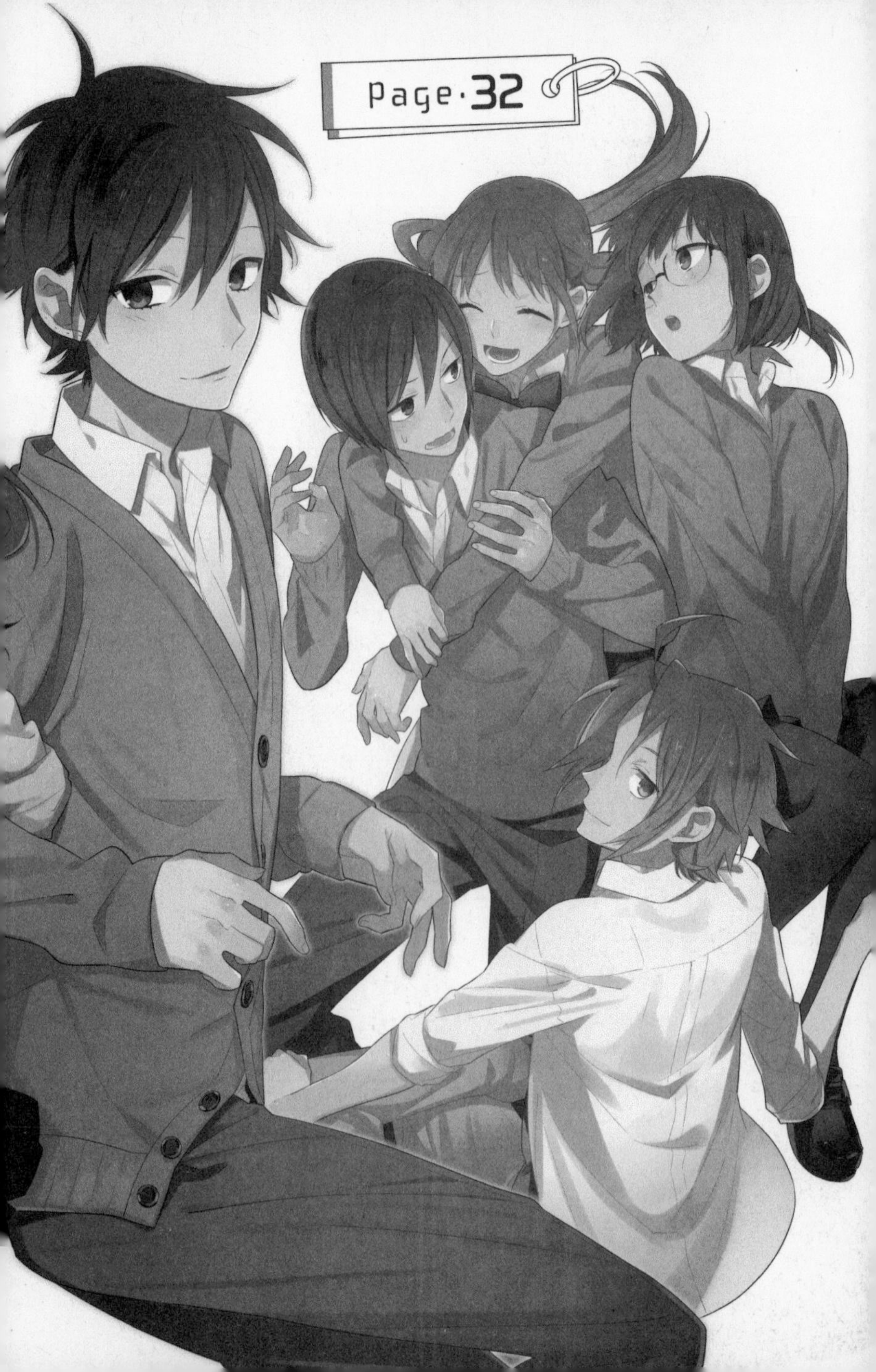

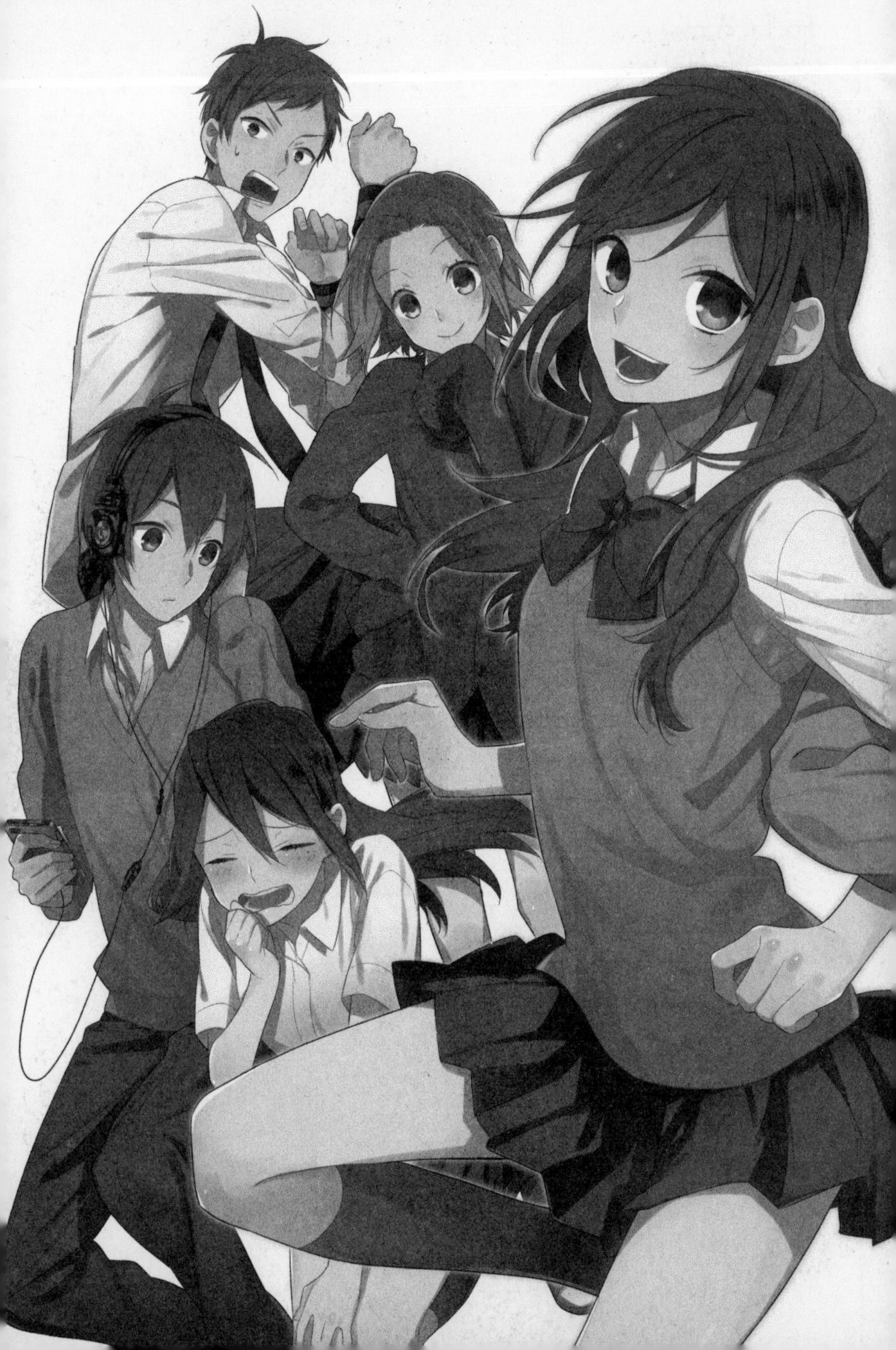

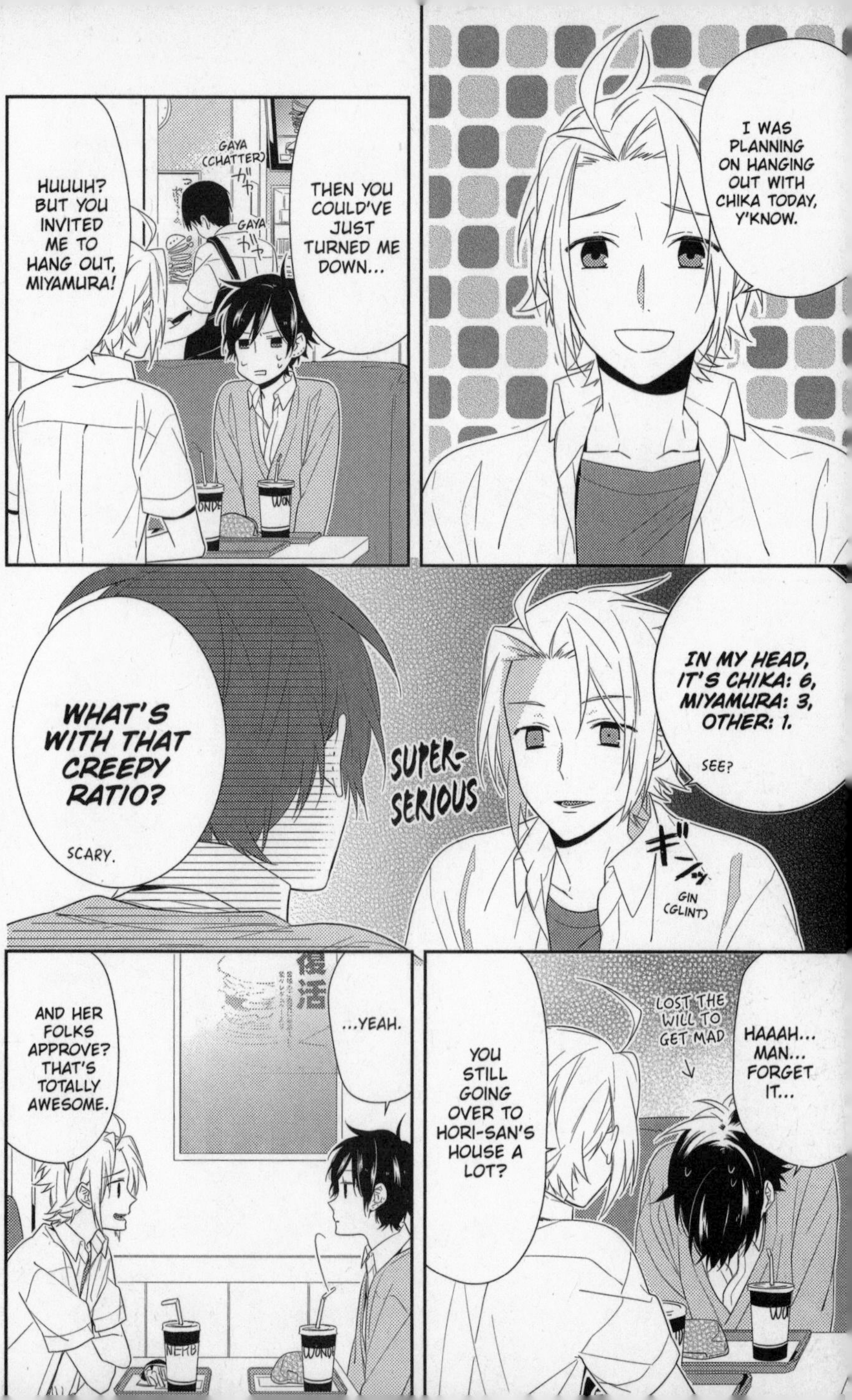
I WAS PLANNING ON HANGING OUT WITH CHIKA TODAY, Y'KNOW.
THEN YOU COULD'VE JUST TURNED ME DOWN...
ガヤ
GAYA (CHATTER)
ガヤ
GAYA
HUUUH? BUT YOU INVITED ME TO HANG OUT, MIYAMURA!
IN MY HEAD, IT'S CHIKA: 6, MIYAMURA: 3, OTHER: 1.
SEE?
ギン
GIN (GLINT)
SUPER-SERIOUS
WHAT'S WITH THAT CREEPY RATIO?
SCARY.
HAAAH... MAN... FORGET IT...
LOST THE WILL TO GET MAD
YOU STILL GOING OVER TO HORI-SAN'S HOUSE A LOT?
...YEAH.
AND HER FOLKS APPROVE? THAT'S TOTALLY AWESOME.

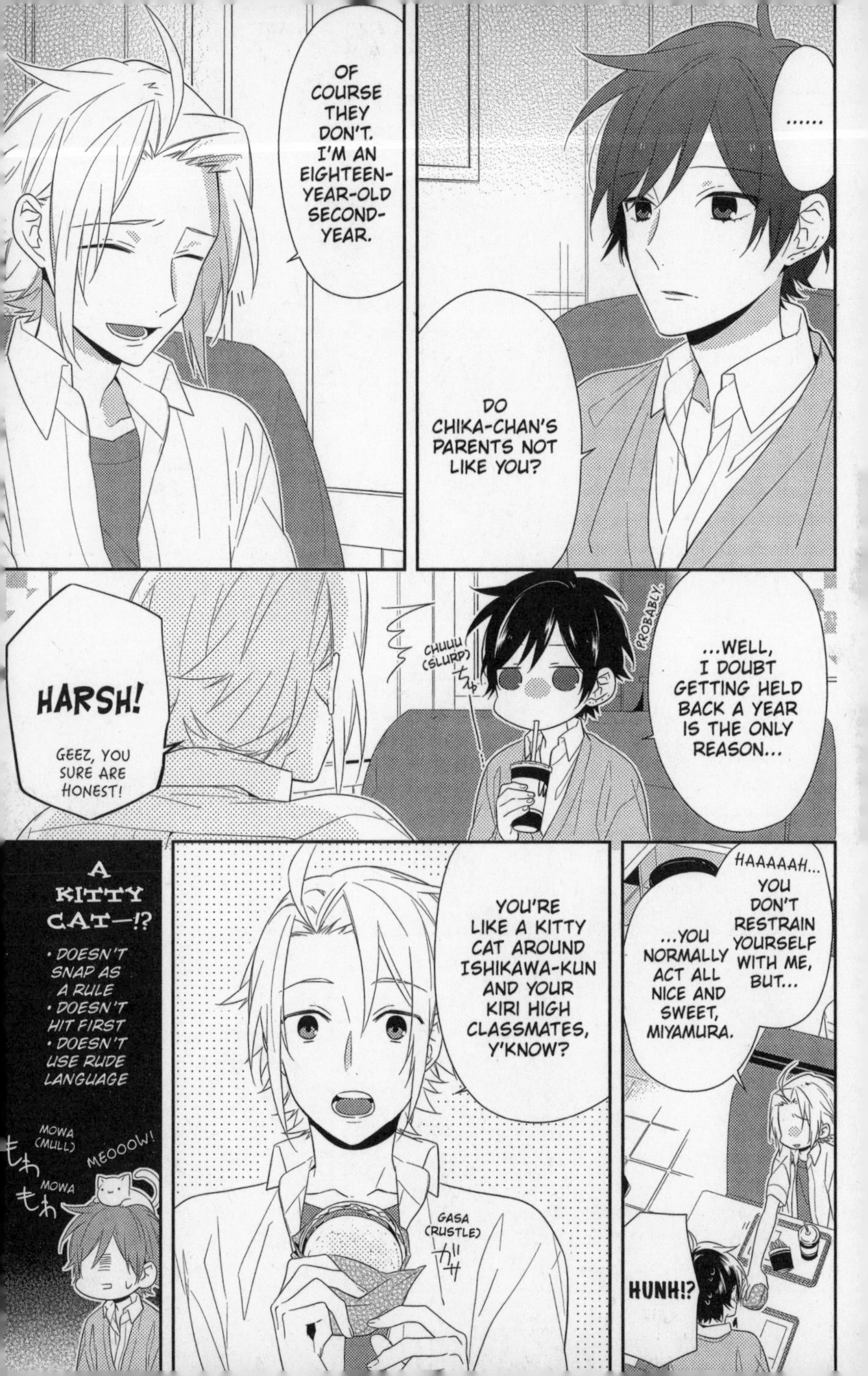

......
DO CHIKA-CHAN'S PARENTS NOT LIKE YOU?
OF COURSE THEY DON'T. I'M AN EIGHTEEN-YEAR-OLD SECOND-YEAR.
...WELL, I DOUBT GETTING HELD BACK A YEAR IS THE ONLY REASON...
PROBABLY.
CHUUU (SLURP)
HARSH!
GEEZ, YOU SURE ARE HONEST!
HAAAAAH... YOU DON'T RESTRAIN YOURSELF WITH ME, BUT...
...YOU NORMALLY ACT ALL NICE AND SWEET, MIYAMURA.
HUNH!?
YOU'RE LIKE A KITTY CAT AROUND ISHIKAWA-KUN AND YOUR KIRI HIGH CLASSMATES, Y'KNOW?
GASA (RUSTLE)
A KITTY CAT—!?
• DOESN'T SNAP AS A RULE
• DOESN'T HIT FIRST
• DOESN'T USE RUDE LANGUAGE
MOWA (MULL) MOWA
MEOOOW!

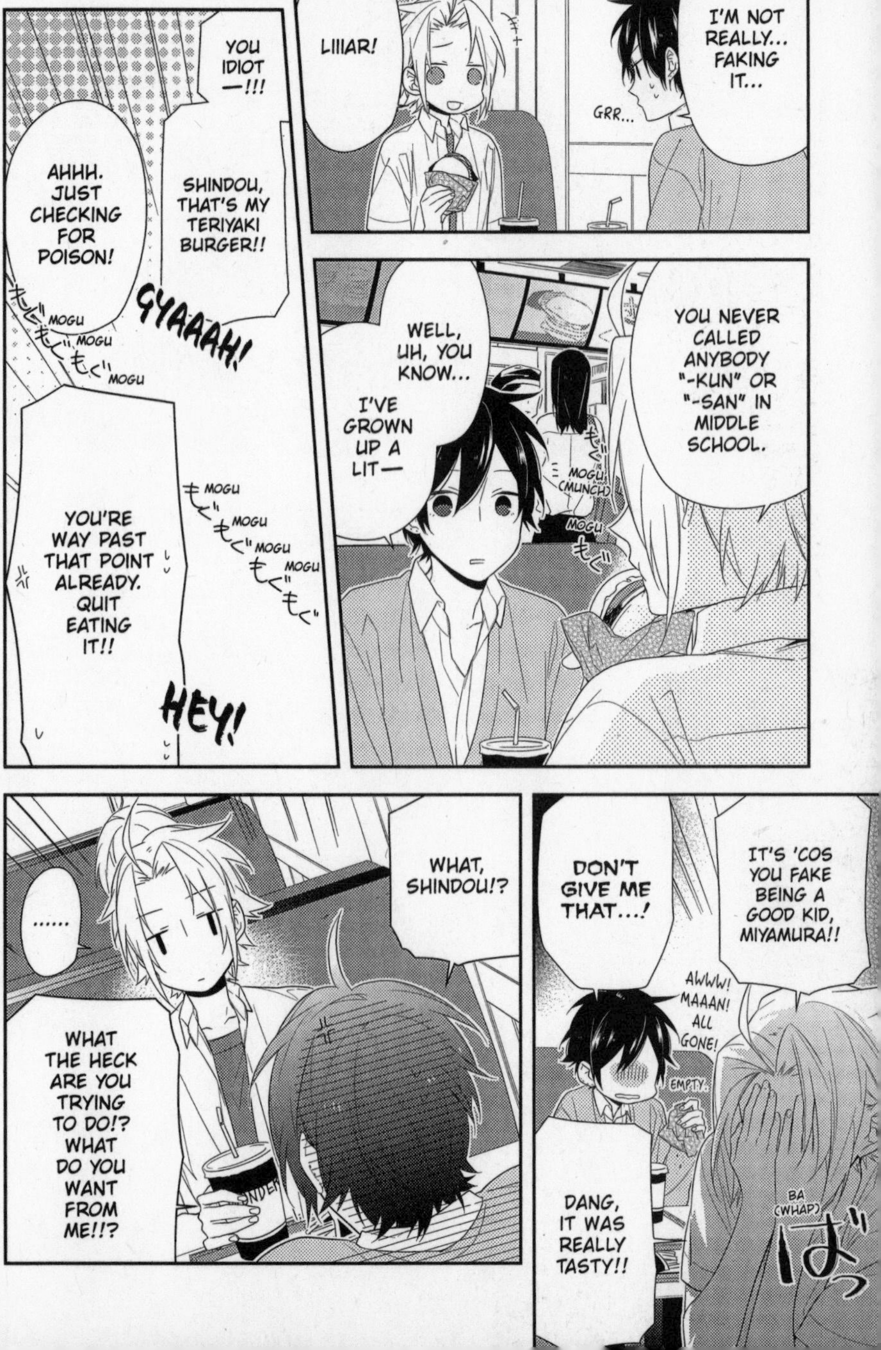
I'M NOT REALLY... FAKING IT...
GRR...
LIIIAR!
YOU NEVER CALLED ANYBODY "-KUN" OR "-SAN" IN MIDDLE SCHOOL.
MOGU (MUNCH) MOGU
WELL, UH, YOU KNOW...
I'VE GROWN UP A LIT—
YOU IDIOT—!!!
SHINDOU, THAT'S MY TERIYAKI BURGER!!
AHHH. JUST CHECKING FOR POISON!
GYAAAAH!
MOGU MOGU MOGU
MOGU MOGU MOGU MOGU
YOU'RE WAY PAST THAT POINT ALREADY. QUIT EATING IT!!
HEY!
IT'S 'COS YOU FAKE BEING A GOOD KID, MIYAMURA!!
DON'T GIVE ME THAT...!
AWWW! MAAAN! ALL GONE!
EMPTY.
BA (WHAP)
DANG, IT WAS REALLY TASTY!!
WHAT, SHINDOU!?
......
WHAT THE HECK ARE YOU TRYING TO DO!? WHAT DO YOU WANT FROM ME!!?

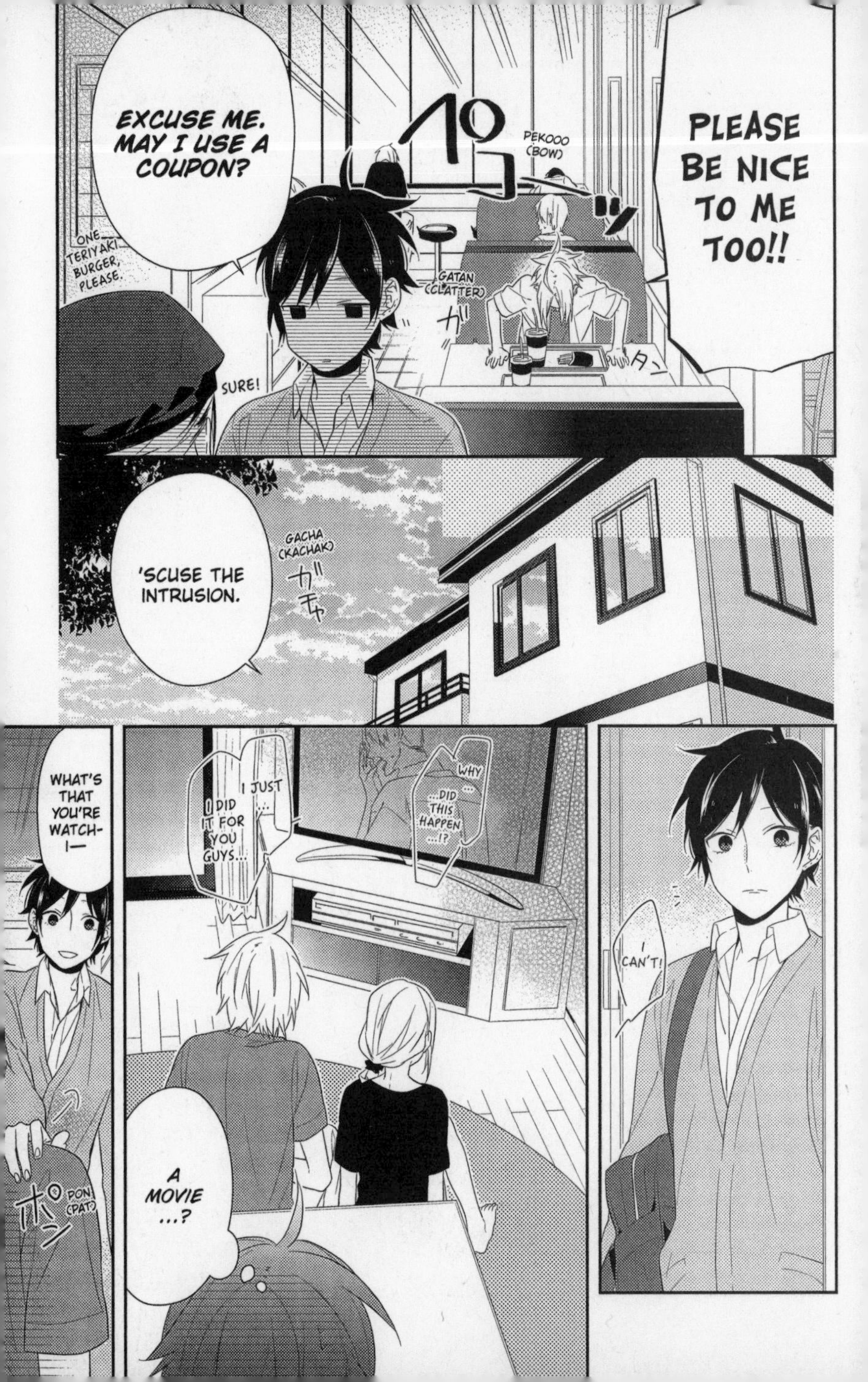
PLEASE BE NICE TO ME TOO!!
PEKOOO (BOW)
EXCUSE ME. MAY I USE A COUPON?
ONE TERIYAKI BURGER, PLEASE.
GATAN (CLATTER)
SURE!
GACHA (KACHAK)
'SCUSE THE INTRUSION.
I CAN'T!
WHY...
...DID THIS HAPPEN ...!?
I JUST ...
I DID IT FOR YOU GUYS...
A MOVIE ...?
WHAT'S THAT YOU'RE WATCH-I—
PON (PAT)

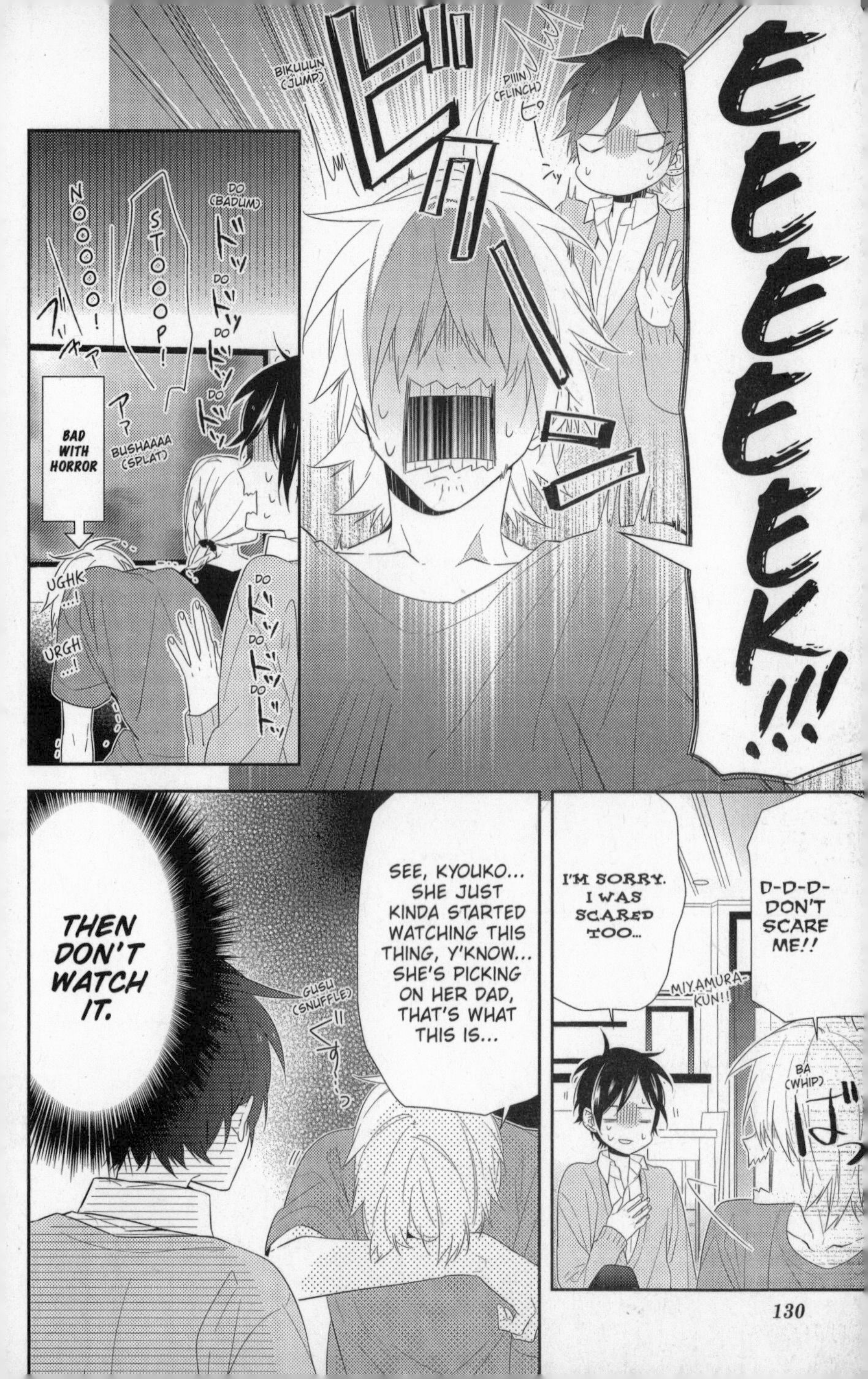
EEEEEEK!!!
PIIIN (FLINCH)
BIKUUUN (JUMP)
DO (BADUM)
DO
DO
DO
STOOOP!
NOOOOOO!
BUSHAAAA (SPLAT)
BAD WITH HORROR
UGHK ...!
URGH ...!
DO
DO
DO
D-D-D-DON'T SCARE ME!!
MIYAMURA-KUN!!
I'M SORRY. I WAS SCARED TOO...
BA (WHIP)
SEE, KYOUKO... SHE JUST KINDA STARTED WATCHING THIS THING, Y'KNOW... SHE'S PICKING ON HER DAD, THAT'S WHAT THIS IS...
GUSU (SNUFFLE)
THEN DON'T WATCH IT.

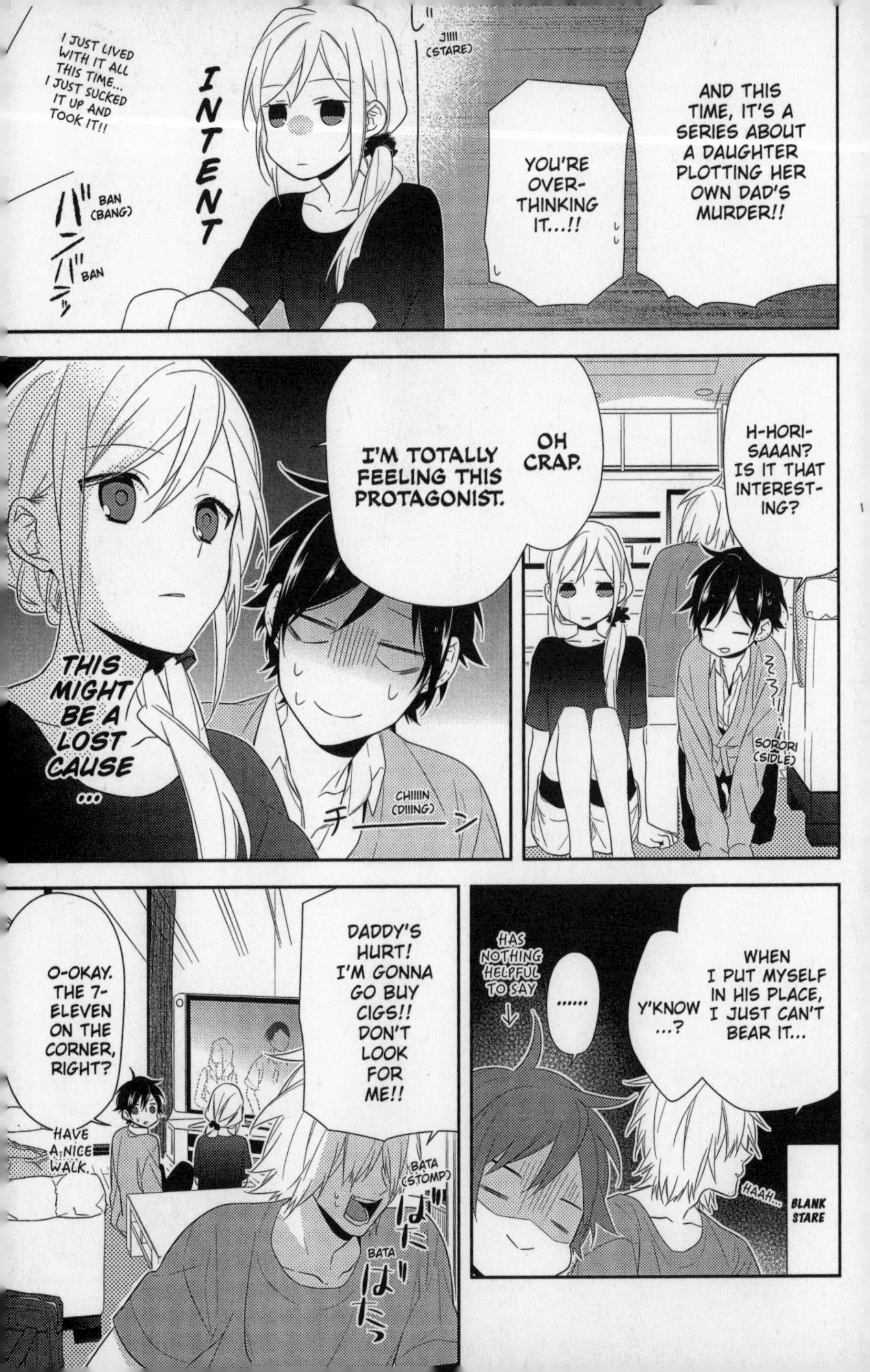
AND THIS TIME, IT'S A SERIES ABOUT A DAUGHTER PLOTTING HER OWN DAD'S MURDER!!
YOU'RE OVER-THINKING IT...!!
JIIII (STARE)
INTENT
I JUST LIVED WITH IT ALL THIS TIME... I JUST SUCKED IT UP AND TOOK IT!!
BAN (BANG)
BAN
H-HORI-SAAAN? IS IT THAT INTEREST-ING?
SORORI (SIDLE)
OH CRAP.
I'M TOTALLY FEELING THIS PROTAGONIST.
THIS MIGHT BE A LOST CAUSE...
CHIIIIN (DIIING)
WHEN I PUT MYSELF IN HIS PLACE, I JUST CAN'T BEAR IT...
Y'KNOW ...?
......
HAS NOTHING HELPFUL TO SAY
HAAH...
BLANK STARE
DADDY'S HURT! I'M GONNA GO BUY CIGS!! DON'T LOOK FOR ME!!
O-OKAY. THE 7-ELEVEN ON THE CORNER, RIGHT?
HAVE A NICE WALK.
BATA (STOMP)
BATA

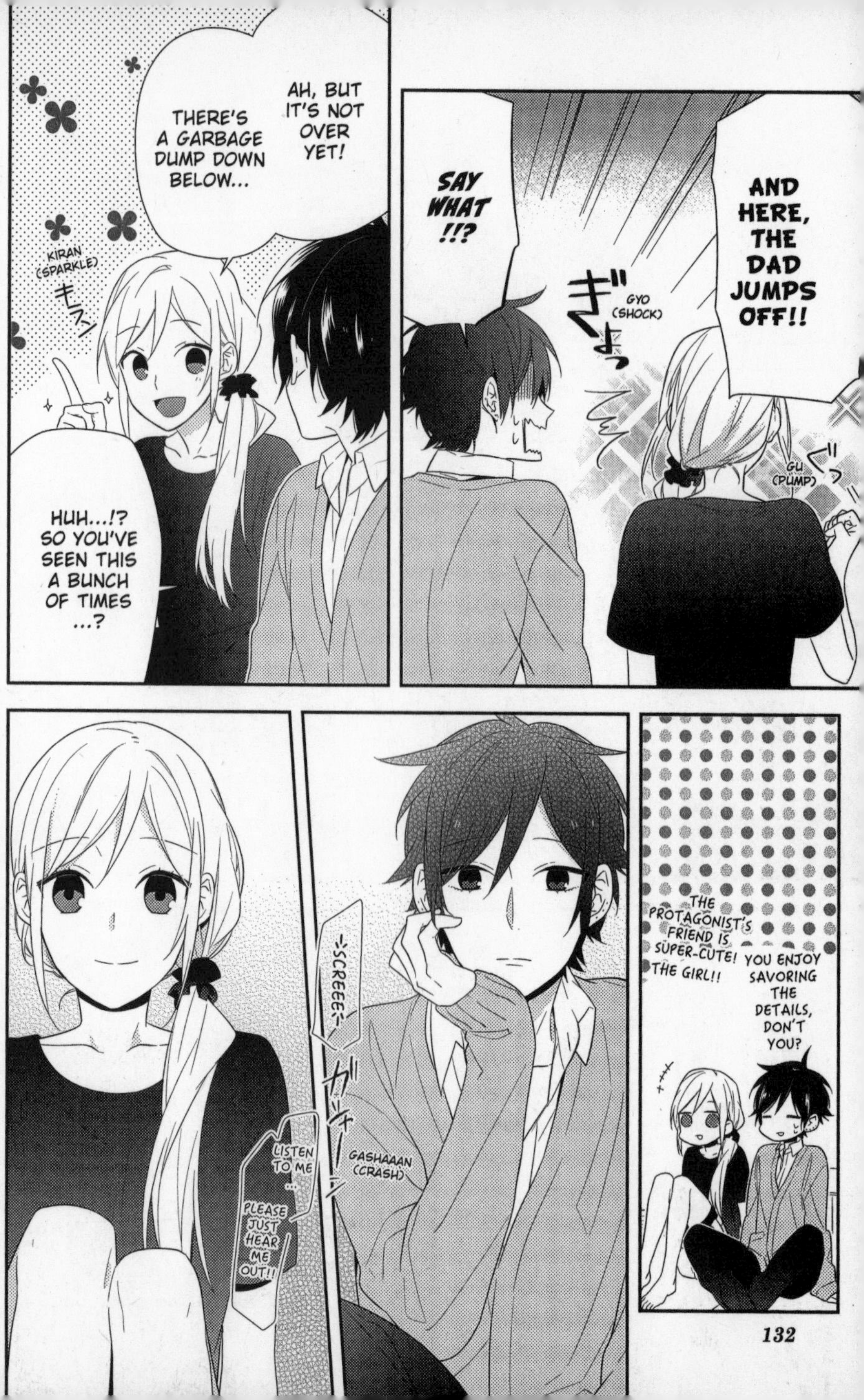
AND HERE, THE DAD JUMPS OFF!!
SAY WHAT!!?
GYO (SHOCK)
GU (PUMP)
AH, BUT IT'S NOT OVER YET!
THERE'S A GARBAGE DUMP DOWN BELOW...
KIRAN (SPARKLE)
HUH...!? SO YOU'VE SEEN THIS A BUNCH OF TIMES ...?
YOU ENJOY SAVORING THE DETAILS, DON'T YOU?
THE PROTAGONIST'S FRIEND IS SUPER-CUTE! THE GIRL!!
SCREEEE
GASHAAAN (CRASH)
LISTEN TO ME ...
PLEASE JUST HEAR ME OUT!!

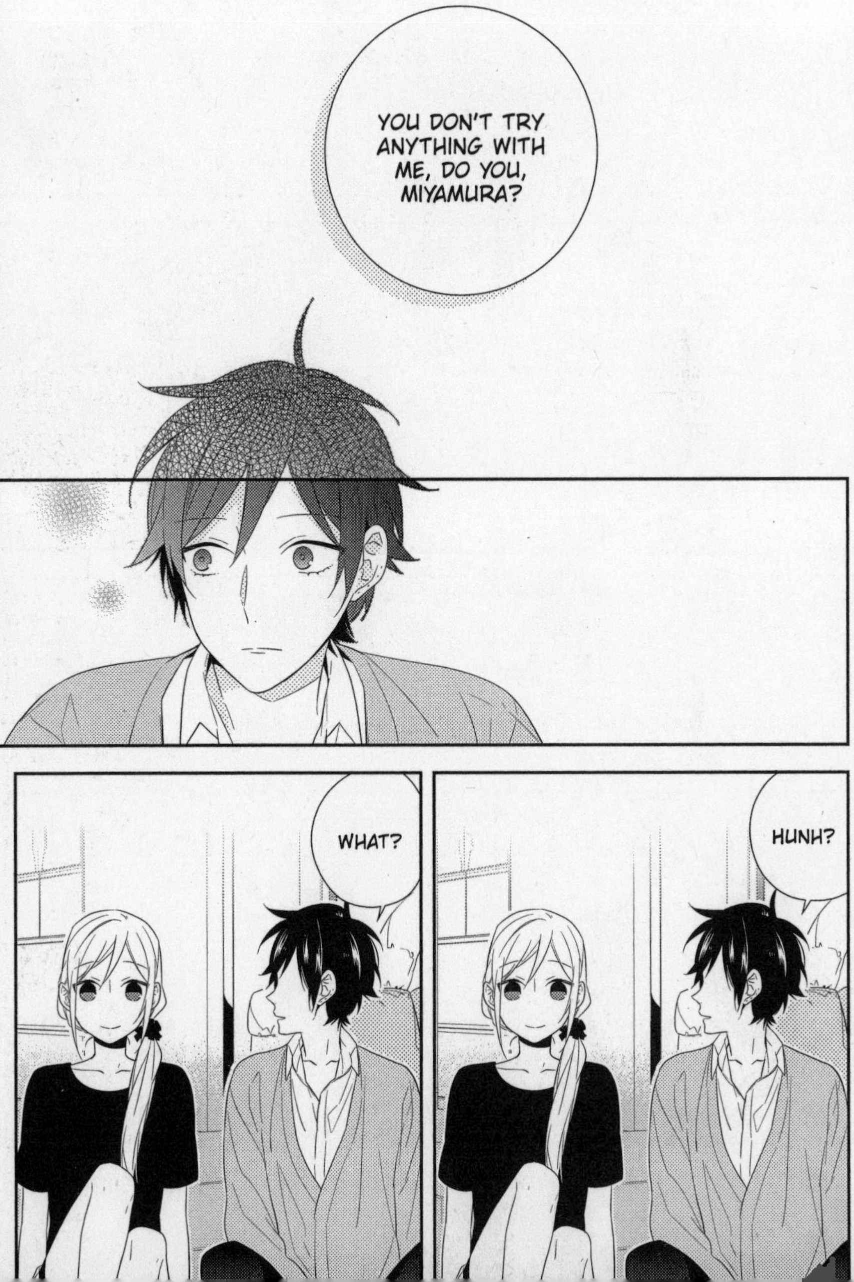
YOU DON'T TRY ANYTHING WITH ME, DO YOU, MIYAMURA?
HUNH?
WHAT?

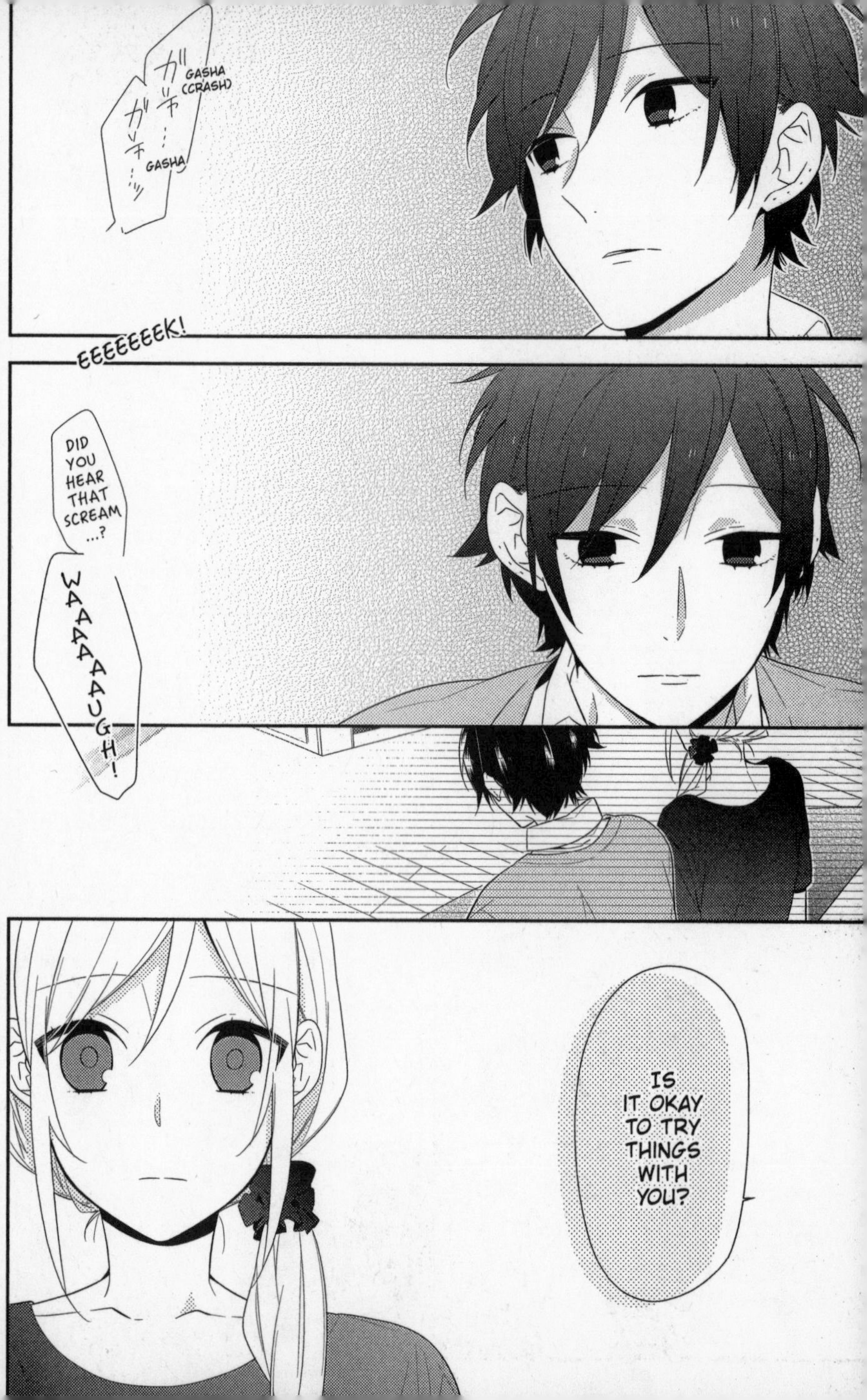
ガチャ
GASHA (CRASH)
ガチャッ
GASHA
EEEEEEEK!
DID YOU HEAR THAT SCREAM ...?
WAAAAAAAUGH!
IS IT OKAY TO TRY THINGS WITH YOU?

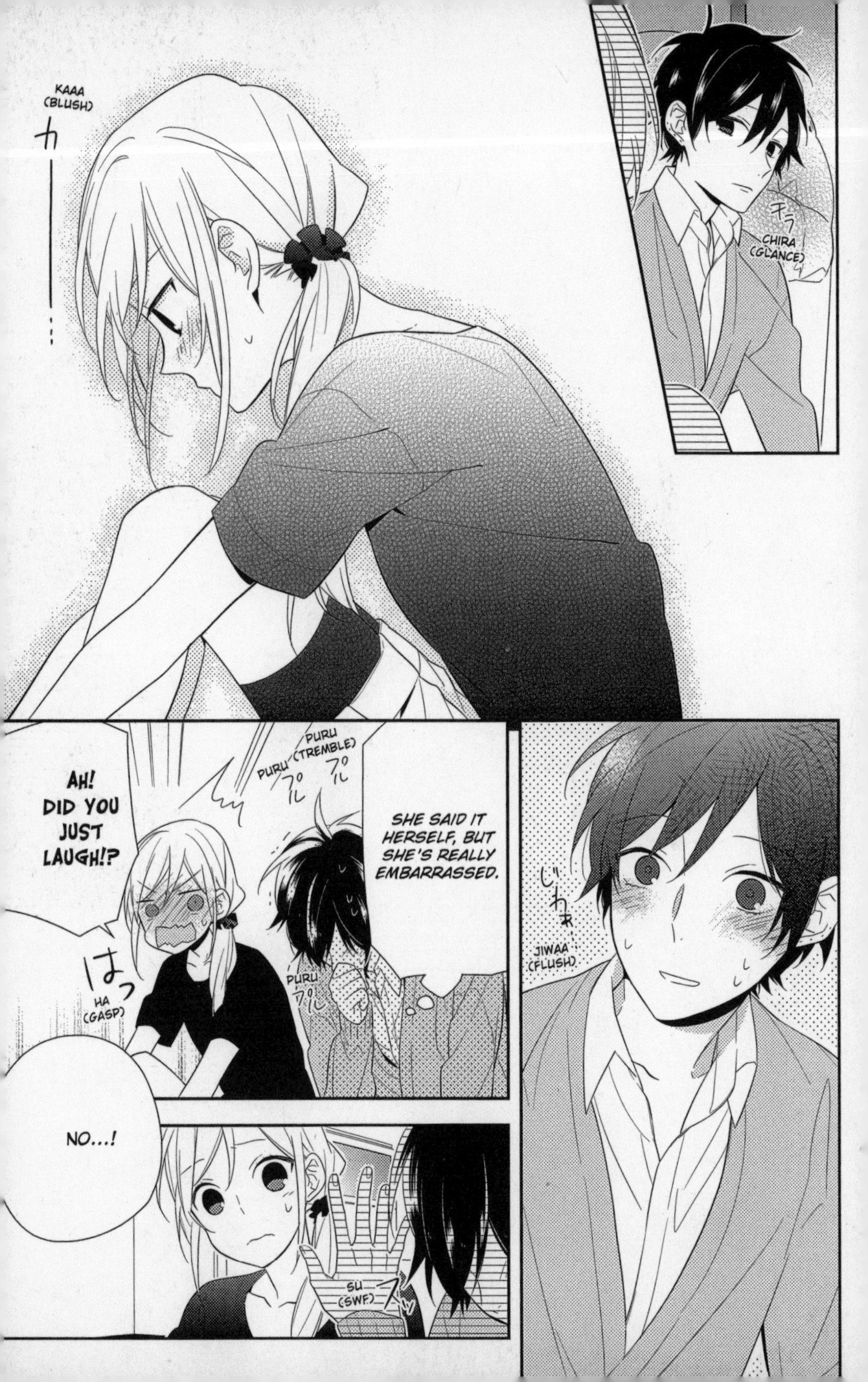
チラ
CHIRA (GLANCE)
カー…
KAAA (BLUSH)
じわぁ
JIWAA (FLUSH)
SHE SAID IT HERSELF, BUT SHE'S REALLY EMBARRASSED.
プル プル
PURU PURU (TREMBLE)
AH! DID YOU JUST LAUGH!?
はっ
HA (GASP)
プル
PURU
スッ
SU (SWF)
NO...!

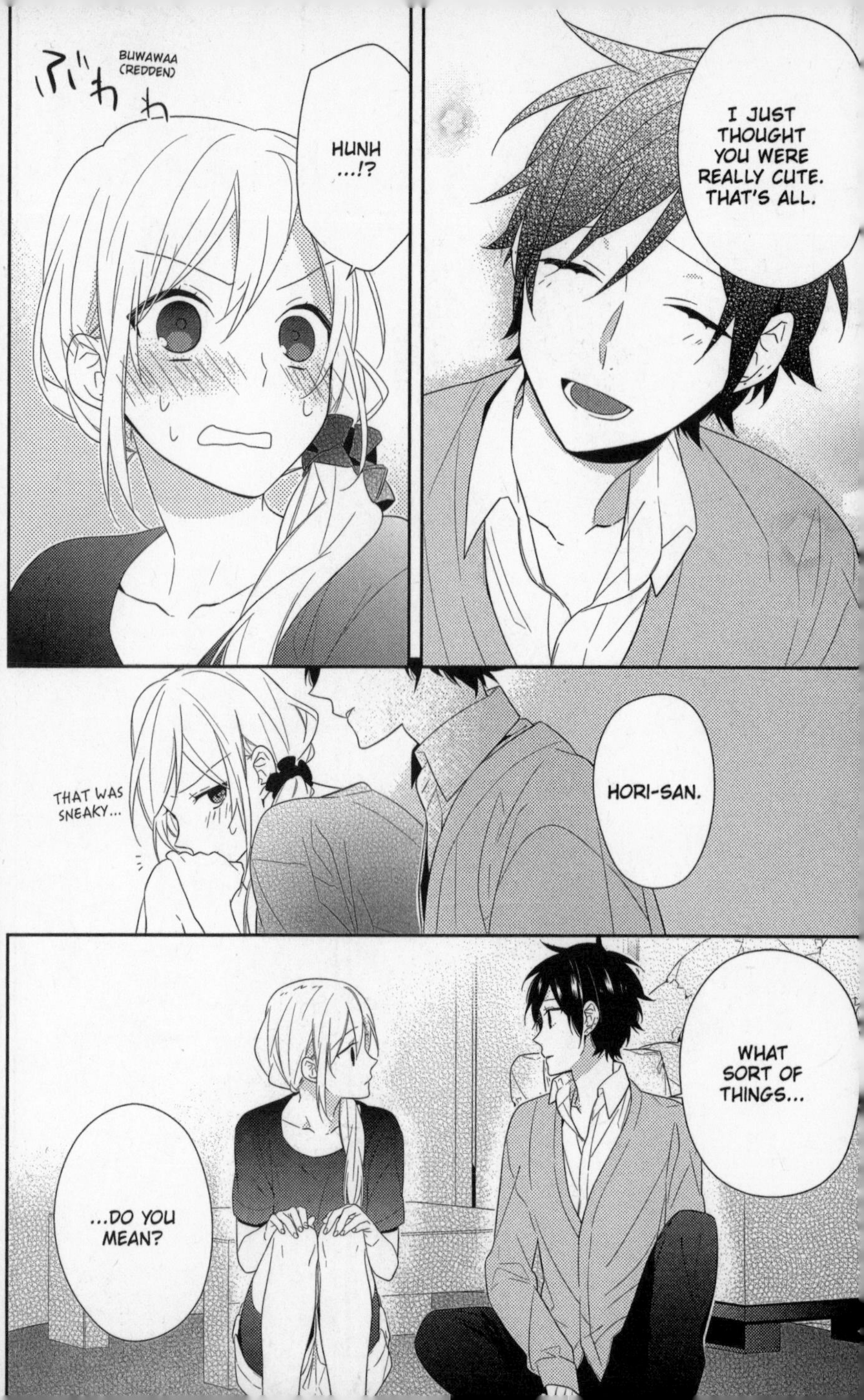
I JUST THOUGHT YOU WERE REALLY CUTE. THAT'S ALL.
ぶわわ
BUWAWAA (REDDEN)
HUNH ...!?
HORI-SAN.
THAT WAS SNEAKY...
WHAT SORT OF THINGS...
...DO YOU MEAN?

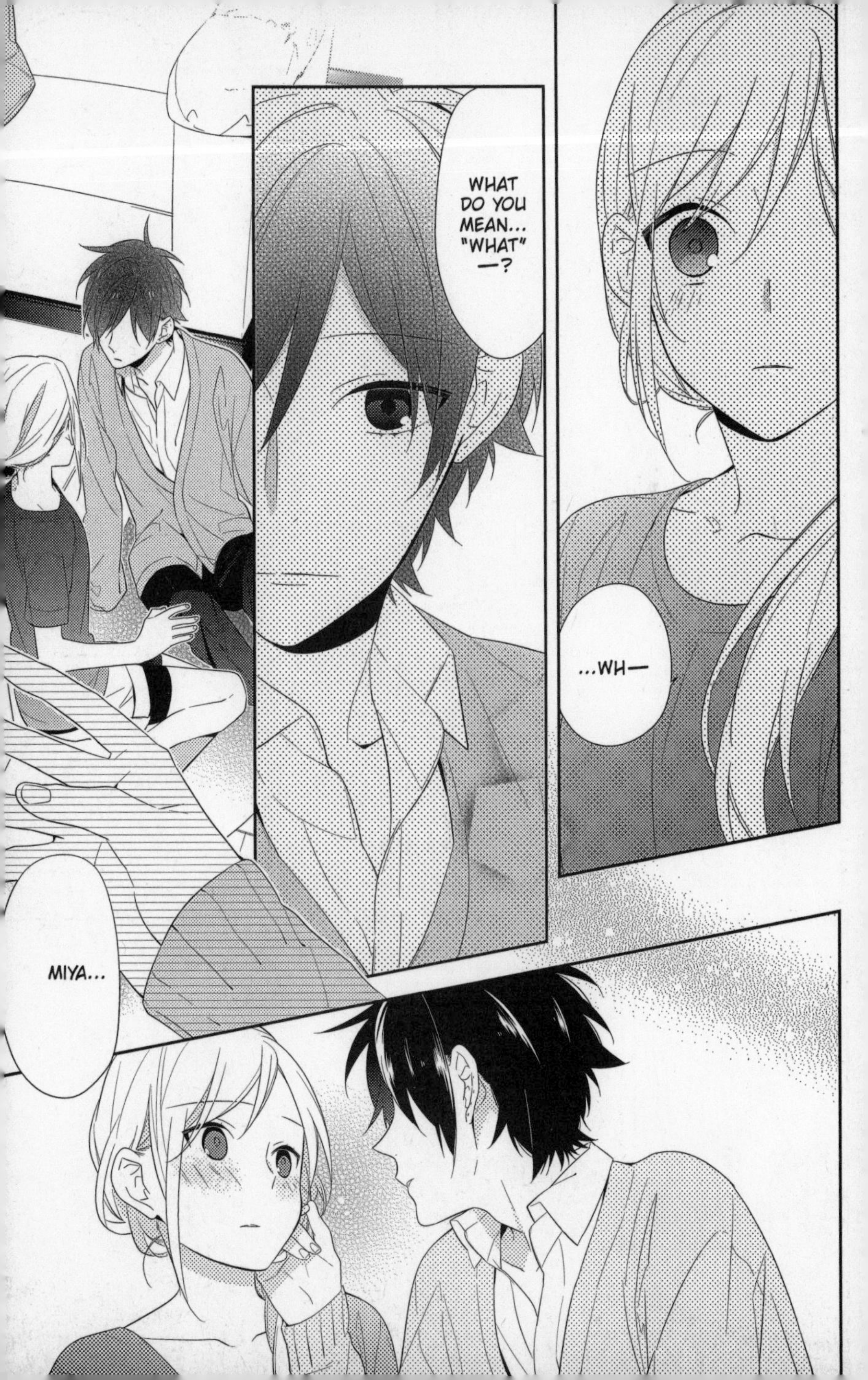
...WH—
WHAT DO YOU MEAN... "WHAT" —?
MIYA...

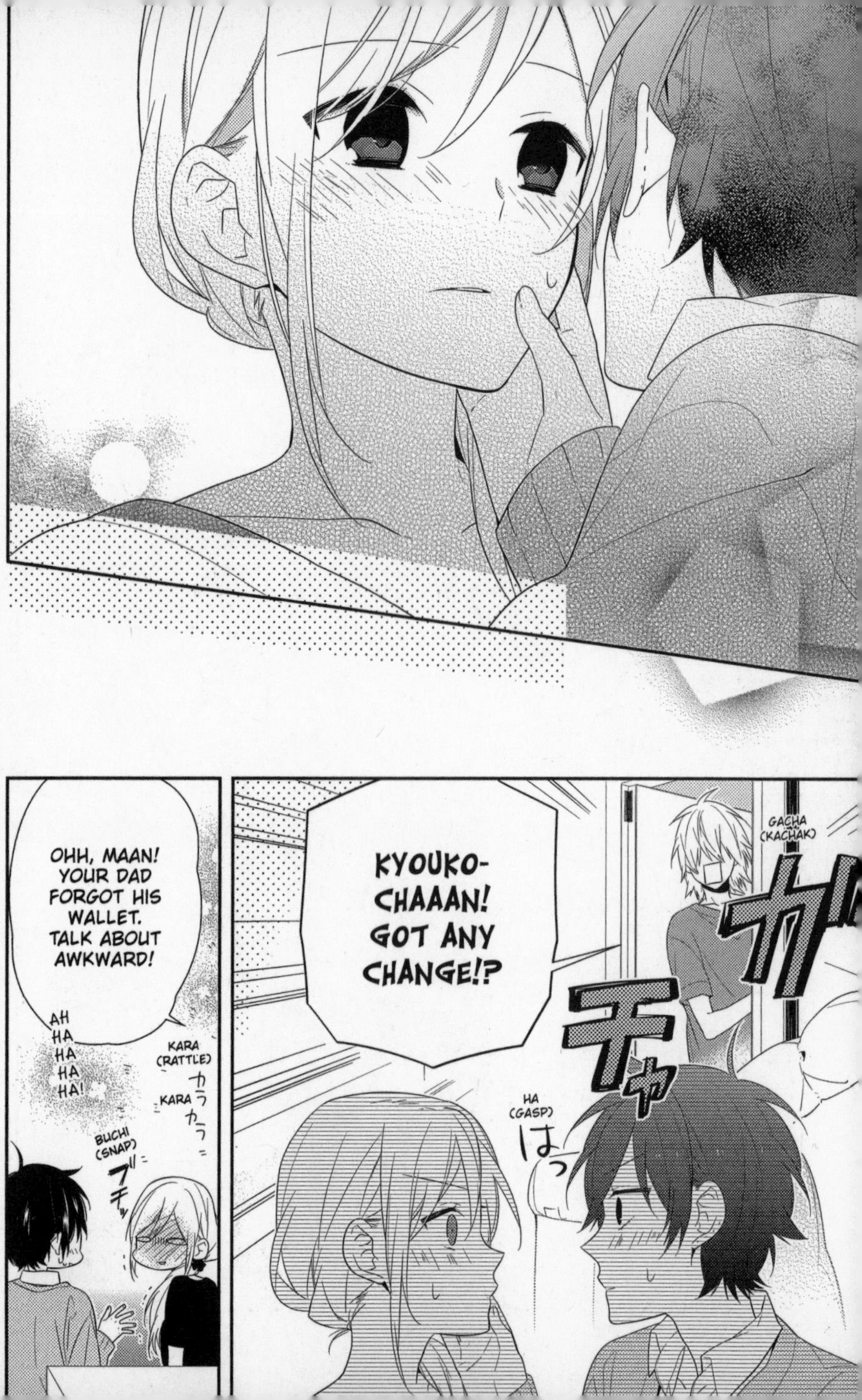
GACHA (KACHAK)
ガチャ
KYOUKO-CHAAAN! GOT ANY CHANGE!?
HA (GASP)
はっ
OHH, MAAN! YOUR DAD FORGOT HIS WALLET. TALK ABOUT AWKWARD!
AH HA HA HA HA!
KARA (RATTLE)
カラ
KARA
カラ
BUCHI (SNAP)
ブチッ

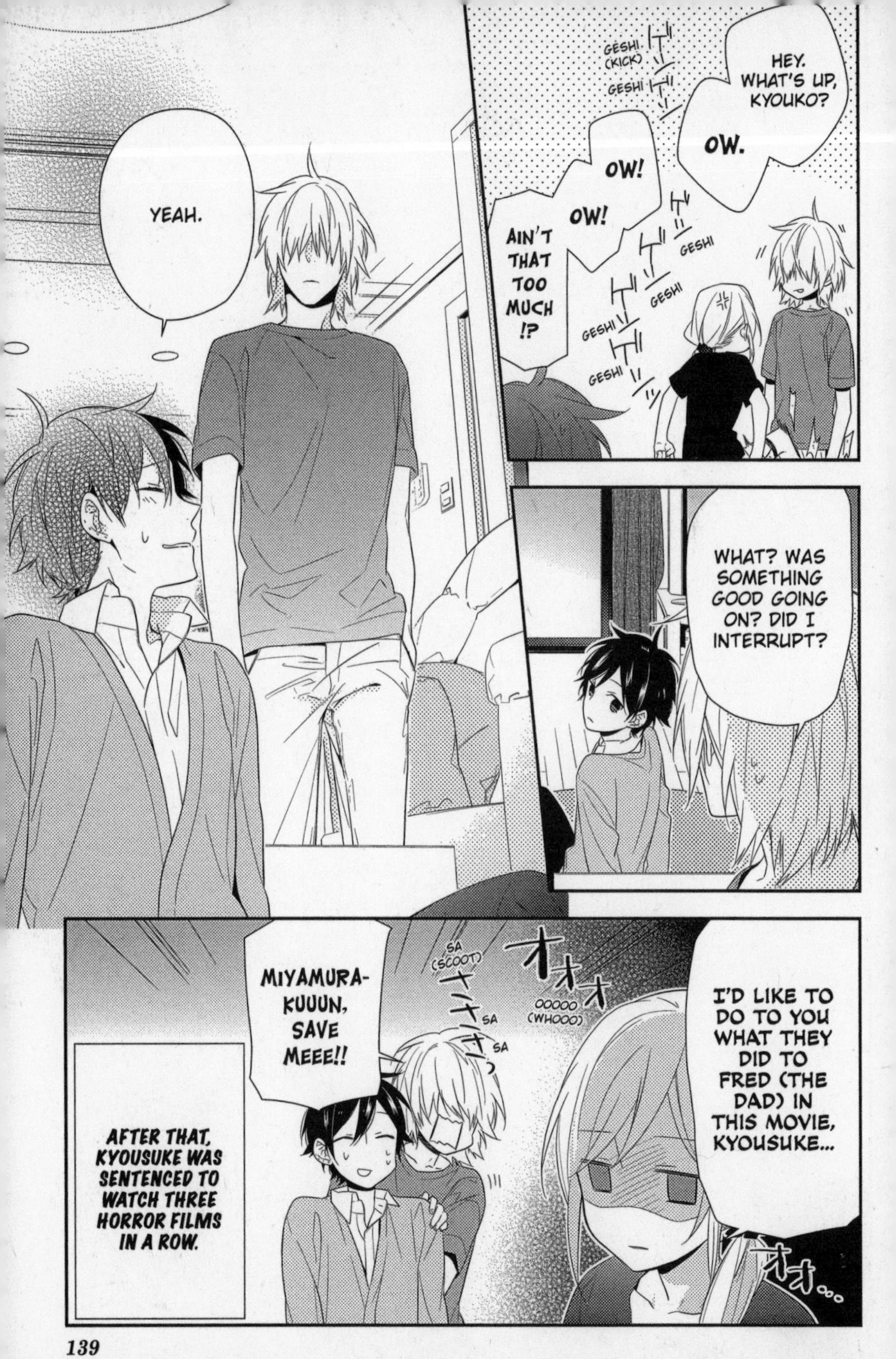
HEY. WHAT'S UP, KYOUKO?
OW.
GESHI (KICK)
GESHI
OW!
OW!
AIN'T THAT TOO MUCH !?
GESHI
GESHI
GESHI
GESHI
WHAT? WAS SOMETHING GOOD GOING ON? DID I INTERRUPT?
YEAH.
I'D LIKE TO DO TO YOU WHAT THEY DID TO FRED (THE DAD) IN THIS MOVIE, KYOUSUKE...
OOOOO (WHOOO)
SA (SCOOT)
SA
SA
MIYAMURA-KUUUN, SAVE MEEE!!
AFTER THAT, KYOUSUKE WAS SENTENCED TO WATCH THREE HORROR FILMS IN A ROW.

HORIMIYA

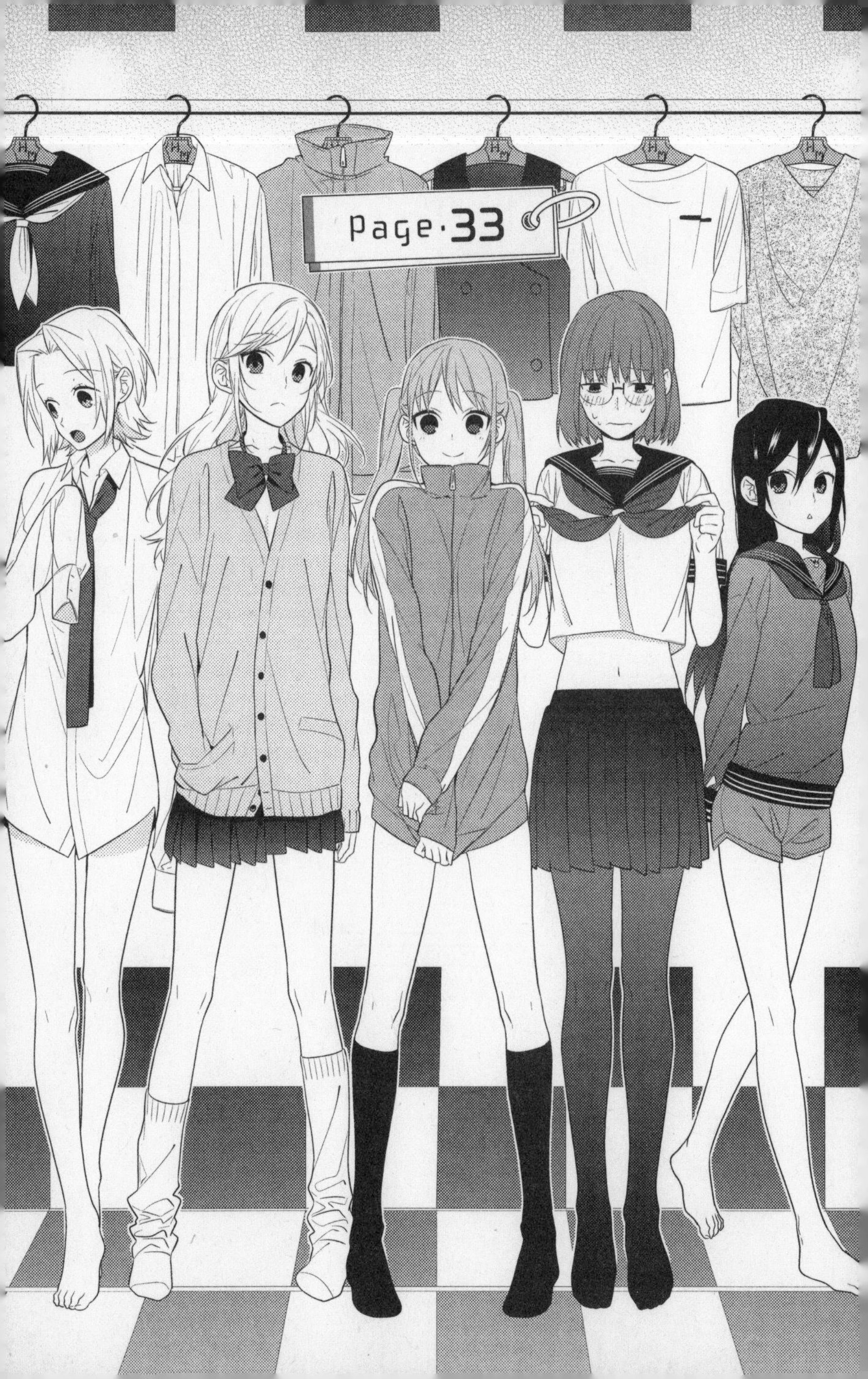
page.33

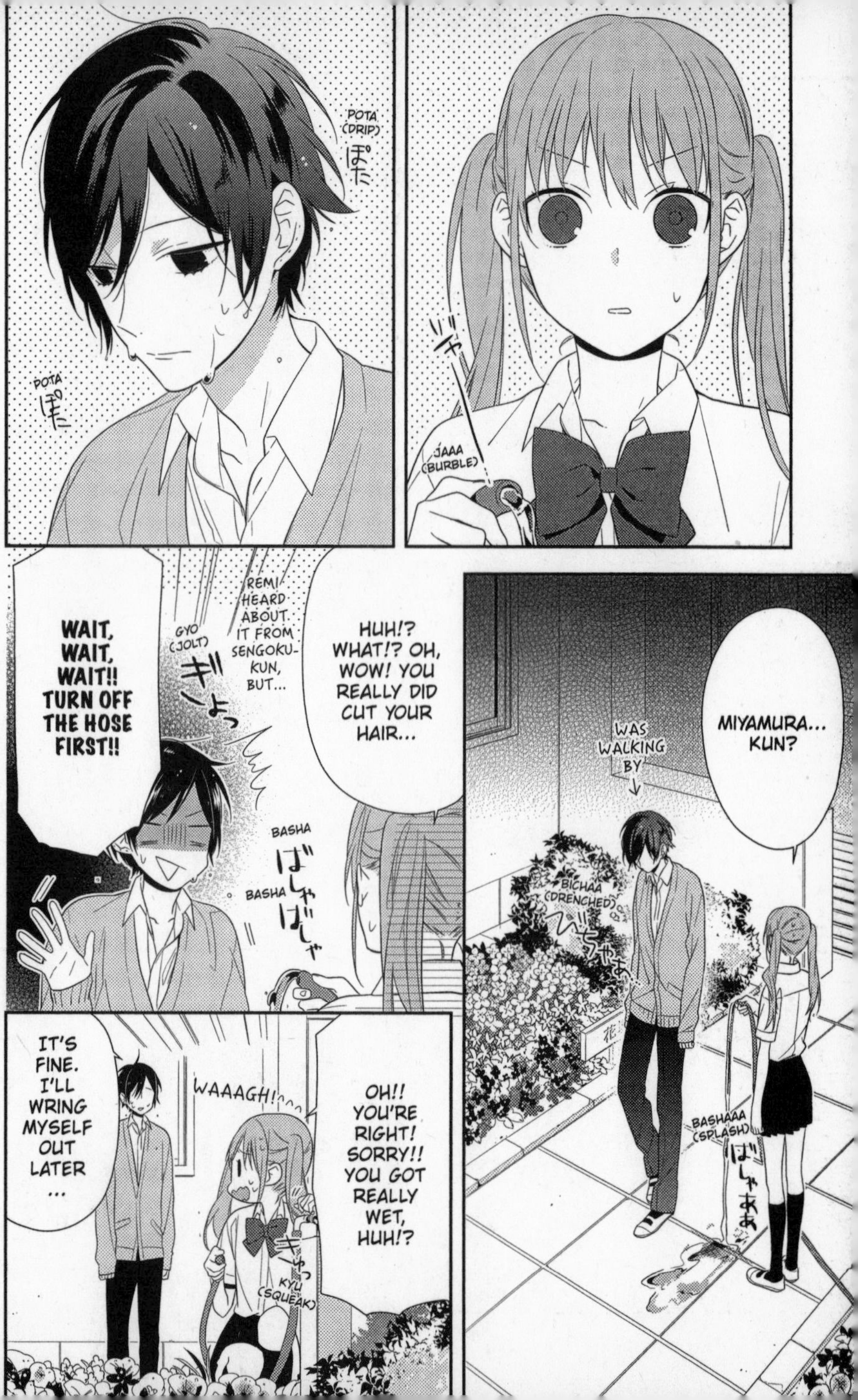
ジャ
JAAA (BURBLE)
POTA (DRIP)
ぽた
POTA
ぽた
MIYAMURA... KUN?
WAS WALKING BY ↓
BICHAA (DRENCHED)
びちゃあ
BASHAAA (SPLASH)
ばしゃあ
HUH!? WHAT!? OH, WOW! YOU REALLY DID CUT YOUR HAIR...
REMI HEARD ABOUT IT FROM SENGOKU-KUN, BUT...
GYO (JOLT)
ぎょっ
WAIT, WAIT, WAIT!! TURN OFF THE HOSE FIRST!!
BASHA
ばしゃ
BASHA
ばしゃ
OH!! YOU'RE RIGHT! SORRY!! YOU GOT REALLY WET, HUH!?
WAAAGH!
きゅっ
KYU (SQUEAK)
IT'S FINE. I'LL WRING MYSELF OUT LATER...

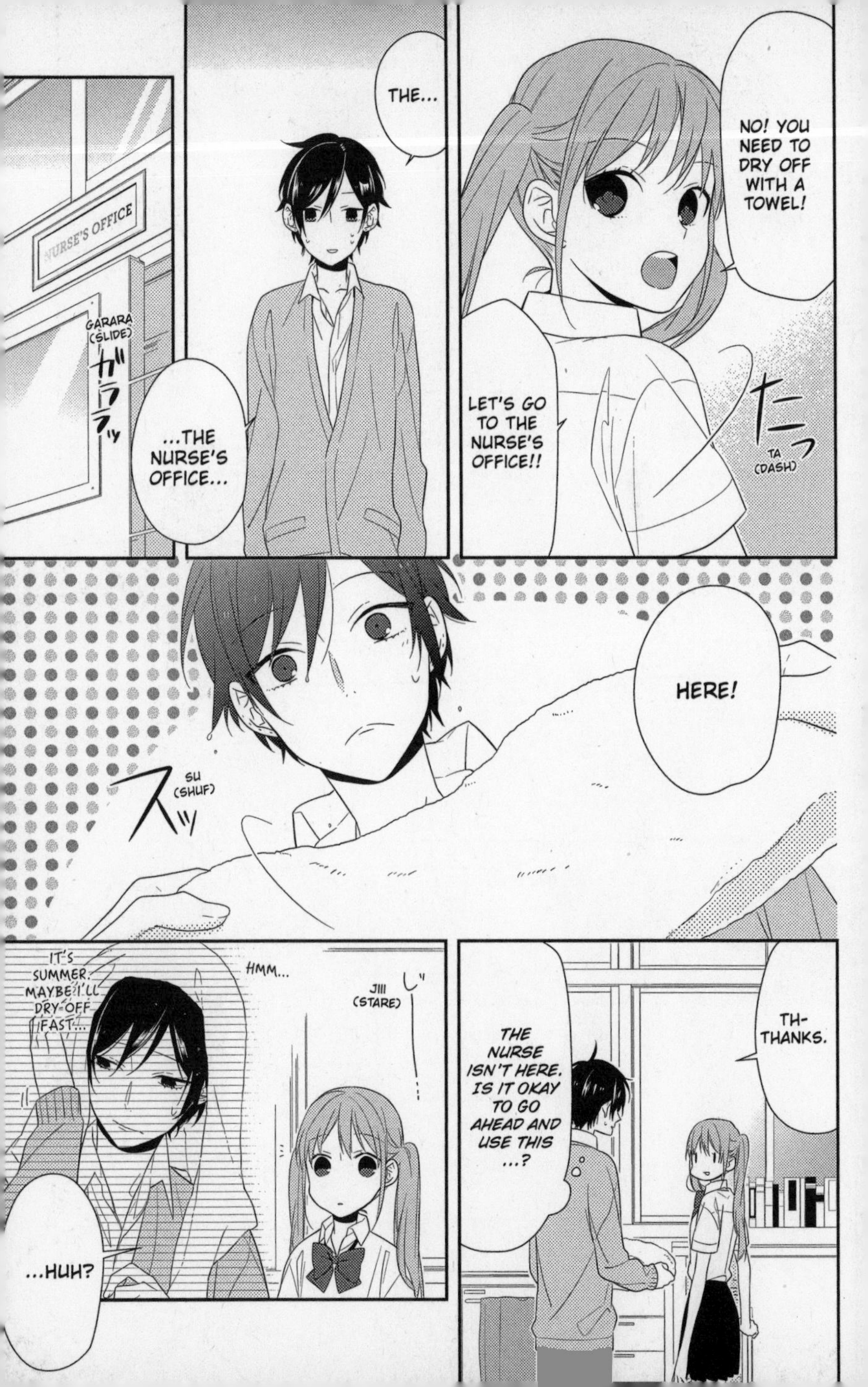
NO! YOU NEED TO DRY OFF WITH A TOWEL!
LET'S GO TO THE NURSE'S OFFICE!!
TA (DASH)
THE...
...THE NURSE'S OFFICE...
NURSE'S OFFICE
GARARA (SLIDE)
HERE!
SU (SHUF)
TH- THANKS.
THE NURSE ISN'T HERE. IS IT OKAY TO GO AHEAD AND USE THIS ...?
JIII (STARE)
HMM...
IT'S SUMMER. MAYBE I'LL DRY OFF FAST...
...HUH?

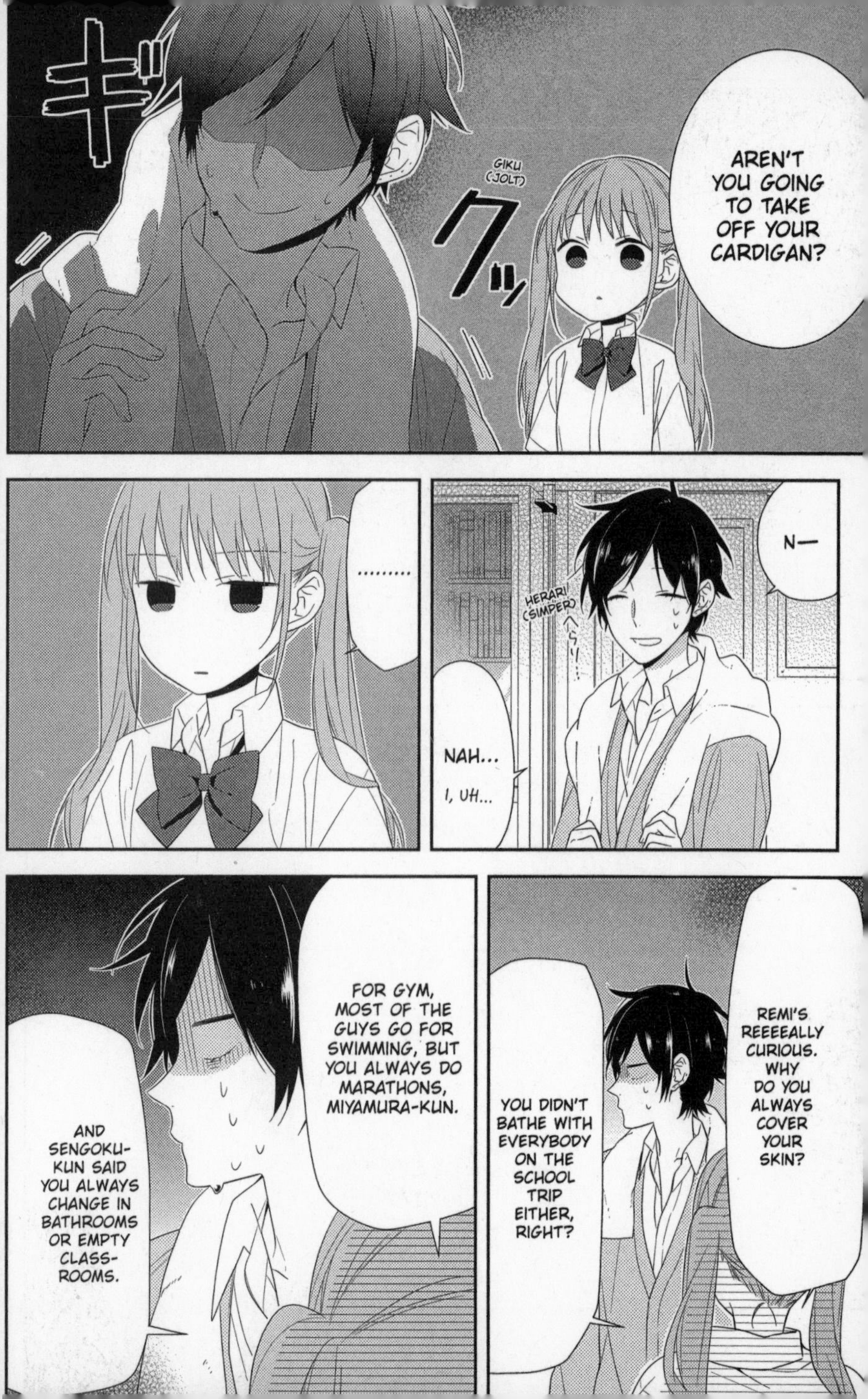
AREN'T YOU GOING TO TAKE OFF YOUR CARDIGAN?
GIKU (JOLT)
ギクッ
N—
HERARI (SIMPER)
NAH... I, UH...
....
REMI'S REEEEALLY CURIOUS. WHY DO YOU ALWAYS COVER YOUR SKIN?
YOU DIDN'T BATHE WITH EVERYBODY ON THE SCHOOL TRIP EITHER, RIGHT?
FOR GYM, MOST OF THE GUYS GO FOR SWIMMING, BUT YOU ALWAYS DO MARATHONS, MIYAMURA-KUN.
AND SENGOKU-KUN SAID YOU ALWAYS CHANGE IN BATHROOMS OR EMPTY CLASS-ROOMS.

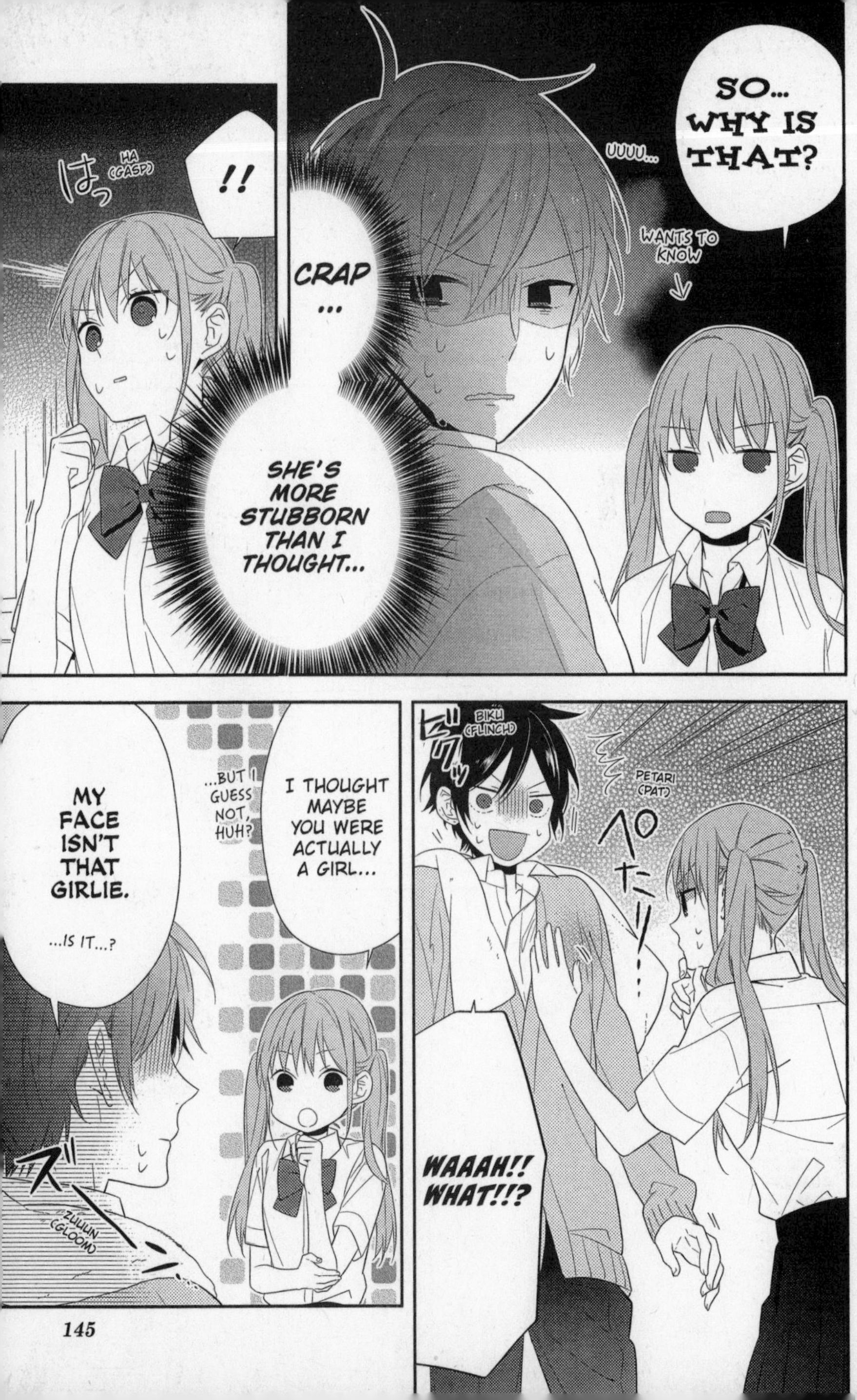
SO... WHY IS THAT?
UUUU...
WANTS TO KNOW
CRAP...
SHE'S MORE STUBBORN THAN I THOUGHT...
はっ
HA (GASP)
!!
BIKU (FLINCH)
PETARI (PAT)
WAAAH!! WHAT!!?
I THOUGHT MAYBE YOU WERE ACTUALLY A GIRL...
...BUT I GUESS NOT, HUH?
MY FACE ISN'T THAT GIRLIE.
...IS IT...?
ZUUUN (GLOOM)

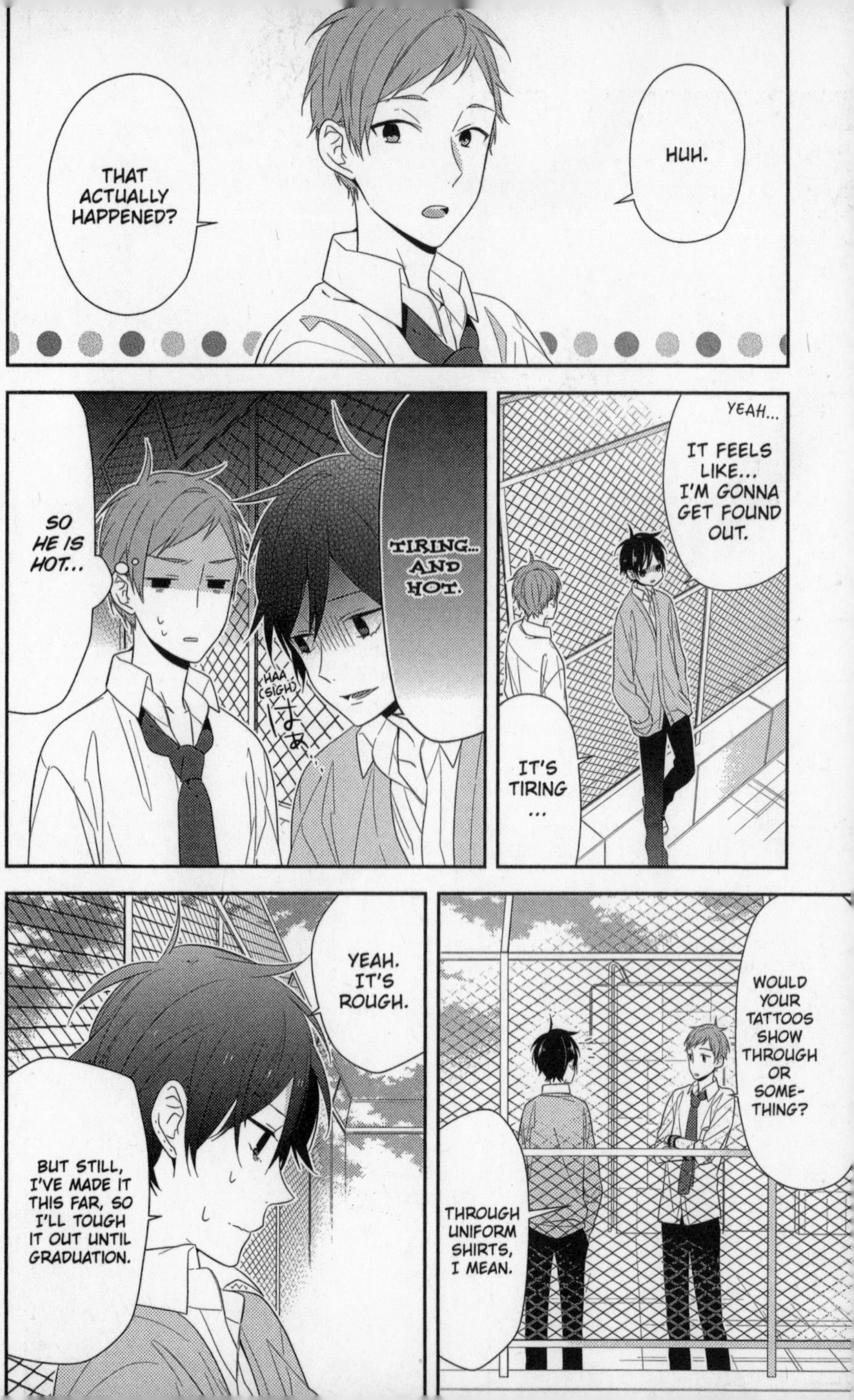
HUH.
THAT ACTUALLY HAPPENED?
YEAH... IT FEELS LIKE... I'M GONNA GET FOUND OUT.
IT'S TIRING ...
TIRING... AND HOT.
HAA (SIGH)
はぁ…
SO HE IS HOT...
WOULD YOUR TATTOOS SHOW THROUGH OR SOME-THING?
THROUGH UNIFORM SHIRTS, I MEAN.
YEAH. IT'S ROUGH.
BUT STILL, I'VE MADE IT THIS FAR, SO I'LL TOUGH IT OUT UNTIL GRADUATION.

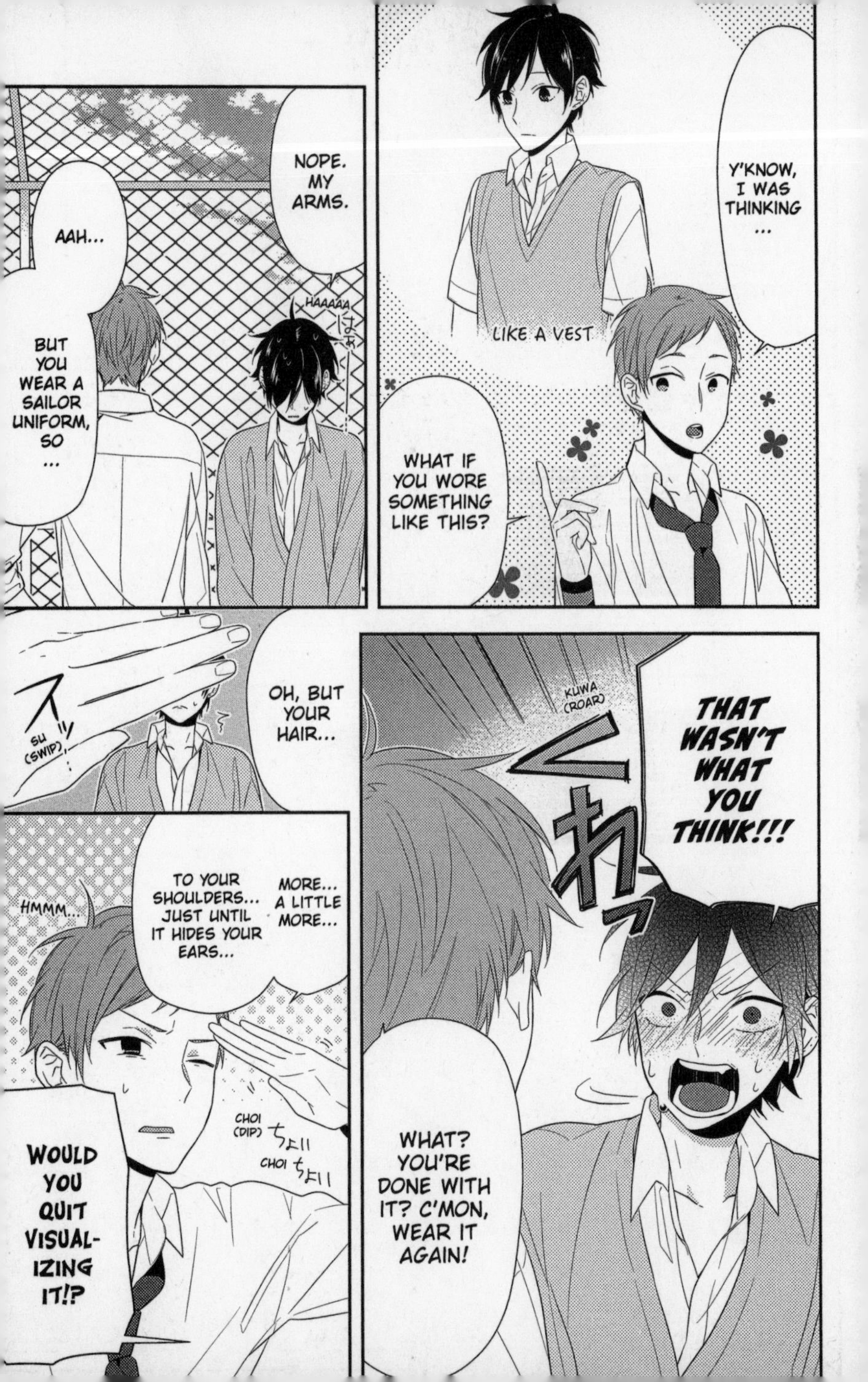
Y'KNOW, I WAS THINKING ...
LIKE A VEST
WHAT IF YOU WORE SOMETHING LIKE THIS?
NOPE. MY ARMS.
HAAAAA
AAH...
BUT YOU WEAR A SAILOR UNIFORM, SO ...
KUWA (ROAR)
THAT WASN'T WHAT YOU THINK!!!
WHAT? YOU'RE DONE WITH IT? C'MON, WEAR IT AGAIN!
OH, BUT YOUR HAIR...
SU (SWIP)
MORE... A LITTLE MORE...
TO YOUR SHOULDERS... JUST UNTIL IT HIDES YOUR EARS...
HMMM...
CHOI (DIP)
CHOI
WOULD YOU QUIT VISUALIZING IT!?

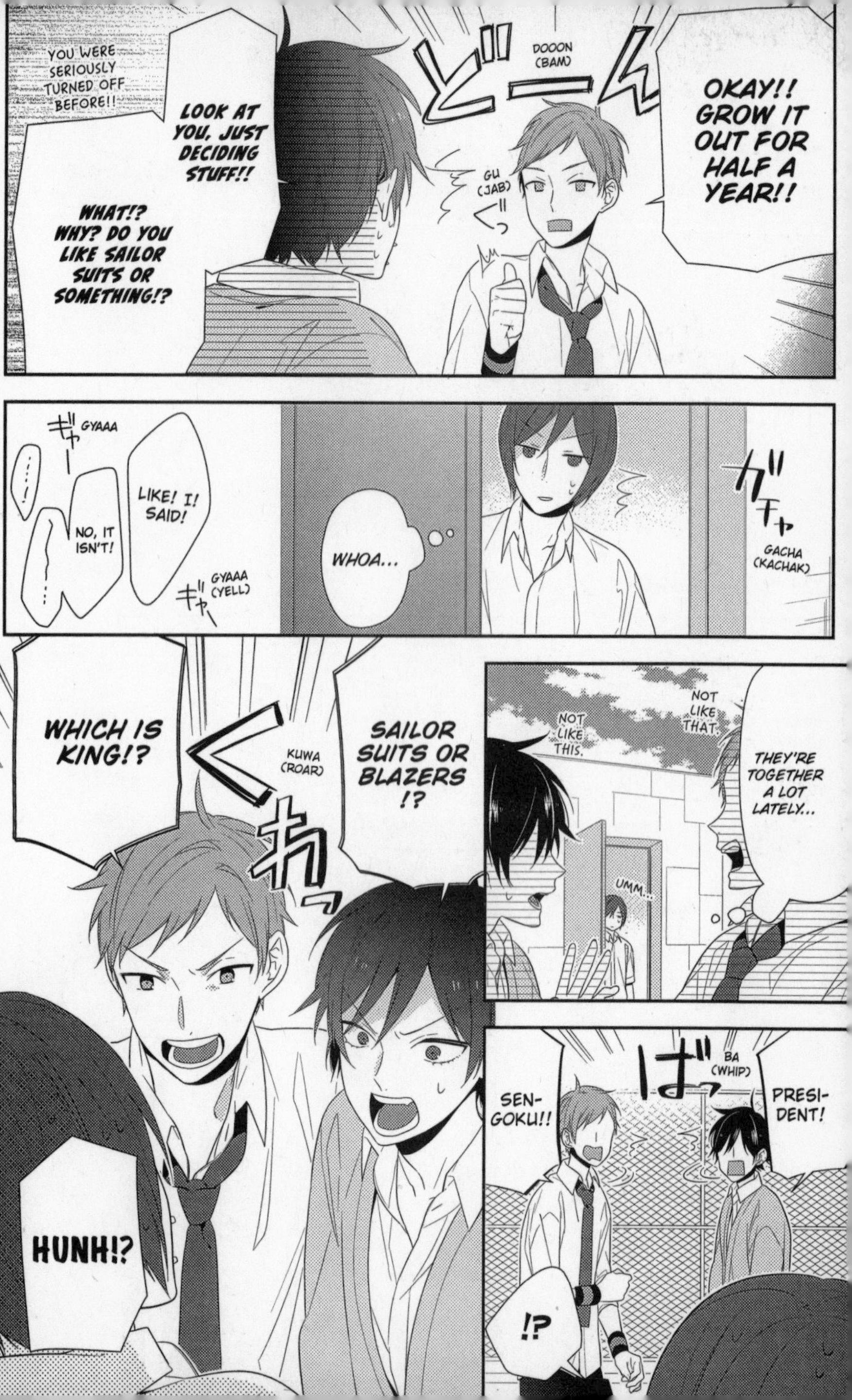
OKAY!! GROW IT OUT FOR HALF A YEAR!!
どーん
DOOON (BAM)
ぐっ
GU (JAB)
LOOK AT YOU, JUST DECIDING STUFF!!
YOU WERE SERIOUSLY TURNED OFF BEFORE!!
WHAT!? WHY? DO YOU LIKE SAILOR SUITS OR SOMETHING!?
ガチャ
GACHA (KACHAK)
WHOA...
LIKE! I! SAID!
ギャー
GYAAA
NO, IT ISN'T!
ギャ
GYAAA (YELL)
THEY'RE TOGETHER A LOT LATELY...
NOT LIKE THAT.
NOT LIKE THIS.
UMM...
PRESI-DENT!
ばっ
BA (WHIP)
SEN-GOKU!!
!?
SAILOR SUITS OR BLAZERS!?
くわっ
KUWA (ROAR)
WHICH IS KING!?
HUNH!?

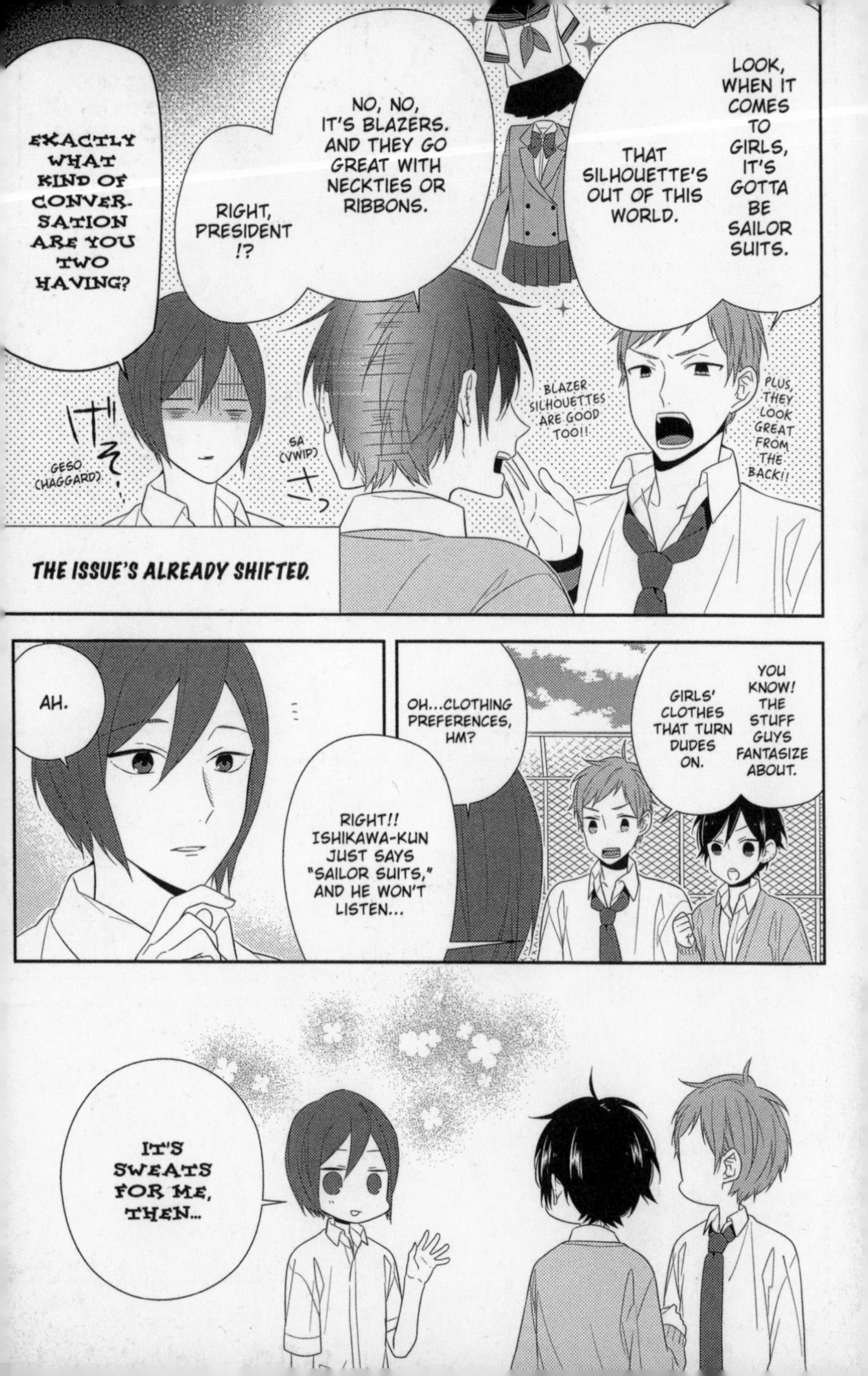
LOOK, WHEN IT COMES TO GIRLS, IT'S GOTTA BE SAILOR SUITS.
THAT SILHOUETTE'S OUT OF THIS WORLD.
NO, NO, IT'S BLAZERS. AND THEY GO GREAT WITH NECKTIES OR RIBBONS.
RIGHT, PRESIDENT!?
EXACTLY WHAT KIND OF CONVERSATION ARE YOU TWO HAVING?
PLUS, THEY LOOK GREAT FROM THE BACK!!
BLAZER SILHOUETTES ARE GOOD TOO!!
SA (VWIP)
GESO (HAGGARD)
THE ISSUE'S ALREADY SHIFTED.
YOU KNOW! THE STUFF GUYS FANTASIZE ABOUT.
GIRLS' CLOTHES THAT TURN DUDES ON.
OH...CLOTHING PREFERENCES, HM?
RIGHT!! ISHIKAWA-KUN JUST SAYS "SAILOR SUITS," AND HE WON'T LISTEN...
AH.
IT'S SWEATS FOR ME, THEN...

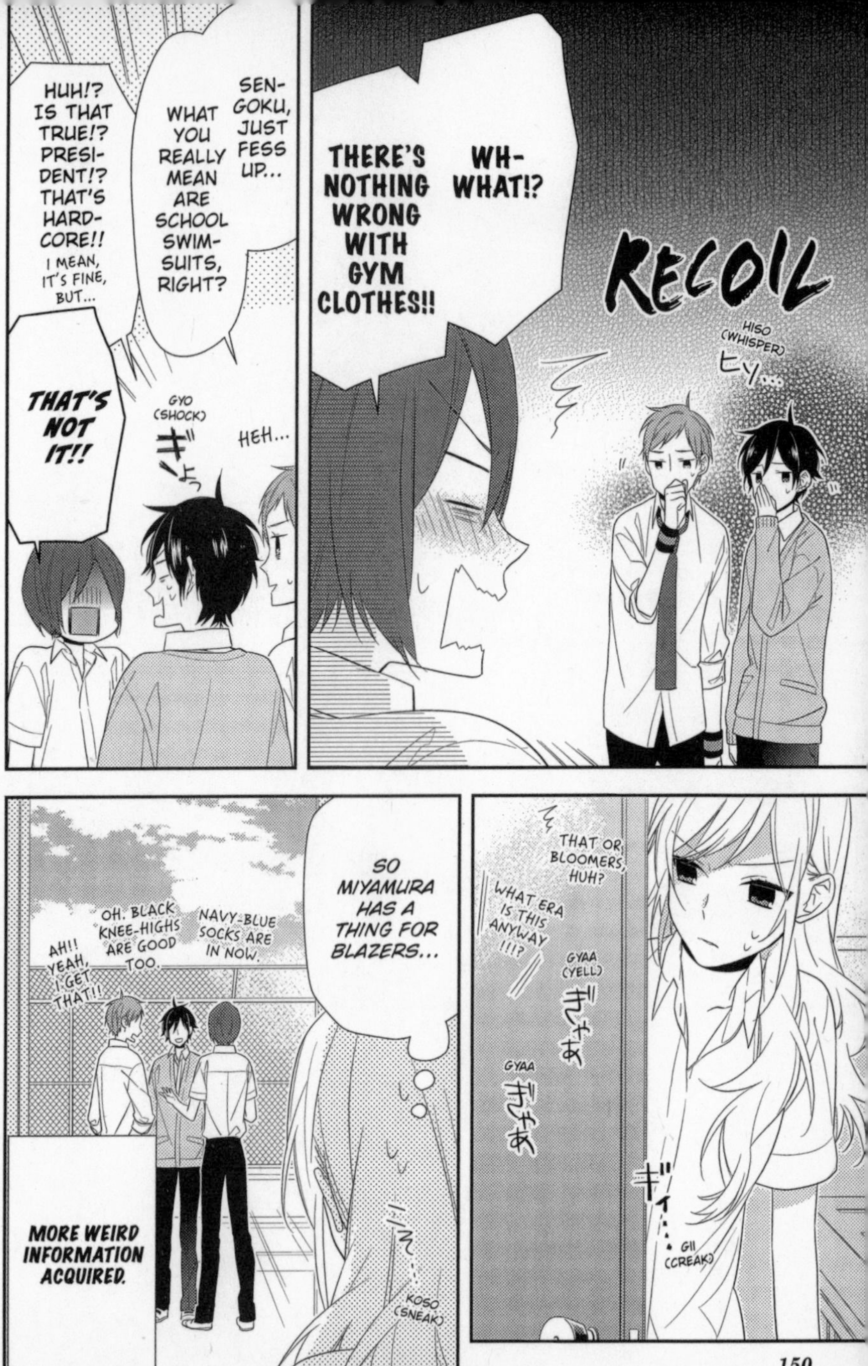

WH-WHAT!?
THERE'S NOTHING WRONG WITH GYM CLOTHES!!
RECOIL
HISO (WHISPER)
ヒソ…
SEN-GOKU, JUST FESS UP...
WHAT YOU REALLY MEAN ARE SCHOOL SWIM-SUITS, RIGHT?
HUH!? IS THAT TRUE!? PRESI-DENT!? THAT'S HARD-CORE!!
I MEAN, IT'S FINE, BUT...
HEH...
GYO (SHOCK)
ギョ
THAT'S NOT IT!!
THAT OR BLOOMERS, HUH?
WHAT ERA IS THIS ANYWAY!!!?
GYAA (YELL)
ぎゃあ
GYAA
ぎゃあ
ギィ…
GII (CREAK)
SO MIYAMURA HAS A THING FOR BLAZERS...
こそ…
KOSO (SNEAK)
NAVY-BLUE SOCKS ARE IN NOW.
OH. BLACK KNEE-HIGHS ARE GOOD TOO.
AH!! YEAH, I GET THAT!!
MORE WEIRD INFORMATION ACQUIRED.

HORIMIYA

HORIMIYA

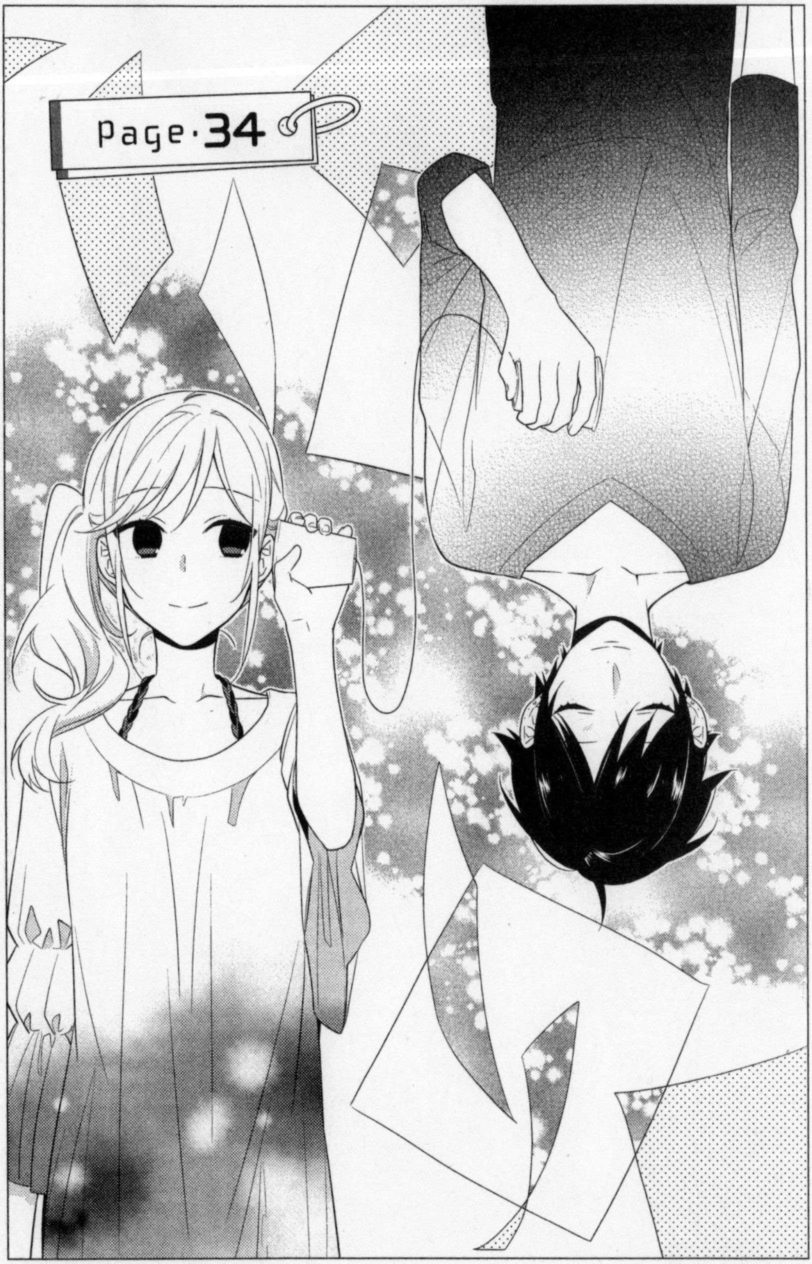
Page.34

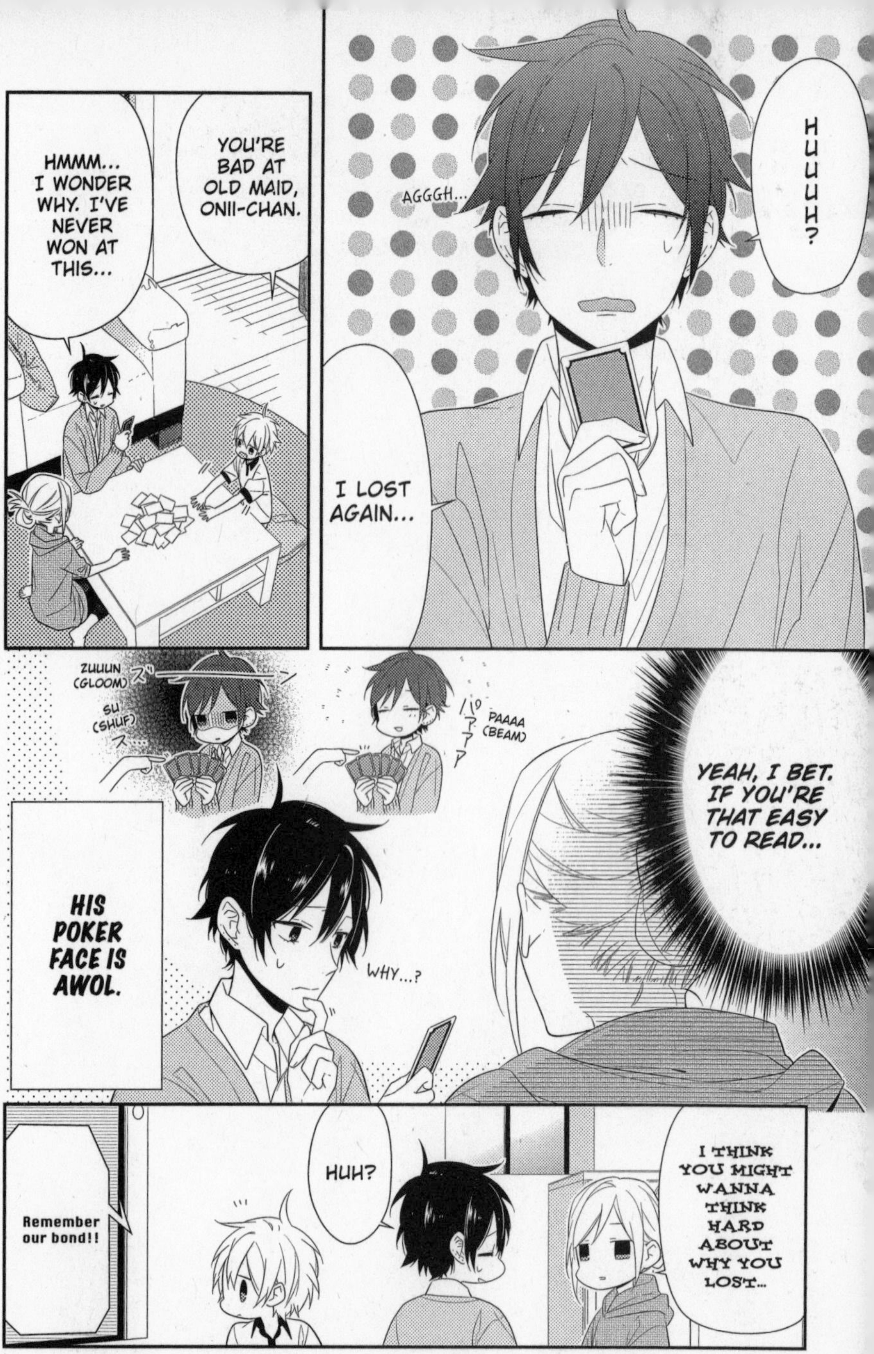
HUUUH?
AGGGH...
I LOST AGAIN...
YOU'RE BAD AT OLD MAID, ONII-CHAN.
HMMM... I WONDER WHY. I'VE NEVER WON AT THIS...
YEAH, I BET. IF YOU'RE THAT EASY TO READ...
PAAAA (BEAM)
ZUUUN (GLOOM)
SU (SHUF)
HIS POKER FACE IS AWOL.
WHY...?
I THINK YOU MIGHT WANNA THINK HARD ABOUT WHY YOU LOST...
HUH?
Remember our bond!!

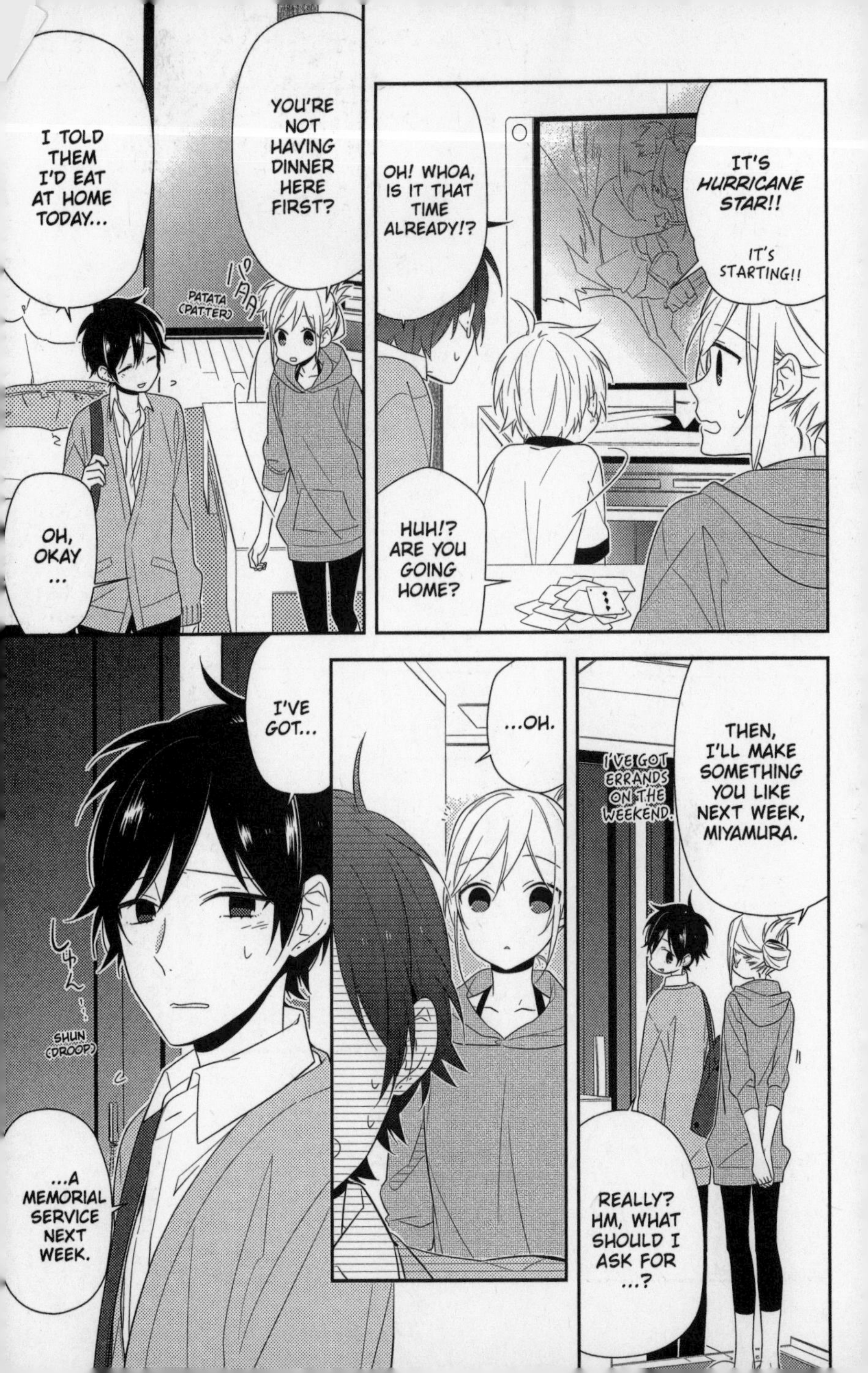
IT'S HURRICANE STAR!!
IT'S STARTING!!
OH! WHOA, IS IT THAT TIME ALREADY!?
HUH!? ARE YOU GOING HOME?
YOU'RE NOT HAVING DINNER HERE FIRST?
PATATA (PATTER)
I TOLD THEM I'D EAT AT HOME TODAY...
OH, OKAY ...
THEN, I'LL MAKE SOMETHING YOU LIKE NEXT WEEK, MIYAMURA.
I'VE GOT ERRANDS ON THE WEEKEND.
REALLY? HM, WHAT SHOULD I ASK FOR ...?
...OH.
I'VE GOT...
SHUN (DROOP)
...A MEMORIAL SERVICE NEXT WEEK.

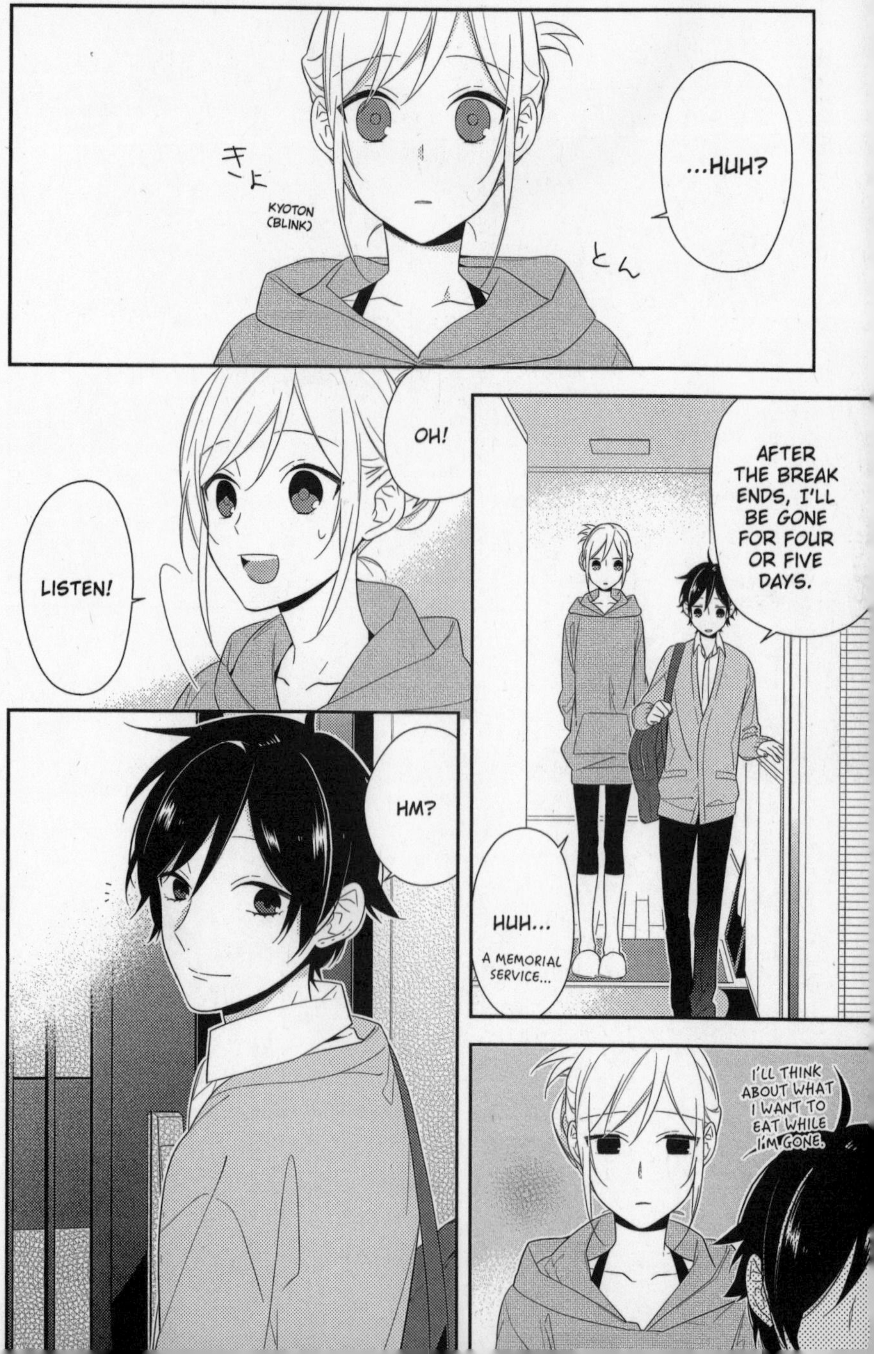

…HUH?
きょ
KYOTON (BLINK)
とん
AFTER THE BREAK ENDS, I'LL BE GONE FOR FOUR OR FIVE DAYS.
HUH… A MEMORIAL SERVICE…
OH!
LISTEN!
HM?
I'LL THINK ABOUT WHAT I WANT TO EAT WHILE I'M GONE.

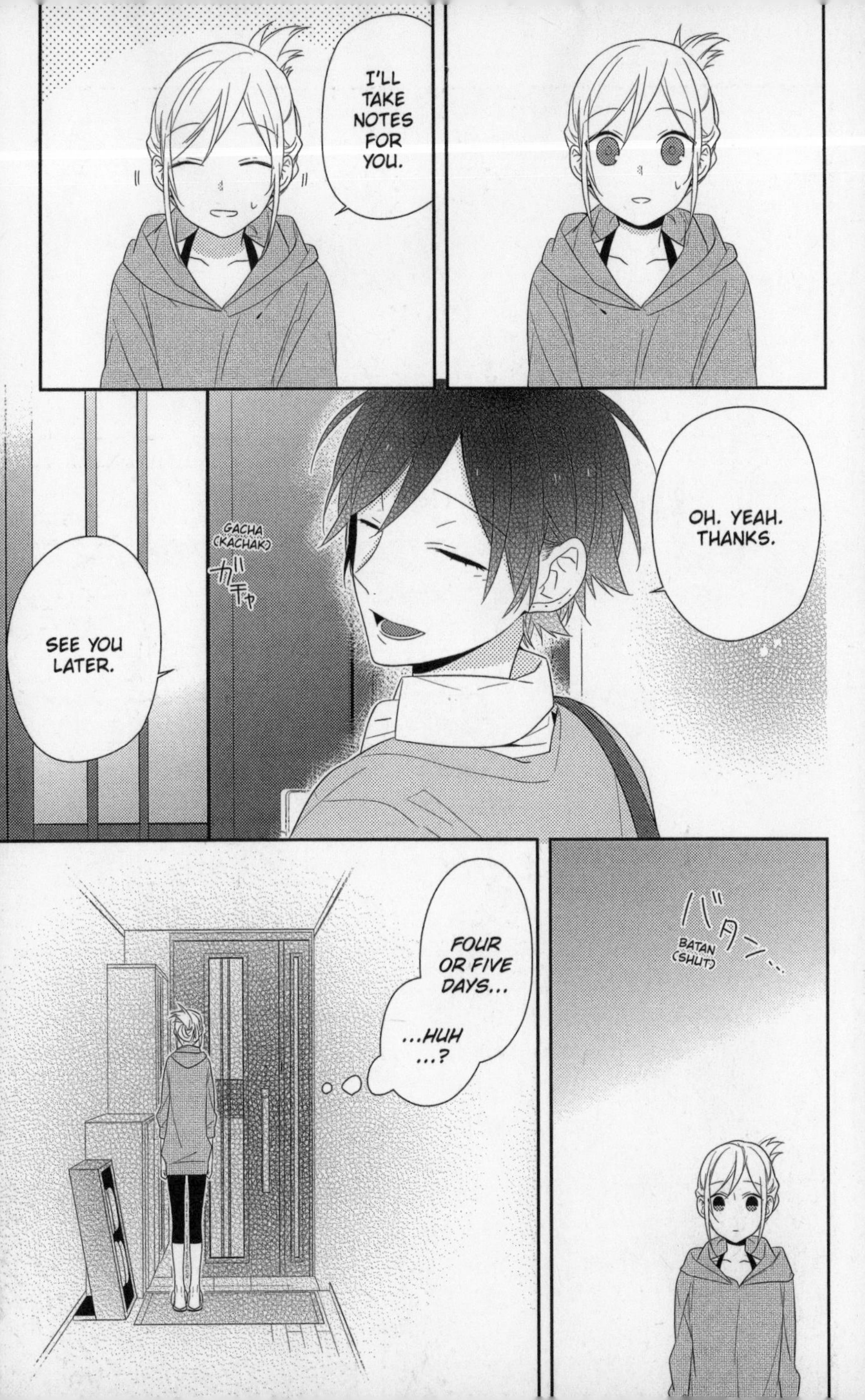
I'LL TAKE NOTES FOR YOU.
OH. YEAH. THANKS.
GACHA (KACHAK)
ガチャ
SEE YOU LATER.
バタン…
BATAN (SHUT)
FOUR OR FIVE DAYS...
...HUH ...?

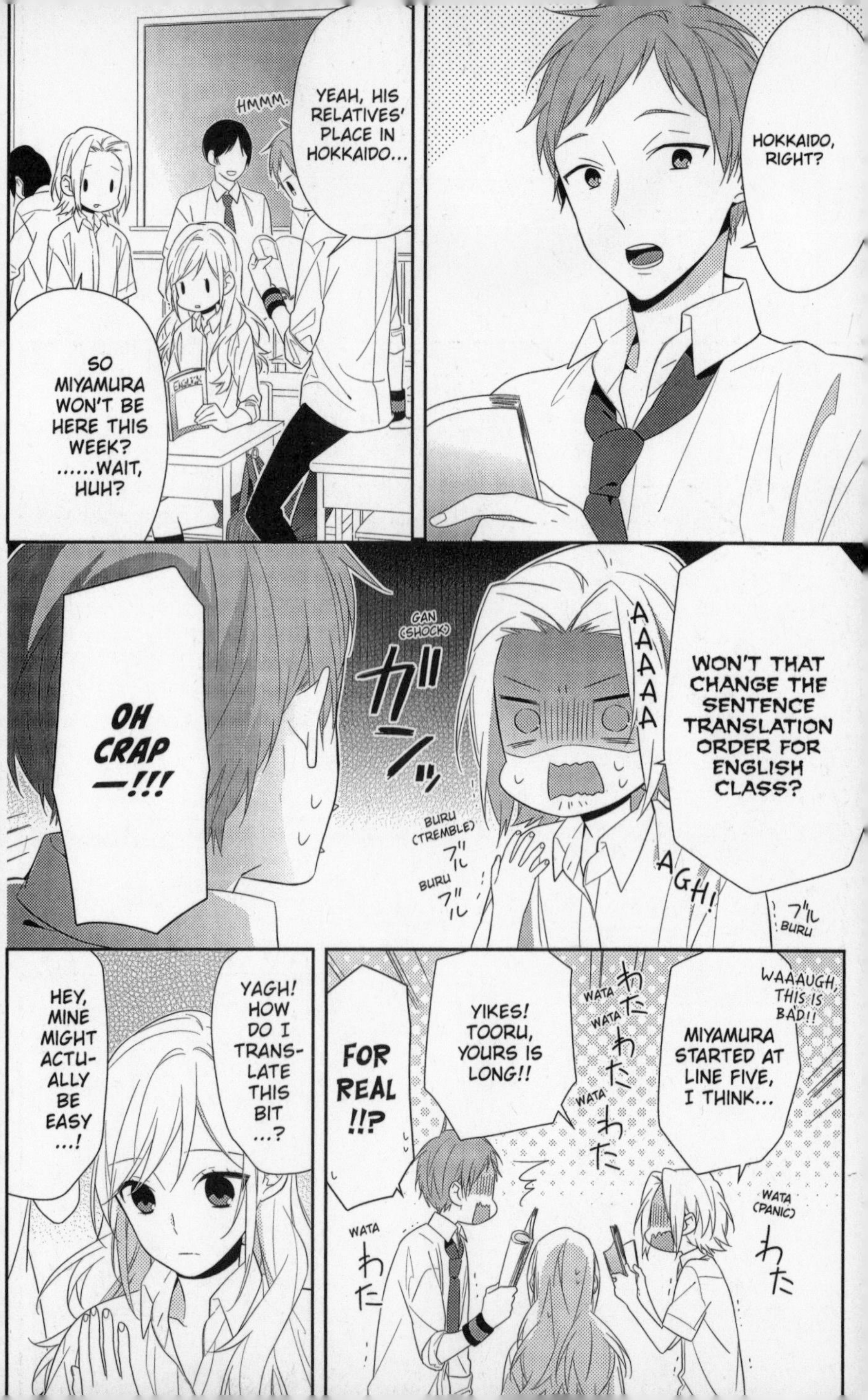
HOKKAIDO, RIGHT?
YEAH, HIS RELATIVES' PLACE IN HOKKAIDO...
HMMM.
SO MIYAMURA WON'T BE HERE THIS WEEK? ......WAIT, HUH?
ENGLISH
WON'T THAT CHANGE THE SENTENCE TRANSLATION ORDER FOR ENGLISH CLASS?
AAAAA
AGH!
ブル
BURU
ガーンッ
GAN (SHOCK)
ブル BURU (TREMBLE)
ブル BURU
OH CRAP—!!!
WAAAUGH, THIS IS BAD!!
MIYAMURA STARTED AT LINE FIVE, I THINK...
わた
WATA (PANIC)
わた わた わた
WATA
WATA
WATA
YIKES! TOORU, YOURS IS LONG!!
FOR REAL!!?
わた
WATA
YAGH! HOW DO I TRANS-LATE THIS BIT...?
HEY, MINE MIGHT ACTU-ALLY BE EASY...!

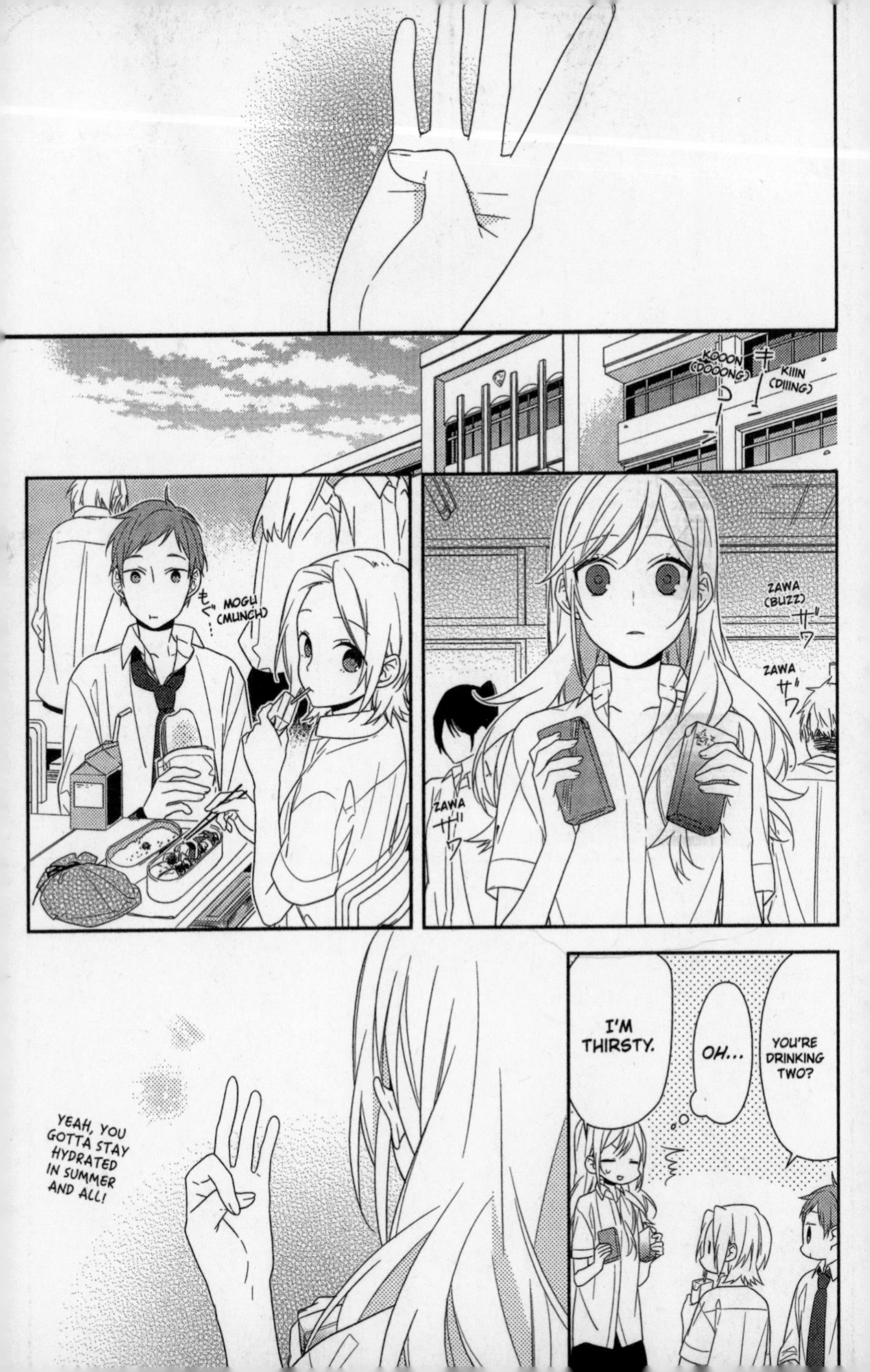
KIIN (DIIING)
KOOON (DOOONG)
ZAWA (BUZZ)
ZAWA
ZAWA
MOGU (MUNCH)
YOU'RE DRINKING TWO?
OH...
I'M THIRSTY.
YEAH, YOU GOTTA STAY HYDRATED IN SUMMER AND ALL!

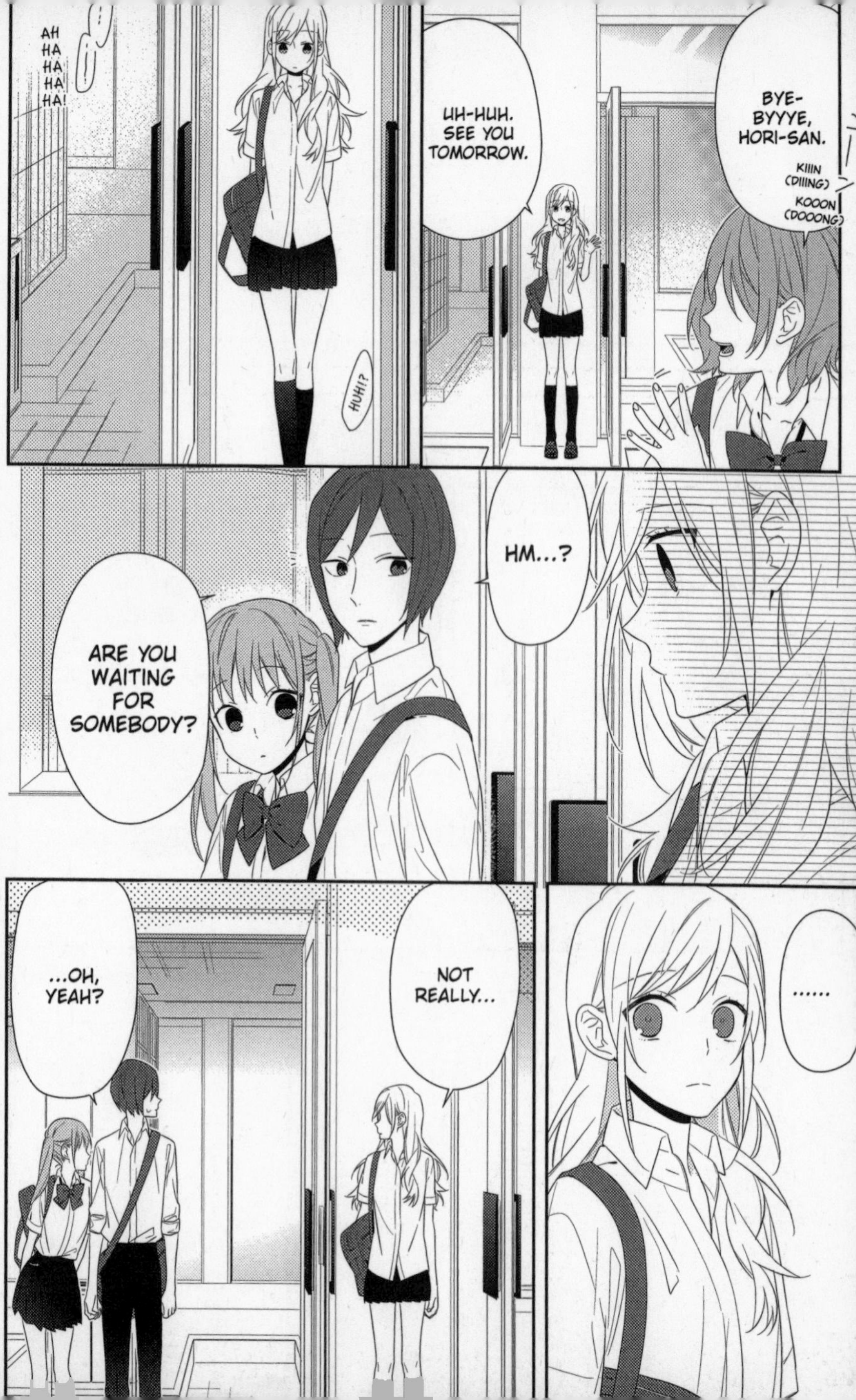
BYE-BYYYE, HORI-SAN.
KIIN (DIIING)
KOOON (DOOONG)
UH-HUH. SEE YOU TOMORROW.
AH HA HA HA HA!
HUH!?
HM...?
ARE YOU WAITING FOR SOMEBODY?
......
NOT REALLY...
...OH, YEAH?

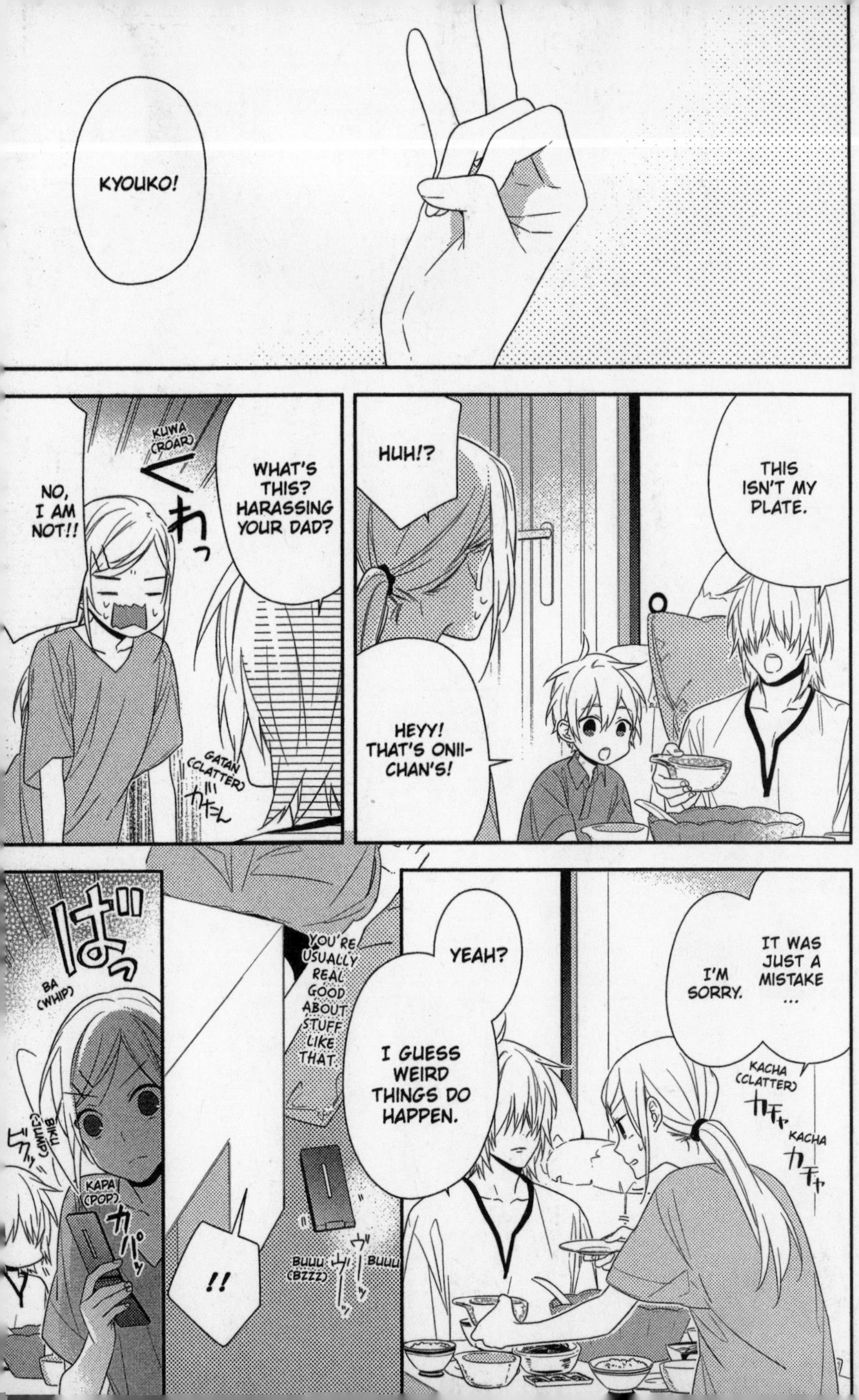
KYOUKO!
THIS ISN'T MY PLATE.
HUH!?
HEYY! THAT'S ONII-CHAN'S!
WHAT'S THIS? HARASSING YOUR DAD?
KUWA (ROAR)
NO, I AM NOT!!
GATAN (CLATTER)
IT WAS JUST A MISTAKE ...
I'M SORRY.
YEAH?
KACHA (CLATTER)
KACHA
I GUESS WEIRD THINGS DO HAPPEN.
YOU'RE USUALLY REAL GOOD ABOUT STUFF LIKE THAT.
!!
BUUU (BZZZ)
BUUU
BA (WHIP)
BIKU (JUMP)
KAPA (POP)

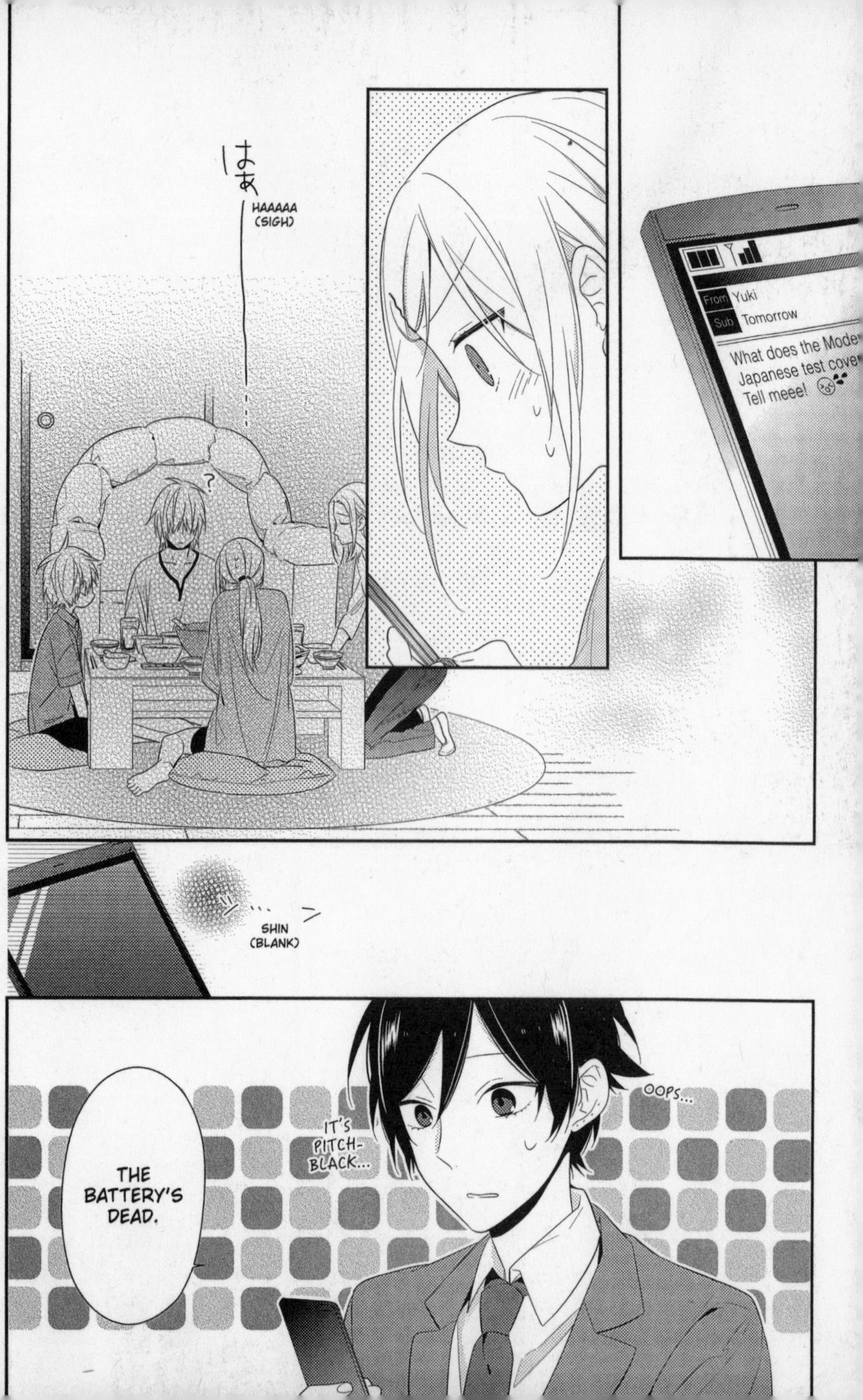

From Yuki
Sub Tomorrow
What does the Mode
Japanese test cove
Tell meee!
はあ
HAAAAA (SIGH)
SHIN (BLANK)
OOPS...
IT'S PITCH-BLACK...
THE BATTERY'S DEAD.

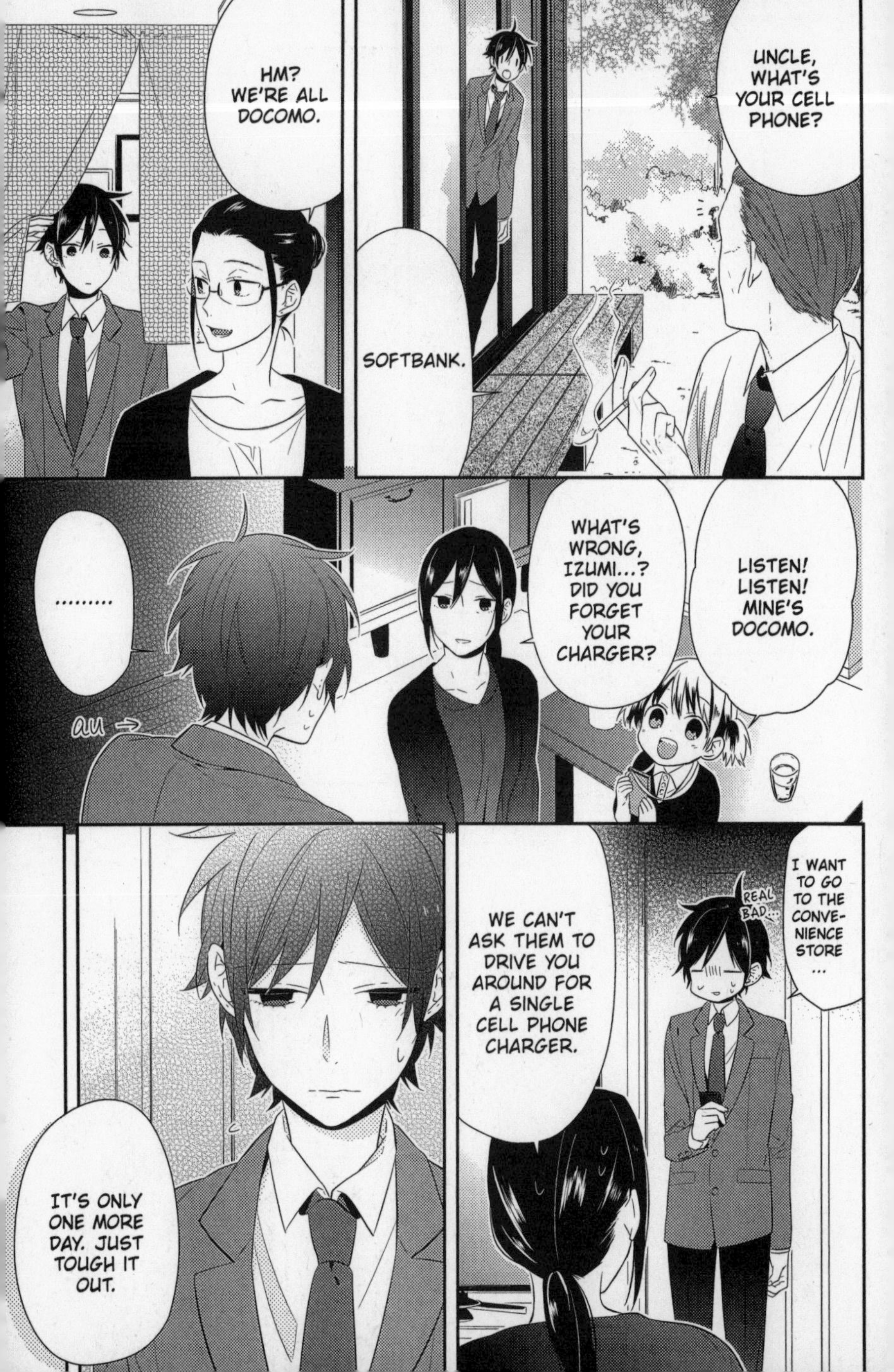
UNCLE, WHAT'S YOUR CELL PHONE?
SOFTBANK.
HM? WE'RE ALL DOCOMO.
LISTEN! LISTEN! MINE'S DOCOMO.
WHAT'S WRONG, IZUMI...? DID YOU FORGET YOUR CHARGER?
....
au →
I WANT TO GO TO THE CONVE-NIENCE STORE ...
REAL BAD...
WE CAN'T ASK THEM TO DRIVE YOU AROUND FOR A SINGLE CELL PHONE CHARGER.
IT'S ONLY ONE MORE DAY. JUST TOUGH IT OUT.

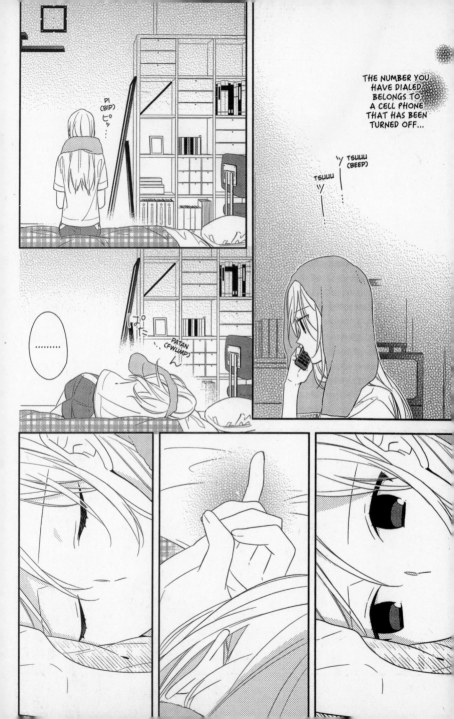

PI
(BIP)

THE NUMBER YOU HAVE DIALED BELONGS TO A CELL PHONE THAT HAS BEEN TURNED OFF...

TSUUU
(BEEP)

TSUUU

....

PATAN
(FWUMP)

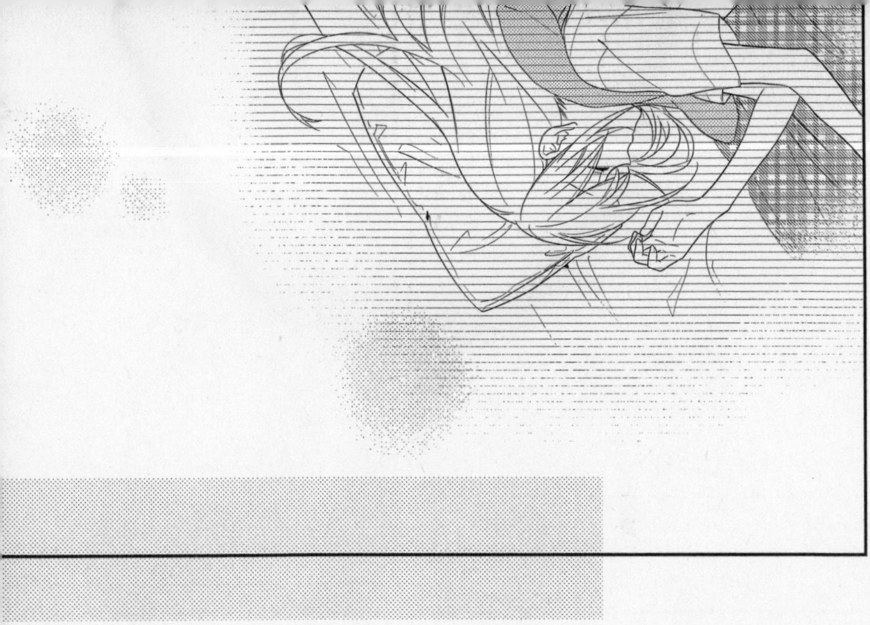

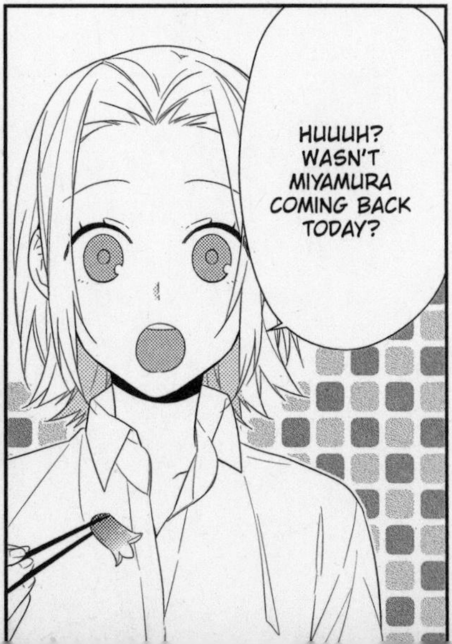
HUUUH? WASN'T MIYAMURA COMING BACK TODAY?

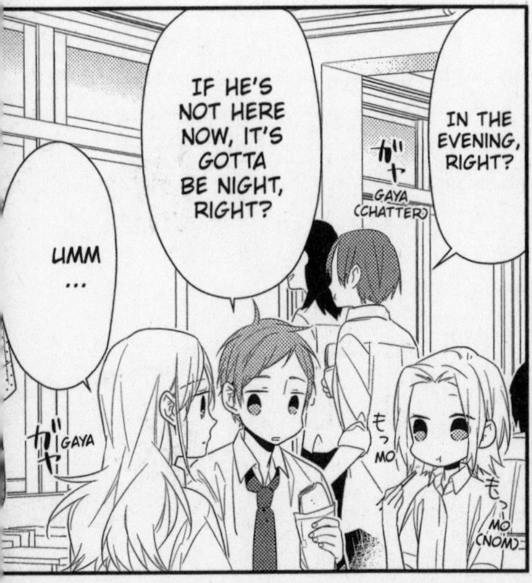
IN THE EVENING, RIGHT?
がや
GAYA (CHATTER)
IF HE'S NOT HERE NOW, IT'S GOTTA BE NIGHT, RIGHT?
UMM ...
もっ
MO
がや
GAYA
もっ
MO (NOM)

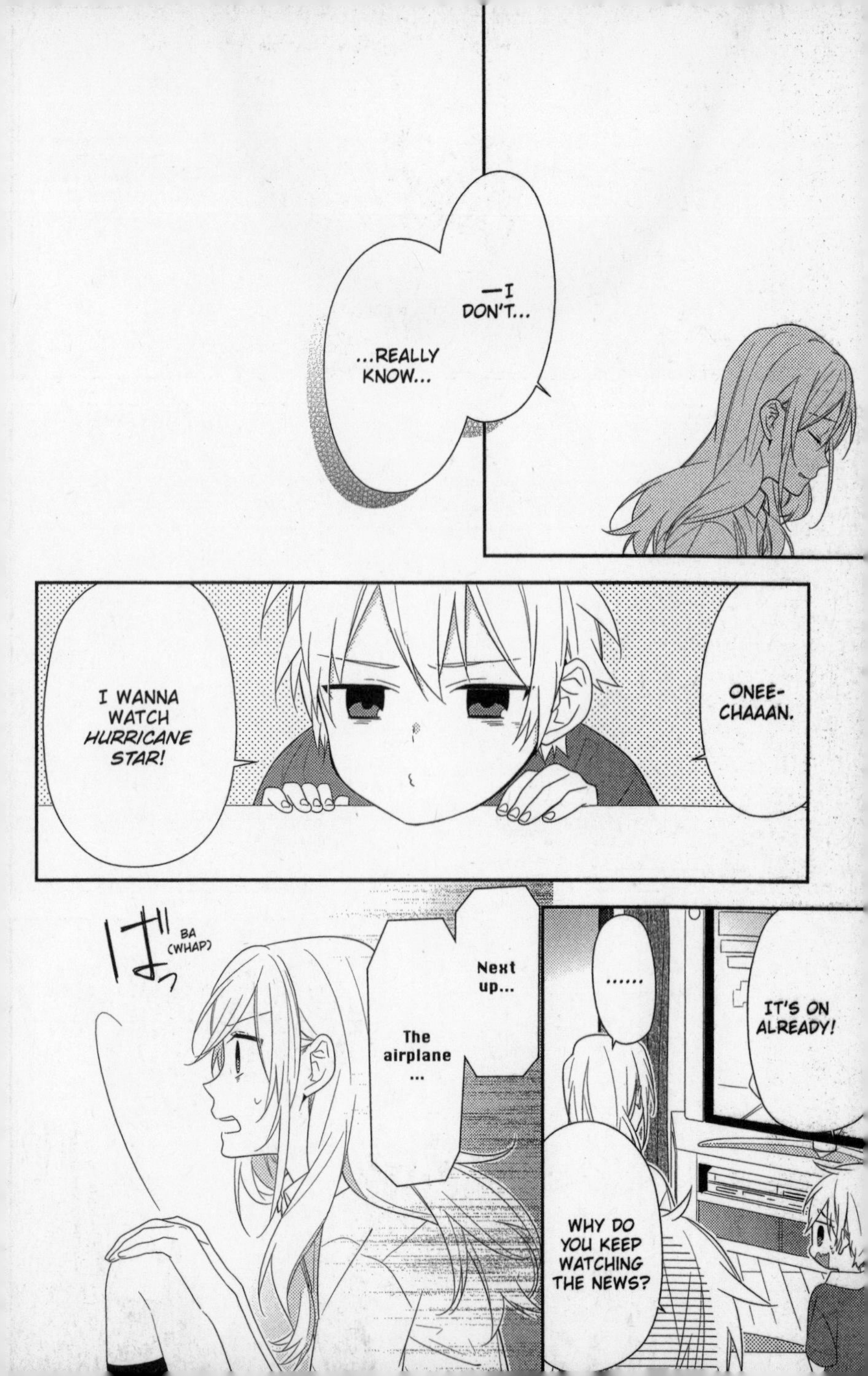
—I DON'T...
...REALLY KNOW...
ONEE-CHAAAN.
I WANNA WATCH *HURRICANE STAR*!
IT'S ON ALREADY!
......
WHY DO YOU KEEP WATCHING THE NEWS?
Next up...
The airplane ...
ぱっ
BA (WHAP)

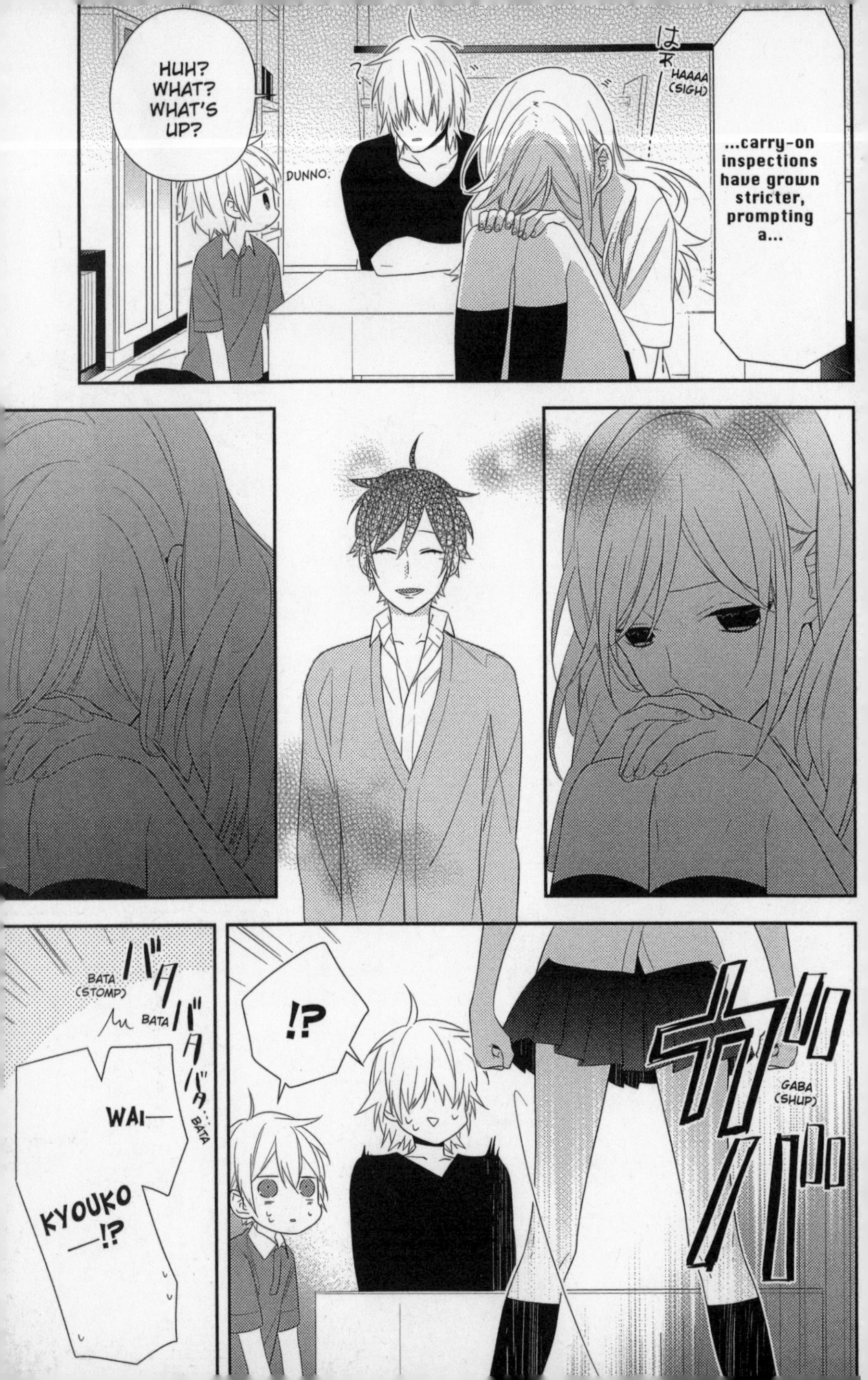
...carry-on inspections have grown stricter, prompting a...
HAAAA (SIGH)
HUH? WHAT? WHAT'S UP?
DUNNO.
GABA (SHUP)
!?
BATA (STOMP)
BATA
BATA
WAI—
KYOUKO—!?

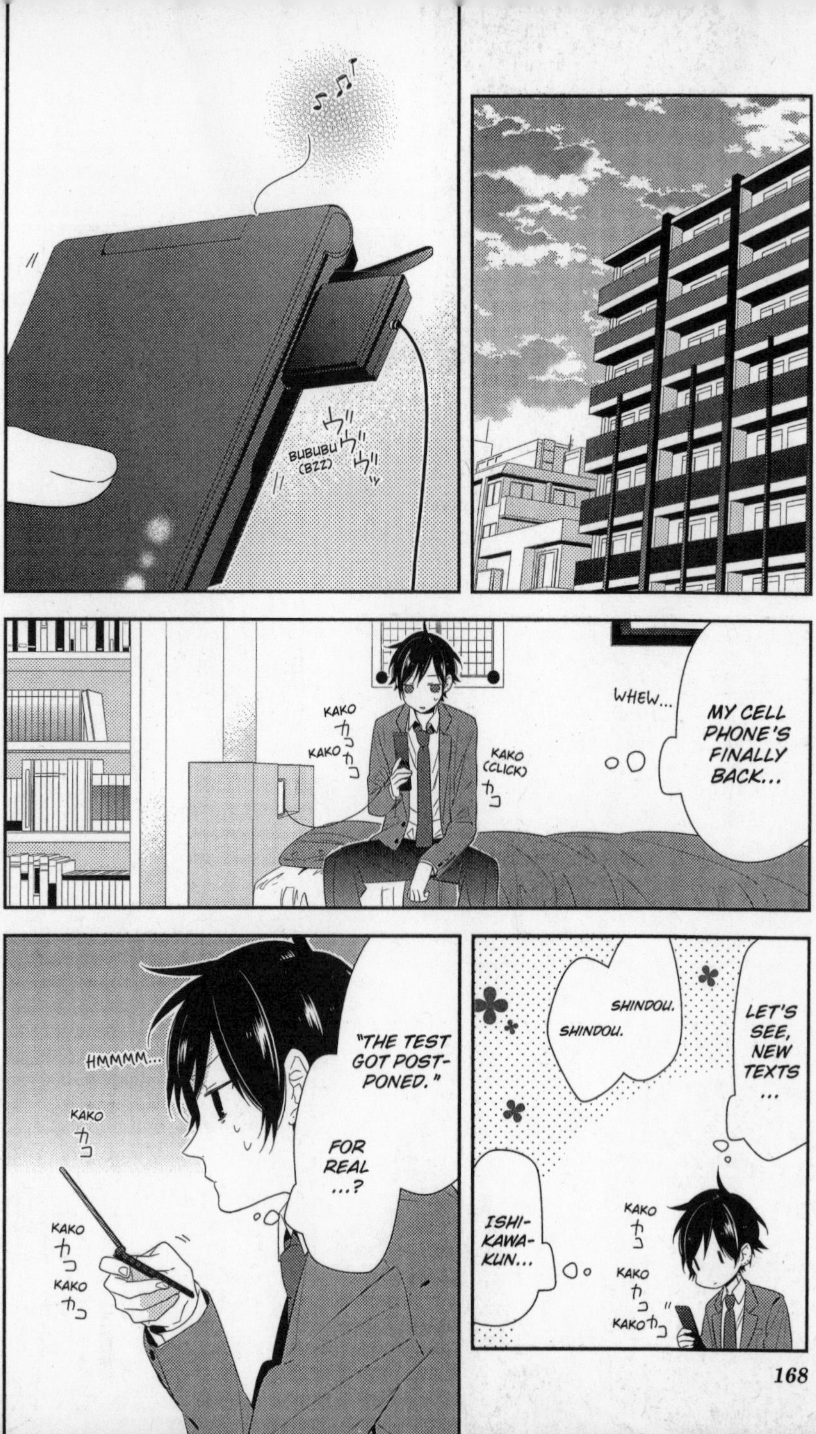

BUBUBU (BZZ)
ヴヴヴ
MY CELL PHONE'S FINALLY BACK...
WHEW...
KAKO (CLICK) カコ
KAKO カコ
KAKO カコ
LET'S SEE, NEW TEXTS...
SHINDOU.
SHINDOU.
ISHI-KAWA-KUN...
KAKO カコ
KAKO カコ
KAKO カコ
"THE TEST GOT POST-PONED."
FOR REAL...?
HMMMM...
KAKO カコ
KAKO カコ
KAKO カコ

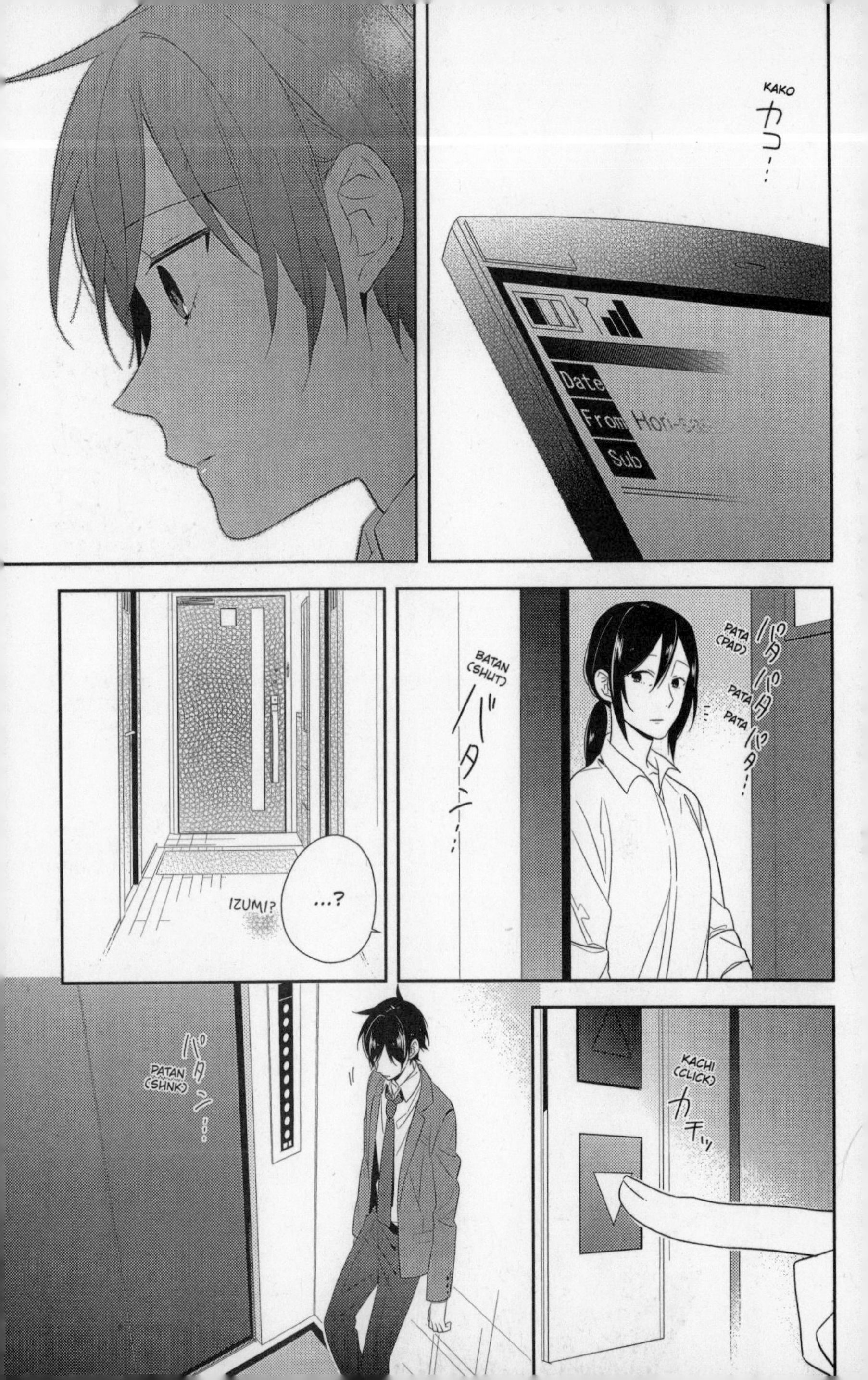

KAKO
カコ…
Date
From Hori-san
Sub
PATA (PAD)
PATA
PATA
パタパタパタ…
BATAN (SHUT)
バタン…
IZUMI?
...?
KACHI (CLICK)
カチッ
PATAN (SHNK)
パタン…

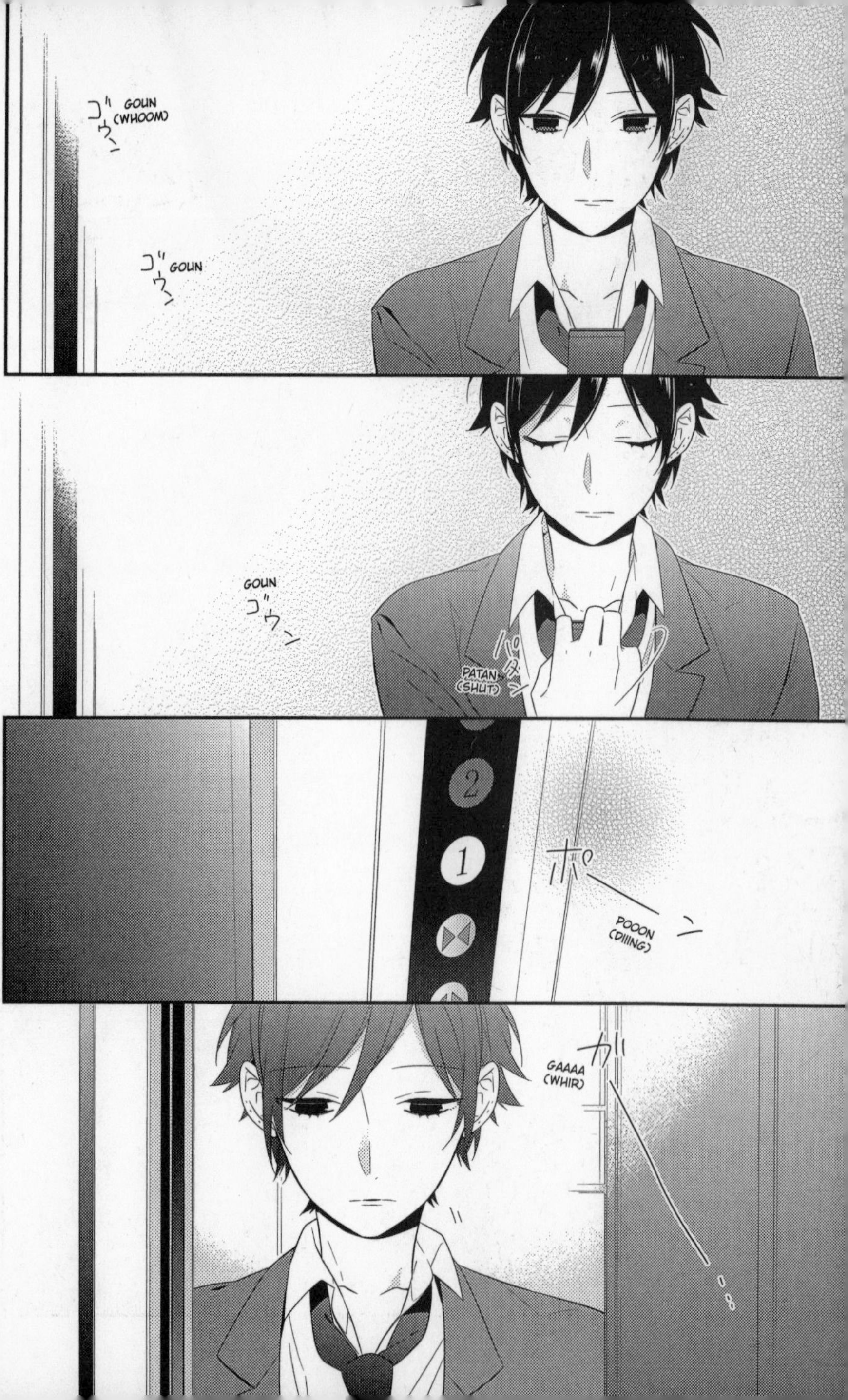
GOUN (WHOOM)
GOUN
GOUN
PATAN (SHUT)
POOON (DIIING)
GAAAA (WHIR)

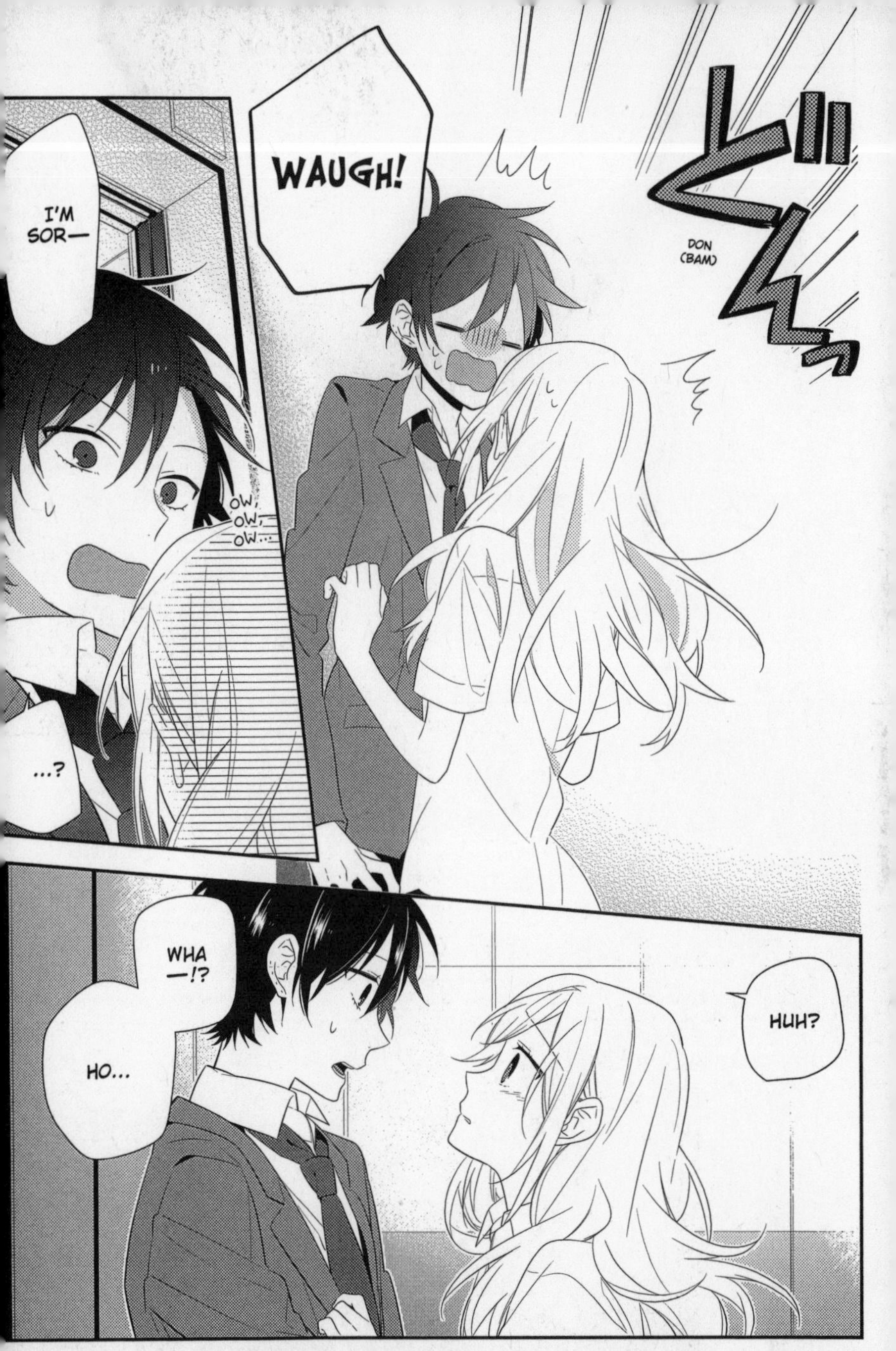
DON (BAM)
WAUGH!
I'M SOR—
OW, OW, OW...
...?
HUH?
WHA—!?
HO...

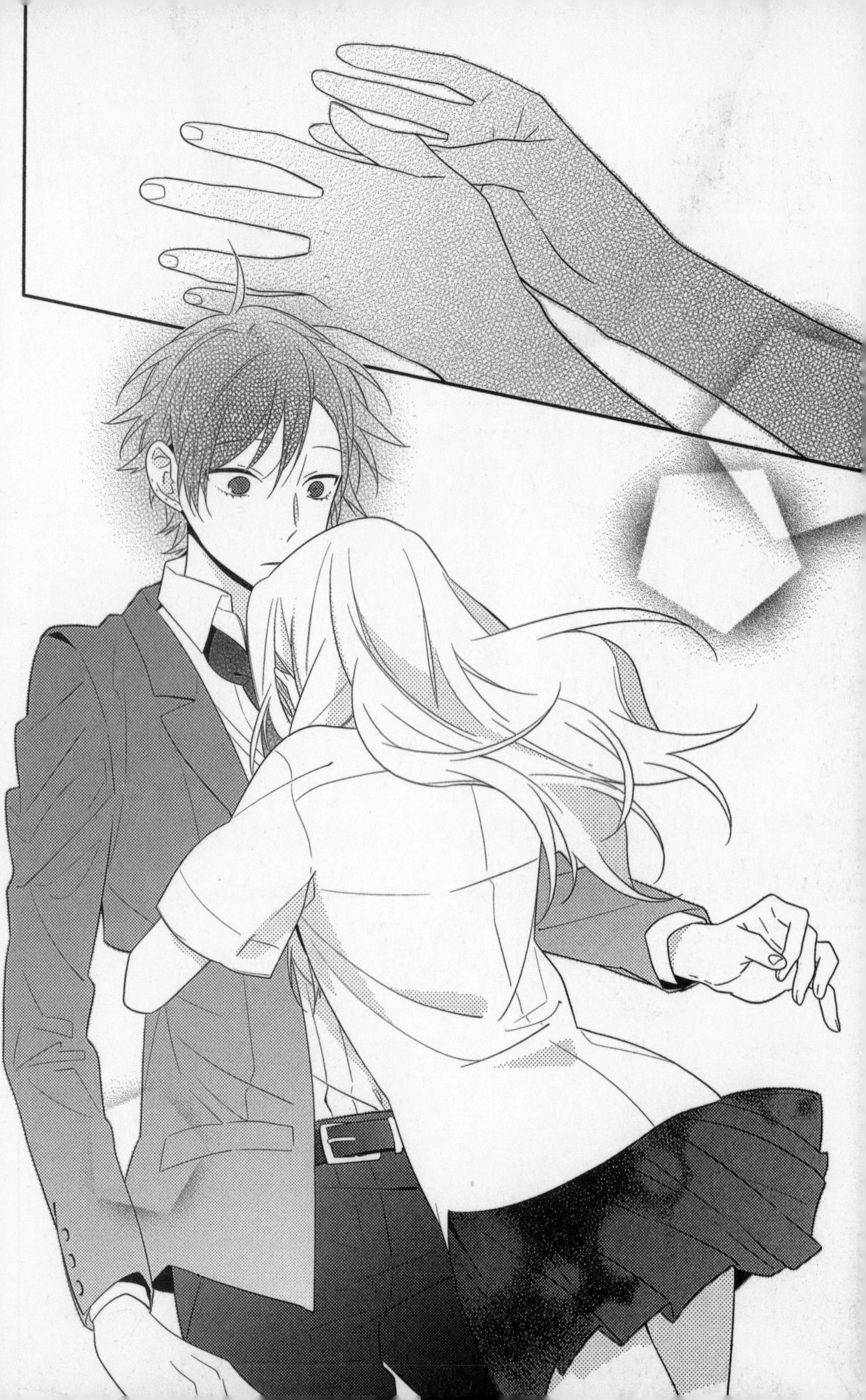

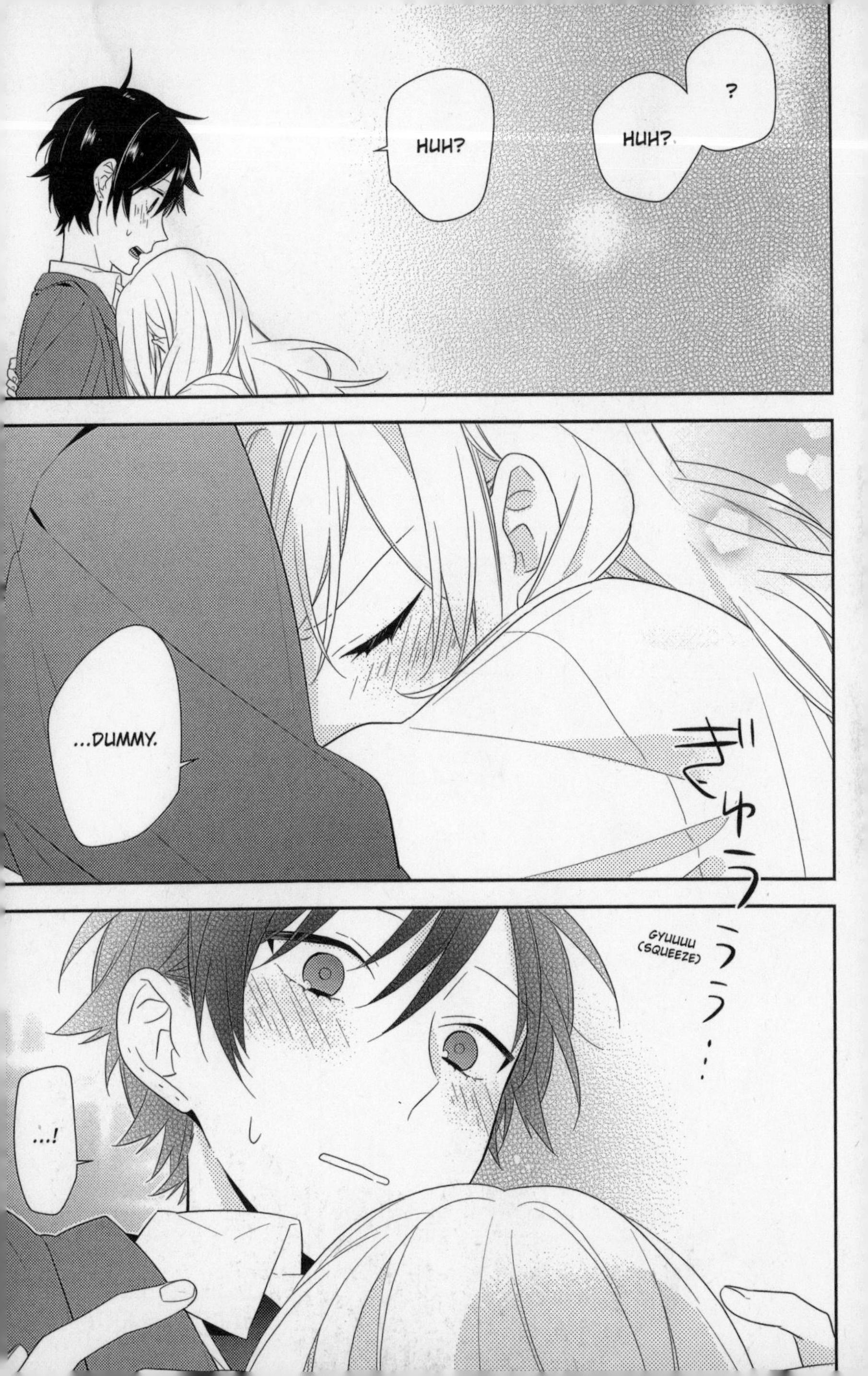
?
HUH?
HUH?
ぎゅううう…
...DUMMY.
GYUUUU
(SQUEEZE)
...!

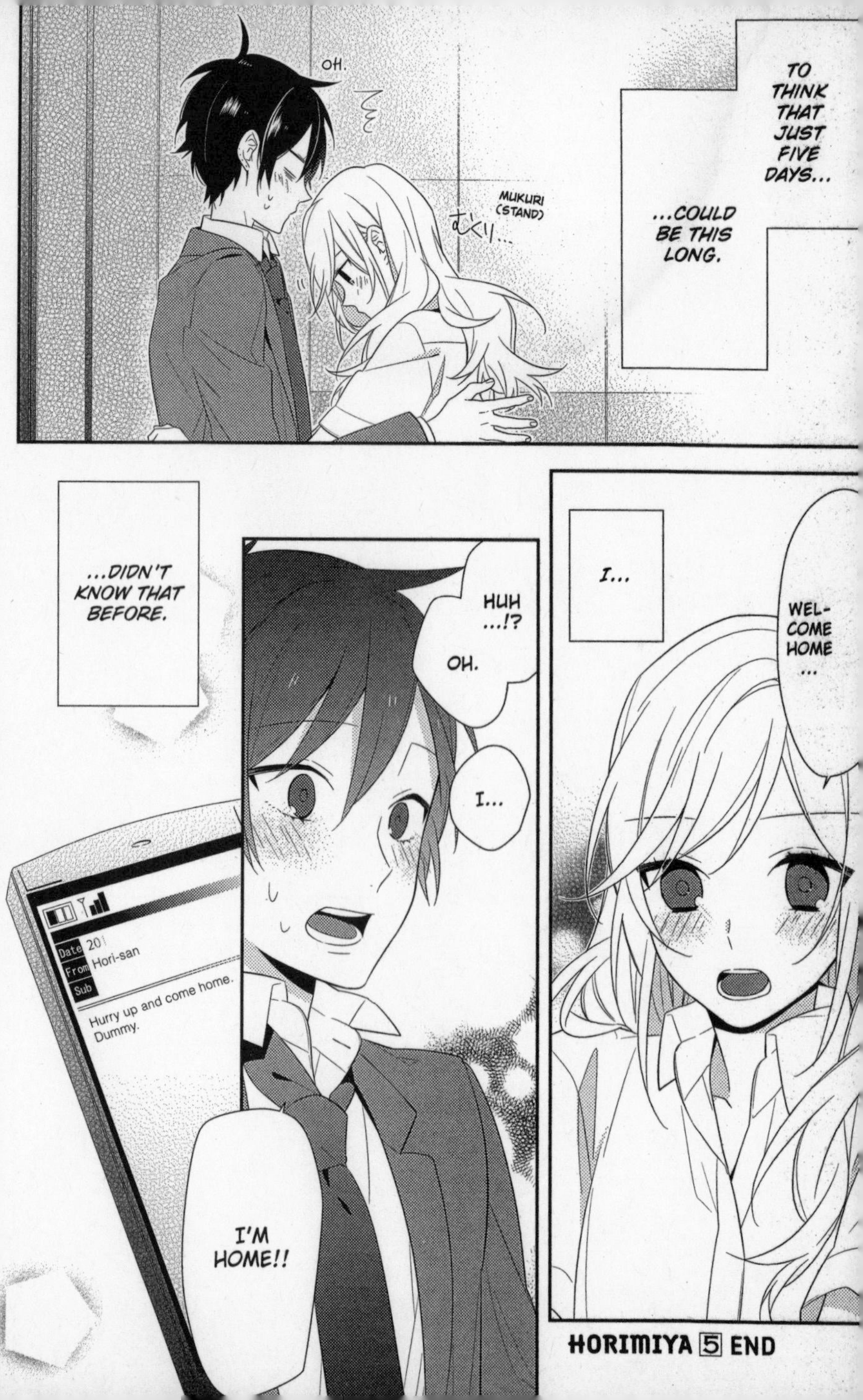
TO THINK THAT JUST FIVE DAYS...
...COULD BE THIS LONG.
OH.
MUKURI (STAND)
むくり…
WEL-COME HOME...
I...
HUH...!?
OH.
I...
...DIDN'T KNOW THAT BEFORE.
Date 20
From Hori-san
Sub
Hurry up and come home. Dummy.
I'M HOME!!
HORIMIYA 5 END

To Be Continued...

BONUS MANGA: MYAMURA ④

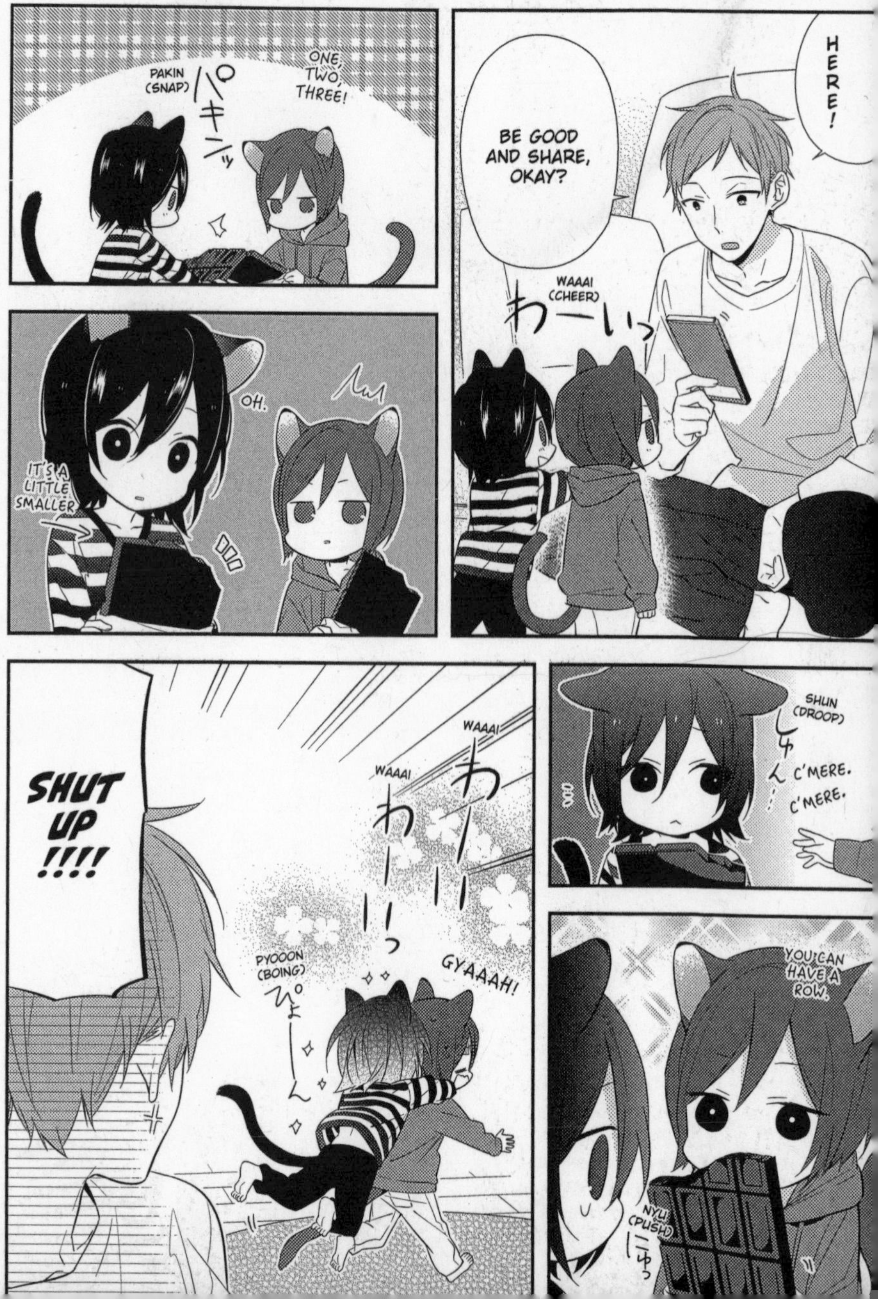
HERE!
BE GOOD AND SHARE, OKAY?
WAAAI (CHEER)
わーいっ
ONE, TWO, THREE!
PAKIN (SNAP)
パキンッ
OH.
IT'S A LITTLE SMALLER
SHUN (DROOP)
しゅん
C'MERE. C'MERE.
YOU CAN HAVE A ROW.
NYU (PUSH)
にゅっ
WAAAI
WAAAI
GYAAAH!
PYOOON (BOING)
ぴょーん
SHUT UP!!!!

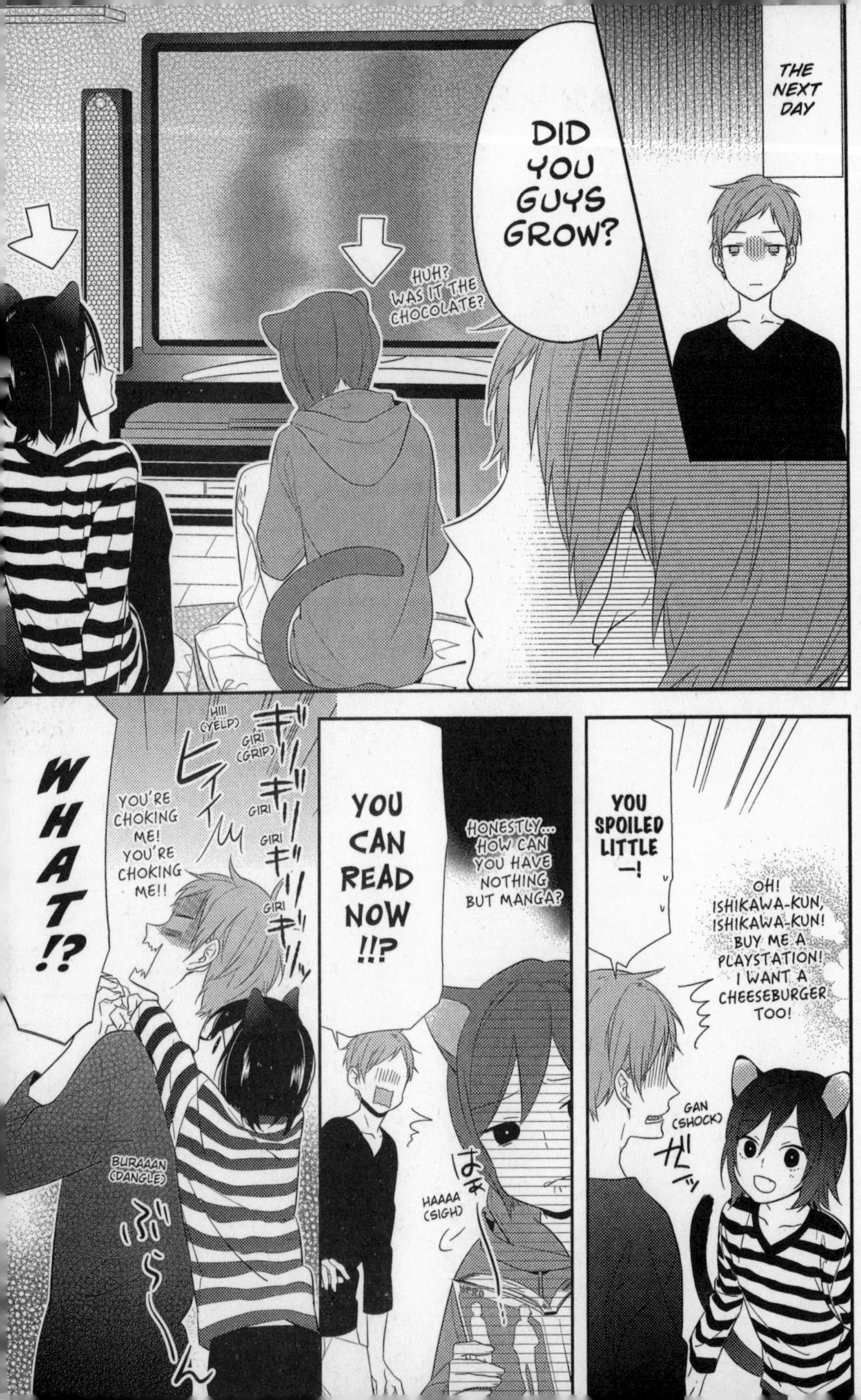
THE NEXT DAY
DID YOU GUYS GROW?
HUH? WAS IT THE CHOCOLATE?
OH! ISHIKAWA-KUN, ISHIKAWA-KUN! BUY ME A PLAYSTATION! I WANT A CHEESEBURGER TOO!
YOU SPOILED LITTLE—!
GAN (SHOCK)
YOU CAN READ NOW!!?
HONESTLY... HOW CAN YOU HAVE NOTHING BUT MANGA?
HAAAA (SIGH)
GIRI (GRIP)
GIRI
GIRI
GIRI
HIII (YELP)
WHAT!?
YOU'RE CHOKING ME! YOU'RE CHOKING ME!!
BURAAAN (DANGLE)

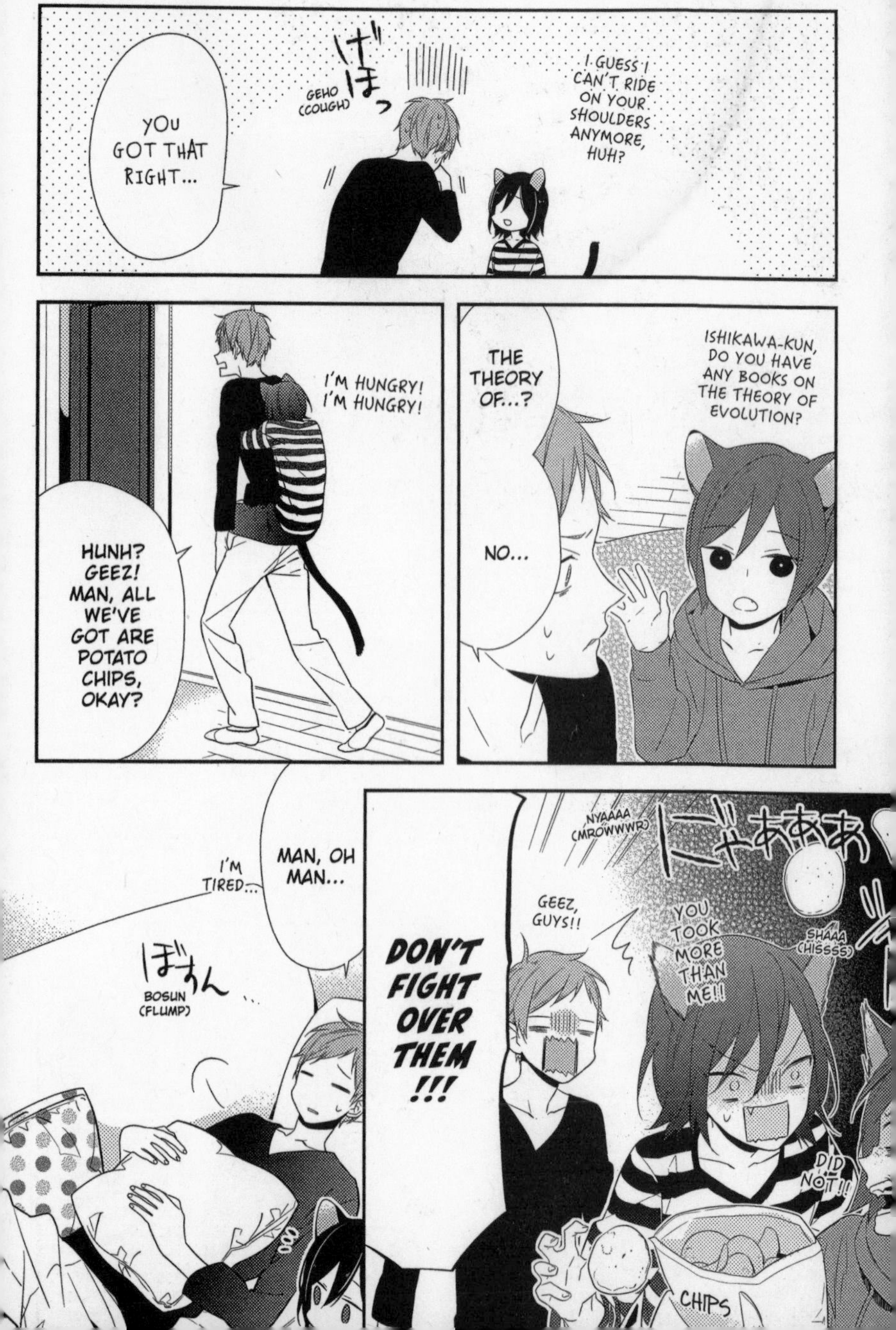
I GUESS I CAN'T RIDE ON YOUR SHOULDERS ANYMORE, HUH?
げほっ
GEHO (COUGH)
YOU GOT THAT RIGHT...
ISHIKAWA-KUN, DO YOU HAVE ANY BOOKS ON THE THEORY OF EVOLUTION?
THE THEORY OF...?
NO...
I'M HUNGRY! I'M HUNGRY!
HUNH? GEEZ! MAN, ALL WE'VE GOT ARE POTATO CHIPS, OKAY?
にゃあああ
NYAAAA (MROWWWR)
SHAAA (HISSSS)
YOU TOOK MORE THAN ME!!
GEEZ, GUYS!!
DON'T FIGHT OVER THEM!!!
DID NOT!!
CHIPS
MAN, OH MAN...
I'M TIRED...
ぼすん
BOSUN (FLUMP)

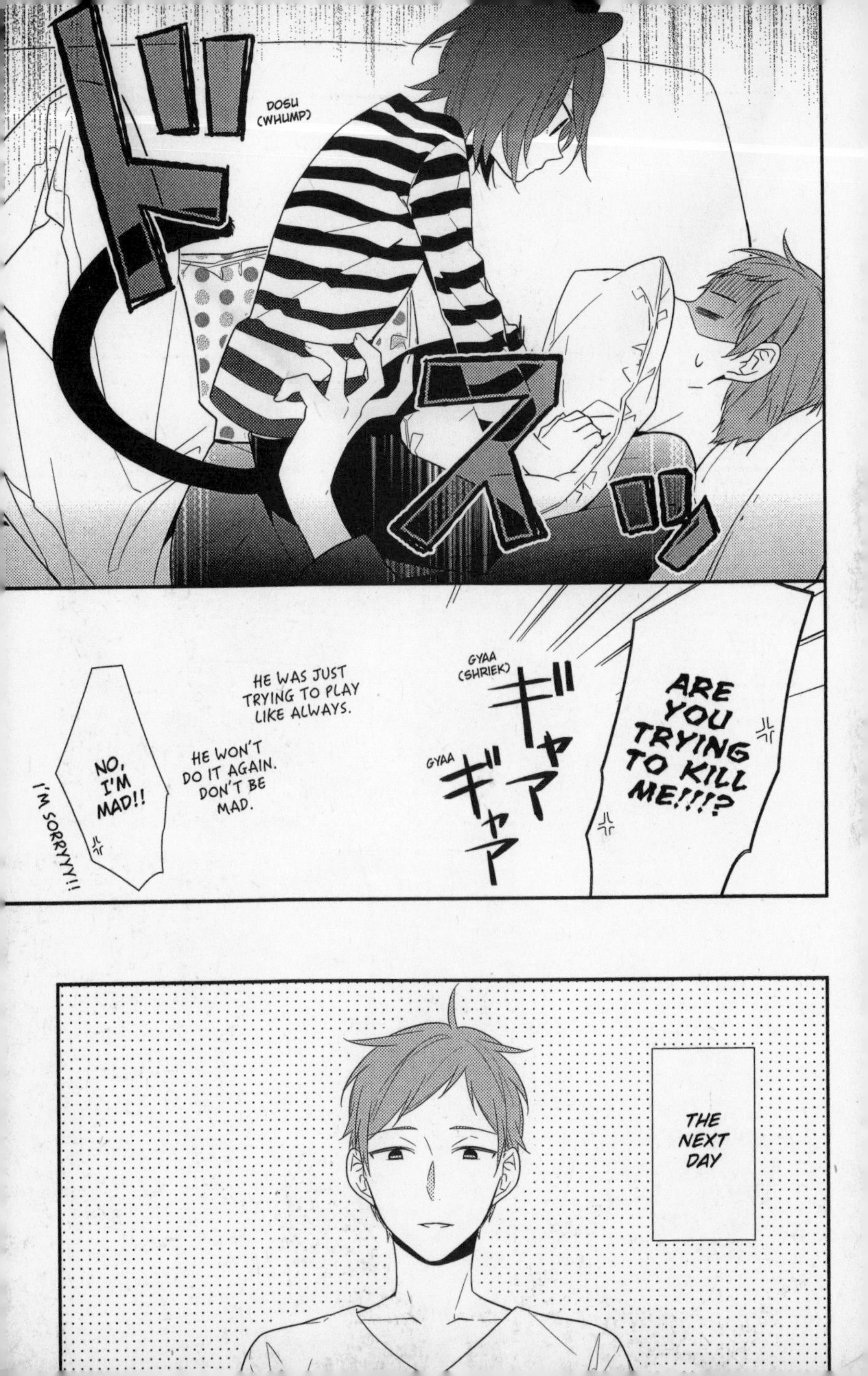
ドスッ
DOSU (WHUMP)
ARE YOU TRYING TO KILL ME!!!?
ギャア
GYAA (SHRIEK)
ギャア
GYAA
HE WAS JUST TRYING TO PLAY LIKE ALWAYS.
HE WON'T DO IT AGAIN. DON'T BE MAD.
NO, I'M MAD!!
I'M SORRYYY!!
THE NEXT DAY

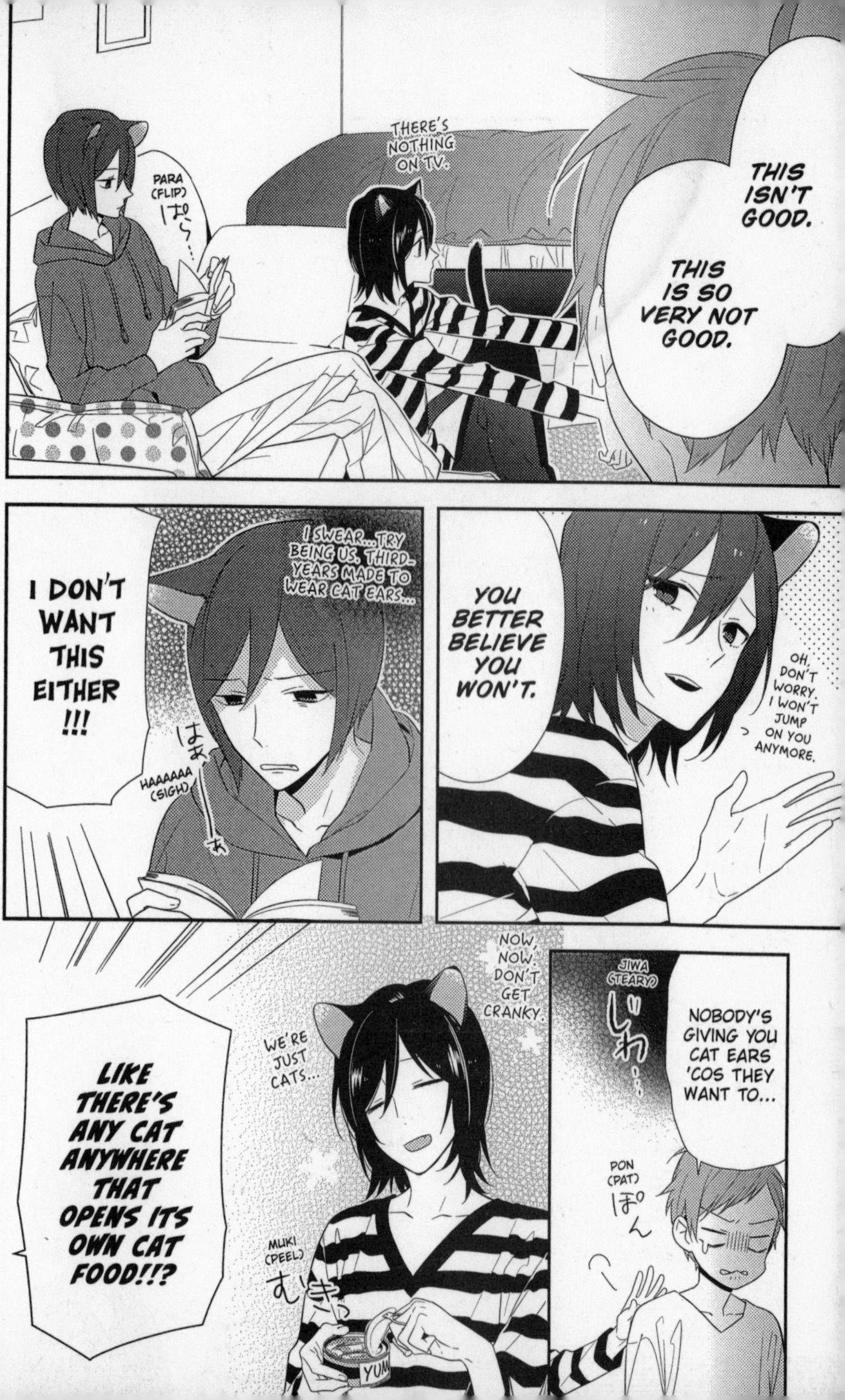
THIS ISN'T GOOD.
THIS IS SO VERY NOT GOOD.
THERE'S NOTHING ON TV.
PARA (FLIP) ぱら…
OH, DON'T WORRY. I WON'T JUMP ON YOU ANYMORE.
YOU BETTER BELIEVE YOU WON'T.
I SWEAR... TRY BEING US. THIRD-YEARS MADE TO WEAR CAT EARS...
I DON'T WANT THIS EITHER!!!
HAAAAAA (SIGH) はぁ…あ
JIWA (TEARY) じわ…
NOBODY'S GIVING YOU CAT EARS 'COS THEY WANT TO...
PON (PAT) ぽん
NOW, NOW. DON'T GET CRANKY.
WE'RE JUST CATS...
LIKE THERE'S ANY CAT ANYWHERE THAT OPENS ITS OWN CAT FOOD!!?
MUKI (PEEL) むきっ
YUM

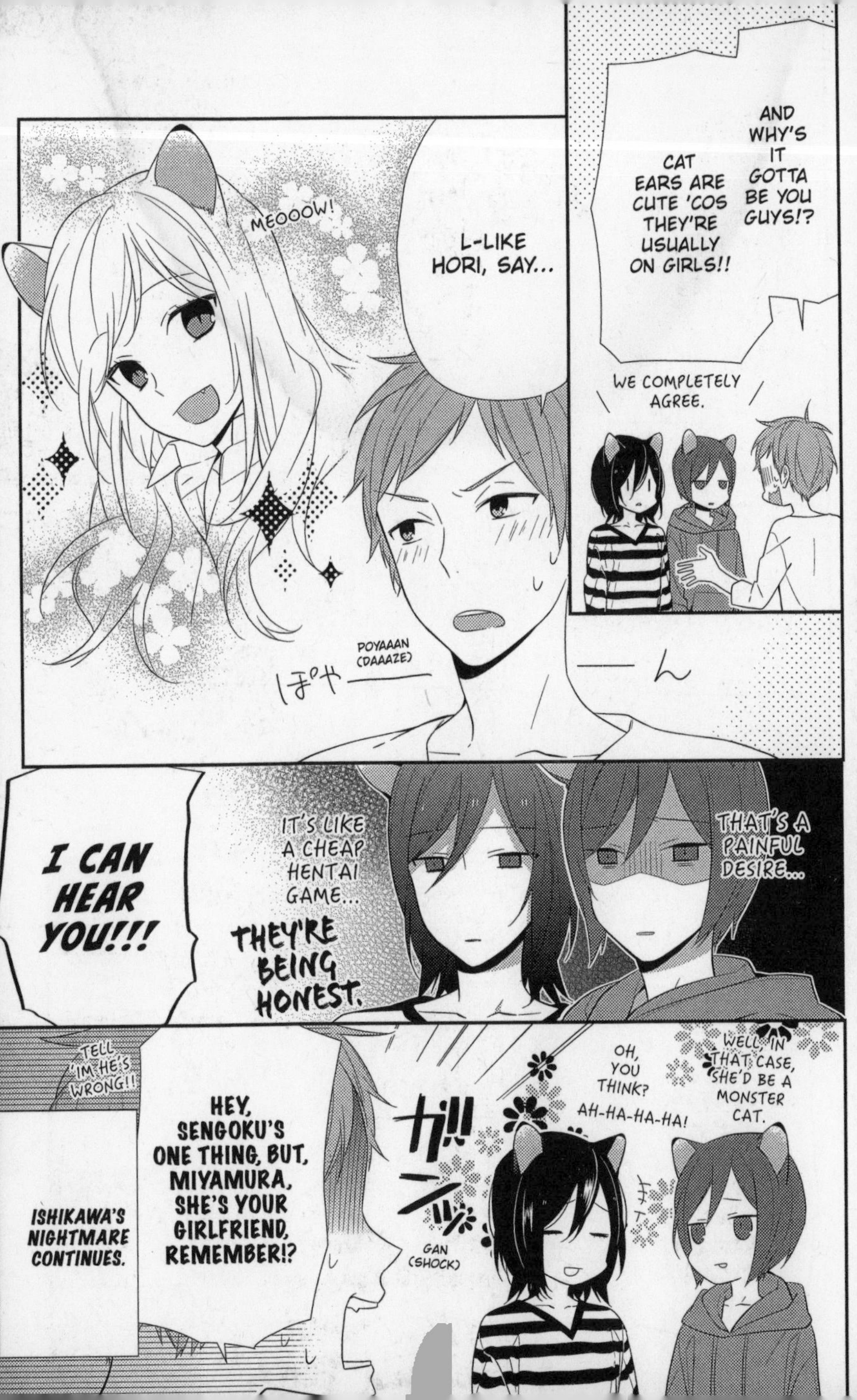
CAT EARS ARE CUTE 'COS THEY'RE USUALLY ON GIRLS!!
AND WHY'S IT GOTTA BE YOU GUYS!?
WE COMPLETELY AGREE.
L-LIKE HORI, SAY...
MEOOOW!
POYAAAN (DAAAZE)
ぽやーーん
THAT'S A PAINFUL DESIRE...
IT'S LIKE A CHEAP HENTAI GAME...
THEY'RE BEING HONEST.
I CAN HEAR YOU!!!
WELL, IN THAT CASE, SHE'D BE A MONSTER CAT.
OH, YOU THINK?
AH-HA-HA-HA!
ガ!!ーンッ
GAN (SHOCK)
HEY, SENGOKU'S ONE THING, BUT, MIYAMURA, SHE'S YOUR GIRLFRIEND, REMEMBER!?
TELL 'IM HE'S WRONG!!
ISHIKAWA'S NIGHTMARE CONTINUES.

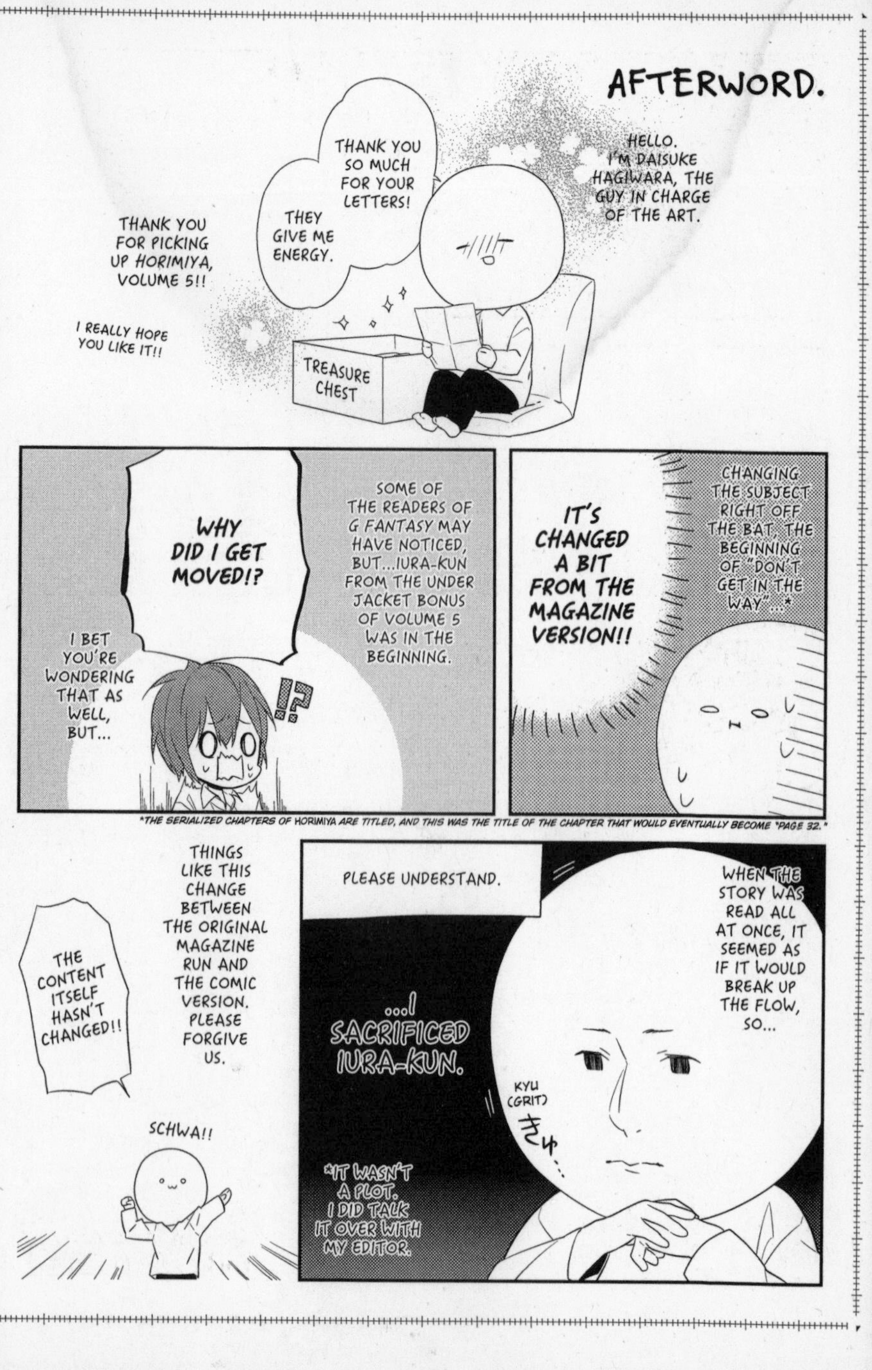
AFTERWORD.
HELLO. I'M DAISUKE HAGIWARA, THE GUY IN CHARGE OF THE ART.
THANK YOU SO MUCH FOR YOUR LETTERS!
THEY GIVE ME ENERGY.
THANK YOU FOR PICKING UP HORIMIYA, VOLUME 5!!
I REALLY HOPE YOU LIKE IT!!
TREASURE CHEST
CHANGING THE SUBJECT RIGHT OFF THE BAT, THE BEGINNING OF "DON'T GET IN THE WAY"...*
IT'S CHANGED A BIT FROM THE MAGAZINE VERSION!!
SOME OF THE READERS OF G FANTASY MAY HAVE NOTICED, BUT...IURA-KUN FROM THE UNDER JACKET BONUS OF VOLUME 5 WAS IN THE BEGINNING.
WHY DID I GET MOVED!?
!?
I BET YOU'RE WONDERING THAT AS WELL, BUT...
*THE SERIALIZED CHAPTERS OF HORIMIYA ARE TITLED, AND THIS WAS THE TITLE OF THE CHAPTER THAT WOULD EVENTUALLY BECOME "PAGE 32."
WHEN THE STORY WAS READ ALL AT ONCE, IT SEEMED AS IF IT WOULD BREAK UP THE FLOW, SO...
PLEASE UNDERSTAND.
...I SACRIFICED IURA-KUN.
KYU (GRIT)
*IT WASN'T A PLOT. I DID TALK IT OVER WITH MY EDITOR.
THINGS LIKE THIS CHANGE BETWEEN THE ORIGINAL MAGAZINE RUN AND THE COMIC VERSION. PLEASE FORGIVE US.
THE CONTENT ITSELF HASN'T CHANGED!!
SCHWA!!

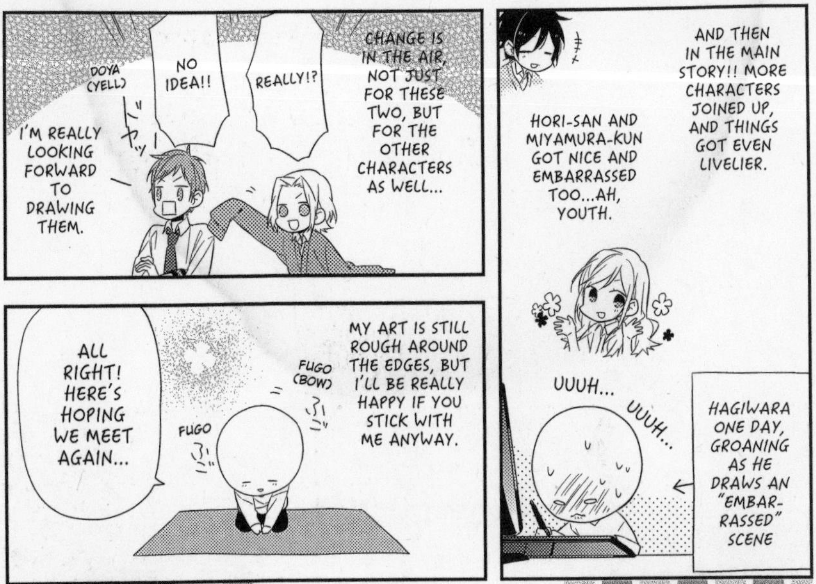
AND THEN IN THE MAIN STORY!! MORE CHARACTERS JOINED UP, AND THINGS GOT EVEN LIVELIER.
HORI-SAN AND MIYAMURA-KUN GOT NICE AND EMBARRASSED TOO...AH, YOUTH.
UUUH...
UUUH...
HAGIWARA ONE DAY, GROANING AS HE DRAWS AN "EMBAR-RASSED" SCENE
CHANGE IS IN THE AIR, NOT JUST FOR THESE TWO, BUT FOR THE OTHER CHARACTERS AS WELL...
REALLY!?
NO IDEA!!
DOYA (YELL)
I'M REALLY LOOKING FORWARD TO DRAWING THEM.
MY ART IS STILL ROUGH AROUND THE EDGES, BUT I'LL BE REALLY HAPPY IF YOU STICK WITH ME ANYWAY.
FUGO (BOW)
FUGO
ALL RIGHT! HERE'S HOPING WE MEET AGAIN...

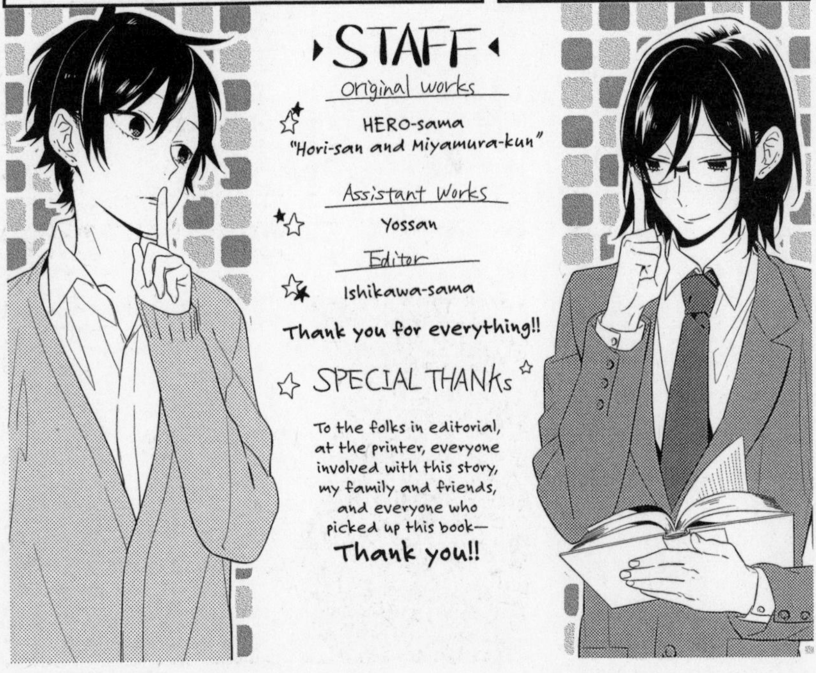
STAFF
Original works
HERO-sama
"Hori-san and Miyamura-kun"
Assistant Works
Yossan
Editor
Ishikawa-sama
Thank you for everything!!
SPECIAL THANKs
To the folks in editorial, at the printer, everyone involved with this story, my family and friends, and everyone who picked up this book—
Thank you!!

Translation Notes

Page 30 – Hannya
A Hannya is a Noh demon mask that symbolizes
female jealousy, anger, or vengefulness.

Page 70 – *Kouhai*
Kouhai is the term for someone in a lower year at school
in relation to an older student. Since Hori's a third-year,
first- and second-year students would be her *kouhai* and
will probably refer to her as *senpai*. The terminology
carries over to companies and the working world, where
employees may use these forms of address in reference to
when they joined the company in relation to one another.

Page 99 – Baths
In Japan, baths are basically just for relaxation. Bathers
shower beforehand, during which they shampoo their
hair, soap up, and rinse off. It's only after the shower
that the bather actually gets into the tub for a soak.

Page 114 – Slimes
Slimes are the mascot monster for the *Dragon Quest*
video game franchise. They're notoriously weak.

Page 163 – SoftBank, Docomo, and AU
These three brands are all Japanese
telecommunication companies.

Page 182 – Schwa!!
"Shuwacchi!" is what the classic Japanese TV superhero
Ultraman says when he transforms. Because Hagiwara's pose
is also classic Ultraman, it's likely that this is a parody.

HORIMIYA

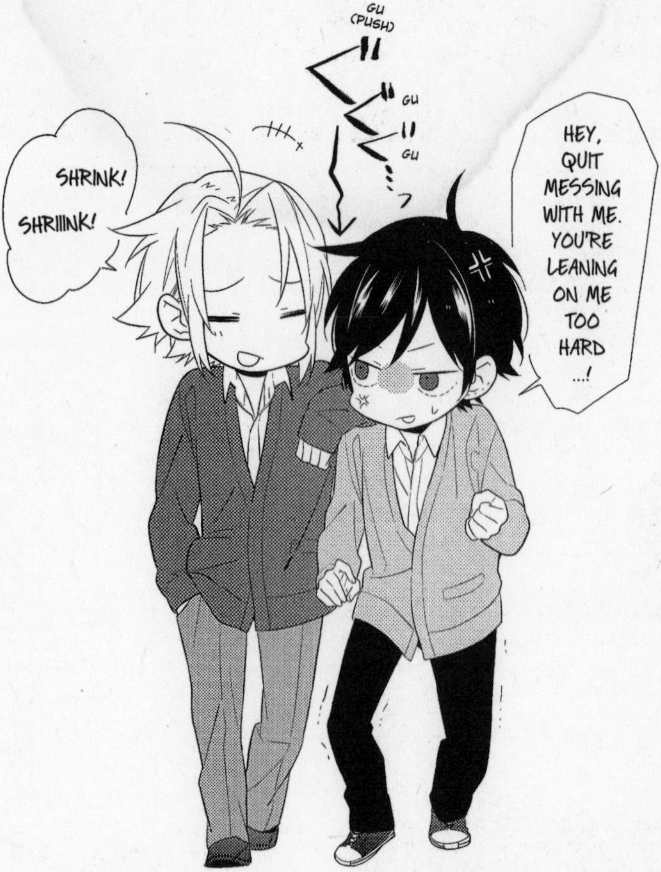
GU (PUSH)
GU
GU
HEY, QUIT MESSING WITH ME. YOU'RE LEANING ON ME TOO HARD ...!
SHRINK!
SHRIIINK!

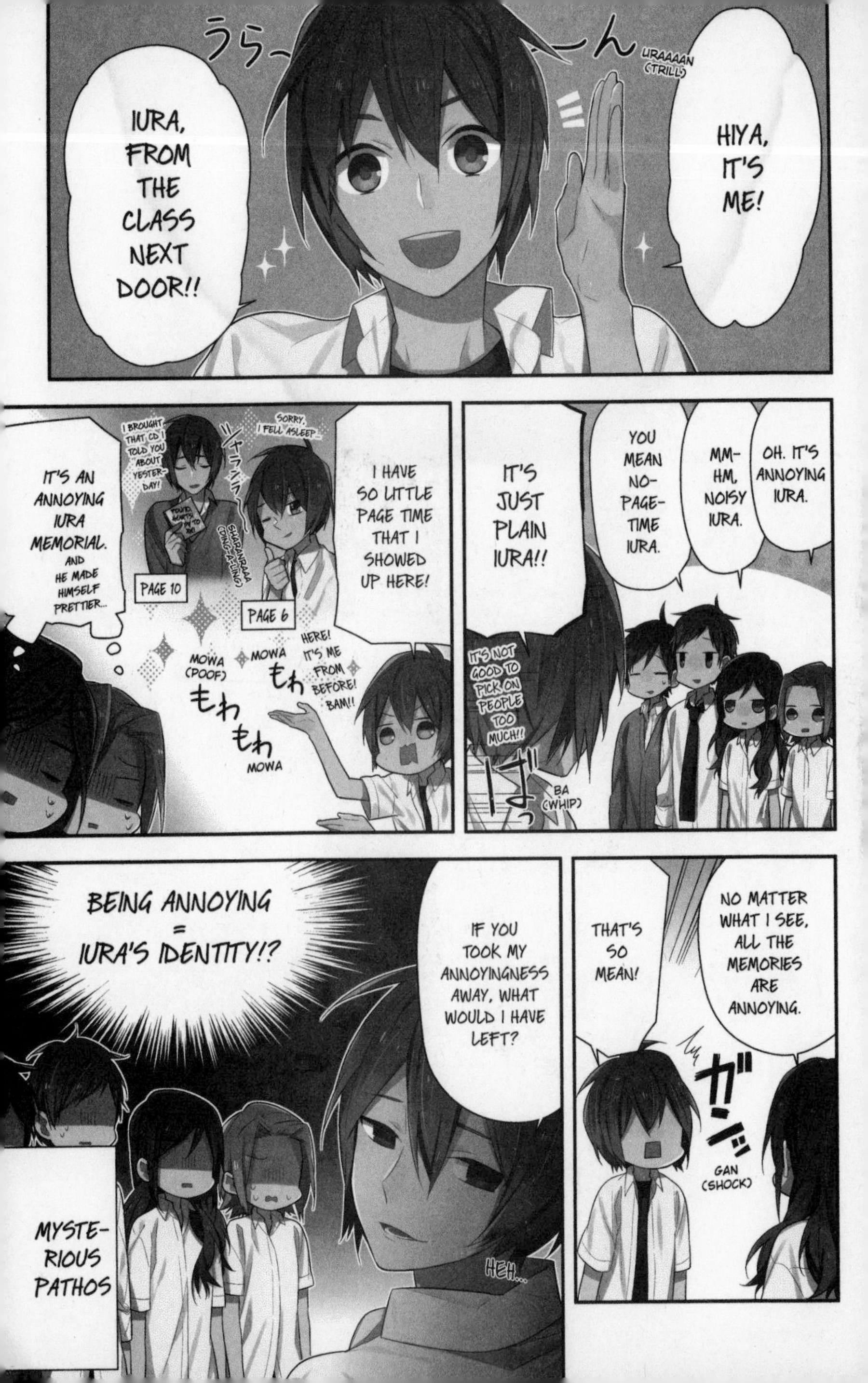
うら〜ん
URAAAAN (TRILL)
HIYA, IT'S ME!
IURA, FROM THE CLASS NEXT DOOR!!
OH. IT'S ANNOYING IURA.
MM-HM, NOISY IURA.
YOU MEAN NO-PAGE-TIME IURA.
IT'S JUST PLAIN IURA!!
IT'S NOT GOOD TO PICK ON PEOPLE TOO MUCH!!
ばっ
BA (WHIP)
I HAVE SO LITTLE PAGE TIME THAT I SHOWED UP HERE!
SORRY, I FELL ASLEEP...
シャランラ〜
SHARANRAA (DING-A-LING)
PAGE 6
I BROUGHT THAT CD I TOLD YOU ABOUT YESTERDAY!
PAGE 10
HERE! IT'S ME FROM BEFORE! BAM!!
もわ
MOWA
MOWA (POOF)
もわ
もわ
MOWA
IT'S AN ANNOYING IURA MEMORIAL.
AND HE MADE HIMSELF PRETTIER...
NO MATTER WHAT I SEE, ALL THE MEMORIES ARE ANNOYING.
THAT'S SO MEAN!
GAN (SHOCK)
IF YOU TOOK MY ANNOYINGNESS AWAY, WHAT WOULD I HAVE LEFT?
HEH...
BEING ANNOYING = IURA'S IDENTITY!?
MYSTERIOUS PATHOS

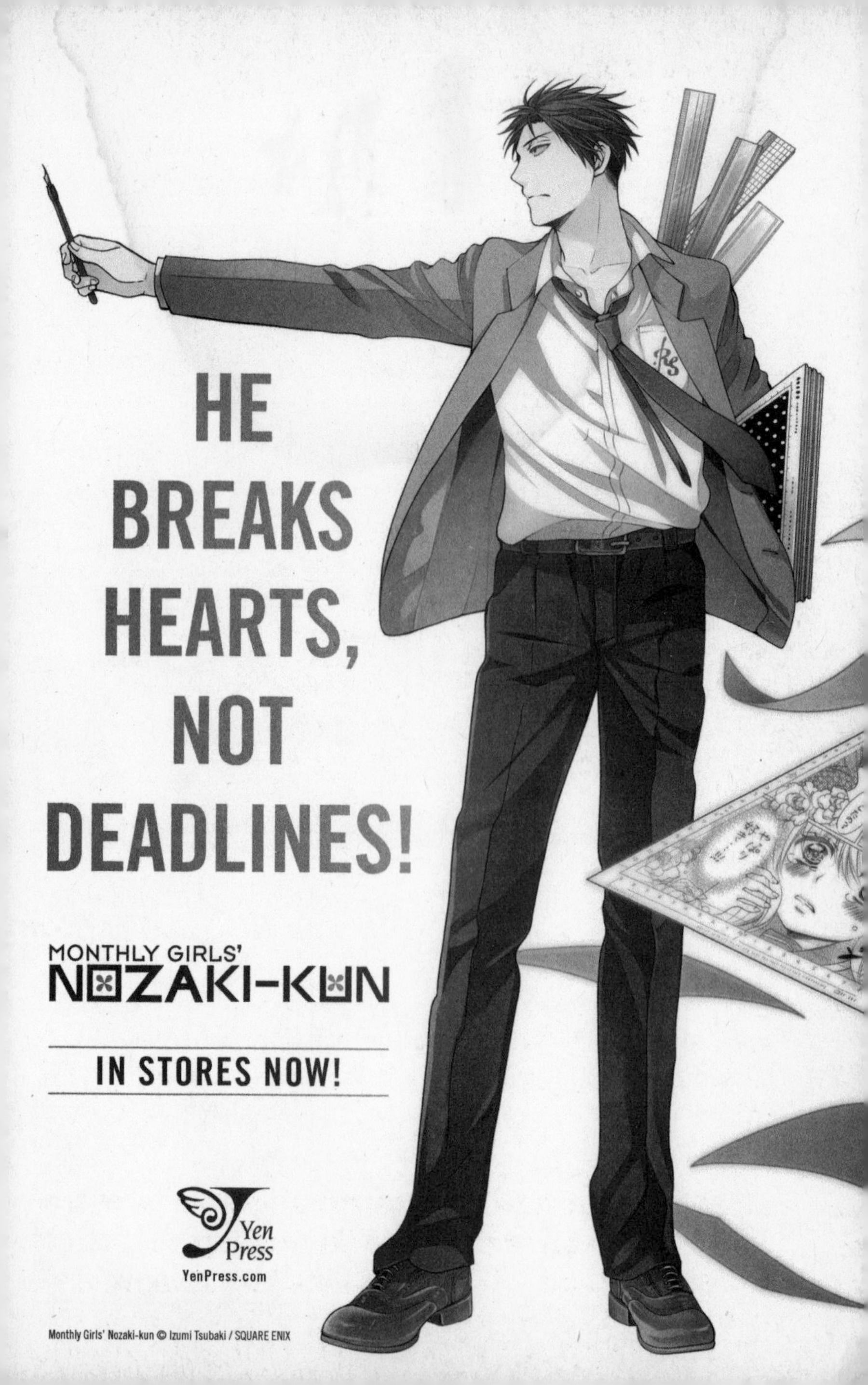
HE BREAKS HEARTS, NOT DEADLINES!
MONTHLY GIRLS'
NOZAKI-KUN
IN STORES NOW!
Yen Press
YenPress.com
Monthly Girls' Nozaki-kun © Izumi Tsubaki / SQUARE ENIX

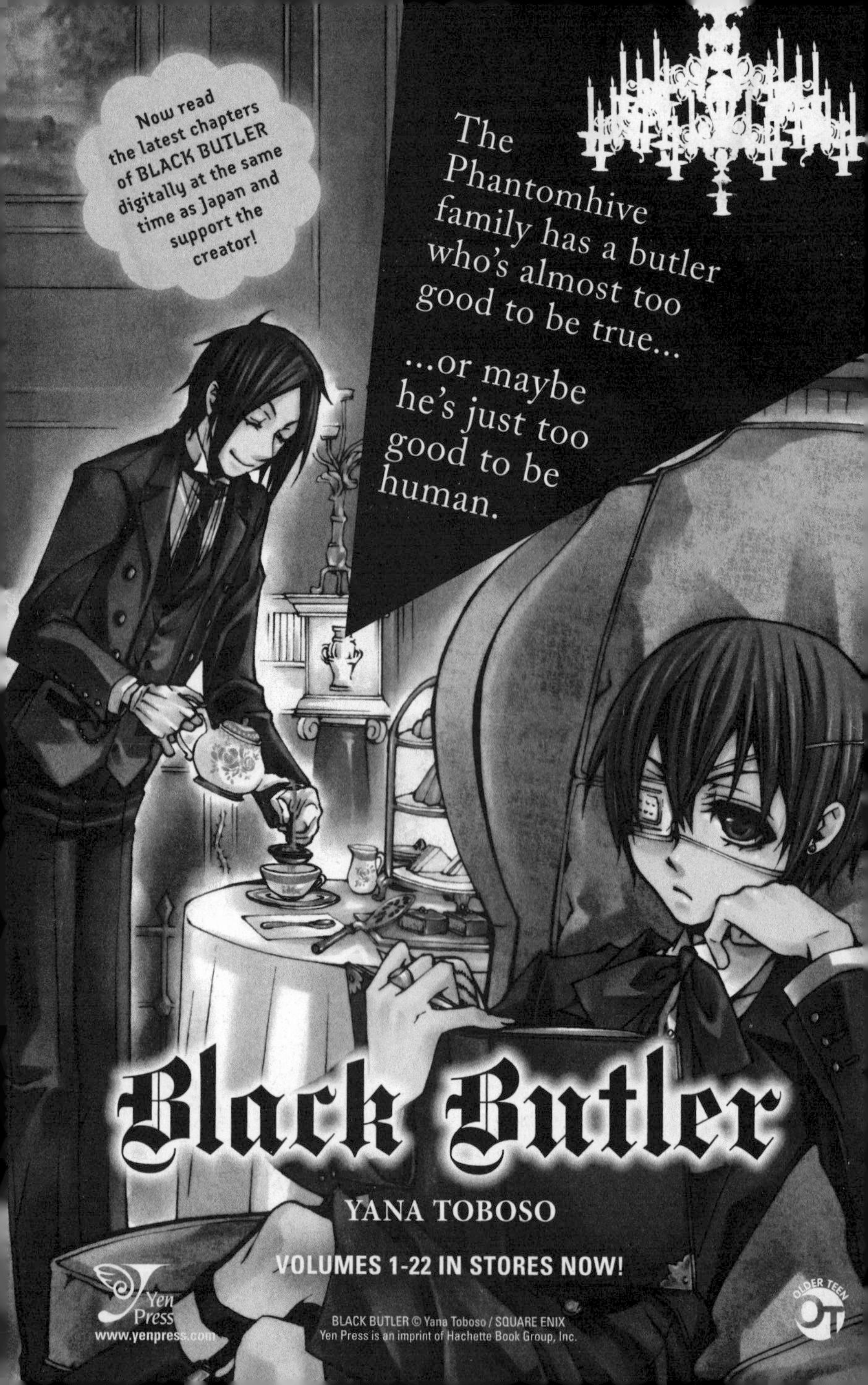
Now read the latest chapters of BLACK BUTLER digitally at the same time as Japan and support the creator!
The Phantomhive family has a butler who's almost too good to be true...
...or maybe he's just too good to be human.
Black Butler
YANA TOBOSO
VOLUMES 1-22 IN STORES NOW!
Yen Press
www.yenpress.com
BLACK BUTLER © Yana Toboso / SQUARE ENIX
Yen Press is an imprint of Hachette Book Group, Inc.
OLDER TEEN
OT

WELCOME TO IKEBUKURO, WHERE TOKYO'S WILDEST CHARACTERS GATHER!!

AS THEIR PATHS CROSS, THIS ECCENTRIC CAST WEAVES A TWISTED, CRACKED LOVE STORY...

AVAILABLE NOW!!

HORIMIYA

HERO × Daisuke Hagiwara

Translation: Taylor Engel
Lettering: Alexis Eckerman

HORIMIYA vol. 5
© HERO・OOZ
© 2014 Daisuke Hagiwara / SQUARE ENIX CO., LTD. First published in Japan in 2014 by SQUARE ENIX CO., LTD. English translation rights arranged with SQUARE ENIX CO., LTD. and Yen Press, LLC through Tuttle-Mori Agency, Inc.

English translation © 2016 by SQUARE ENIX CO., LTD.

Yen Press
1290 Avenue of the Americas
New York, NY 10104

Visit us at yenpress.com • facebook.com/yenpress •
twitter.com/yenpress • yenpress.tumblr.com •
instagram.com/yenpress

First Yen Press Edition: October 2016

Yen Press is an imprint of Yen Press, LLC.
The Yen Press name and logo are trademarks
of Yen Press, LLC.

The publisher is not responsible for websites
(or their content) that are not owned by the
publisher.

Library of Congress Control Number:
2015960115

ISBNs: 978-0-316-27012-0 (paperback)
978-0-316-35667-1 (ebook)

10 9 8 7 6 5 4 3 2

BVG

Printed in the United States of America